The Rand McNally
ALMANAC of ADVENTURE

The Rand McNally

ALMANAC of ADVENTURE

A Panorama of Danger and Daring

by Richard Whittingham

Foreword by Sir Edmund Hillary

Rand McNally & Company

Chicago • New York • San Francisco

Uncaptioned Pictures

p. 2: Climbers in Mount Hood National Forest. *U.S. Forest Service*
p. 21: Early print depicting Timbuktu (detail). *Library of Congress*
p. 81: Grierson's Raiders entering Baton Rouge, 1863 (detail).
    Library of Congress
p. 147: The eyes of spy Evelyn Lewis. *United Press International*
p. 193: Rugged mountain terrain in Mount Hood National Forest.
    U.S. Forest Service
p. 233: Whitewater rafting. *Gerald S. Ratliff*
p. 285: *Double Eagle II* nearing landing in France, 1978.
p. 323: Japanese ama divers. *Japan National Tourist Organization*
p. 377: Print depicting Galveston tidal wave, 1900 (detail).
    Library of Congress

Permissions

The permissions appearing on page 18 are hereby made part of this
copyright page.

Copyright © 1982 by Rand McNally & Company
All rights reserved
Printed in the United States of America
First printing, 1982

Library of Congress Cataloging in Publication Data
_____

    The Rand McNally almanac of adventure.
    1. Adventure and adventurers.   I. Title.
G525.P24   1982   904'.7   82-13297
ISBN 0-528-81118-5
ISBN 0-528-88063-2 (pbk.)

For Paige, David, and Amy,
whose adventures still lie ahead of them

Contents

Spies and Other Secret Warriors

On the Land and in the Mountains

On the Water

Foreword

An Adventurer Speaks Out About the Art
by Sir Edmund Hillary

Adventure is available for everyone, whatever his or her physical capacity. Call it challenge, testing oneself, building confidence, tasting fear—yet sensibly handled, adventure is good for all of us. When a civilization loses its sense of adventure, then it will surely decline.

In our modern society we devote much attention to safety and security. This is not a bad thing in itself, as long as our young are given every opportunity to take part in challenging activities. If there is an unfortunate disaster, people are very quick to make a public outcry demanding more rules, more regulations, more restrictions. Little thought is given to the thousands who enjoy the freedom to choose their own adventures—and happily succeed.

Adventurous activities can be tremendous fun for the participants. There will be occasions that are rather grim and even frightening, but most of the time adventure can be exhilarating and can result in a great sense of achievement. Adventure doesn't necessarily have to involve violent or exuberant activity. It may be pitching a tent in a peaceful corner of the woods, or sniffing the salty tang of the sea on some lonely coastline. It could be fishing in a high mountain lake, or floating down a foaming river. Adventure doesn't even require physical danger. There are substantial challenges to be found in the business and community world, and dealing with social problems may demand a moral courage greater than any needed on a mountain.

But to most of us, adventure is synonymous with danger, difficulties, and fear.

I believe that, young or old, you have the right to risk your life in a challenge if you wish to do so—as long as you aren't taking a gamble with an unwilling person's life at the same time.

Some years ago I met the famous Italian mountaineer Walter Bonatti. Someone asked him if he would want his son to become a mountaineer. The reply from this fabulous climber, who had probably taken as many chances as anyone, was very definite: "Never! I know too much about the risks and dangers," he told us. "Better that he should play tennis." I can understand his feelings, and I would never encourage an unwilling person to extend himself beyond his limits. There is nothing very clever about getting involved in some foolish disaster; it's often an admission of inefficiency or failure. Sheer common sense demands that we recommend caution, good planning, sufficient experience, consideration of others. But once these matters have been taken into account, then those who wish to do so have the right to try themselves out, even if they chance risking their lives in the process.

In 1961 my Himalayan Expedition made the first ascent of the fantastic peak Mount Ama Dablam, 22,300 feet, by a route up the southwest ridge. Many years later my son, Peter, himself an accomplished mountaineer, decided to attempt Ama Dablam with three companions "directissimo"—straight up the formidable unclimbed west face. It was not my responsibility, I believed, to try to dissuade Peter from this task. Only when he asked my views of the climb did I express my concern about the great masses of ice clinging to the face, providing a potential avalanche danger. But Peter had his answers ready: He had spent many days watching the face and had never seen any major avalanche coming down; his small team was technically very competent and could move very fast through the danger areas; he believed they could bivouac safely at night in protected positions. I still had my doubts but believed that the decision was up to Peter.

Overcoming extreme technical challenges, they made their way up this appalling face. All was going well and they were barely a thousand feet from the summit . . . then the avalanche broke loose— great chunks of ice leaping downward, right over the four-man team. One member was swept to his death, but somehow the main belay held. All the others were battered, and Peter had a broken arm and a badly sprained ankle. For three days they crept down the face at the limit of their endurance, then ultimately reached safety at the foot of the mountain. They had almost succeeded in this superb climb, but luck had been against them. I was deeply relieved that Peter had survived. Maybe they had been a little crazy; it was certainly something I would never have attempted myself. But they had wanted to do it and had nearly succeeded. At least they had the right to try.

All adventurous activities demand a certain degree of leadership ability. There is the need to plan, to make sound decisions, to persist even when the going is difficult. Some people seem to have natural leadership qualities, an almost instinctive ability to think quickly and soundly in an emergency. But like most things, leadership can be learned. Nearly everyone has the capacity to become a competent leader if he or she is prepared to make the effort and the sacrifices. I have frequently had members in my expeditions who were much more technically competent than myself or who were of considerably greater intellectual capacity. How is it possible to lead people like that?

There are a number of answers to this. Experience, of course, can give you an important ability to make decisions. Then "doing your homework" is of prime importance. Before going off to sleep at night, I have adopted the habit of running through my mind the potential problems of the next day and assessing what to do about them if they should occur. This enables me to be ready if a decision needs to be made. If someone else puts forward a good idea, don't try to crush it because you didn't think of it first. Build it into your plan and use it so it becomes yours, too; then everyone is happy. I am sure that none of us has to be a "natural" to be a leader—you can develop the skill with common sense and application.

Many adventures are solo efforts, and these usually demand considerable personal skill and ability. But team projects can sometimes be just as successful even though the individual members may have more modest attributes. The important thing is that the whole team should have a combined devotion toward its common objective.

In 1951 I made my first visit to the Himalayas, and the four in our team climbed some pretty good mountains, too. I was back in the Himalayas again in 1952, and then in 1953 Sherpa Tenzing and I stood on the top of Mount Everest. It was the culmination of much effort by many hardy expeditions and many tough climbers. I have good memories of those great days, memories of difficulties and danger, but even more so, memories of comradeship and team spirit.

I remember when Tenzing and I did a trial run up through the icefall just to prove how fit we were. We set off from base camp early in the morning and made our way up through crevasses and icewalls, certainly the most dangerous part of the mountain. We were traveling very strongly and we reached advanced base camp at 21,000 feet well ahead of schedule. We had time for a leisurely drink and some food, and then we turned downward again. Time was now against us—we must get back through the icefall before dark. We were roped together and I pounded along in the lead. Halfway down the icefall we approached still another of the innumerable crevasses, not particularly wide this one, but very deep. It was too wide to easily step across, but stuck onto the wall on the lower lip of the crevasse was a great chunk of ice, which we had earlier used as a cautious stepping-stone to enable us to reach the other side.

I came belting down the hill and reached the crevasse. Then, without thinking too sensibly, I just leaped in the air and landed with both my feet square on the chunk of ice. Whereupon the chunk of ice broke off and dropped into the crevasse with me on top of it.

We've all heard how sometimes in moments of stress your whole life may pass before your eyes. Well, I don't remember that happening to me, but one strange thing did occur—everything seemed to start going slowly. The walls of the crevasse were passing by, but it was only as if I were going down in a slow elevator, and I had plenty of time to think.

Time passed . . . and I came to the reluctant conclusion that if the rope didn't come tight pretty soon I would come to a sticky end on the bottom of the crevasse. At that moment up top, Tenzing whacked in a belay, the rope came tight with a twang, and I swung in against the icewall. The block of ice smashed to smithereens at the bottom of the crevasse. Then it was just a matter of cutting steps in the wall and carefully climbing my way up to the top.

People have often said to me, "Surely you must have felt a great sense of appreciation for Tenzing having saved your life like that." Well, I don't know that I really did! We were a team, and I expected Tenzing to carry out the right procedure in an emergency, as I would have expected myself to do if our roles had been reversed. Teamwork can be very important, and it was certainly teamwork that got Tenzing and me to the top of Everest.

Even on a mountain there can be a wide variety of adventurous activities. On one occasion a climbing friend, George Lowe, and I plus three Sherpas made the first crossing of the 19,000-foot Nup La Pass in the Himalayas. We'd been caught by heavy monsoon snows, and we had to descend a steep and complicated icefall. We couldn't see a thing, and avalanches were rumbling down all around us. I probably fell into more crevasses that day than most climbers do in a lifetime, and only the rope saved my life. We all got desperately tired—and pretty scared, too.

We thought we'd never find our way out of the maze of icecliffs and deep holes. Then, almost miraculously, we were on the easy glacier at the bottom and all the danger was behind us. Most people wouldn't have regarded it as an ideal camping spot—it was rough ice littered with boulders—but we put up our tents as best we could and crawled inside. The avalanches were still rumbling above us, and the wind and snow were whipping around, but we were cozy in our sleeping bags with a pot of stew bubbling on the pressure stove. We were immensely content and wouldn't have exchanged our tent for a palace. Maybe that's one of the good things about effort and danger—it's always so nice when it stops.

A couple of years ago I flew to the Canadian Arctic, to Resolute Bay and Grise Fjord at 77° north latitude. We saw Eskimos, ice-capped peaks, hundreds of miles of pack ice, and a 30-strong herd of muskox. We had a superb pilot at the controls of our Twin Otter aircraft, and he landed us on a steeply sloping bouldery beach. It was Beechey Island, about 76° north and a most uncomfortable landing site. We clambered out of the aircraft and walked up a hundred feet to some piles of weathered timber, to the graves of four of Sir John Franklin's men who had died there in 1846. I have rarely been in a more amazing place: the sea frozen hard; the abrupt rock cliffs of Beechey head; the feeling of space and isolation—it was all incredibly impressive. And men had gone there of their own free will, and in the end all of them had died.

Of course, you don't expect to die when you start out. Otherwise, I guess, none of us would leave home.

The moments you remember most clearly are not always the most dramatic ones. Certainly, the summit of Everest was important to me, but there have been many other occasions that were equally impressive at the time.

In the middle of October 1957, I set off from Scott Base in McMurdo Sound with a group of farm tractors, bound for the South Pole. Very few people in McMurdo Sound had any confidence in the traveling ability of our simple tractors, and our neighboring Americans and most of the New Zealanders at Scott Base openly doubted that we would get 50 miles out on the Ross Ice Shelf before having to be rescued. But the more opposition we got, the more determined I became to prove them wrong.

Our journey across the Ross Ice Shelf started off very slowly indeed; 6 miles were covered that first day. But then we started to improve—23 miles, 30 miles, 32 miles, and then 38 miles. On the sixth day we drove for 13 hours and covered a massive 50 miles, massive, that is, for us with our maximum 4 mph speed. We had reached our depot at the foot of the Skelton Glacier.

Ahead of us now was the great iceflow of the glacier, peppered with steep slopes and deep crevasses. For 130 miles it climbed up to 8,000 feet, where we had established the Plateau Depot with small ski planes. Would we be able to make it up there with our modest tractors?

For day after day we battled our way upward through drifting snow, breaking through the bridges over innumerable crevasses, being battered by constant strong winds. Whenever the sun appeared I'd hastily work out our position and then turn the tractors back to the right heading. Slowly we made height and reached the snowfields at the head of the glacier. Dense fog surrounded us, but still we pushed on. We knew we must be somewhere near the depot . . . but would we ever find it?

Suddenly the mist began to thin and we emerged into clear visibility. I looked anxiously ahead, and there on the horizon several miles away was a tiny black triangle—a tent. It was the Plateau Depot.

I have never felt more relieved or excited. Alone in my vehicle, in an unaccustomed outburst of emotion, I shouted and sang at the top of my voice. Despite all the doubts of others, and even ourselves, we had made it. We were still 900 miles from the South Pole, but that was one of the best moments I can ever remember.

There is no doubt that to be first on any adventure has a special attraction that nothing else can quite match. To first set foot on an unknown glacier or cross a great desert; to be first to cross the Atlantic by balloon or the first to drop over Niagara in a barrel—there is a special reward in such challenges, although why this is so, I sometimes do not know.

But adventure is not only achieving the obvious firsts. Nature itself provides a constant variety of challenges, and human beings are always seeking excitement in a multitude of ways. Life is an adventure in itself from birth to death. It can be mundane and even boring, or stimulating and demanding—the decision is largely up to us.

JANUARY 15, 1982

Acknowledgments

A book of this nature involves the time and efforts of many people as well as the cooperation and assistance of a large variety of organizations. It would be impossible to credit everyone who contributed to the book, but some stand out, and I wish to extend my deep appreciation.

Special thanks to: Sir Edmund Hillary, who sat for a long and involved interview and who graciously contributed the Foreword; rodeo rider Donnie Gay; Bob St. John of the Dallas *Morning News*; former CIA director William E. Colby; Sergeant Ron McCarthy of the Los Angeles SWAT team and the Los Angeles Police Department; Policewoman Carol Scannell and the Chicago Police Department; Richard Bangs and George Wendt of Sobek Expeditions, Angels Camp, California; Colonel Lewis L. Millett, U.S. Army, Ret.; hydroplane racer the late Dean Chenoweth and Budweiser, his sponsor; aerobatics ace Debbie Gary; rock climber Dan Goodwin; Lou Weber of Publications International, Ltd., Skokie, Illinois; Carter Smith of Media Projects Incorporated, New York; and fellow authors Weston W. George, Carol MacConaugha, Jim Hargrove, and Dereck Williamson.

Thanks also to these organizations: Himalaya Expeditions, Berkeley, California; Lufthansa Airlines; O.A.R.S. (Outdoor Adventure River Specialists), Angels Camp, California; New York *Times*; The Associated Press; Chicago *Tribune*; Chicago *Sun-Times*; Workman Publishing Company; Museum of Science and Industry, Chicago; National Aeronautics and Space Administration; and Lloyds of London.

The concept for this book was the brainchild of Stephen Sutton, senior editor at Rand McNally, who perished in the American Airlines DC-10 crash at Chicago's O'Hare Airport in May 1979, on his way to attend the American Booksellers Association convention in Los Angeles. The work was carried on, and I am deeply indebted to Steve for launching the project. I would also like to express sincere appreciation to the entire Rand McNally editorial staff, whose efforts, patience, and guidance were instrumental in bringing the book to fruition. Special mention should also be made of Milton Kaplan, for his assistance in photo research.

To everyone else who participated, added to, and otherwise complemented the work, cordial thanks are extended.

R. W.

Permissions

The author gratefully acknowledges permission to reprint the following items:

The Rand McNally
ALMANAC of ADVENTURE

Explorers and World Rovers

A Modern Adventurer Explores the Past

In the 20th century, what could be a more meaningful adventure than to experience in authentic detail the voyages of the world's earliest mariners? What could be more exciting and illuminating than to face the same challenges, hardships, and perils as those encountered in the dawn of civilized humankind? And what could be a more appropriate place from which to launch such an enterprise than from a land believed by many to be the very cradle of civilization?

It was only natural that one of the world's foremost modern adventurers, Thor Heyerdahl, would choose such an undertaking. To demonstrate the seafaring capabilities of early cultures, the Norwegian-born amalgam of explorer, scientist, historian, and author had sailed the Pacific from Peru to Polynesia in 1947 on his now famous raft *Kon-Tiki* and in 1969 had traversed the Atlantic from Morocco to Barbados in a vessel built of papyrus. Now, he wanted to reenact the exploits of mariners from ancient Sumer, the oldest known civilization.

The people of Sumer, whose culture preceded that of Babylonia and Assyria in Mesopotamia, had settled in what is today southern Iraq. On reliefs and other artifacts, they left behind illustrations of the boats they crafted of reeds, and cuneiform writings that, deciphered, tell us how they built the vessels as well as the lore of some of their travels. It was Heyerdahl's aim to demonstrate that the primitive watercraft could traffic beyond the local rivers and were perhaps used to spread the Sumerians' burgeoning culture to civilizations on the African continent and to lands in what are known today as Pakistan and India.

The project was named the Tigris Expedition. The site chosen for building the vessel, to be known as the *Tigris*, was the confluence of the Tigris and Euphrates rivers, on a spit of land lush with date palms and emblazoned by magnificent sunsets, said to be the lost paradise of Adam and Eve. It is also where adventurous Sumerians collected the resilient reeds called *berdi* and lashed them together to form their boats.

The *Tigris* sailed under the flag of the United Nations, appropriate certainly because of the apolitical nature of the venture, but also because the crew was a microcosm of that modern body. Besides the Norwegian Heyerdahl, the crew included two Americans, the navigator and the National Geographic Society filmmaker; a Soviet physician; a German merchant seaman; an Italian mountain climber; an underwater cameraman from Japan; a Mexican film producer; and students from Norway, Denmark, and Iraq. In addition, a group of Aymara Indians, experienced reed-boat builders from Lake Titicaca in Bolivia, were brought over to help in the intricate construction of the ship.

The pulp-filled *berdi* reeds had to be harvested in the month of August if they were to be used for boat-building, Heyerdahl learned; otherwise they would be too absorbent and a craft made of them would quickly become waterlogged and sink like a giant bale of hay. And that created a problem because during August in that torrid area of the globe daily temperatures range from 100 degrees to 120 degrees Fahrenheit. Such heat obviously would severely curtail the activities of Heyerdahl and his associates, but it hardly disturbed the Marsh Arabs (or Madans) who live there and who were employed to wade out into the marshes and harvest the enormous amount of reeds necessary to build a 60-foot-long, 20-foot-wide boat. The Marsh Arabs also seemed unaffected by the bilharzia that infest the swamps, tiny and extraordinarily obnoxious worms that drill through human skin and then multiply inside the body.

Working from diagrams created from ancient writings and drawings, Heyerdahl's team of builders constructed the Tigris totally from materials that were natural to the time and locale of the Sumerians. It took nearly a year to build the boat and bring in the stores and supplies necessary for the extended voyage.

By November 1977, the Tigris was ready for launch. Cheered on by an excited, waving crowd of local Marsh Arabs, the odd-shaped vessel, which Heyerdahl referred to as "a floating haystack," moved out into the water. Its sail was hoisted, and the craft was maneuvered into the current of the river Shatt al-Arab, the name given to the waterway formed by the conjunction of the Tigris and

Euphrates rivers. The intrepid crew, re-creators now of ancient marine adventure, watched the verdant point of land believed to be the site of the Garden of Eden steadily diminish as they sailed downriver toward the Persian Gulf.

The distance to the gulf was about 100 miles as the proverbial crow flies. The river route was much lengthier, weaving snakelike through a land that, by the 1970s, was one of great historic contrasts. At one extreme were the small villages built along the banks, with houses of reeds, date plantations, grazing water buffalo and goats, women cloaked in long black robes, men fishing or seining from slender, hand-built canoes, half-naked children and their yapping dogs, a culture uninfluenced by time or technology. Far removed from that life was the shattering reality of the modern world not too many miles farther down the river: dreadfully polluted water, palm trees displaced by smokestacks and radio towers, modern buildings, new bridges, and an immense traffic of oceangoing tankers and barges. The Tigris, as it passed through this environment and into the gulf, was a startling anachronism.

Once in the open sea—called the Persian Gulf by the Iranians, who inhabit the eastern coastline, and the Arabian Gulf by the Arabs, who control the western coast—the Tigris began the calculated test of its seagoing capability, in which Heyerdahl so strongly believed.

The destination of the ancient Sumerians who had set sail from the mid-Asian mainland was often an island referred to in their writings as Dilmun, their ancestral home. Dilmun is believed today to be either Bahrain or Faylakah, two islands along the Arabian coast of the gulf.

And so Heyerdahl set the course of the *Tigris* for Faylakah, the closer of the two islands, resting just off the coast of Kuwait. But the approach to the island, surrounded by shallows and jagged reefs, is treacherous. The winds carried the *Tigris* directly toward the worst of the shoals, and desperate, Heyerdahl anchored in the shallows so that his buoyant but certainly vulnerable vessel would not be swept into the roaring reefs. The only way out was a tow, obtained by barter from a crew of Arab pirates on a motorized dhow.

The *Tigris* suffered some damage, including a rather disconcerting hole in the outer layer of the bow of the ship, but the deep layering of the *berdi* reeds prevented water from getting in and swamping the boat. Heyerdahl moved on down the gulf to Bahrain, where repairs were made using some *berdi* reeds he had brought along as well as native palm stalks bought from the Bahrainians.

The Persian (or Arabian) Gulf at Bahrain and the peninsula of Qatar forms a right angle, so *Tigris* sailed east to the Strait of Hormuz, which leads to the Gulf of Oman.

As they floated in these warm waters, Heyerdahl and his crew viewed with amazement and ultimate caution a most dazzling spectacle, great schools of sea snakes. All were brightly, shockingly colored. They floated lazily on the surface or swam lethargically, but however indolent they were deadly poisonous.

There was another floating peril for the occupants of the *Tigris*, this one man-made. Pollution. Black oil slicks, congealing asphalt wastes, sudsy white sludges from paper mills, and a variety of other chemical contaminants were commonplace, testament to the size of the oil industry of the Middle East and the modernization of the cities of that region. The crew of the *Tigris*, unlike the ancient Sumerians, had to be constantly on the alert to avoid, or at least be able to quickly escape, these maritime hazards because the acrid material could eat away at the structure of the ship and cause it irreparable damage.

The Strait of Hormuz is an ever-moving maze of congestion. Huge tankers and oilers are everywhere, anchored or plying the narrow waterway. There was perhaps no greater danger on the entire expedition than weaving amid these behemoths of the sea.

The *Tigris* paid a visit to the port of Muscat, the capital of Oman. Until 1970, no foreigners had been allowed into that country, which encompasses the southeastern segment of the Arabian Peninsula. Even after that time, only those personally approved by the supreme Sultan Qaboos were permitted to visit the land.

From Muscat, the *Tigris* made its way across the Arabian Sea and along the coast of Pakistan, near the site of the Indus Valley civilization. The culture that once flourished there was perhaps as ancient and as advanced as that of the Sumerians.

The Arabian Sea is the northernmost region of the Indian Ocean, and out on its vast waters the *Tigris* was constantly accompanied by patrolling sharks—some friendly and innocuous, but others, like the hammerhead, huge and menacing—as well as by great schools of multicolored fish that moved along with the craft as if drawn by some invisible magnet. There were occasional schools of porpoises who rose and fell in the water in their own inimitable dance. Even a few curious whales, including killer whales, surfaced and cruised beside the strange-looking craft ·of reeds. The crew caught or speared fish almost at will to bring aboard a variety of fresh food, and at night errant but tasty flying fish made the fatal mistake of choosing the *Tigris*'s deck for their landing.

At Ormāra, an ancient and primitive village in Pakistan, the *Tigris* moored for a visit. Here, camel trains came and went, the men wore turbans, and the women, clad in brightly colored robes, could be seen carrying jugs of water on their heads. Ormāra is a "shark village." The main industry is catching sharks and selling them as food. Heyerdahl and his crew observed the process. The decapitated bodies of huge sharks are submerged in ponds, then stomped on by villagers, the pressure expunging the ammonia from the shark's flesh, making the fillets edible.

The *Tigris* sailed on to Karachi, Pakistan, the now vast seaport of more than 5 million inhabitants.

From there, Heyerdahl and his crew decided to recross the Arabian Sea and head for the east coast of Africa. It was a long voyage, about 1,900 miles, and a supreme test of the oceanic durability of the reed boats of the Sumerians. The *Tigris* fared just as Heyerdahl had expected, without a problem.

Then, however, an insurmountable difficulty arose, and it was of human making. The countries of Somalia and Ethiopia, whose coastlines stretch for 1,500 miles along eastern Africa, were at war. Heyerdahl was told that to land anywhere in either country could be extremely dangerous and at the least might result in imprisonment.

The plan was therefore altered. Instead of sailing down the coast of Africa, Heyerdahl would navigate the *Tigris* into the Gulf of Aden and through the narrow strait of Bāb el-Mandeb into the Red Sea to continue the journey northward. But that plan foundered too, as soon as word was received that the politically sensitive governments of Yemen and South Yemen would not grant permission for the explorers to land on either of their coasts.

Only the small African republic of Djibouti, perched precariously between the warring nations of Somalia and Ethiopia, offered hospitality, and Heyerdahl had no choice but to accept it.

Because of political conditions in Africa and southern Arabia, the *Tigris* Expedition could proceed no farther. It ended at Djibouti, after a remarkable 4,200-mile, 143-day odyssey on the water. As Thor

Heyerdahl later wrote in his book about their adventure:

> There was suddenly nowhere to sail in any direction. . . . I took a hard decision. Instead of being left to rot, *Tigris* should have a proud end, as a torch that would call to men of reason to resume the cause of peace in a corner of the world where civilization first took foothold. We would set the reed bundles ablaze at the entrance to the Red Sea as a fiery protest.

And so ended the *Tigris*, the sturdy, stable ship of reeds that had served 20th-century adventurers as its ancestral ships had the world's earliest mariners. It went up in a dazzling conflagration, but it left an indelible mark on modern-day adventure.

A Motive to Move:
The Making of an Explorer

The call of the unknown and the hitherto unvisited, and the desire to discover new cultures have motivated humankind since the earliest times. What stirs human beings to explore their world (and now the one beyond it) and the romance involved form the heart of this piece, which has been excerpted from The Rand McNally World Atlas of Exploration, *by Eric Newby.*

The story of man the hunter is one of continual adaptation to an almost always hostile environment. What impelled him to travel were probably the same reasons that still cause the lesser animals to migrate. The exhaustion of game and other foods due to overkilling, overcropping, and the changing seasons; natural cataclysms and disasters, such as earthquakes and forest fires; and in the long term, changes in the earth's climate. When he began to make weapons of stone about 50,000 years ago, man's capacity to kill was vastly increased and the need to find new hunting grounds became urgent. His tenacity of purpose, powers of reasoning and imagination, which continued to increase in the face of difficulty and disaster, enabled him to survive the four great ice ages, which, in the space of a million years, covered great tracts of the Northern Hemisphere with enormous sheets of ice, altering its physiognomy. His retreat before them may have been the occasion of the first mass migrations. His crossing of the land bridge between Asia and America about 20,000 years ago, during the last Ice Age, was made possible, it is thought, by the shallowness of the sea. When the ice melted and the water rose, the bridge was submerged and the continents were separated.

Whatever the reasons for man's peregrinations, there would soon be few regions of the earth where a human footprint was unknown: from the west coast of Greenland, high above the Arctic Circle in the Northern Hemisphere, to as far south as Tierra del Fuego, beyond the [Strait of Magellan]. The only continent where no evidence of human occupation has so far been found has been Antarctica; yet even there, on an island close to the Antarctic peninsula—one of the visible summits of a land bridge that may have linked South America with the southern continent—mysterious spherical stone artifacts were discovered in the 19th century.

It is for this reason—the astonishing ubiquity of man on the face of the earth (even in the heart of the 250,000-square-mile Rub'al Khali in Arabia, "The Abode of Emptiness," the 20th-century explorers Bertram Thomas and Wilfred Thesiger found that there were men ready to kill them)—that in the entire history of exploration, there are comparatively few instances that can be given of man discovering virgin territories that were not already known or inhabited. The assumption, for instance, that the interior of Africa was "discovered" by members of the nations of the West is in a sense as absurd as a claim by an inhabitant of the Congo to have "discovered" New York because he was the first to have traveled there. When [David] Livingstone found what he named the Victoria Falls, "the most wonderful sight I have witnessed in Africa," he learned from the indigenous inhabitants that they already had a name for it—Mosiottatunya, "The Smoke that Thunders," by which it is still known to the present inhabitants of Zambia, who consider the name of a foreign and long-dead monarch an affront.

"Westerners," Henri Cordier wrote in his *Histoire Generale de la Chine*, "have singularly narrowed the history of the world in grouping the little that they knew of the human race around the peoples of Israel, Greece, and Rome. Thus they have ignored all those travelers and explorers who in their ships plowed to the China Sea and the Indian Ocean or rode across the immensities of central Asia to the Persian Gulf."

Although Western man has tended to see the opening-up of the world as a preeminently occidental achievement, in his search for what are to him new lands, he has invariably come across other civilizations already long established there. When in 1492 B.C. the Egyptian queen Hatshepsut dispatched an expedition to the mysterious land of Punt to obtain myrrh trees to embellish the great mausoleum and temple at Deir el-Bahri, its members were greeted by people of a high order of civilization who fully appreciated the value of gold, silver, ivory, leopard skins, and very probably of the myrrh tree also. When the Portuguese explorer Vasco da Gama "discovered" the ports on the east coast of Africa in 1498, he found that they were already populated by Arabs, Persians, and various mixtures compounded with the blood of the indigenous inhabitants and that Moorish ships were carrying on a brisk trade with India and beyond, laden with gold and silver, which were exchanged for cloves, peppers, and ginger, "as also quantities of pearls, jewels, and rubies, all of which articles are used by the people of this country." When da Gama reached India, he found that the Moors had preceded him there and enjoyed a monopoly of trade with the inhabitants. Even the Moors had been anticipated by the Chinese, who had already traded with India and the coast of Africa from Somaliland and Madagascar between the 9th and 12th centuries.

The instances are innumerable. When Marco Polo, "the first traveler to trace a route across the whole longitude of Asia, naming and describing kingdom after kingdom that he had seen with his own eyes," reached Khan-balek, the capital of the Great Khan on the site of present-day Peking, he found it to be a city of splendor with walls 24 miles in circumference, which contained eight vast palaces. In one of them there was a banqueting hall that could seat 6,000 persons (the same number that can be accommodated in the banqueting hall of the present Communist Great Hall of the People [in Peking]. When [Hernando] Cortes and his conquistadors reached Tenochtitlan, the Aztec capital, on the present site of Mexico City, they found a remarkable people whose members were able to achieve stupendous works of engineering without the aid of metal tools, beasts of burden, or

the use of the wheel and had a civilization even more bloodthirsty than their own. When [Francisco] Pizarro set out to take the great Inca city of Cuzco, which had 250,000 inhabitants, he and his men traveled to it along a magnificent trunk road hundreds of miles long, thousands of feet above the sea in the high sierras, a road that crossed great chasms by means of highly sophisticated suspension bridges. Even that most legendary of legendary cities, Timbuktu, had been flourishing for centuries before the first foreign traveler, the indefatigable Arab ibn-Batuta, set foot in it. The city was to remain a mystery to European man for another 500 years, and it was not until 1826, when it had long been in decline, that the first European, Alexander Laing, succeeded in reaching it. We cannot say that Laing "discovered" Timbuktu, nor for that matter that ibn-Batuta did so.

What in recorded time have been the principal motives that inspired men to risk their lives in search of the unknown? Trade, especially to satisfy the demand for luxurious and exotic merchandise; the need to found colonies to relieve overcrowding at home or else to escape from invading peoples; sheer curiosity (evinced at a surprisingly early date); the dispatch of missions and embassies to obtain some favorable alliance; the desire to convert the heathen, which often went hand in hand with a policy of national aggrandizement; the study of geography; the desire for gold and silver; the urge to find alternative routes from Europe to the East that engrossed mankind for centuries; the trade in slaves; the belief in the existence of Terra Australis, a great southern continent; scientific inquiry and reconnaissance. In the 20th century, a new motive became apparent—exploration for its own sake, sometimes inspired by a desire for personal or national glory or a mixture of the two—to be the first to reach the Poles; to be the first to climb the highest mountain in the world, "because it is there." This motive too inspired to some extent the race to be first in space, first on the moon.

If it all sounds a little dry, the records left by the explorers themselves are not. They cover the whole range of human experience: of suffering and endurance, exultation, splendor, and misery, abominable cruelty to the people they encountered, and sometimes self-sacrifice. The temptation was to go on beyond human limits, beyond the possibility of return, which often led them to "the undiscovered country from whose bourn no traveler returns." Many failed to take the advice tendered to Alexander the Great, on the banks of the river Jhelum, when he proposed to extend his conquests and explorations to the entire world. "Sir," said Coenus, "if there is one thing above all others that a successful man should know, it is *when to stop.*"

Bravery is the thread that binds them. When the monk [William of] Rubruck reached the camp of the Tartar khan Mangu, after a journey of 3½ months from the Volga in the 13th century, he was told by the great ruler, "Fear not." Rubruck replied,

"If I had been afraid, I would not have come."

Henry de Tonty, prisoner of the Iroquois on the shore of Lake Michigan, one of whom "plunged a knife into my breast, wounding a rib near the heart . . ." had "a man behind me with a knife in his hand, who every now and then lifted up my hair. They were divided in opinion. Tegantouki, chief of the Isonoutouan, desired to have me burnt. Agoasto, chief of the Onnoutagues, wished to have me set at liberty as a friend of M. de la Salle, and he carried his point."

Of another sort was the 19th-century traveler [Johann Ludwig] Burckhardt, of whom it was written:

He was of that small company of profoundly wise and foreseeing travelers who go with ease where others may not even go with pain and knowing no stirring moments in a land wherein to some every hour brings peril. He testifies that he was never more at peace than in Mecca, and nowhere in Arabia suffered any hap more inconvenient than falls to the ordinary lot of wayfarers and pilgrims in the Hijaz.

It is the sea and the reaching of land that have inspired what are perhaps the most memorable descriptions. Coming ashore on an island of the New World after a perilous voyage at the beginning of the 11th century, the Viking crew of Leif [Ericson], son of Erik the Red, found, to [its] great delight, "dew on the grass, and the first thing [the crewmen] did was to get some of it on their hands and put it to their lips, and to some of them, it seemed the sweetest thing they had ever tasted." Anchored off Tahiti in 1767, Louis Antoine, Comte de Bougainville, wrote of the moment when the inhabitants first came out to the ship in their canoes "crying 'tayo' which means friend. . . . They pressed us to choose a woman and to come on shore with her. . . . It was very difficult to keep at their work 400 young French sailors who had seen no woman for six months."

Such moments of happiness were rare for the early sailors. On [Ferdinand] Magellan's voyage to the Pacific [in 1519], they were:

three months and 20 days without taking in provisions, and we only ate old biscuit reduced to powder, and stinking from the dirt that the rats had made on it . . . and we drank water that was yellow and stinking. We also ate the ox hides that were under the main yard . . . also the sawdust of wood, and rats that cost half a ducat each . . . and the upper and lower gums of most of our men grew so much that they could not eat [due to scurvy] . . . and in this way, 19 died . . . besides 25 or 30 fell ill of divers sicknesses, both in the arms and legs and other places.

In such ships, the great gales of high latitudes were an awesome experience. Of [Sir Francis] Drake's ship in the strait between Cape Horn and the South Shetlands it was written that it was driven back again "into 55 degrees, toward the pole Antarctic, as a pelican alone in wilderness . . . [with] the most mad seas, the lee shores, the dangerous rocks, the contrary and most intolerable winds—the most impossible passage out. . . ."

John Davis's description, in 1587, of the mouth of the Hudson Strait was equally evocative:

eight or nine great races, currents, or overfalls, loathsomely crying like the rage of waters under London Bridge. . . . [The next day] coming close by a foreland or great cape, we fell into a mighty race, where an island of ice was carried by the force of the current as fast as the bark could sail with lum [light] winds . . . where at our great admiration we saw the sea falling down into the gulf with a mighty overfall, and roaring, and with divers circular motions like whirlpools.

The Antarctic explorer [Ernest] Shackleton, sailing with three companions in a 20-foot open boat through the stormiest seas in the world from Elephant Island to South Georgia in search of help for his ship's crew, gives a graphic description:

At midnight, I was at the tiller and suddenly noticed a line of clear sky between the south and southwest. I called to the other men that the sky was clearing, and then a moment later, I realized that what I had seen was not a rift in the clouds but the white crest of an enormous wave. During 26 years' experience of the ocean in all its moods, I had not encountered a wave so gigantic. It was a mighty upheaval of the ocean, a thing apart from the big, white-capped seas that had been our tireless enemies for many days. I shouted, "For God's sake, hold on! It's got us!" Then came a moment of suspense that seemed drawn out for hours. White surged the foam of the breaking sea around us. We felt our boat lifted and flung forward like a cork in breaking surf. We were in a seething chaos of tortured water; but somehow the boat lived through it, half full of water, sagging to the dead weight and shuddering under the blow. . . .

Hunger and thirst to the last extremity were a common experience of explorers, whether on land or sea. When the Australian explorer Ernest Giles walked out of the great Gibson Desert in 1873, having lost his companion in the sands, he carried a 45-pound keg of water on his shoulders for 60 miles and, at the end of the stage, finding a small, dying wallaby weighing not more than two pounds, in his own terrible words, "the instant I saw it, I pounced upon it and ate it, living, raw, dying—fur, skin, bones, skull, and all."

When Major Egerton Walker attempted to cross the [Australian] continent from Alice Springs to the Indian Ocean that same year in drought conditions with 17 camels, the animals began to collapse and die one by one. Those that did were either cut up and jerked (dried) or eaten on the spot:

No shred was passed over. Head, feet, hide, tail, all went into the boiling pot. . . . The tough, thick hide was cut up and parboiled. The coarse hair was then scraped off with a knife and the leather-like substance replaced in the pot and stewed until it became like the inside of a carpenter's glue pot, both to the taste and the smell. . . .

In a desperate bid to assuage the tortures of thirst, another Australian explorer, Alexander Forrest, drank the blood of a dead hawk. Not surprisingly, this dire measure failed.

But in spite of all the danger, suffering, trials, and tribulations, it was worth it, even if individual discoveries, such as that made by the Venetian navigator [Alvise da] Cadamosto, were only steps—often accidental—on the long road to knowledge of the world. Cadamosto was striving to find a way to the Indies when he became the first Westerner to observe the Southern Cross (albeit a rather disappointing constellation) off the coast of West Africa in 1455:

During our stay at the mouth of the river, we only saw the Pole Star once; and then it sank so low that it seemed to touch the sea, apparently standing only one-third of a spear-shaft above the water. There we also saw six large and wonderfully bright stars. We measured them with the compass. We believed them to be the Great Bear of the Southern Hemisphere.

It was a heartening sight but hardly the longed-for goal. Twenty-seven years passed before Diogo Cão finally succeeded in sailing south of the equator.

[Robert E.] Peary reached the North Pole, realizing his life's ambition, and then pushed on for five miles with two Eskimo companions, from which point he was looking southward down the other side of the world. "East, west, and north had disappeared for us," he wrote. "Only one direction remained, and that was south. Every breeze that could possibly blow upon us, no matter from what point of the horizon, must be a south wind. Where we were, one day and one night constituted a year, a hundred such days and nights constituted a century. . . ."

Beneath the Pole in the Arctic Ocean, Peary found no bottom in 1,500 fathoms. The year was 1908. Fifty-two years later, Jacques Piccard and Don Walsh sank in the bathyscaph *Trieste* to the floor of the world at 35,000 feet in the Mariana Trench . . . "the last extreme on our earth that remained to be conquered. . . ."

Perhaps the greatest experience reserved for man . . . has been to gaze down on the planet that was his birthplace and see it for the first time as a whole. . . .

Eugene Cernan, one of the two men in Gemini 9, one of the spacecraft used to produce the first color photographic survey of the earth, described how,

> without blinking an eye I could see the high Andes, the Pacific Ocean, the great Altiplano with a jewel-like Lake Titicaca, the rain forest of the Amazon basin and the Chaco plains on down our or-

bital path. The broad western bulge of Africa was the most interesting area of the world to see from space. Its dry, desolate terrain was nearly always free of clouds, and it was a delight to photograph because there was so little haze to dim its beauty. The tiny Indian subcontinent was especially fascinating, representing the lives of 500 million people whose lives were dependent upon the scattered pre-monsoon cloud cover so clearly visible. Also conspicuous were individual houses in haze-free Nepal, the wake of a ship on the Brahmaputra, an oil refinery near Perth, Australia, and numerous other phenomena such as the Four Corners power plant in New Mexico, whose smoke emission was detectable from 620 miles out in space, submarines, individual city streets, blast furnaces and a wealth of hurricanes, storms, cyclones, as well as the launch facilities at Cape Kennedy [Canaveral]. . . .

In a matter of seconds lands were traversed that took the 14th-century Arab explorer ibn-Batuta (who is estimated to have covered 75,000 miles, without taking into account detours) 30 years of his life.

In one way nothing has changed. Man, with all his efforts, is still poised on the edge of the unknown. We are very dependent on one another and we are not masters of our destiny—a fact of which the early mariners, venturing forth in their fragile vessels, were all too conscious.

Two Days in the Life of Captain Cook

James Cook, one of the greatest English explorers, was born in the village of Marton-in-Cleveland, Yorkshire, in 1728. A onetime apprentice to a grocer and haberdasher, he chose a life on the sea at the age of 18. Cook worked his way up through the ranks of the Royal Navy and took his first command in 1764, as master of the schooner Glenville.

Cook, remembered for his productive explorations of the Pacific coast of North America, the islands of the south Pacific, and of New Zealand and Australia, was also the first man in history to sail across the Antarctic Circle. He made three famous voyages to the Pacific: the Endeavour, 1768–1771; Resolution, 1772–1775 (Cook was finally promoted to captain after this voyage); and Resolution, 1776–1780, which resulted in great contributions not only to geography but to various other areas of science, medicine, and navigation as well. And his voyages were often as extraordinary as they were adventurous. Take for instance these two days logged in Captain Cook's journal.

January 16, 1770, in the south Pacific

Variable light airs and clear settled weather. At 1:00 P.M. hauled close round the southwest end of the island, on which stands the village before mentioned, the inhabitants of which were all in arms. At two o'clock we anchored in a very snug cove, which is on the northwest side of the bay facing the southwest end of the island in 11 fathoms water; soft ground, and moored with the stream anchor. By this time several of the natives had come off to the ship in their canoes, and after heaving a few stones at us and having some conversation with Tupia [a Tahitian whom Cook had picked up to serve as a guide and interpreter], some of them ventured on board, where they made but a very short stay before they went into their boats again, and soon after left us altogether. I then went ashore in the bottom of the cove, accompanied by most of the gentlemen on board. We found a fine stream of excellent water, and as to wood the land is here one entire forest. Having the seine with us we made a few hauls and caught 300 pounds weight of different sorts of fish, which were equally distributed to the ship's company. Morning, careened the ship, scrubbed and payed the larboard side. Several of the natives visited us this morning, and brought with them some stinking fish, which, however, I ordered to be bought up to encourage them in this kind of traffic, but trade at this time seemed not to be their object, but [they] were more inclinable to quarrel, and as the ship was upon the careen I thought they might give us some trouble, and perhaps hurt some of our people that were in the boats alongside. For this reason I fired some small shot at one of the first offenders; this made them keep at a proper distance while they stayed, which was not long before they all went away. These people declared to us this morning that they never either saw or heard of a ship like ours being upon this coast before. From this it appears that they have no tradition among them of Tasman [Abel Tasman, a Dutch explorer of the mid-17th century] being here, for I believe Murtherer's Bay, the place where he anchored, not to be far from this place; but this cannot be it from the latitude, for I find by an observation made this day at noon that we are at an anchor in 41 degrees 5 minutes 32 seconds south, which is 15 degrees to the southward of Murtherer's Bay.

January 17, 1770

Light airs, calm and pleasant weather. Afternoon, righted ship and got the other side ready for heeling out, and in the evening hauled the seine and caught a few fish. While this was doing some of us went in the pinnace [a small sailing boat] into another cove, not far from where the ship lays; in going thither we met with a woman floating upon the water, who to all appearance had not been dead many days. Soon after we landed we met with two or three of the natives who not long before must have been regaling themselves upon human flesh, for I got from one of

them the bone of the forearm of a man or woman that was quite fresh, and the flesh had been but lately picked off, which they told us they had eat; they gave us to understand that but a few days before they had taken, killed, and eat a boat's crew of their enemies or strangers, for I believe they look upon all strangers as enemies. From what we could learn the woman we had seen floating upon the water was in this boat and had been drowned in the fray. There was not one of us that had the least doubt but what these people were cannibals; but the finding this bone with part of the sinews fresh upon it was a stronger proof than any we had yet met with, and, in order to be fully satisfied of the truth of what they had told us, we told one of them that it was not the bone of a man, but that of a dog; but he, with great fervency, took hold of his forearm, and told us again that it was that bone: and to convince us that they had eat the flesh he took hold of the flesh of his own arm with his teeth and made signs of eating. Morning, careened, scrubbed, and payed the starboard side of the ship; while this was doing some of the natives came alongside seemingly only to look at us. There was a woman among them who had her arms, thighs, and legs cut in several places; this was done by way of mourning for her husband who had very lately been killed and eat by some of their enemies as they told us and pointed toward the place where it was done, which lay somewhere to the eastward. Mr. Banks got from one of them a bone of the forearm, much in the same state as the one before mentioned; and to show us that they eat the flesh, they bit and gnawed the bone and drawed it through their mouths, and this in such a manner as plainly showed that the flesh to them was a dainty bit.

Ten years later, on February 14, 1779, Captain Cook encountered another, even more dangerous group of Polynesian natives. At Kealakekua Bay in the Hawaiian Islands (known then as the Sandwich Islands), in full uniform and carrying a double-barreled shotgun, Cook went ashore with a guard of sailors and British marines to confront the natives there about the theft of one of the rowboats

from his anchored ship. The Polynesians were immediately hostile. Cook stood his ground, then made his demands. Things got very unruly. The British raised their arms, cocked their rifles, even fired several warning shots. Despite their muskets, however, the British were attacked. The enraged natives, throwing stones, wielding spears, and totally disregarding the enemy's guns, forced the British mariners into a retreat back to the shore. And with the waves lapping at his feet, Captain Cook was bludgeoned and stabbed to death, ending a magnificent career as an explorer in His Majesty's service.

13 Ill-Fated Explorers

Exploring new and forbidding worlds has always produced an inordinate share of risks. Some intrepid souls have sailed right through—making their discoveries; establishing themselves as eminent explorers; and then in their twilight years, writing about their exploits, lecturing, or merely retelling their stories in the corridors of geographic societies or universities. Other adventurers—often successful contributors to the story of the earth's exploration—have not been so fortunate, bravely accepting the challenge to expand human horizons and daring to go where no one else had gone before but paying the ultimate price in the quest.

Juan Ponce de León
(Spanish, 1460?–1521)

Juan Ponce de León set out to explore the New World and perhaps discover the legendary Fountain of Youth in the early 1500s but lost his life in the quest. Born in Tierra de Campos, Spain, Ponce de León spent most of

his life as an explorer and was killed in his early sixties without ever having gazed upon or tasted the "miraculous waters."

As a young man, Ponce de León first sampled adventure by fighting in the Moorish Wars. In 1493, however, he sought a more peaceful challenge as one of the 1,500 men to man the 17-ship fleet composing Christopher Columbus's second voyage to the New World. Ponce de León did not return with Columbus; instead he settled on the island of Hispaniola (today the countries of Haiti and the Dominican Republic). From there, he launched his own explorations and eventually settled in Puerto Rico in 1508. King Ferdinand of Spain named him governor of that island the following year, but in 1511 the king bestowed the office on Christopher Columbus's son Diego. In conciliation for his ouster—which had been a political move on the king's part—Ponce de León was given three ships and the commission to explore the Caribbean area and, in particular, to seek out the Fountain of Youth, which was believed to be on the Caribbean island of Bimini.

Instead, on April 3, 1513, one month after he had set sail from Puerto Rico, Ponce de León happened on a mass of land to the north of the Caribbean. Although he thought it to be a large island, it was in fact a peninsula. Claiming his new discovery for Spain, he named it *Pascua Florida* (roughly translated as "Easter") because he had reached its shore during the Lenten season. The location of that first landing on Florida soil was in the vicinity of St. Augustine.

For the next eight years, Ponce de León continued to sail the Caribbean, establishing settlements there at the direction of the king of Spain, and to search for the Fountain of Youth. During that time, he explored much of the Bahamas, the Florida keys, and a set of islands inhabited by a large number of land turtles, naming the islands the Dry Tortugas in their honor. In September 1513, he returned to Puerto Rico to serve as governor for several years. But in February 1521, he again sailed to Florida, traveling with two ships and 200 men. Midway up its west coast, he and his crew went ashore at Charlotte Harbor. They found the Indians to be unfriendly there and so sailed a short distance to Sanibel Island, where they found the Indians to be even less friendly. In the skirmish that followed, Ponce de León was hit by an Indian arrow and, seriously wounded, was taken aboard ship. His crew took him to Havana, Cuba, to recuperate, but he died there in July 1521 as a result of the wound.

Willem Barents
(Dutch, died 1597)

The Dutch navigator Willem Barents is best known for his exploration of the frigid Arctic sea bounded by Scandinavia to the south, Spitsbergen to the west, and Novaya Zemlya to the east. The sea now bears his name, but for such recognition he paid a grave price.

Barents was in search of a Northeast Passage, a waterway that would link Europe to China, launching his first voyage in this quest from Amsterdam in 1594. Two ships, making their way up the North Sea into the Arctic Circle and around the northernmost coast of Norway, sailed as far north as the desolate twin islands of Novaya Zemlya, which extend north of 75 degrees latitude above the coast of the Soviet Union. A year later, Barents embarked on another voyage, leading seven ships through the strait that separates Vaygach Island (just south of Novaya Zemlya) and the Soviet mainland, and then into the Kara Sea.

The third voyage, Barents's most productive and historic, was also his last. On May 10, 1596, he set sail from Vlieland, an island off the northwest coast of the Netherlands. There were only two ships, and this time instead of rounding the northern coast of Norway, Barents continued due north. On June 9, in latitude 74 degrees 30 minutes north, he sighted an island whose southern face was a sheer cliff of ice that rose 1,300 feet above the ocean waters. Barents and his shipmates became the first Europeans to discover what would become known as Bear Island. They then sailed north to Spitsbergen and followed its west coast to latitude 80 degrees 10 minutes north. Then the two vessels separated because Barents and the captain of the other ship, Jan Rijp, disagreed on which course they should take to find the Northeast Passage. Barents's ship headed east, while the other ship went farther north.

Barents reached the extreme northern tip of Novaya Zemlya and rounded it at Cape Mauritus, just above the Kara Sea. There, however, the ice, ever-forming as the northern summer was coming to an end, locked the ship in an inescapable vise. Barents and his crew abandoned the ship and made their way to the mainland of the island at a bay known today as Ice Haven. It was early September, and the brutal Arctic winter had begun. The stranded sailors were able to gather driftwood, however, and built a crude shelterhouse that they hoped would see them through the winter.

Some men went back to the ship and gathered their supplies and equipment—oil lamps, an hourglass, a clock, a barrel, bunks, and blankets—and brought them to the house. By late September the men had exhausted their food supply. Some of them were given the chore of trapping foxes, and others set out to hunt polar bears. They lived on the meat of the animals they trapped or shot and used the fat extracted from the polar bears for their lamps. Then in November, the sun disappeared into the Arctic night and was not to reappear for more than three months.

When the sun shone again at the end of January, most of the men were barely alive to greet it. They were weak and racked with scurvy. By June, the ice had broken up enough to allow them to set out in two open boats salvaged from their ship. The hull of the ship itself had been crushed by the ice and would never be seaworthy again. After seven days at sea, as the boats weaved their way through the ice-ridden waters, Willem Barents died and was buried at sea. The other men continued down the west coast of Novaya Zemlya, living on seabirds and their eggs as well as a kind of growth called "scurvy grass." Some survived, and in November they reached the Russian coast at Kola, where they met Jan Rijp's ship, which had already arrived in port.

In 1871, Elling Carlsen, a Norwegian seal hunter, discovered Barents's driftwood house, still intact nearly 300 years after it had been abandoned. Many artifacts were found at the site: crude pieces of furniture, fashioned implements, lamps, a clock, a musket, a powder horn, a flute, portions of Barents's journal, and the writings of the crew members. Today, these items are on display at a museum in The Hague, Netherlands.

John Davis

(English, 1550?–1605)

John Davis was one of the first British explorers determined to discover the Northwest Passage to the Pacific Ocean. Today, the great strait that lies between Greenland and Baffin Island, an area of ocean he often sailed in pursuit of the elusive opening to a sea lane to Asia, is named for him.

Davis, the son of a yeoman farmer, was born about 1550 in Sandridge, England. But it was not until June 1585 that he set out on his first northwest expedition. With two ships, the *Sunshine* and the *Moonshine*, and 26 men, he sailed to the icebound east coast of Greenland, followed it south, rounded its southern tip (which he named Cape Farewell), and then headed north up the strait that now bears his name. On August 6, as the ships angled northwest, Davis and his crew found the coast of Baffin Island in latitude 66 degrees 40 minutes north. They then discovered Cumberland Sound, the huge inland waterway flanked on the north by mountains 8,000 feet tall, in about latitude 65 degrees north, and

believed it to be the Northwest Passage. As winter approached and the ice began to form, however, Davis and his crew were forced to return to England.

On his second voyage into the North Atlantic, launched in May 1586, Davis cruised along the west coast of Greenland and sailed into the inlet that he had passed on his first voyage and had named Gilbert Sound. In June, he landed on one of the islands and made contact with friendly Eskimos who lived there. Davis and his shipmates sang English country ballads for their amusement and even taught them how to play soccer. As the Englishmen left, however, they kidnapped one of the Eskimos, forever dooming any further relationship they could have had with the colony. Still having found no passage, they returned to England.

A third and similar expedition was launched in 1587. Davis sailed up the coast of Baffin Island as far as latitude 72 degrees 12 minutes north but then was forced to turn back. Later, Davis drew new maps based on his findings, chartings of the Arctic regions that would prove quite helpful to such explorers as Henry Hudson and William Baffin.

He returned to England in time to command a ship, the *Black Dog*, against the invading Spanish Armada in 1588, and during the 1590s Davis explored the southern route to the Pacific. He sailed with Thomas Cavendish between 1591 and 1593 and then later on his own. Part of his objective was to enter the Pacific Ocean, sail north, and find a western entrance to the Northwest Passage. He then would return through the passage to England. On one of these voyages, in 1592, he discovered the Falkland Islands off Tierra del Fuego at the southern tip of South America.

During this time, Davis also invented a 45-degree backstaff, later known as the Davis quadrant. An important addition to navigation instruments (it is the predecessor of the sextant), it enabled the sun's altitude to be measured in high latitudes without sunblinding the user. He also wrote two important books: *The Seaman's Secrets*, on navigation, and *The Worlde's Hydrographical Description*, about the Northwest Passage.

Davis sailed with the East India Company for four years, until 1605, when his ship was attacked by Japanese pirates off Bintang near Sumatra. Davis was killed in the battle with the pirates on December 27, 1605.

Henry Hudson
(English, died 1611)

One of the most famous explorers to cross the Atlantic Ocean, Henry Hudson met his demise at the hands of his crew in the early summer of 1611, and according to what is recorded in history, with some justifiable cause.

Hudson is best known for his explorations along the upper east coast of the United States and Canada and in the bay that bears his name, but he began his career by searching for a route to the Pacific Ocean in another direction. The Muscovy Company (a consortium of English merchants who were carrying on trade with Russia) commissioned him to sail the Arctic Ocean to seek out a Northeast Passage to Asia—in effect, to discover a "Northern Passage ." In 1607, he sailed on his first voyage, heading north until he reached Spitsbergen in latitude 80 degrees 23 minutes north. There an ice barrier forced his return to England. The next year, he was financed again by the Muscovy Company, and this time he sailed as far east as Novaya Zemlya in the Barents Sea.

The Muscovy Company, however, either gave up on the idea of a Northeast Passage or had lost faith in Hudson's ability to find it, and so he signed with the Dutch East India Company, setting sail on his third voyage in the *Half Moon* on April 13, 1609. With a crew composed of Dutch and English sailors, he again headed to the northeast, but he encountered an impassable ice floe before he reached Novaya Zemlya. Then the crew, unaccustomed to the harsh weather conditions, staged a mutiny, quelled only by Hudson's decision to change course in search of a Northwest Passage.

The *Half Moon* turned sail and reached the east coast of the United States, at Virginia, in the late summer of 1609. In early September, Hudson sailed into New York harbor, exploring 150 miles up the river that today is named for him. Then he returned to Europe.

Sailing under the flag of England, Hudson, bringing along his young son, John, embarked on what was to be his last voyage on April 17, 1610.

Setting out aboard the *Discovery*, a 55-ton vessel, Hudson once again struck out to the west but he traveled much farther north this time. After two months at sea, the *Discovery* reached what is today known as Hudson Strait, an inland waterway at about latitude 60 degrees north. During the next six weeks, he explored and charted the strait, and by July he had entered what he thought at first to be an ocean but was in fact an enormous bay—about 480,000 square miles—to which he also gave his name. For the next three months, Hudson explored the 500-mile eastern shore of the bay, but he stayed too long.

It was the beginning of November, and the ice prevented Hudson and his crew from sailing out of the bay, and so they set up a winter camp in its southwest corner, known today as James Bay. Throughout the winter, Hudson parceled rations to his men, their meager diet supplemented by the wild game, mostly birds, that they could obtain hunting. It was a brutal winter, one that lasted longer than normal in that frigid climate, and the hardships were overwhelming. Spring did not bring a respite from the cold, and there was barely enough food for survival. By the time the ice began to break up, the starving crew was almost uncontrollable.

The *Discovery* broke free of the ice in early June 1611, but bitter words were still being passed among the crewmen. Three days later, suspecting their captain had not been fair in apportioning the food, they rose in mutiny. According to the journal of a mate, Abacuck Prickett, the men found various food items in Hudson's cabin: "200 of biscuit cakes, a peck of meal, of beer to the quantity of a butt." It signaled the end for Henry Hudson. The mutineers seized him, his young son, and seven others deemed to be involved in the chicanery, pushed them aboard a small boat, and then set them adrift, with no provisions, into the ice-ridden bay. Henry Hudson, his son, and the others were never seen again.

The mutineers, however, did not fare much better than Hudson. On their return trip to England, they stopped at Greenland, where they were attacked by Eskimos. Many of them were killed. Only a handful of survivors reached London in September 1611. They were put on trial for mutiny but were found not guilty.

Vitus Bering
(Danish, 1680–1741)

In 1719, Peter the Great, czar of Russia, ordered a scientific exploration of the north and east coasts of Asia; his hope was to find a land passage that would connect Asia and North America. The first few voyages yielded nothing substantial. Then in 1725, the same year that Czar Peter died, he commissioned Vitus Bering, a Danish explorer, to sail in that quest under the flag of Russia.

But the first ship in this new venture, called the Kamchatka Expedition, did not take to the water until 1728. The reason was a credible one: Bering and his crew first would have to gather their equipment at St. Petersburg and haul it across the great expanses of Russia and Siberia to the Sea of Okhotsk. There they would transport it by boat to the Kamchatka Peninsula; cross that mountainous, ice-ridden tract of land; and then stow it at the mouth of the Kamchatka River, where they would build a ship to take them on their first voyage. It took Bering three years to accomplish this, and perhaps never in the history of exploration had the initial preparation been so arduous.

But in July 1728, Bering and a crew of 44 men set sail on the *Gabriel*. Moving north, Bering charted the barren coastline of eastern Siberia and then entered the vast sea that today is named for him. Here, in August, he discovered St. Lawrence Island, just south of the easternmost tip of Siberia and less than 200 miles from Nome, Alaska. Then for fear of becoming icebound, Bering turned his ship homeward. He sighted and named the Diomede Islands, not knowing that he was passing through the narrow strait that separates Asia from the New World, the strait that one day would bear his name. But Bering and his crew did not sight the mainland of Alaska; it lay just a few short miles beyond their horizon.

Several other Russian expeditions followed, but the Great Northern Expedition, personally ordained and financed by Empress Anne of Russia, called for the most elaborate plans. It was designed primarily to survey the north coast of Russia and especially the mouths of the great Russian rivers—the Ob, the Lena, and the Yenisey. Bering was put in command of this grandiose opera-

tion that involved 600 men, but he never went to sea with it. In fact, he was not to be under sail again for eight years.

It was June 4, 1741, before Bering captained a ship again—the St. *Peter*. Another explorer, Aleksey Chirikov, was placed in command of a sister ship, the St. *Paul*. Both sailed out of Avacha Bay on the east coast of Kamchatka Peninsula, but a storm arose shortly afterward, and the two ships lost contact with each other and went their separate ways. Bering took the St. *Peter* north and then east and on July 17, in latitude 58 degrees 14 minutes north, Bering saw for the first time the coast of a great land mass. What rose before him was 18,000-foot Mount St. Elias in southeastern Alaska. He believed correctly that he had discovered a part of the New World. For the next month, Bering charted the Gulf of Alaska, passing Kodiak Island and continuing down the Alaska Peninsula and the Aleutian Islands.

The trip, however, was exceptionally difficult. Strong, gale-force winds continually threw the ship off course, and in October scurvy took hold aboard ship and soon debilitated the crew. Bering, who also was plagued with the illness, set a course toward Avacha Bay. By early November, however, Bering and his crew were so ill that they had to put in at an island about 100 miles east of the Kamchatka Peninsula. Winter came upon the island (later to be named in Bering's honor), and they existed with only sails from the ship for shelter and, for food, the raw flesh of seals, seabirds, and sea otters that they were able to trap or shoot. But the onslaught of scurvy could not be combated, and Bering and almost half the crew died of it during that brutal winter of 1741. Forty-five members of the original crew survived, built a small boat, and made it back to Russia in the fall of 1742 to tell of their discoveries and ordeal.

Jean de la Pérouse
(French, 1741–1788?)

Jean François de Galaup, Comte de la Pérouse, joined the French navy when he was 15 years old and experienced his first taste of adventure when he fought off the east coast of North America during the French and Indian War in the early 1760s. During the American War of Independence, La Pérouse returned to North America to aid the Americans in their conflict with England. He commanded a French ship that conducted daring raids on British trading posts in Hudson Bay.

La Pérouse, however, was not to be remembered foremost as a warrior, but rather as an intrepid explorer who sailed the length and breadth of the Pacific Ocean and finally lost his life there. After the war, he was commissioned to command two corvettes, l'Astrolabe and la Boussole, on an expedition funded by Louis XVI, king of France. The object was to explore the Pacific Ocean, essentially to extend the explorations of the British explorer James Cook.

On August 1, 1785, La Pérouse set sail from the French port of Brest, beginning what would be a 2½-year journey from which neither he nor his crew would return. The two ships crossed the Atlantic Ocean, rounded Cape Horn in late January 1786, and then entered the Pacific. They continued up the coast of South America, angled west to stop at the Sandwich Islands (now called the Hawaiian Islands), and then sailed along the northwest coast of North America as far north as Mount St. Elias in Alaska. They had been under sail for more than a year.

La Pérouse then guided the two ships down the west coast of North America, and in September, after stopping for several days at Monterey Bay, just below the present site of San Francisco, he headed back out across the Pacific. By this time, La Pérouse had noted in his journal that the existence of a Northwest Passage seemed highly doubtful. He had also refuted some of Captain Cook's findings.

On his trek west, La Pérouse stopped again at the Hawaiian Islands; continued on to the Philippines; and reached the port of Macao, China, in late January 1787. He then guided the two ships up Korea Strait, between Japan and Korea; north beyond the Japanese island of Hokkaidō; and through Soya Strait, which separates Hokkaidō from Sakhalin, an island in the Soviet Union. From there, La Pérouse sailed up the east coast of the Kamchatka Peninsula. Stopping at the desolate port of Petropavlovsk, he dispatched Baron Jean de Lesseps with his journals, giving him instructions to carry them overland to France. Jean de Lesseps not only completed the trip, a journey covering a distance almost halfway around the world, but also became the only survivor of the expedition.

The voyage was far from over, however. In September 1787, La Pérouse set sail for the South Pacific, where he visited the Navigators Islands (now known as Samoa), Tonga, and Norfolk Island, and then sailed to Port Jackson, New South Wales.

By February 1788, La Pérouse was once again at sea, heading northeast on his way to chart the Solomon Islands. But when he and his crew reached Vanikoro Island in the Santa Cruz Islands, just south of the British Solomons, they were beset by a torrential storm. The ships were damaged so badly that the men had to go ashore. Hostile natives attacked them on sight, and about half the French sailors were slaughtered. The others managed to escape, built a small boat, and left the island but were never heard from again. It is not known whether La Pérouse died at the hands of the natives or was drowned in the swells of the sea.

Mungo Park
(Scottish, 1771–1806)

Born in Selkirk, Scotland, Mungo Park had a background more diversified than most explorers of his day. A surgeon, a friend of the famous Scottish novelist Sir Walter Scott, and a happily married man, he was also a victim of wanderlust, costing him first his freedom and later his life.

Shortly after entering his twenties, Park signed on as an assistant surgeon for an exploratory voyage—his first journey—aboard an East In-

diaman bound for the island of Sumatra. By the time Park was 24 years old, the African Association, a group of wealthy gentlemen who met regularly at St. Alban's Tavern in London and who were dedicated to searching for the Niger River and the fabled African city of Timbuktu, had commissioned Park to carry out such an expedition.

In May 1795, Mungo Park set sail from England and 30 days later arrived at the mouth of the Gambia River on the west coast of Africa. After following the river for 200 miles to the east, Park reached a British trading post known as Pisania and stayed there for almost six months while studying the Mandingo language and otherwise preparing for his trip in search of the mysterious Niger.

In December, Park left Pisania and started on what was to be a difficult journey across the Senegal Basin. He and his party not only had to contend with the heat (their route was in about latitude 12 degrees north), the tropical diseases, and the wild animals, but also harassment by the tribal chieftains. In some areas, the explorers were able to buy their way through with trinkets, but in others they had to give the chieftains more substantial possessions—clothes, pack animals, and supplies.

After heading east for two months, Park was accosted by an irate Muslim chieftain, who had him imprisoned in a squalid jail for four months. The others fled for their lives. But on July 1, 1796, Park managed to escape on horseback, and with the tenacity of a Scotsman, he continued his quest alone.

Twenty days later, he finally came upon the Niger River at Ségou, a river village (in modern-day Mali) about 700 miles east of the Atlantic Ocean. From there, Park navigated a makeshift canoe down the river about 80 miles to Silla. By this time, however, Park was worn down by sickness and fatigue and was helped back to the port at Gambia by a native slave trader whom he had met along the way. Weathered, shaken, but triumphant, Park arrived in England in December 1797.

Park then wrote a book about his adventures in the Dark Continent. *Travels in the Interior Districts of Africa* was published in 1799 and became a British best-seller.

In October 1801, Park went back to the practice of medicine in Scotland. But almost four years later, he was on his way to Africa again, leaving England from Portsmouth harbor with a party of 40 on January 31, 1805. After cruising up the Gambia River to Pisania, he and his party embarked by canoe and portage to the Niger. This trip would prove to be more difficult than the first one, the tropical rains and the diseases ravaging them to such a degree that by August 19, when they reached the Niger at Bamako, 29 men in the party of 40 had died from malaria, sleeping sickness, or dysentery. At Sansanding, a village just above Ségou, the remaining 11 members of the expedition rested to prepare for the arduous journey down the Niger, but they were weak and some of them succumbed.

When Park was finally ready to explore the river in November, only four members of the group were still alive. With them, three slaves he had purchased, and a native interpreter, Park launched a strange-looking vessel that they had fashioned from two decayed canoes, lightweight wood, thatch, vines, and a variety of other products of the jungle. The group followed the flow of the river to the east and then to the south for a full 1,000 miles, a journey never before taken by any European. In the spring of 1806 it ended, however, not at the Atlantic Ocean, as Park believed it would, but at a series of rapids near the village of Bussa (in modern-day Nigeria). There, just 500 miles short of the Niger delta, the small group was attacked by natives. Park and most of the others were pitched into the roiling waters of the rapids and drowned. One of the slaves escaped to later tell the story of Mungo Park's fate.

Park's legacy was a major one in the annals of exploration. His journal, which he had sent back to Gambia before he departed on his final journey, gave the first authentic picture of the West African interior.

Johann Ludwig Burckhardt
(Swiss, 1784–1817)

The obsession to find and enter the notoriously mysterious city of Timbuktu stirred Europeans in the early 19th century to concoct some daring and bizarre plots. The members of the African Association of London thought they had the answer when they approached Johann Ludwig Burckhardt, a 25-year-old orientalist and adventurer from Lausanne, Switzerland. Burckhardt would go to

Egypt; disguise himself as an Arab; join one of the caravans that periodically traveled through Egypt en route to Timbuktu; and, as a part of it, clandestinely gain admission to the fabled city.

Burckhardt agreed and left England in March 1809, fully aware of the dangers of impersonating a Muslim or of infiltrating any of the holy places in Arabia or Africa. That same year, Ulrich Seetzen, a German botanist and Arabist, pawned himself off as a dervish to enter the holy cities of Mecca and Medina and later was murdered in the desert.

According to the plan, Burckhardt first went to Syria, arriving in Aleppo in July. During the next 2½ years, he mastered the Arabic language, learned the customs of the people, and studied Islamic doctrine and laws in depth. He was not to be an ordinary Muslim but a devout and scholarly one as well.

By June 1812, Burckhardt was ready. Dressed in the robes of a Muslim and traveling under the name Shaikh Ibrahim ibn-Abdullah, he journeyed from Syria, down through Jordan, and across the Sinai to Egypt. There he planned to join a caravan that would take him across the Sahara Desert, on to the Niger River, and finally to Timbuktu, an arid journey of nearly 2,400 miles.

On the way to Cairo, Burckhardt happened on the village of Petra, an ancient city of Jordan, which had been inhabited by the Edomites in biblical times and had been home to the Nabateans, an Arab tribe, since the 2nd century B.C. Rich with the ruins of its own civilization, as well as those from Roman occupation about A.D. 200, the city had not been visited by a European since the Crusaders stopped there and built a citadel in the 12th century.

By September 1812, Burckhardt had arrived in Cairo but could not find a reliable caravan heading west. So he decided to explore the virgin deserts of Dongola and Nubia, in southern Egypt, and on March 22, 1813, he discovered the two great temples at Abu Simbel. Pharaoh Ramses II had the temples built into the sandstone cliffs on the west bank of the Nile south of Aswan to honor himself and his queen, Nefertari. The larger temple had four enormous statues of Ramses II, each 67 feet tall, sculpted at the entrance. (This temple was dismantled piece by piece in the 1960s and moved to higher ground, so that it would not be submerged in the lake formed by the Aswan High Dam.)

Burckhardt then continued on to Isna, a village about 75 miles north of Aswan. And it was here that he decided to take a different route to reach Timbuktu. Instead of returning to Cairo, he would cross the Nubian Desert, then the Red Sea, and join the Muslims on their way to Mecca and Medina. There he would link up with a caravan that would take him to Timbuktu. Certainly it was a precarious and indirect route but, he thought, one that would eventually get him there.

Burckhardt floated south on the Nile to Shendi, a center for the slave trade, about 100 miles north of Khartoum in modern-day Sudan. There he joined a camel caravan, which took him to the Sudanese port of Suakin on the Red Sea. With a group of other pilgrims, he crossed the sea and landed at the Arabian port of Jidda. Burckhardt then made his way into the holy city of Mecca and in January 1815 followed the holy trail to Medina.

Despite all the dangers of his masquerade, Burckhardt survived. His surreptitious entry into the high holy places of Islam was historic, and he later cataloged all he saw and experienced. But he could not combat the perils of nature, being stricken with malaria in Medina, and so set out for Cairo in the hope of recuperating there. He still had plans to reach his initial goal, Timbuktu, but two years after his arrival in Cairo in 1815, he died there as a result of acute dysentery and malaria.

Hugh Clapperton
(Scottish, 1788–1827)

Hugh Clapperton did not survive to see his 40th birthday, but during his relatively short life, he became an eminent explorer, discovering Lake Chad in Africa and almost, *almost*, becoming the first European to reach the sought-after city of Timbuktu.

Born in Dumfriesshire, Scotland, Clapperton began his roving career at an early age, putting out to sea as a cabin boy in his early teens. In his twenties, he served in the Royal Navy and then began a career as an explorer, first visiting the South Pacific with the East India Company and later exploring the North American forests surrounding the Great Lakes. By the time Clapperton was 32 years old, he was ready to take on the interior of the African continent.

In 1820, Clapperton and two British explorers, Walter Oudney and Dixon Denham, were invited to join an expedition to Bornu (today a central African kingdom extending from northeastern Nigeria to the western savanna of Chad). Clapperton and Oudney landed in Tripoli, Libya, where Denham joined them, and in October 1821 the group headed south across the desolate expanses of North Africa. In December, the three men reached Bornu, discovering Lake Chad on February 4, 1823, and the Chari River, which flows into the southern end of the lake, two months later. After spending more than a year in Bornu, Clapperton and Oudney set out together for the Niger River, which they knew was somewhere directly to the west of them. Oudney, however, became ill and died on the way, and Clapperton went on alone. But after reaching the village of Sokoto, about 150 miles east of the Niger, Clapperton, ill himself from the rigorous journey in the tropics and unable to employ a guide, decided to return to England. He rejoined Denham in Kuka, where both of them linked up with a caravan to Tripoli. They then voyaged to England, arriving there in June 1825.

Clapperton did not stay in London for a full two months, however, before he again set sail for Africa. This time, he hired a helper, Richard Lander (who later discovered the Niger delta and proved finally that the Niger River did flow into the Atlantic Ocean). Clapperton wanted to take up where he had left off—to reach the Niger River and travel up it to Timbuktu. Instead of traveling down from Tripoli, he decided to sail around the upper west coast of the continent into the Gulf of Guinea and land on the shore of the Bight of Benin, apparently not fearing the warning sung by seafarers, "Beware and take care of the Bight of Benin; for one that comes out, there are 40 goes in."

On March 31, 1826, after traveling inland for three months, Clapperton and Lander came upon the Niger River at Bussa, confronting the white water that had claimed the life of Mungo Park 20 years earlier. But the thrill of finding the river and the prospect of navigating it northward to Timbuktu were overshadowed by a tropical fever that almost totally disabled Clapperton. Realizing that he could not continue in his condition, he traveled, with the help of Lander, to the village of Sokoto in the hope of obtaining medical treatment. The journey took three days, but when they entered the village on April 13, 1827, Clapperton died (becoming, as the old salt's chantey predicted, one of the 40 that goes in but does not come out). Richard Lander was the fortunate "one" to survive the Bight of Benin. But seven years later, when on another expedition, he was killed by natives on a bank of the Niger River.

Jedediah Smith
(American, 1799–1831)

In the 1820s, Jedediah Strong Smith was described as intelligent, tough, and adaptable, but a mild man and a pious Christian. By the age of 30, he had earned a small fortune as a fur trader and a substantial reputation as one of the foremost explorers of the American West and Southwest.

Born in Jericho (now Bainbridge), New York, Smith set out on his first westward expedition in 1822, his goal to travel up the Missouri River and to trap and hunt for furs in the Rocky Mountains. It was a frightening initiation to the wilds of the unexplored West. Just past the Black Hills in South Dakota, Smith suffered a severe mauling by a wounded grizzly bear before the members of his expedition were finally able to kill it. Then they encountered the blizzards and the freezing cold of an especially brutal Rocky Mountain winter.

Smith searched for a way through the rugged mountains of Wyoming, but it was March before he found one. Friendly Indians had told him of a pass that would get his party through; it later became known as South Pass, the "gateway to the American West."

Smith and his party of fur trappers crossed the Continental Divide, and continuing about 75 miles to the southwest, they came upon the Green River and then followed it south, working it for beaver down to Flaming Gorge at the northern border of Utah and the northern slopes of the Uinta Mountains. Then they explored north, and after reaching the Clark Fork of the Columbia River in the northwest corner of Montana, Smith led his party back south, hooking up with the Snake River in Wyoming. They did some trapping and hunting along the river for a while before they started on their return trip to the Great Salt Lake in Utah.

In August 1826, Jedediah Smith led another major expedition. Setting out from the Great Salt Lake with 16 men and 50 horses, he was about to become the first explorer to reach the Pacific Ocean by traveling diagonally across the forbidding desert terrain of Utah, Nevada, and southern California. Smith and his party battled the rapids of the Colorado River, crossed the searing Mojave Desert, and scaled the San Bernardino Mountains to reach the Pacific, at San Gabriel, not far from modern-day Los Angeles.

After a skirmish with the Mexican government (which controlled the southern portion of California in the 1820s) that led to Smith being placed under house arrest for a short time, he led his party back to the Great Salt Lake, and in returning, according to historian Helen Delpar, "They accomplished what no white men and probably no Indians had done... crossed North America's highest mountains and its largest desert, the Great Basin."

On July 13, 1827, not quite two weeks after his return, Smith again set out for California. By the fall of that year, he had reached San Jose, where once again he became involved with the Mexican authorities, this time being accused of and arrested for trespassing and making illegal claims for the United States. The charges, based on an Indian's accusations, were eventually dropped, and Smith continued his trek up the coastline into Oregon, charting the land along the way. One year later, in Oregon, near the Umpqua River, he

and his partners were attacked by the Kelawatset Indians. The only member of the expedition to escape alive was Smith, who managed to reach the Hudson Bay Company outpost at Fort Vancouver.

While Smith had been exploring and charting new frontiers in the American West and Southwest, he had also carried on a trade in furs, and by 1830 he was a rather wealthy young man. Whether it was his suddenly realized affluence or his close brush with death in Oregon, Smith decided that he would no longer explore the West. In October 1830, he bought a house in St. Louis, Missouri, intending to settle down to a quiet life, but within a year he agreed to ride scout on a wagon train bound for Santa Fe, New Mexico. On May 27, 1831, as he rode ahead of the wagon train to search for water along a bank of the Cimarron River, 32-year-old Jedediah Smith was attacked and brutally murdered by a marauding band of Comanche Indians.

Ludwig Leichhardt
(German, 1813–1848)

Ludwig Leichhardt was not the typical swashbuckling adventurer who explored new and mysterious lands in the 18th and 19th centuries. He graduated from the University of Berlin in 1836; avoided work as best he could; joined the Prussian army, only to desert later; and then fled to Australia.

Leichhardt had credentials as a natural scientist—botany and geology principally—but he would never become an eminent explorer, although he had hoped to gain fame from his ventures in Australia.

In February 1842, Leichhardt arrived in Sydney, where he lectured on botany and geology until 1844, when he had raised enough money to finance his first expedition. He was an unlikely-looking leader—bearded and rather handsome, yes, but garbed in a Malay coolie hat and knickers with a long sword hung from his waist. The group, which included John Gilbert, an ornithologist, set sail in August 1844, traveling north from Sydney to Brisbane on the east coast of Australia. From there, the party would head northwest to explore the swamps, forests, and plains around the Gulf of Carpentaria and then move north overland and, in the vicinity of Cape York Peninsula, cross the Great Dividing Range and carry on to the gulf. But it took the party a full seven months to reach a pass through the Great Dividing Range, and in the words of the historian Helen Delpar, "Leichhardt calculated that only one-quarter of the journey had been completed but three-quarters of the provisions had been consumed." Undaunted, however, the men continued.

By June 1845, the party had reached the banks of the Mitchell River, which snakes a little more than 100 miles before flowing into the Gulf of Carpentaria. There the party was attacked by aborigines, Gilbert being speared to death and two others suffering injuries. Leichhardt and the others who managed to escape were able to entice a few friendly aborigines to guide them to the west, traveling north across the gulf coastal lands to Port Essington (modern-day Darwin) on the northern coast.

In December, the decimated, scurvy-ridden group reached the port city, recuperated, and then in March 1846 sailed back to Sydney. There they were given a hero's welcome, the government of Australia awarding Leichhardt an honorarium of £1,500 and the king of Prussia having sent him a pardon for his desertion from the king's army.

In early 1848, Leichhardt set out on an even more ambitious project. He planned to lead a small party of men on a northwest course across the continent. The group would travel from Darling Downs, on the west side of the Great Dividing Range, near Brisbane on the east coast, to the Victoria River in the north; follow the river to its mouth in the Timor Sea; and then travel the coast south to the Swan River. In a somewhat disjointed way, the party would be semicircling the great island. However, the men never got farther than 300 miles on their 2,000-mile expedition. Near the Barcoo River, the group of seven men and more than 70 pack animals disappeared. Two of their campsites were later discovered, but no trace of the men or their animals has ever been found.

Salomon Andrée
(Swedish, 1854–1897)

With the dawn of the 20th century came the great rush to become the first human being to set foot on the North Pole. Among those in search of the historic honor was Salomon Andrée, who at the age of 40 resigned from his job as the chief engineer at the Swedish Patent Office and announced his plans to travel to the Pole in a unique way. He would float there aboard a hot-air balloon. The funds for the flight, which would carry Andrée and his two companions to the top of the earth, were elicited from Oscar II, king of Sweden, and Alfred Nobel, the inventor of dynamite and by his last will the founder of the Nobel Prizes. The craft was the Örnen (the Eagle), an enormous balloon almost 100 feet tall and 65 feet in diameter, its Chinese silk casing capable of containing 212,000 cubic feet of hydrogen. Hung from it was a gondola large enough for the three men and their Spartan cache of supplies.

The launch was set for July 1896; the site chosen was Dane Island, just off the west coast of Spitsbergen. Accompanying Andrée were Knut Fraenkel, a young sportsman, and Nils Strindberg, a physicist, a photographer, and a nephew of the Swedish playwright August Strindberg. Everything was in order, except the wind, which remained unfavorable while the summer wore on. Finally, the flight had to be scrubbed.

The next summer, however, Andrée and his two mates were back on Dane Island with the Örnen, and this time the winds were favorable. So on July 11, 1897, the Örnen lifted from the ground, caught the gentle wind, and drifted toward the North Pole.

Besides playing the various wind currents, Andrée also had devised a steering gear, which in effect was a dragline. After flying for approximately 250 miles, about one-third the distance to the Pole, however, the three men ran into erratic, gusty winds, which caused them to lose their steering apparatus. Then on July 12, they entered a dense fog. Ice began to form on the great balloon, weighing down the craft, and on July 14, in latitude 82 degrees 56 minutes north and longitude 29 degrees 52 minutes east, the aeronauts were forced to crash land on the ice.

The only hope they had, Andrée felt, was to attempt to make it across the ice and water to Spitsbergen, an extraordinary trek under the best of conditions. But with only random ice floes for navigation and their meager supplies for survival, they packed up and moved out on foot. Along the way, the three men supplemented their diets with the meat from the polar bears that they were able to kill, and despite the cold and the Arctic storms, they managed to reach White Island, only about 50 miles from the coast of Spitsbergen, on October 5. They were forced to set up camp in their attempt to survive the Arctic winter, but they did not succeed, their diary notes indicating that the men perished in October.

No one learned of the fate of Salomon Andrée and his companions for the next 33 years. Then on August 5, 1930, Gunnar Horn of Norway, a geologist, and a group of seal hunters happened on their camp and found their frozen bodies. Also at the site were their individual journals and rolls of film, which surprisingly were able to be developed—all of which chronicled their tragic ordeal.

Robert F. Scott
(English, 1868–1912)

Robert Falcon Scott was no stranger to the desolate, frozen continent of Antarctica when he set out to reach the South Pole in 1911. As a young lieutenant in the Royal Navy, he led the National Antarctic Expedition into McMurdo Sound in 1902 and set up a base camp on Ross Island, where he remained for more than two years conducting a series of inland explorations and scientific projects on the continent.

Seven years later, he was ready to strike out for the South Pole, where no human being had ever set foot. He not only would be combating the cold, the ice, the fury of the Antarctic blizzards, and the treacherous, crevasse-ridden terrain but also would be competing against the Norwegian explorer Roald Amundsen, who was launching his own assault on the Pole via a different route.

Scott reached Cape Evans on Ross Island in January 1911 and immediately probed inland to set up way stations (called "depot laying" in the jargon of polar explorers), stocking them with provisions for the trek to come. Then during the dark Antarctic winter (May to September), Scott finalized the route and personally attended to all the other details of the expedition.

Scott's force consisted of 33 men, 33 sled dogs, and 17 ponies, although only a party of four men— Scott; Lieutenant Edward Evans, second in command; Dr. Edward Wilson, a scientist and an artist; and Lawrence ("Titus") Oates, an old Es-tonian cavalry officer—was scheduled to make the final march to the Pole. Amundsen, on the other hand, had no ponies but brought 118 sled dogs, which he knew would provide not only hauling power but also food, if it came to that (and it did— only 11 dogs returned; most of the others were consumed by the men and the surviving dogs).

The journey to the Pole was approximately 800 miles over the ice, but standing awesomely between Scott and his destination was the imposing Beardmore Glacier, 100 miles long and 30 miles wide, which leads to the 10,000-foot-high Antarctic Plateau. On November 1, 1911, Scott's main party and several support parties moved their sleds out from the base camp. By late December, they had ascended the glacier and were about half the distance to the Pole. Most of their ponies, however, had died from exposure, and the others, weakened, had to be shot. The hauling now had to be a joint effort between the dogs and the men. Scott then led the group across the great Antarctic Plateau, and on January 4, 1912, the last support party left Scott to return to the base camp.

Scott had added a fifth man to the main party, Lieutenant H. R. Bowers, a Royal Indian Marine, to accompany him and the others through the last five depots. And on the morning of January 18, they descended to the spot that Scott had calculated to be the South Pole. There they found a tent with a small Norwegian flag flying above it. Amundsen had beaten them, arriving on December 14,

1911. He had stayed there for three days and now was well on the way back to his base camp at the Bay of Whales.

Bitterly disappointed, Scott and his party started back. But the temperatures were lower and the blizzards more frequent and severe than they had anticipated. Two members of the party were badly frostbitten. Lieutenant Evans died just after the group had descended the Beardmore Glacier in February, and one month later Titus Oates, realizing he could go no farther, hobbled out of the tent one evening and was never seen again. The three surviving men struck out for the next depot, but the blizzards were so severe that they had to stop, pitch camp, and try to wait it out. The temperatures of the Antarctic autumn were dropping below −40 degrees Fahrenheit at night, and the party's supply of food was all but gone.

On March 29, 1912, Scott wrote in his journal:

> Every day we have been ready to start for our depot only 11 miles away, but outside of the tent it remains a scene of whirling drift. I do not think we can hope for any better things now. We shall stick it out to the end, but we are getting weaker, of course, and the end cannot be far.... It seems a pity, but I do not think that I can write more.

The following November, a search party found their tent, the bodies of Scott and his two companions frozen in their sleeping bags. There were also a collection of fossils and other geological specimens and, of course, Scott's journal.

The Fabled City of Timbuktu

In the Middle Ages, Europeans exchanged stories of the splendor and the mystery of a city hidden somewhere in the heart of Africa and known as Timbuktu. It was rumored that the city, forbidden to all except the Muslims of Africa and Arabia, was a world of great wealth and sublime culture. Gold was traded as freely there as wheat in the marketplaces of Europe. Non-Muslims had approached the city, and sometimes had been captured and brought to it, but none were ever heard from again.

Timbuktu does exist; but it is not a Shangri-la or an El Dorado. Timbuktu is situated on the southern fringe of the great Sahara Desert and on the banks of the Niger River. About A.D. 1000, it had been nothing more than a well amid the sand dunes, where the Tuareg and other nomadic tribes of the Sahara would gather to trade their goods. According to legend, its name comes from a beautiful Bellah slave girl, Buktu, who had been left by the well to guard the possessions of her Tuareg masters. (*Tin* in Tuareg means "the place of.") Eventually, some of the tribespeople took up permanent residence there; tents, straw huts, and then mud houses began to appear. It became a central stopping point for Muslim merchants and traders, and by the 14th century it had become a thriving market and an established city with its own grand mosque, built by the Mandingo king Gongo Musa in 1310.

Word of this great city began to filter back to Europe from Egypt and other more accessible parts of Africa. And by the 1500s, Timbuktu lived up to the stories that were being told about it in the capitals of Europe. Gold was traded profusely in the markets there, as was salt, mined in nearby pits, and such other commodities as grain, sugar, tea, and handicrafts, particularly rugs. A university was built, and it had become a major center of Muslim culture. The population of the city had grown to an estimated one million. Then in 1591, the city was captured by the sultan of Morocco and subsequently was ruled by pashas appointed by the sultan and his successors.

During all the years of the city's exotic splendor, however, no Europeans traded or even visited there and lived to tell of its charms, the rumors of its inhospitality being not in the least exaggerated.

Still, it became the goal of intrepid European explorers. One after the other, they sailed to Africa and set out across the deserts and savannas in search of the city. Some even disguised themselves as Muslims and tried to infiltrate Arab caravans headed for the city. But it was not until 1826 that an outsider entered the city and survived the effort—at least for a little while. And what he found was not the fabled city he had heard about but one that had been in constant decline for two centuries and now was nothing more than a village of earthen huts that was home to about 10,000 Muslims.

Alexander Laing, a Scottish explorer, was the first European to visit Timbuktu. The trip there was not easy. Laing and his party of three other men landed at Tripoli, Libya, in May 1825 but did not start out for Timbuktu until January of the following year. On the way there, his party was attacked by Tuareg natives. Laing was the sole survivor, and though he was badly wounded, he managed to escape and continue on to Timbuktu, arriving there on August 13, seven months after the journey had begun. During the five weeks he stayed there, Laing wrote a series of letters, sending them back to England by Arab caravans, in which he described for the first time the mysterious city. (His descriptions for the most part were inaccurate, extolling a splendor that was not there but was believed by those back home.) Then a local sheik told Laing that his life would be in grave danger if he was to stay in the city any longer. So Laing fled, but he was not outside the city for two full days before he was slain by his Tuareg guide.

Two years later, René Caillié, a French explorer, visited Timbuktu and managed to return to Europe un-

(continued on page 56)

Thor Heyerdahl Names Eight Places Still to Explore

Thor Heyerdahl, born in Norway in 1914, achieved lasting fame as an adventurer and explorer because of three major expeditions he led. The first was the 101-day float trip across the Pacific Ocean from Peru to Polynesia, aboard the balsa-log raft named Kon-Tiki *(1947). That was followed by the* Ra *expeditions, on the second of which he crossed the Atlantic Ocean, from Morocco to the Caribbean island of Barbados, in a boat built of papyrus reeds (1969). The third was the re-creation of a Sumerian sailing vessel of about 3000 B.C. (dubbed* Tigris*) and the subsequent 4,200-mile, 143-day voyage through the Persian Gulf, Gulf of Oman, Arabian Sea, and part of the Indian Ocean (1977–78).*

Here, in a list first published in 50 Plus magazine, he names eight unique places still awaiting the modern adventurer.

Iraq

A biblical land with many many search sites, most of them only partially uncovered, Iraq is getting ready for outsiders. Hotels are being built and work is in progress to improve transportation. The Tower of Babel, really a pyramidlike structure, has yet to be found. But there are existing ruins of Nineveh, Uruqu, and Ur, where Abraham was born. Here, too, is where the Sumerian version of Noah and his ark originated. Abraham brought the legend of Noah with him from Ur to the Holy Land long before the Old Testament was written.

Russian and Iraqi archeologists digging at Ur have found Sumerian cuneiform inscriptions on clay tablets dated circa 2,800 B.C., 1,000 years before Abraham. They speak of the flood. Their version of Noah puts him and his ark in what is now Bahrain. I believe they're right.

Oman

Stand in line on the day they start issuing tourist visas for Oman! There are 5,000-year-old copper mines where the ancient Babylonians came to fetch copper to make their bronze. Professional archeologists and scientists are aching for a chance to dig there. The photographic possibilities are endless because the scenery is spectacular, and there are mountain villages that have never seen a Western face.

Pakistan

There is much to be found in Pakistan. For example, at the end of World War II scientists discovered that a third civilization as important as Egypt and Mesopotamia once existed in the Indus Valley region. Two cities, Mohenjo-Daro and Hapappa, only partially uncovered, await the digger's tools. Both date from 2,000 B.C.

Colombia
In the area of St. Augustine on the northern coast of Colombia, there are remnants of a lost civilization we still know very little about. Statues and other artifacts are scattered about the region. We can only imagine what lies beneath the surface of the earth.

Cyprus
Archeologists are looking for something rather unusual in Cyprus—1,500 missing years. No one knows exactly what happened on this Mediterranean island between 5,000 B.C. and 3,500 B.C. At the moment Brandeis University has a team digging at Khirokitis, the oldest site on the island, where they've found evidence of a Stone Age settlement that may have existed at that time, but they've only been there a year and have barely scratched the surface.

Peru
There is more to Peruvian history than the Inca lore we've read so much about. There are still many important sites of pre-Inca civilizations to be investigated. Most archeological teams head for the mountains, but I would dig along the coast. The ancient Peruvians were seafarers and they had ports no one has found yet. The Peruvian government welcomes outsiders who can contribute, economically or professionally, to their excavating programs.

Bolivia
Bolivia's most famous archeological site, Tiahuanaco, is largely undug. I am not very familiar with the area, but I know there is much to be found there.

The Marquesas
This group of French islands in the mid-South Pacific are virtually untouched by scientific explorers. There are remains of pre-European times on some of the islands, and it is generally accepted that the islands were the first mid-Pacific territories to be reached by early Polynesian peoples. Excavations have started, but years of digging lie ahead.

scathed. He brought the true if somewhat disappointing description of Timbuktu back with him:

> I looked around and found that the sight before me did not answer my expectations. . . . The city presented, at first view, nothing but a mass of ill-looking houses built of earth. Nothing was to be seen in all directions but immense plains of quicksand of a yellowish white color. The sky was a pale red as far as the horizon; all nature wore a dreary aspect, and the most profound silence prevailed. . . .

Today Timbuktu (or Tombouctou, as it is often spelled), situated near the center of the republic of Mali, has a population of about 12,000 and is not much larger than it was in 1893, when the French took over governance of the city. It is still surrounded by rolling sand dunes, dotted with a scattering of thorn bushes and mimosa trees. Occasionally, the city is whipped by sandstorms. There is still a marketplace and several mosques, which were built in the 15th century. Many of the flat-roofed, sun-dried-mud houses, built by the early residents, are still intact. Today most of the inhabitants are members of the Songhai, a Muslim tribe, but there are also Arabs and Moors. The Tuareg, still nomads, come to the city to trade, as they have for centuries, and then disappear into the desert. But there is also a modern hotel, where Europeans, Americans, and Asians can stay in safety and relative comfort. Both the splendor and the inhospitality have long since vanished from the historic city of Timbuktu.

Overland to the Pacific: The Journals of Lewis and Clark

Among the most exciting adventures in the history of man was the exploration of the American West. Here was a wilderness made up of virgin forests, vast plains, towering mountains, arid deserts, raging rivers, and a climate where temperatures were hotter in the desert and colder on the windy plains and in the mountain passes than any the settlers had ever experienced before. There were also grizzly bears, black bears, mountain lions, wolves, rattlesnakes, water moccasins, copperheads, and tarantulas, not to mention bands of hostile Indians.

Two of the most illustrious explorers of the New World were Meriwether Lewis and William Clark. During the period from 1804 through 1806 their river and overland expedition took them from the Midwest to the Rocky Mountains, across the Continental Divide, on to the Columbia River, and eventually to the Pacific Ocean. The expedition, initiated by President Thomas Jefferson, became one of the most productive and famous in American annals of exploration. The two articulate adventurers kept diaries, and the excerpts from them reproduced here from American Odyssey *by Ingvard Henry Eide give a sharply focused picture of the situations they and other westward-bound explorers encountered in the untamed American West. (Note: Words or phrases enclosed in brackets [ ] are later insertions or emendations made by Clark himself or by the editors of early editions of the diaries.)*

Lewis: November 16, 1803

Passed the Missippi this day . . . a respectable looking Indian offered me three beverskins for my dog [Scannon] . . . of the newfoundland breed one that I prised much for his docility and qualifications generally for my journey and of course there was no bargan . . . Capt. Clark and myself passed over to the . . . W. side of the river from the point of junction of the rivers. . . .

Clark (Orderly Book): June 29, 1804

Ordered—A Court Martiall will Set this day at 11 oClock, to consist of five members, for the trial of *John Collins* and *Hugh Hall*, Confined on Charges exhibited against them by Sergeant Floyd. . . .

The Court Convened agreeable to order and proceeded to the trial of the Prisoners Viz

John Collins Charged "with getting drunk on his post this Morning out of whiskey put under his charge as a Sentinal, and for Suffering *Hugh Hall* to draw whiskey out of the Said Barrel intended for the party."

To this Charge the prisoner plead *not Guilty*.

The Court after mature deliv[b]er-

ation on the evidence adduced &c are of oppinion that the prisoner is *Guilty* of the Charge exibited against him, and do therefore sentence him to receive *one hundred Lashes on his bear Back*.

Hugh Hall was brought before the Court Charged with takeing whiskey out of a Keg this morning which whiskey was stored on the Bank (and under the Charge of the Guard) Contrary to all order, rule, or regulation."

To this Charge the prisoner "Pleaded Guilty."

The Court find the prisoner Guilty and Sentence him to receive fifty Lashes on his bear Back. . . .

Clark: September 24, 1804

. . . The Tribes of the Seauex Called the Teton, is Camped about 2 Miles up on the N.W. Side, and we Shall Call the River after that Nation, Teton   This river is 70 yards wide at the mouth of Water, and has a considerable Current   we anchored off the Mouth. . . .

. . . we prepare to Speek with the Indians tomorrow. . . .

Clark: September 25, 1804

. . . Envited those Cheifs on board to Show them our boat and such

Curiossities as was Strange to them, we gave them ¼ a glass of whiskey which they appeared to be verry fond of, Sucked the bottle after it was out & Soon began to be troublesom, one of the 2d Cheif assumeing Drunkness, as a Cloake for his rascally intentions   I went with those Cheifs ... to Shore with a view of reconsileing those men to us, as Soon as I landed the Perogue three of their young Men Seased the Cable of the Perogue, [in which we had pressents &c] the Chiefs Soldr [each Chief has a soldier] Huged the mast, and the 2d Chief was verry insolent both in words & justures ... I felt My self Compeled to Draw my Sword [and Made a Signal to the boat to prepare for action] at this Motion Capt Lewis ordered all under arms in the boat, those with me also Showed a Disposition to Defend themselves and me, the grand Chief then took hold of the roap & ordered the young Warrers away, I felt My Self warm & Spoke in verry positive terms.

Most of the Warriers appeared to have ther Bows strung and took out their arrows from the quiver. as I [being surrounded] was not permited [by them] to return, I sent all the men except 2 Inps [Interpreters] to the boat, the perogue Soon returned with about 12 of our determined men ready for any event. this movement caused a no: of the Indians to withdraw at a distance, [leaving their chiefs & soldiers alone with me] .... I turned off & went with my men on board the perogue, I had not prosd more the 10 paces before the 1st Cheif 3rd & 2 Brave Men Waded in after me. I took them in & went on board. ...

Clark: January 27, 1805

a fine day, attempt to Cut our Boat and Canoos out of the Ice, a deficuelt Task I fear as we find water between the Ice, I bleed the man with the Plurisy to day & Swet him, Capt Lewis took off the Toes of one foot of the Boy who got frost bit Some time ago. ...

Lewis: May 9, 1805

... Capt. Clark killed ... 2 buffaloe, I also killed one buffaloe which proved to be the best meat ... we saved the best meat, and from the cow I killed we saved the necessary materials for making what our wrighthand cook Charbono, calls *boudin (poudingue) blanc*, and immediately set him about preparing them for supper; this white pudding we all esteem one of the greatest delicacies of the forrest. ... About 6 feet of the lower extremity of the large gut of the Buffaloe is the first morsel ... the mustle lying underneath the shoulder blade next to the back, and fillets are next saught, these are needed up very fine with a portion of kidney suit; to this composition is then added a just proportion of pepper and salt and a small quantity of flour ... all is compleatly filled with something good to eat, it is tyed at the other end, but not any cut off, for that would make the pattern too scant; it is then baptised in the missouri with two dips and a flirt, and bobbed into the kettle; from whence, after it be well boiled it is taken and fried in bears oil until it becomes brown, when it is ready to esswage the pangs of a keen appetite, or such as travelers in the wilderness are seldom at a loss for. . . .

Lewis: May 11, 1805

. . . About 5.P.M. my attention was struck by one of the Party runing at a distance towards us and making signs and hollowing as if in distress . . . I immediately turned out with seven of the party in quest of this monster [grizzly], we at length found his trale and persued him about a mile by the blood . . . these bear being so hard to die reather intimedates us all; I must confess that I do not like the gentlemen and had reather fight 2 Indians than one bear; there is no other chance to conquer them by a single shot but by shooting them through the brains. . . . the flece and skin were as much as two men could possibly carry. . . . directed the two cooks to render the bear's oil and put it in the kegs which was done. there was about eight gallons of it.

Lewis: August 13, 1805

. . . we set out, still pursuing the road down the river. we had marched about 2 miles when we met a party of about 60 warriors mounted on excellent horses who came in nearly full speed, when they arrived I advanced towards them with the flag leaving my gun with the party about 50 paces behind me. the chief and two others who were a little in advance of the main body spoke to the women, and they informed them who we were and exultingly shewed

the presents which had been given them   these men then advanced and embraced me very affectionately in their way which is by puting their left arm over your wright sholder clasping your back, while they apply their left cheek to yours and frequently vociforate the word âh-hí-e, âh-hí-e that is, I am much pleased, I am much rejoiced. bothe parties now advanced and we wer all carresed and besmeared with their grease and paint till I was heartily tired of the national hug. I now had the pipe lit and gave them smoke; they seated themselves in a circle around us and pulled off their mockersons before they would receive or smoke the pipe. this is a custom among them as I afterwards learned indicative of a sacred obligation of sincerity in their profession of friendship . . . as much as to say that they wish they may always go bearfoot if they are not sincere; a pretty heavy penalty if they are to march through the plains of their country . . . the principal chief Ca-me-âh-wait made a short speach to the warriors. I gave him the flag which I informed him was an emblem of peace among whitemen and now that it had been received by him it was to be respected as the bond of union between us. . . .

Clark: November 7, 1805

. . . our Small Canoe which got seperated in the fog this morning joined us this evening. . . .

Great joy in camp   we are in view of the Ocian . . . this great Pacific Octean which we been so long anxious to See. and the roreing or noise made by the waves brakeing on the rockey Shores (as I suppose) may be heard disti[n]ctly

We made 34 miles to day as computed.

Lewis: March 19, 1806

... The Killamucks, Clatsops, Chinnooks, Cathlahmahs and Wâc-ki-a-cums [Qu: Wackms] resemble each other as well in their persons and dress as in their habits and manners. their complexion is not remarkable, being the usual copper brown of most of the tribes of North America.... the most remarkable trait in their physiognomy is the peculiar flatness and width of forehead which they artificially obtain by compressing the head between two boards while in a state of infancy and from which it never afterwards perfectly recovers. this is a custom among all the nations we have met with West of the Rocky mountains. ... this process seems to be continued longer with their female than their mail children, and neither appear to suffer any pain from the operation.... the large or apparently swolen legs particularly observable in the women are obtained in a great measure by tying a cord tight around the ankle. their method of squating or resting themselves on their hams which they seem from habit to prefer to siting, no doubt contributes much to this deformity of the legs by preventing free circulation of the blood.... The dress of the women consists of a robe, tissue, and sometimes when the weather is uncommonly cold, a vest.... The garment which occupys the waist, and from thence as low as nearly to the knee before and the ham, behind, cannot properly be denominated a petticoat .... when the female stands erect to conceal those parts usually covered from formiliar view, but when she stoops or places herself in many other attitudes, this battery of Venus is not altogether impervious to the inquisitive and penetrating eye of the amorite. This tissue is sometimes formed of little twisted cords of the silk-grass knoted at their ends and interwoven. ...

The favorite ornament of both sexes are the common coarse blue and white beads.... they are also fond of a species of wampum which is furnished them by a trader whom they call Swipton.... I think the most disgusting sight I have ever beheld is these dirty naked wenches. The men of these nations partake of much more of the domestic drudgery than I had at first supposed. they collect and prepare all the fuel, make the fires, assist in cleansing and preparing the fish, and always cook for the strangers who visit them. they also build their houses, construct their canoes, and make all their wooden utensils. the peculiar provence of the woman seems to be to collect roots and manufacture various articles which are prepared of rushes, flags, cedar bark, bear grass or waytape. the management of the canoe for various purposes seems to be a duty common to both sexes....

Clark: June 17, 1806

... I with great difficulty prosued ... to the top of the mountain where I found the snow from 12 to 15 feet deep . . . here was Winter with all it's rigors; the air was cold my hands and feet were benumed. . . . if we proceeded and Should git bewildered in those Mountains the certainty was that we Should lose all of our horses and consequently our baggage enstrements perhaps our papers and thus eventually resque the loss of our

discoveries which we had already made if we should be so fortunate as to escape with life. . . . we therefore come to the resolution to return with our horses while they were yet strong and in good order, and indeaver to keep them so untill we could precure an indian to conduct us over the Snowey Mountains. . . .

Exploration of Planet Earth: A Historical Time Line

Year	Explorer (Nationality)	Area Explored
c. 630 B.C.	Diogenes (Greek)	East Africa
c. 600 B.C.	Scylax (Greek)	Red Sea, Indus River, Gulf of Oman
c. 470 B.C.	Hanno (Phoenician)	Sierra Leone
c. 460 B.C.	Herodotus (Roman)	Nile River
334–27 B.C.	Alexander the Great (Greek)	Persia, Asia Minor, India
326 B.C.	Hephaestion (Greek)	Khyber Pass
302 B.C.	Megasthenes (Ionian)	India
c. 140 B.C.	Eudoxus (Greek)	Arabian Sea
c. 138–27 B.C.	Chang Chi'en (Chinese)	Central Asia
25 B.C.	Aelius Gallius (Roman)	Red Sea
c. 10 B.C.	Julius Maternus (Roman)	Sahara Desert
A.D. 14	Hippalus (Greek)	Indus River
60	Roman centurions	Nile River
413	Fa-Hsien (Chinese)	Ceylon
629–45	Hsuan-Tsang (Chinese)	Tashkent, Samarkand, Hindu Kush, Assam, Ceylon
850	Soleiman (Arab)	Maldive Islands, Ceylon, Malacca, Canton
860	Chinese sailors	East coast of Africa, Malindi, Madagascar
860	Irish monks	Iceland
c. 860	Vikings	Orkney Islands, Shetland Islands, Faeroe Islands
862	Rurik (Viking)	Novgorod (Russia), Dnieper River

Year	Explorer (Nationality)	Area Explored
c. 950	Al Mas'udi (Arab)	Aral Sea
c. 950	Gunnbjörn Ulfsson (Icelandic)	East coast of Greenland
978	Snaebjord Galti (Icelandic)	East coast of Greenland
982	Erik the Red (Icelandic)	West coast of Greenland
986	Bjarni Herjolfsson (Viking)	Northeast coast of North America
c. 986	Icelanders	Greenland
c. 1000	Leif Ericson (Viking)	Labrador
c. 1000	Erling Sighvatsson (Icelandic)	Greenland
c. 1004	Thorvald Ericson (Viking)	Labrador, Newfoundland
1245–47	John de Carpini (Italian)	Dnieper River, Don River, Volga River, Karakoram Mountains
1253	William of Rubruck (Flemish)	Caspian Sea
1262–69	Niccolo Polo (Venetian) Maffeo Polo (Venetian)	Bukhara, Samarkand, Yellow River, Peking
1271–95	Marco Polo (Venetian)	Central Asia, Gobi Desert, China, Burma, East Indies, Ceylon
1291	John of Monte Corvino (Italian)	China, Persia
1318–30	Odoric of Pordenone (Italian)	Constantinople, India, East Indies, China, Tibet, Sumatra, Java, Borneo
1325–53	ibn-Batuta (Arab)	Egypt, east coast of Africa, Timbuktu, Sudan, Mali, Iraq, Saudi Arabia, Indus River, Maldive Islands, Ceylon, Sumatra, Canton
c. 1400	Niccolo de Conti (Venetian)	East Indies
1405–09	Cheng-Ho (Chinese)	Indochina, East Indies, Siam
1417–19	Hou-Hsien, Cheng-Ho (Chinese)	Maldive Islands, East Indies, Ryukyu Islands
1444	Nuño Tristão (Portuguese)	Senegal River
1455	Alvise da Cadamosto (Venetian)	Gambia River, Cape Verde Islands
1457	Diogo Gomez (Portuguese)	Loma Mountains
1469	Gregory Istoma (Russian)	North coast of Norway

Year	Explorer (Nationality)	Area Explored
1476	Nicholas Pining (Danish)	Gulf of St. Lawrence
1482	Diogo Cão (Portuguese)	Mouth of Congo River
1488	Bartolomeu Dias (Portuguese)	Cape of Good Hope
1490	Pedro de Covilhão (Portuguese)	Mozambique
1492–1502	Christopher Columbus (Genoese)	West Indies, coast of Venezuela
1497–98	John Cabot (Genoese)	Cape Breton Island, coast of Newfoundland
1497–1503	Amerigo Vespucci (Florentine)	Amazon River, south and southeast seaboard of U.S.
1498	Vasco da Gama (Portuguese)	East coast of Africa, Malabar coast of India
1499	Amerigo Vespucci (Florentine) Alonzo de Ojeda (Spanish)	Coasts of Venezuela and Brazil
1500	Pedro Alvares Cabral (Portuguese)	Coast of Brazil
1500	Diogo Dias (Portuguese)	Madagascar
1500	Vincente Yañez Pinzón (Spanish)	Coast of Brazil
1501	Gaspar Corte Real (Portuguese)	Coasts of Labrador and Newfoundland, Strait of Belle Isle
1501–02	Amerigo Vespucci (Florentine)	Rio de Janeiro, Patagonia
1502–08	Lodovico di Varthema (Italian)	Persia, India, Malacca, Sumatra, Java, Borneo, Moluccas
1505	Lourenço de Almeida (Portuguese)	Ceylon, Maldive Islands
1506	Vincente Yañez Pinzón (Spanish) Juan Díaz de Solís (Spanish)	Yucatan Peninsula, Honduras
1509	Diego López de Sequeira (Portuguese)	Malacca
1510	Vasco Nuñez de Balboa (Spanish)	Isthmus of Panama
1511–12	Ferdinand Magellan (Portuguese)	Malay Archipelago

Year	Explorer (Nationality)	Area Explored
1513	Vasco Nuñez de Balboa (Spanish)	Pacific Ocean
1513	Juan Ponce de León (Spanish)	Florida, Bahamas, Dry Tortugas
1513	Francisco Serrão (Portuguese)	Malay Archipelago
1514	Andrea Corsali (Italian) Giovanni da Empoli (Italian)	Canton
1515	Affonso d'Albuquerque (Portuguese)	Malacca
1515	Juan Díaz de Solís (Spanish)	Rio de la Plata
1517	Hernandes de Cordova (Spanish)	Yucatan Peninsula
1517–22	Hernando Cortés (Spanish)	Yucatan Peninsula, Vera Cruz, Mexico City
1519	Alonso de Pineda (Spanish)	Mouth of Mississippi River
1519–21	Ferdinand Magellan (Portuguese)	Strait of Magellan, Phoenix Islands, Philippines
1520–26	Francisco Alvarez (Portuguese)	Central Ethiopia
1523	Pedro de Alvarado (Spanish)	Guatemala
1524	Jorge de Meneses (Portuguese)	Coast of New Guinea
1524	Giovanni de Verrazano (Italian)	East coast of North America
1526	Leo Africanus (Arab)	Sudan, Timbuktu
1526–28	Sebastian Cabot (Venetian)	Recife (Brazil), Rio de la Plata, Paraná River, Paraguay River
1527	Alvaro de Saavedra (Spanish)	Mexico, Moluccas, New Guinea, Admiralty Islands, Marshall Islands
1528	Pánfilo de Narvaez (Spanish)	Florida, Gulf of Mexico, coast of Texas
1528	Hernando de Soto (Spanish)	Guatemala, Yucatan Peninsula
1528–36	Alvar Núñez Cabeza de Vaca (Spanish)	Texas, Mexico, Gulf of California
1532	Francisco Pizarro (Spanish)	Peru

Year	Explorer (Nationality)	Area Explored
1535–36	Jacques Cartier (French)	St. Lawrence River
1535–36	Hernando Cortés (Spanish)	Gulf of California
1536	Pedro de Mendoza (Spanish)	Buenos Aires
1537	Diego de Almagro (Spanish)	Andes Mountains, Concepción (Chile)
1537	Hernando de Grijalva (Spanish)	Gilbert Islands, New Guinea
1539	Marcos de Niza (Savoyard)	New Mexico, Arizona
1539–42	Hernando de Soto (Spanish)	Florida, Mississippi River, Great Smoky Mountains, Ozark Mountains
1539	Francisco de Ulloa (Spanish)	Gulf of California
1540	Hernando de Alarcón (Spanish)	Colorado River
1540	García López de Cárdenas (Spanish)	Grand Canyon
1540–42	Francisco Vásquez de Coronado (Spanish)	Colorado River, Grand Canyon, Rio Grande, Texas, Oklahoma, Kansas
1540–52	San Francisco de Xavier (Portuguese)	Malacca, Moluccas, Japan
1541	Pedro de Valdivia (Spanish)	Santiago (Chile)
1541–42	Francisco de Orellana (Spanish)	Amazon River, Napo River
1542	Luis de Moscoso de Alvaro (Spanish)	Arkansas River, Mississippi River, Mexico
1542	Juan Rodríguez Cabrillo (Portuguese)	San Diego
1542	Alvar Núñez Cabeza de Vaca (Spanish)	Paraná River, Asunción (Paraguay)
1542	Francisco Zeimoto (Portuguese)	Japan
1545	Iñigo Ortiz de Retes (Spanish)	New Guinea, Moluccas
1553–54	Richard Chancellor (English)	Moscow, White Sea
1561–62	Anthony Jenkinson (English)	Moscow, Kazan, Volga River Basin, Astrakhan

Year	Explorer (Nationality)	Area Explored
1564–65	Alonso de Arellana (Spanish) Andras de Urdaneta (Spanish)	Philippines, Mariana Islands
1565	Pedro Menéndez de Aviles (Spanish)	St. Augustine
1567	Alvaro de Mendana (Spanish) Pedro Fernandes de Quiros (Portuguese)	Solomon Islands
1569–71	Gonzalo Jiménez de Quesada (Spanish)	Orinoco River
1570s	Oliver Brunel (Dutch)	Ob River
1576–78	Martin Frobisher (English)	South coast of Greenland, Resolution Island, Frobisher Bay, Hudson Strait
1577–80	Francis Drake (English)	Coast of Brazil, Strait of Magellan, Chile, Peru, west coasts of North America and South America, Philippines, Moluccas, Java
1578–1601	Matteo Ricci (Italian)	Canton, Nanking, Peking
1579	Yermak Timofieiev (Russian)	Ural Mountains
1581	John Newberry (English)	Euphrates River
1582	Antonio de Espejo (Spanish)	New Mexico
1584–85	Walter Raleigh (English)	Virginia, Roanoke Island, North Carolina
1585–92	John Davis (English)	Gilbert Sound, Davis Strait, Cumberland Sound, Baffin Island, Sukkertoppen, Hudson Strait, Cape Chidley, Falkland Islands (The Arctic)
1586–88	Thomas Cavendish (English)	Philippines, Mariana Islands, Java
1591	Walter Raleigh (English)	Orinoco River
1594–97	Willem Barents (Dutch)	Novaya Zemlya, Bear Island, northwest coast of Spitsbergen (The Arctic)
1595–96	Alvaro de Mendana (Spanish) Pedro Fernandes de Quiros (Portuguese)	Marquesas Islands, Ellice Islands

Year	Explorer (Nationality)	Area Explored
1598–1601	Oliver van Noort (Dutch)	Mariana Islands, Philippines, East Indies
1601–05	John David (English)	Moluccas, East Indies
1602	Bartholomew Gosnold (English)	Massachusetts Bay, Cape Cod
1602	Wybrand van Warwijk (Dutch)	Sumatra, Borneo, Malacca, Java
1602	George Waymouth (English)	Hudson Strait
1603	Stevan van der Hagen (Dutch)	Moluccas
1603	Martin Pring (English)	Coasts of Maine, New Hampshire, Massachusetts
1603–05	Samuel de Champlain (French)	St. Lawrence River, Saguenay River, Bay of Fundy
1603–05	Benedict de Goes (Spanish)	Lahore (Pakistan), India, Tien Shan Mountains, Gobi Desert
1604–05	Henry Middleton (English)	Sumatra, Java
1605	William Jansz (Dutch)	Java, south coast of New Guinea
1605–06	Pedro Fernandez de Quiros (Portuguese)	North Cook Island, New Hebrides
1606	Luis Vaez de Torres (Spanish)	South coast of New Guinea
1607	John Smith (English)	East coast of North America, Chesapeake Bay, Potomac River
1608–11	Samuel de Champlain (French)	Richelieu River, Lake Champlain, Ottawa River
1608–12	John Jourdain (English)	Yemen, East Indies
1608–15	Etienne Brulé (French)	Lake Huron, Georgian Bay, Susquehanna River
1609–11	Henry Hudson (English)	Hudson River, Hudson Strait, Hudson Bay
1611–13	John Saris (English)	Java, Sumatra, Buru, Halmahera
1615	Samuel de Champlain (French)	Georgian Bay, Lake Ontario, Lake Oneida
1615–19	Willem Schouten (Dutch)	Cape Horn, Tuamotu Island, Friendly Islands, Horno Island, Admiralty Island, north coast of New Guinea, Moluccas

Year	Explorer (Nationality)	Area Explored
1616	William Baffin (English) Robert Bylot (English)	Lancaster Sound, Smith Sound, Jones Sound, Baffin Bay (The Arctic)
1618	Jan Coen (Dutch)	East Indies
1618	Pedro Paez (Portuguese)	Source of Blue Nile River
1619	Frederik Houtman (Dutch)	Perth (Australia)
1621	Etienne Brulé (French)	Lake Huron
1622–33	Manoel de Almeida (Portuguese)	Ethiopia
1624–26	Antonio de Andrada (Spanish)	Tibet
1624–33	Manoel Barradas (Portuguese)	Tigre (Ethiopia)
1627	Francois Thijszoon (Dutch) Pieter Nuyts (Dutch)	Southern Australia
1628	Jerome Lobo (Portuguese)	Blue Nile Falls
1628	Gerrit de Witt (Dutch)	Eastern Australia
1631	João Cabral (Portuguese)	Katmandu, Ganges River
1631	Thomas James (English)	James Bay
1633–34	Jean Nicolet (French)	Straits of Mackinac, Lake Michigan, Green Bay, Fox River
1637–38	Pedro Teixeira (Spanish)	Amazon River, Napo River, Ecuador
1642–44	Abel Tasman (Dutch)	Tasmania, coast of New Zealand, Friendly Islands, Fiji, New Guinea
1643	Vasili Poyarkov (Russian)	Aldan River, Amur River, Sea of Okhotsk
1647	Buldakov (Russian)	Kolyma River
1648	Matlas Abad (Spanish)	Colombia
1648	Semyon Dezhnev (Russian)	Siberia, Kolyma River, Lena River, Bering Strait
1652	Onufrei Stepanov (Russian)	Lake Baykai, Shilka, Amur River
1654–58	Sieur de Groseilliers (French) Pierre Radisson (French)	Green Bay, Wisconsin River, Mississippi River
1660s	Jean Peré (French)	Hudson Bay to Lake Superior
1661–62	John Grueber (Austrian) Albert d'Orville (Belgian)	Tibet, India
1668	Stenka Razin (Russian)	Volga River, Astrakhan

Year	Explorer (Nationality)	Area Explored
1669	Louis Joliet (French)	Lake Huron, Lake St. Clair, Detroit River, Lake Erie
1669	René Cavelier, Sieur de la Salle (French)	Niagara River, Ohio River
1669–70	John Lederer (German)	Blue Ridge Mountains
1671–73	Louis Joliet (French) Jacques Marquette (French)	Wisconsin River, Mississippi River, Illinois River
1676	Nicolas Spafarik (Greek)	Tien Shan Mountains, Peking
1681–84	René Cavelier, Sieur de la Salle (French)	Great Lakes, Illinois River, Mississippi River, Gulf of Texas, Arkansas River
1684–91	William Dampier (English)	New Hebrides
1687–1711	Eusebio Francisco Kino (Spanish)	California, Arizona
1689–90	Henry Kelsey (English)	Canadian plains
1691–92	Samuel Fritz (Bohemian)	Amazon River
1696–99	Vladimir Atlassov (Russian)	Kamchatka Peninsula
1698	André Brüe (French)	Senegal River
1698	Beauchêne Gouin (French)	Cape Horn, Galapagos Islands
1708–11	William Dampier (English)	New Guinea
1712	Amadée Frézier (French)	Tierra del Fuego
1714–16	Ippolito Desideri (Italian) Manuel Freyre (Portuguese)	Kashmir, Lhasa (Tibet)
1719	Bernardo de la Harpe (French)	Red River, Santa Fe
1720–27	Philip Strahlenberg (Swiss) Daniel Messerschmidt (German)	Ob River, Yenesei River
1722	Jacob Roggevven (Dutch)	Juan Fernández Islands, Tuamotu Archipelago, Easter Island
1722	Carl Thunberg (Swedish) Anders Sparrman (Swedish)	Southwest Africa
1728–33	Vitus Bering (Danish)	St. Lawrence Island, Bering Strait
1731–43	Pierre Gaultier de Varennes (French)	Saskatchewan River, James River, Lake Winnipeg, Missouri River

Year	Explorer (Nationality)	Area Explored
1733–42	Great Northern Expedition (Russian)	Arctic coast of Siberia
1735–45	Charles de la Condamine (French)	Esmeraldas River, Mount Chimborazo, Amazon River, Negro River
1736	Jorge Juan y Santacilia (Spanish) Antonio de Ulloa (Spanish)	Gulf of Guayaquil, Quito
1740	George Anson (English)	Cape Horn, coast of Peru, Pacific Ocean
1741	Vitus Bering (Danish)	Kodiak Island, Gulf of Alaska, Aleutian Islands, Bering Island
1741	Alexei Chirikov (Russian)	Alaska
1742–73	Jean Godin des Odonais (French)	Quito, Amazon River, Cayenne
1749	João de Sousa de Azevedo (Portuguese)	Amazon River, Arinos River
1749–50	Thomas Walker (American)	Cumberland Gap
1760–75	Daniel Boone (American)	Tennessee, Cumberland River, Mississippi River, Kentucky
1761–1808	José Celestino Mutis (Spanish)	Bogotá
1762–67	Carsten Niebuhr (German)	Middle East, India
1764–66	John Byron (English)	Coast of Brazil, Falkland Islands, Tuamotu Archipelago, King George Islands, Gilbert Islands
1766–67	Louis Antoine de Bougainville (French)	Tahiti, Samoa, New Hebrides, Great Barrier Reef, New Guinea, Louisiade Archipelago, Solomon Islands, New Britain, Buru
1766–68	Marqués de Rubí (Spanish) Nicolas de Lafora (Spanish)	Mexico, Texas
1767–68	William Pink (English)	Mackenzie River
1767–68	Samuel Wallis (English)	Tahiti, Tinian
1767–69	Philip Carteret (English)	Tuamotu Archipelago, Tahiti, Society Islands, Pitcairn Island, Santa Cruz Island, Solomon Islands
1768	Fernando de Rivera y Moncada (Spanish)	Mexico, California

Year	Explorer (Nationality)	Area Explored
1768	Junipero Serra (Spanish)	Coast of California
1768–70	James Cook (English)	Tahiti, coast of Brazil, Tierra del Fuego, east coast of New Zealand
1768–73	James Bruce (Scottish)	Source of Blue Nile River
1769–72	Samuel Hearne (English)	Churchill River, Coppermine River, Great Slave River, Great Slave Lake
1770–75	James Cook (English)	Cook Strait, east coast of Australia, Cape Desolation, Cape Horn, Society Islands, Friendly Islands, Easter Island, New Hebrides, Antarctica
1773	Constantine Phipps (English)	Spitsbergen
1773–76	Francisco Garcés (Spanish)	Colorado River
1776	Francisco Dominguez (Spanish) Francisco de Escalante (Spanish)	New Mexico, Great Salt Lake
1776–80	James Cook (English)	Christmas Island, Hawaiian Islands, Kuril Islands, west coasts of United States and Canada
1778	Peter Pond (American)	Saskatchewan River
1779–80	Alexander von Humboldt (German)	Venezuela, Orinoco River, Negro River
1780	Michel Adanson (French)	Coast of Senegal
1784–1801	Félix de Azara (Spanish)	Paraná-Paraguay River Basin
1785–87	Jean François de la Pérouse (French)	Hawaiian Islands, Philippines, Macao, Korea Strait, Sea of Japan, Samoa, Tonga, La Pérouse Strait, Friendly Islands
1785–88		
1787–94	Alessandro Malaspina (Lombard)	Coasts of Brazil and Argentina, Falkland Islands, Chile, Peru
1789	Alexander Mackenzie (Scottish)	Northwest Canada
1791	Antonine Bruni (French)	Solomon Islands, Admiralty Islands, Friendly Islands, Java
1791–92	Daniel Houghton (English)	Gambia River
1792	Alexander Baranov (Russian)	Prince William Sound, Alexander Archipelago (Alaska)

Year	Explorer (Nationality)	Area Explored
1792	Robert Gray (American)	Northwest coast of North America, Columbia River
1792	George Vancouver (English)	West coast of North America, Vancouver
1794	Andrew Henry (American)	Madison River, Continental Divide
1795–1806	Mungo Park (Scottish)	Gambia River, Senegal River, Niger River
1797–1811	David Thompson (Welsh)	Great Lakes, Columbia River
1801	John Barrow (English)	Orange River
1801–03	Alexander von Humboldt (German)	Magdalena River, Ecuador, Peru
1802	Francis Barrallier (English/French)	Blue Mountains (Australia)
1802	Nicolas Baudin (French)	Cape Banks, Nuyts Archipelago (Australia)
1802	Matthew Flinders (English)	Nuyts Archipelago (Australia)
1803–06	Meriwether Lewis (American) William Clark (American)	St. Louis to mouth of Columbia River
1805–06	Zebulon Pike (American)	Mississippi River, Arkansas River, Red River
1806	William Scoresby (English)	Spitsbergen (The Arctic)
1807	Manuel Lisa (American)	Yellowstone River
1807–08	John Colter (American)	Grand Teton Mountains
1809	Ulrich Seetzen (German)	Mecca, Medina
1811	Thomas Manning (English)	Lhasa (Tibet)
1811–13	John Jacob Astor (American)	Missouri River, Columbia River
1813–15	Johann Ludwig Burckhardt (Swiss)	Petra, Nile River, Abu Simbel, Nubian Desert
1815	Frédéric Caillaud (French)	Nubia
1817	Stephen H. Long (American)	Minnesota River, St. Croix River
1817	William Scoresby the Younger (English)	East coast of Greenland
1817–18	Johann Baptist von Spix (German)	Rio de Janeiro, São Paulo, Amazon River

Year	Explorer (Nationality)	Area Explored
1818	David Buchan (English) John Franklin (English)	Northwest Spitsbergen (The Arctic)
1818	Joseph Ritchie (British) George Lyon (British)	North Africa
1819	George Sadlier (British)	Arabia
1819	William Smith (English)	King George Island (Antarctica)
1819–21	William Parry (English)	Melville Sound, Frozen Strait, Fury and Hecla Strait (The Arctic)
1820–24	Ferdinand von Wrangel (Russian)	Coast of Siberia
1821	Nathaniel Palmer (American) George Powell (English)	South Orkney Islands
1821–22	William Becknell (American)	Southwestern United States
1822	James Weddell (English)	Weddell Sea (Antarctica)
1822–25	Hugh Clapperton (British)	Lake Chad
1822–28	Jedediah Smith (America)	West and southwestern United States
1823–27	Johann Natterer (Austrian)	Minas Gerais, Goiás, Mato Grosso
1824	Jim Bridger (American)	Bear River, Great Salt Lake, Yellowstone Valley
1825–26	Alexander Laing (Scottish)	Sahara Desert, Timbuktu
1825–26	Frederick William Beechay (English)	Point Barrow (Alaska)
1825–27	Hugh Clapperton (British) Richard Lander (British)	Niger River, Badagri, Bussa, Kano, Sokot (Africa)
1825–28	René Caillié (French)	Timbuktu
1825–30	Peter Ogden (American)	John Day River, Klamath River, Mount Shasta, Humboldt River, San Joaquin and Sacramento valleys
1826–27	James Pattie (American)	Gila River
1827	Dumont d'Urville (French)	New Zealand
1827–32	Eduard Peoppig (German)	Peru, Amazon River
1829	Juan de Grijalva (Spanish)	Yucatan Peninsula
1829	Alexander von Humboldt (German)	Ob River, Altai Mountains, Volga River, Don River
1829	Ewing Young (American)	Salt River, San Joaquin Valley

Year	Explorer (Nationality)	Area Explored
1829–31	James Ross (Scottish)	King William Island, Magnetic North Pole
1830–32	John Biscoe (English)	Prinsesse Astrid Kyst, Enderby Land, Graham Land, Adelaide Island (Antarctica)
1830–31	Richard Lander (English) John Lander (English)	Mouth of Niger River
1831–35	Charles Darwin (English)	Galapagos Islands, Tahiti, Rio de la Plata, Tierra del Fuego, Argentina, Falkland Islands, Chile
1832–35	Johann Natterer (Austrian)	Solimões River, Casiquiare Canal, Negro River
1833	Joseph Walker (American)	Great Salt Lake, Humboldt River, Yosemite Valley, High Sierras
1836–37	James Alexander (Scottish)	Cape Town, Walvis Bay
1837–39	Thomas Simpson (English)	Great Bear Lake, Coppermine River
1837–48	Antoine d'Abbadie (French) Arnaud d'Abbadie (French)	Ethiopia
1839–40	Johann von Tschudi (Swiss)	Chile, Peru, Southern Andes, Minas Gerais
1840	Charles Wilkes (American)	Oates Land, Knox Coast, Shackleton Ice Shelf (Antarctica)
1841–42	John C. Frémont (American)	Des Moines River, Wind River, Oregon, California
1841–43	James Ross (English)	Cape Adare, Possession Islands, Victoria Land, Ross Island, Mt. Erebus, Mt. Terror, Ross Ice Shelf, Weddell Sea (Antarctica)
1844–48	Ludwig Leichhardt (German)	Northern Australia
1846	William H. Edwards (American)	Amazon River
1847	Graham Gore (English)	Victoria Island (The Arctic)
1847–50	John Richardson (English) John Rae (English)	Canadian Arctic Archipelago
1848	Johann Rebmann (German)	Mt. Kilimanjaro
1848–50	John Richardson (English) John Rae (English)	Mackenzie River, Coppermine River

Year	Explorer (Nationality)	Area Explored
1848–51	Henry Kellet (English)	Bering Strait, Wrangel Island, Herald Island
1849	Johann Krapf (German)	Mt. Kenya
1849	Ladislaus Magyar (Hungarian)	Zambezi River, Congo River
1849	David Livingstone (Scottish)	Lake Ngami
1849–50	Alfred Wallace (English)	Amazon River, Negro River
1850	Heinrich Barth (German)	North Africa, Lake Chad
1850	John Franklin (English)	Canadian Arctic Archipelago
1850–51	Henry Bates (English)	Amazon River
1850–59	E. J. De Haven (American)	Grinnel Land (The Arctic)
1850–54	Richard Collinson (English)	Amundsen Gulf, Dease Strait (The Arctic)
1850–54	Robert McClure (Irish)	McClure Strait, Northwest Passage (The Arctic)
1851–56	David Livingstone (Scottish)	Zambezi River, Victoria Falls
1852–54	Leopold McClintock (Irish)	Melville Island, Prince Patrick Island (The Arctic)
1852–54	Frederick Mecham (English)	Eglinton Island, Prince Patrick Island (The Arctic)
1853	Richard Burton (English)	Mecca
1853	Joseph Ives (American)	Arkansas to California, Colorado River, Mohave Desert, Grand Canyon
1853	John Petherick (English)	Congo
1853–56	Eduard Vogel (German)	Lake Chad
1854	Richard Burton (English)	Ethiopia
1854	William Norton (American)	Cape Constitution, Greenland
1854	John Rae (Scottish)	Pelly Bay, Boothia Peninsula (The Arctic)
1854–60	Isaac Hayes (American) William Godfrey (American)	Ellesmere Island, Greenland
1858	Richard Burton (English) John Speke (English)	Lake Tanganyika, Lake Victoria

Year	Explorer (Nationality)	Area Explored
1858–61	Otto Toreli (Norwegian) Erik Nordenskiöld (Swedish)	Spitsbergen (The Arctic)
1858–63	David Livingstone (Scottish)	Lake Shirwa, Lake Nyasa, Shire Highlands
1860–72	Ferdinand von Richthofen (German)	Ceylon, Japan, China
1860–71	Charles Hall (American)	Baffin Island, Hall Basin (The Arctic)
1861–62	Erik Nordenskiöld (Swedish)	Spitsbergen
1861–62	Klaus von der Decken (German)	Mt. Kilimanjaro
1861–63	Alexandrine Tinne (Dutch)	Nile River, Congo
1863–65	Samuel Baker (English)	Lake Albert, Murchison Falls
1865–67	Mani Singh (Tibetan)	Tibet
1868	James Orton (American)	Napo River, Amazon River
1869–70	George Musters (English)	Falkland Islands, Argentina
1869–75	Gustav Nachtigal (German)	Bornu, Kukawa (Africa)
1870–72	Nikolai Przewalski (Russian)	Ulan Bator, Gobi Desert, Peking, Yellow River
1870–80	Erik Nordenskiöld (Swedish)	Greenland, Yenesei River, New Siberian Islands
1872–74	Julius von Payer (Austrian)	Franz Josef Land, Rudolph Island (The Arctic)
1872–75	Ernest Giles (English)	Gibson Desert, Great Victoria Desert
1872–76	Charles Thompson, George Nares (English)	Fiji, Mariana Islands, Hawaiian Islands, Tahiti
1872–92	Frederick Selous (English)	Rhodesia
1873	Peter Warburton (English)	Great Sandy Desert
1874	George Nares (English)	Antarctic Circle
1874–77	Henry M. Stanley (British/American)	Lake Edward, Congo River
1875	Allen Young (English)	Prince of Wales Island, Peel Sound (The Arctic)
1876	L. A. Beaumont (English)	North coast of Greenland
1876	Romolo Gessi (Italian) Carlo Piaggia (Italian)	Lake Albert

Year	Explorer (Nationality)	Area Explored
1876–78	Charles Doughty (English)	Saudi Arabia
1879	Wilfrid Blunt (English)	Saudi Arabia
1879–82	Sarat Chandra Das (Bengali)	Sikkim, Lhasa (Tibet)
1879–82	Jules Crevaux (French)	Paraguay River, Gran Chaco
1879–83	Gaetano Casati (Italian)	Sudan, Congo River Basin
1879–84	Henry M. Stanley (British/American)	Lake Leopold II, Congo River tributaries
1880	Oscar Lenz (German)	North Africa, Senegal River
1880	Hermann von Wissman (German)	Angola
1882–83	James Booth Lockwood (American)	Lockwood Island, Greely Fjord, Ellesmere Island (The Arctic)
1886–89	Francis Younghusband (English)	Manchuria, China, Mandalay, Rawalpindi, Yarkand
1886–99	Robert E. Peary (American)	Greenland
1887–89	Louis Binger (French)	Niger River, Volta River
1888–89	Henry M. Stanley (British/American)	Ruwenzori Mountains
1888–96	Fridtjof Nansen (Norwegian) Otto Sverdrup (Norwegian)	Greenland, Arctic Ocean
1890–96	Jean-Baptiste Marchand (French)	Source of Niger River, Sudan, Ivory Coast, Congo River to Nile River
1892–1904	Francis Younghusband (English)	Kunar Valley, Oxus River, Lhasa (Tibet)
1893–94	Percy Sykes (English)	Iran
1894–97	Sven Anders Hedin (Swedish)	Bukhara, Samarkand, Tien Shan Mountains, Tashkent, Gobi Desert
1895	Leonard Kristensen (Norwegian)	Antarctica
1897	Salomon Andrée (Swedish)	Arctic Ocean
1898	Adrien de Gerlache (Belgian)	South Shetland Islands, Palmer Archipelago, Alexander I Land (Antarctica)
1898–1902	Otto Sverdrup (Norwegian)	Arctic Ocean, Grant Land
1900	Carstens Borchgrevink (Norwegian)	Robertson Bay, Newnes Land, Ross Ice Shelf (Antarctica)

Year	Explorer (Nationality)	Area Explored
1902–03	Robert F. Scott (English) Ernest Shackleton (Irish)	McMurdo Sound, King Edward VII Land, Ross Ice Shelf (Antarctica)
1902–04	Robert F. Scott (English)	Ross Island (Antarctica)
1902–08	Robert E. Peary (American)	Grant Land, North Pole (The Arctic)
1902–12	Knud Rasmussen (Danish)	North and East Greenland
1903	Robert F. Scott (English)	Ferrar Glacier (Antarctica)
1903–05	Roald Amundsen (Norwegian)	Northeast Passage
1904	Jean-Baptiste Charcot (French)	Palmer Archipelago, Wiencke Island, Graham Land (Antarctica)
1904	Godfred Hensen (Norwegian)	King William Island, Victoria Island (The Arctic)
1904–05	Vilhjalmur Stefansson (Canadian)	Iceland, Canadian Arctic Archipelago
1906–08	Alfred Wegener (German)	Greenland
1908	Frederick A. Cook (American)	North Pole
1908–09	Ernest Shackleton (Irish)	Bay of Whales, Ross Island, Beardmore Glacier, Polar Plateau (Antarctica)
1909	Edgeworth David (Australian)	Magnetic South Pole
1909–10	Jean-Baptiste Charcot (French)	Graham Land, Marguerite Bay, Fallières Coast (Antarctica)
1911	Roald Amundsen (Norwegian)	South Pole
1911–12	Robert F. Scott (English)	South Pole
1911–16	Thomas Lawrence (English)	Syria, Euphrates River, Sinai Peninsula, Saudi Arabia
1912	John King Davis (Australian)	Davis Sea, Shackleton Ice Shelf (Antarctica)
1912	Johan Koch (Danish) Alfred Wegener (German)	Greenland
1912	Choku Shirase (Japanese)	Ross Ice Shelf (Antarctica)
1912–13	Douglas Mawson (Australian)	King George V Land, Terré Adélie (Antarctica)
1912–13	Frank Wild (Australian)	Queen Mary Land, Knox Coast (Antarctica)
1913–14	Gertrude Bell (English)	Syria, Euphrates River

Year	Explorer (Nationality)	Area Explored
1914	Theodore Roosevelt (American)	Mato Grosso, Roosevelt River, Madeira River, Amazon River
1915	Vilhjalmur Stefansson (Canadian)	Borden Islands, Brock Islands, Meighen Island, Lougheed Island (near North Pole)
1915–16	Ernest Shackleton (Irish)	Weddell Sea, Elephant Island, South Georgia (Antarctica)
1917	Harry St. John Philby (English)	Saudi Arabia
1925	Percy Fawcett (English)	Mato Grosso
1925–26	Roald Amundsen (Norwegian)	Arctic Ocean, North Pole
1926	Richard E. Byrd (American)	North Pole
1928	Eimar Lundborg (Swedish)	Spitsbergen (The Arctic)
1928	Charles Masson (American)	Afghanistan
1928	Umberto Nobile (Italian)	North Pole
1928	George Wilkins (Australian)	Spitsbergen (The Arctic)
1929	Richard E. Byrd (American)	South Pole
1929–31	Douglas Mawson (Australian) John King Davis (Australian)	Banzare Coast, Knox Coast (Antarctica)
1930–31	Gunnar Isachsen (Norwegian) Hjalmar Riiser-Larsen (Norwegian)	Prinsesse Ragnhild Kyst
1933–34	Richard E. Byrd (American)	Marie Byrd Land (Antarctica)
1934–37	John Rymill (English)	Coast and islands of Graham Land (Antarctica)
1935	Lincoln Ellsworth (American) Herbert Hollick-Kenyon (Canadian)	South Pole
1935–39	Cecil T. Madigan (Australian)	Simpson Desert (Australia)
1948–50	Wilfred Thesiger (English)	Oman
1955	Richard E. Byrd (American)	Wilkes Land (Antarctica)
1957	Vivian Fuchs (English)	South Pole

Year	Explorer (Nationality)	Area Explored
1958	*Nautilus* (U.S. submarine)	North Pole (under the Arctic ice)
1960–62	Wally Herbert (English)	Queen Maud Range
1964–65	Sebastian Snow (English)	South American rivers
1965	Arne Rubin (Swedish)	Blue Nile
1967–69	Sir Edmund Hillary (New Zealander)	Antarctica
1968–69	Wally Herbert (English)	North Pole
1971	Sir Ranulph Fiennes (English)	Nahanni River
1973	Dennis Wickham (Australian)	Australian Desert
1974–75	Major John Blashford-Snell (English)	Zaire River
1974–76	Naomi Uemura (Japanese)	Greenland
1977–81	Wally Herbert (English)	Greenland
1978	Robyn Davidson (Australian)	Australian Desert
1979–82	Sir Ranulph Fiennes (English)	Transglobe Expedition (Antarctica/Arctic)
1980	John Wilde (English)	Sun Kosi River (Nepal)

At War

The Great Locomotive Chase

During the Civil War, a raiding party of 19 Union Army volunteers, members of the Second, Twenty-first, and Thirty-third Ohio infantries, disguised as civilians, infiltrated the South to carry out a mission that would later earn for each of them the Congressional Medal of Honor, the first ever awarded by the U. S. government.

The objective of the mission was to penetrate the Confederate states and sabotage the railroad link between Atlanta, Georgia, and Chattanooga, Tennessee. The group reached Big Shanty, Georgia, in April 1862, where they launched what would become known as "The Great Locomotive Chase." Their story, told here by two of the raiders who survived, Private William Knight of Company E and Private Wilson Brown of Company F, both of the Twenty-first Ohio Infantry, first appeared in The Story of American Heroism.

In the early part of April 1862, twenty-four men were detailed from three Ohio regiments of General J. W. Sill's brigade, forming a portion of that division of Buell's army in East Tennessee under command of General Mitchel.

They were told that the service required of them was "secret and dangerous." No other explanation was given, but when the adjective "dangerous" is used during a campaign such as was being carried on at that time, the soldier well knows it is not a meaningless term.

Each man was ordered to clothe himself in such costume as was generally worn by the inhabitants in that section of the country, to leave behind all weapons except revolvers, and rendezvous a short distance east of Shelbyville on the evening of April 7. . . .

At the appointed time the little party, in general appearance a group of farmers who were trying to escape the horrors of war, arrived at the place of meeting, where they were met by James J. Andrews, a man who for some time had been in the employ of Major General D. C. Buell, as a spy.

Although those who met him were not aware of the fact, Andrews had, some time prior to this, led an expedition to destroy communication between Atlanta and Chattanooga, but had failed in his purpose.

With Andrews was William Campbell, a citizen of Kentucky, who had volunteered for this "secret and dangerous" mission.

In the gloom of the evening, a short distance from the road, the Ohio men listened to the details of the scheme which this man placed before them, and many a heart, however brave, must have quailed on learning what was expected of this band of 24.

They were to divide themselves into detachments of three or four, and travel 200 miles to Marietta, Georgia, in such manner as was most expeditious and possible.

For such transportation no arrangements had been made. Each man, or each detachment, was to consider the ways and means, and decide for himself, or themselves, as to the best course; but all were expected to be at the rendezvous not later than Friday, the 11th.

Once there, it was proposed to capture a locomotive, travel along the line of the road at all hazards, destroying bridges and tearing up rails behind them, until death came to each, or the end of the journey had been reached.

Could this be accomplished General Beauregard's source of supplies would be cut off to a certain extent.

To realize the magnitude of such an undertaking it is well to consider the dangers which would beset the party before they should even arrive at the scene of their proposed operations.

They were to enter the Confederacy, where naturally every man was an enemy, and where, since they were in civilian's costume, capture meant almost instant and ignominious death. During this march of 200 miles they must of necessity encounter many people who would be curious as to the purpose of their journey, and who must be deceived on every point.

It would have seemed as if the obstacles of this 200-mile march must have daunted everyone, and yet there were no murmurings, no attempts to turn back, no thought of bringing reproach upon the State of Ohio through one of her sons proving himself—not a coward in such a case as this, but—a man who feared to attempt the apparently impossible.

They were told that in case of suc-

cess it might be possible for General Mitchel to deal the enemy a severe blow in the vicinity of Chattanooga; if they failed, the Union Army would not suffer because of the disaster, save in the loss of 24 men, for death would probably be the result of non-success.

With this thought in their minds, the men divided into bands, as had been ordered, and without loss of time started.

To be traversed were muddy roads, rendered almost quagmires by 72 hours of continuous rain, swollen streams, which in many cases must be crossed by swimming, and the inhabitants of the country were to be avoided so far as possible.

The majority of the party succeeded in the attempt—the last arriving on the morning of the day set.

One failed to get through in time; a second, by mistaking the directions, passed beyond the town. The enemy captured two, and two more were missing. There were now, therefore, 20 men.

Up to this time matters had progressed, despite the many obstacles, exactly in accordance with the schedule made by Andrews, who now, believing Mitchel's advance on Huntsville would be delayed because of the condition of the roads, decided to make a change in his plans, and it was this decision which probably contributed to the defeat of the party, and it certainly was the primary cause of the ignominious death of eight.

It can hardly be said that Andrews erred in judgment in thus making a change of plans. Friday, the 11th of April, was the day set.

Surely it would not seem that the chapter of accidents could hold for them such a chance as that 24 hours must be fatal, since thus far the enemy were in total ignorance of the purpose of this little band, and with no suspicions as to why these particular 20 men were within the Confederate lines.

Another reason for this delay might have been found in the fact that the original scheme contemplated the capture of a locomotive at Big Shanty, now known as Kenesaw. Immediately on their arrival it was learned that the Confederate forces had established a military camp at Big Shanty, and the dangers of the undertaking had increased a hundredfold, since, if the scheme was to be carried through, it would be necessary for this band of 20 to perform their work in the very midst of several thousand Confederate soldiers.

The change of date was made, and the Ohio boys passed the time as best they could in the very heart of the enemy's country, not knowing what instant they might be arrested as spies, and undoubtedly seeing in each innocent movement of those around them signs betokening that their secret had been discovered.

This short delay must have been the most trying of all their experiences; but finally the time for action arrived. . . .

All the details had been decided upon the night previous. It only remained for each man to lounge as unconcernedly as possible to the railway depot, purchase a ticket to some station beyond the one at which he intended to stop, and, as if strangers to each other, board the train.

The eight miles around the base of the Kenesaw Mountains were traversed slowly because of the heavy rain, and then, every nerve tingling with excitement, the 20 heroes stepped upon the platform at Big Shanty as if to procure breakfast.

On either side could be seen the white camps of the Confederate forces; the tramp, tramp, of the sentry was distinctly heard by these apparently calm adventurers. The hum of the soldiery sounded painfully distinct to their ears.

The train they were expecting to capture was drawn up in front of the low building which served as a depot. It consisted of three empty baggage cars and three passenger cars.

Hardly more than 20 feet away stood a sentry.

The conductor, engineer, and a number of the passengers had alighted for breakfast.

The time for action had arrived.

At a signal from Andrews, Brown and Knight leaped with him on board the engine.

That member of the party who had been detailed to unshackle the box cars from the remainder of the train performed his work.

Wilson jumped upon the third car to act as brakeman, the others clambering on board as best they could, and in the shortest possible space of time. Wide open did Knight pull the throttle valve.

The locomotive started with a plunge, the wheels revolving for an instant ineffectually, and the hoarse cry of escaping steam startled the dozing sentry. In another moment, with a scream and snort of defiance, the iron horse was thundering over the narrow ribbons of iron, and the first act in this daring drama had been played.

Now every desperate chance must be taken; the steam was to be increased until it might become master rather than servant, and the ordinary dangers of the road were heeded no more than they could be if they were the usual incidents of travel.

Knight and Brown, both engineers, both understanding the duties as well as the dangers of their position, turned all their attention to the smoothly working, perfectly moving machinery, the former with his hand on the throttle valve, the latter acting as fireman.

Perhaps never before had this engine been driven forward at such speed, but five minutes after the start the huge wheels were brought to a standstill, in order that the telegraph wires might be cut, lest those who had been tricked should flash the news ahead by the aid of electricity, thus bringing to naught all which had been accomplished.

Was a special on this road? Then the fatal collision must come, since they would be powerless to prevent it. Neither of the party had a timetable, but all knew that extra trains were being run to serve the exigencies of the army.

All that had been learned regarding the movements of the trains was that two were to be met at a certain point, and a local freight, not set down on the passenger timetable, was somewhere on the road.

It was necessary they should obtain information from one of the employees, and this was to be gained at some point ahead, when they would be for a moment free from pursuit.

On, on the engine dashed with the speed of the wind, along this single track, stopping here to cut wires, and there to load on railway ties as fuel to burn bridges, until they arrived at a station.

Once more is the engine brought to a standstill that Andrews may get that for which he stands so sadly in need—official instructions to the employees.

A tank-tender, never suspecting that his visitors are other than what they seem, readily complied with the leader's request, but quite naturally asked the question as to why they are running wild, for he knows no train should be at that point at that particular time.

"An ammunition train. Powder for Beauregard. Everything to be side-tracked for us," was the reply, and once more the engine is leaping madly over the rails, bound for Oostenaula bridge, which is the first on the program to be destroyed.

Thirty miles had been traversed in less than twice that number of seconds per mile, and then they were at Kingston.

Here was found a train waiting to connect with the one whose engine had been stolen, and here also, as was learned by the information obtained from the tank-tender, a freight must be met.

Now it is necessary to run on the side track until once more the road shall be cleared. All save four of the party are hidden in the box cars, which are supposed to be filled with ammunition, and it can well be fancied to what a tension their nerves must have been strung as second after second ticked laggingly by, while they were forced to remain inactive, fearing each instant lest the rumble of wheels from the rear should tell them that pursuit had already begun.

Finally the anxiously awaited train arrived; but to the dismay of those brave hearts who saw it, on the rear platform was carried a red flag, denoting that another train was following.

This meant more delay and increase of danger.

Again it was necessary to tell the story of ammunition for Beauregard, and here was learned, to their surprise, that Mitchel had already captured Huntsville, was on his way to Chattanooga, and everything movable was being hurried from the threatened city.

The second train arrived, and it also bore that flag of ominous color—ominous to this daring party—telling of yet another train for which they must wait.

Now all began to understand what that delay of 24 hours in beginning the enterprise would mean to their party.

Had the original program been carried out they would have run over the road when every train was traveling on schedule time, and where were no extras.

This day, however, owing to Mitchel's success, everything was in confusion, and such confusion as might bring death to those who had made the venture.

Sixty-five minutes, and at such a time each minute must have been increased fivefold, did they wait, and only then was it possible to continue the perilous flight.

Sixty-five precious minutes, during which it might have been possible for those left behind at Big Shanty to procure means of pursuit.

Perhaps it was well that for yet a short time longer this handful of men were ignorant of the fact that pursuers had already started with a powerful locomotive, and were bringing down the road intelligence of what had been done.

When the raiders left Big Shanty there were two men who did not lose their heads; one the conductor of the train that had been captured, and the other the foreman of the Atlanta railway machine shops.

These two, without loss of time or stopping to speculate, ran at full speed up the track, as if expecting to overtake the iron horse, not stopping until they found a handcar, on which they continued what seemed a useless journey.

Arriving at the first break in the rails they were hurled from the track, but not disabled, and once more continued the pursuit on foot until they reached Etowah, where was found the locomotive Yonah, with a full pressure of steam already on. A dozen soldiers were near at hand, and these were taken on board, that the pursuers should be sufficiently strong to cope with the daring raiders when they were overtaken.

Ignorant of what was occurring in the rear, the Ohio boys pressed on, Knight forcing the engine to her utmost speed, slackening it only that they might cut telegraph wires or take up rails, until, at one of these brief halts, the thundering of the pursuing engine could be heard.

The delay at Kingston had been sufficient to bring death very close upon the little party.

Now remains only one hope that pursuit may be checked, and this is to burn Oostenaula bridge.

If that can be done before the engine in the rear shall cross the river, all pursuit is necessarily checked, and the raiders, for the time being, are safe.

Andrews orders one of the baggage cars to be unshackled with the brakes set, in order that it may impede the oncoming engine; but the Confederates push it readily before them, and as the roadbed runs out fair and straight in the distance, the raiders see behind them the huge, snorting, shrieking machine, bristling with the guns of the Confederate soldiers. In that sight is the menace of their liberty.

Each man is working for life now. The cross-ties which have been taken aboard for fuel are dropped on the track, but the speed of the pursuing monster is so great that they are hurled aside like straws.

Just ahead is the bridge.

There is no time to stop for elaborate preparations in firing it, and all that can be done is to trust to chance.

Every ounce of steam that can be raised is now on, the locomotive trembling, groaning, and swaying under its impulse, while those in the cars behind are whittling wood into shavings, tearing boards from the side of the structure, and Knight, on the engine, is shoveling into this flammable mass bushel after bushel of burning coals at the expense of the fuel they will need so badly.

Then, as the engine leaps on the first planks of the bridge, this blazing mass is hurled upon the woodwork, but alas, again, for the delay of 24 hours! The rain which began in the morning had so saturated the timbers that they resisted the fiery element.

One day previous the structure, dry as it was, would have been fanned into flames.

Looking back the raiders see that there is no longer any hope of destroying Oostenaula bridge.

The last chance of carrying out the proposed plan had disappeared. It is now a question simply of life or death, with no possibility of working injury to the enemy.

Five minutes later and the loss of fuel is seriously felt. The needle of the steam gauge drops quiveringly, showing the decrease in force pound by pound, and the velocity of the huge wheels diminishes in proportion, until the locomotive creeps forward like some wounded creature. The moment has come when it must be abandoned.

Now it is each one for himself, and necessary for the safety of all that they separate.

As the engine rounds a curve, its steam is spent, the word is given, and that devoted band leap one by one from the disabled monster to seek in his own fashion a means of saving his life.

To follow the movements of the different members of the party during this short flight, would be to extend the story beyond the limit of the reader's patience. Suffice it to say that when the chase was over, all had been captured.

The remainder of the narrative is not dissimilar to hundreds which have been already told.

Captured in the enemy's camp, in civilian's clothes, there could be but one sequel—a court-martial and condemnation as spies.

At Atlanta were hanged:

> James J. Andrews
> William Campbell
> George D. Wilson
> Marion A. Ross
> Perry G. Shadrack
> Samuel Slavens
> Samuel Robertson
> John Scott

The remainder were confined in prison as spies, to be dealt with later when it should be discovered who were the engineers of the party.

Every effort was made by the Confederates to gain this information, but without success. Threats and bribes were alike unavailing, for not a man would reveal that which would bring to Knight and Brown certain and immediate death.

Until the following October those members of the little band who had escaped the hangman's noose were confined in jail at Atlanta, and then, agreeing among themselves that

death by a bullet would be preferable to the scaffold, they made one more venture, quite as desperate as that upon which they had started from Shelbyville, but, fortunately, more successful.

Attacking the prison guards with the desperation of men on whom death has already set its seal, they succeeded in escaping from prison, and eight of them reached their homes, after such suffering as cannot be described by the poor medium of paper and ink.

The others were captured and taken back to prison, where they remained until March 1863, when they were exchanged as prisoners of war.

Of this flight Brown writes:

> In just 48 days and nights—for the nights should be counted, since under cover of darkness we made the most progress—we reached the Federal lines, footsore and worn to skeletons. We were forced to wade across streams, swim swiftly-running rivers, scale mountains, and at the same time be constantly on the alert against the enemy, who surrounded us on every hand. There were times when it seemed as if our hearts would break because of the clouding of hope and the weakness of our bodies. The knowledge that capture meant certain death alone kept us on the march. No pen can describe our sufferings, God only knows what we were forced to endure. To gain rest from sleep was impossible. When our eyes closed in the un-

consciousness of slumber it was only to dream of pursuit by bloodhounds; of the huge scaffold on the outskirts of Atlanta where our friends had been hanged and where it had been said we should share the same fate; or of a sudden attack in which a bullet would have been more merciful than man.

... That which was done should be given full mede of praise, and those who received the Congressional Medal of Honor for "special service under General Mitchel" are worthy of the honor Congress has bestowed upon them, since they followed even to death the man under whose command their own commanding officer had placed them.

A Civil War Profile

Edward Hatch, born December 23, 1832, in Bangor, Maine, was a colonel in the Union Army during the American Civil War. He was a cavalry officer—handsome as he rode astride a noble horse; some might even have called him "swashbuckling" in those days. Colonel Hatch was the predecessor of Generals John Pershing and George Patton, but he lived in a time when the army's armor divisions moved by the hooves of horses.

Colonel Hatch once commented on the cavalry's battles in the Civil War and later on the conquest of the American West. "They will remember the things we did here, but they will forget how we did it," he said, "and they will forget who we were who did do it." That fortunately isn't altogether true.

Colonel Hatch participated in over 50 battles and skirmishes in southern Missouri, Tennessee, Mississippi, and northern Alabama. His contribution to the northern effort was substantial, but ironically enough his most important single contribution was made at a battle in which he did not even take part—the famous battle of Vicksburg.

It was in the spring of 1863 when General Ulysses S. Grant began his advance on Vicksburg. As a means of diverting the attention of the Confederate Army and of cutting off its communications from the east, he sent a cavalry raiding force into Mississippi. The force came to be known as Grierson's Raiders, and it was composed of three regiments, one of which was under the command of Colonel Hatch. His regiment was given the most important task of destroying a vital railroad line between Columbus and Macon.

After a fierce battle at Columbus, Colonel Hatch and his regiment successfully completed the mission and returned to their base of operations in Tennessee. Meanwhile, Grant made his assault on Vicksburg and emerged victorious in one of the Civil War's most famous battles. In *The Personal Memoirs of Ulysses S. Grant*, the general said that the action of Grierson's Raiders, and Colonel Hatch in particular, "was of great importance, for it successfully attracted the attention of the enemy from the main movement against Vicksburg."

After Atlanta fell in September of 1864, Colonel Hatch was given command of part of General William Sherman's cavalry. He organized it into a division and prepared to march to Tennessee to help defend the state against an impending invasion by Confederate General John B. Hood and his Army of Tennessee.

Hatch's division was deployed along the Tennessee River to observe the approach of General Hood and delay him as long as possible. After successfully carrying out his assignment, Colonel Hatch and his unit became known as "the eye of the army." General Hood was decisively set back in his attempt to retake Tennessee.

Throughout the war, Colonel Hatch was involved in numerous battles all over the area. Some were major, such as Nashville, Franklin, Iuka, Corinth, and Rienzi; others were minor, at such little-known places as Hurricane Creek, Duck River, Inghrams Mill, Brill's Point, Guntown, and Roar's Mill. Through all of these battles, the colonel was wounded only once—in an encounter at Moscow, Tennessee. He was shot in the chest but remained on the battlefield in an ambulance until the rebel force was routed. The wound hospitalized him for three months.

During the battles of Nashville and Franklin, Colonel Hatch was brevetted a brigadier general and a major general. Often awarded during the Civil War, brevet rank was, for all practical purposes, an honorary title awarded for gallant or meritorious service during time of war.

After the Civil War ended, he was mustered out of the U.S. volunteer forces and was commissioned a regular army colonel in the Ninth U.S. Cavalry. Under this title, he was, for a time, in command of the Department of Arizona and New Mexico.

Among his many encounters with Indians, Colonel Hatch in 1880 commanded the force that pursued the Apache chief Victorio after he had escaped from the Mescalero Indian Reservation. Victorio was captured shortly after he fled the territory under Hatch's jurisdiction.

Colonel Hatch was still active in the army at the age of 67, when he was thrown from his carriage and severely injured. He died shortly afterward on April 11, 1889, at Fort Robinson, Nebraska. His remains were later interred in the National Cemetery at Fort Leavenworth, Kansas.

During his long career, Edward Hatch was considered one of the best cavalry officers in the army. Contrary to what he once thought, time has not obscured the memory of him or his deeds.

Escaping the Boers

In 1899, a 25-year-old Britisher, a correspondent for the London *Morning Post*, was assigned to cover the Boer War in South Africa. In October of that year, he was about to embark on one of the most personally perilous wartime adventures in his life—a life that would be intimately involved in a number of wars. The adventure, dramatic in its own right, gained a grander significance because the youthful protagonist was Winston S. Churchill.

Fresh from a four-year tour of duty with the Fourth Hussars, which took him from England to Cuba to India to Egypt, Churchill had not been on South African soil a full month before he was taken prisoner by the Boers.

It occurred on the afternoon of November 15, when he was riding on an armored train that was inauspiciously known as Wilson's death trap, because it steamed its way dangerously close to the battle lines and to Boer entrenchments. Churchill learned · the appropriateness of the sobriquet when the train was attacked and sent careening off the rails. The British soldiers on board climbed from the derailed train, took cover, and then opened fire on their attackers. Young Winston got out of his overturned coach car and suddenly found himself isolated from the others.

Churchill recalls the incident in his autobiography, *A Roving Commission: My Early Life:*

Fifty yards away was a small plate-layers' cabin of masonry; there was cover there. About 200 yards away was the rocky gorge of the Blue Krantz River; there was plenty of cover there. I determined to make a dash for the river. I rose to my feet. Suddenly, on the other side of the railway, separated from me by the rails and two uncut wire fences, I saw a horseman galloping furiously—a tall, dark figure holding his rifle in his right hand. He pulled up his horse almost in its own length and shaking the rifle at me shouted a loud command. We were 40 yards apart. That morning I had taken with me, correspondent-status notwithstanding, my Mauser pistol. I thought I could kill this man. . . . I put my hand to my belt; the pistol was not there. . . . I was quite unarmed. Meanwhile, I suppose in about the time this takes to tell, the Boer horseman, still seated on his horse, had covered me with his rifle. . . . I looked toward the river; I looked toward the plate-layers' hut. The Boer continued to look along his sights. I thought there was absolutely no chance of escape. If he fired, he would surely hit me, so I held up my hands and surrendered myself a prisoner of war.

(The Boer horseman who captured Churchill was Louis Botha, later to be a general and also South Africa's first prime minister.)

Churchill and the other prisoners were herded together and transported to a makeshift prison compound in Pretoria, the Boer capital in the Transvaal province of the South African Republic. Churchill immediately thought about the possibility of escape. So along with Captain Aylmer Haldane, who had been the commander of the ill-fated train, and others taken prisoner, Churchill formulated a plan during the next month. Their scheme centered on a lavatory propitiously close to the least-patrolled section of the compound wall. A prisoner could hide there; then after the sentry passed and remained out of sight for a few moments, the prisoner could race out and scale the relatively low wall. The prisoners could proceed one at a time that way and then rendezvous on the other side of the wall.

Churchill was the first in line to attempt the daring escape, crouching silently in the lavatory on the night of December 12, 1899. As the guard passed on his round, Churchill stood and ran for the wall, scrambled over it, and dropped unnoticed into the bushes of a garden on the other side. He waited for the others, but no one came. After an hour, he realized that other sentries had taken up patrolling the wall inside, making it impossible for the others to escape. He would have to go it alone.

Churchill's path to freedom was a precarious one. First, he would have to get out of the garden. He was in a courtyard, and there was only one walkway that led out to the road about 75 yards away. To get there he would have to walk right past the guards' sentry house.

I said to myself, "*Toujours de l'audace,*" put my hat on my head, strode into the middle of the garden, walked past the windows of the house without any attempt at concealment and so went through the gate and turned to the left. I passed the sentry at less than five yards. Most of them knew me by sight. Whether he looked at me or not I do not know, for I never turned my head. I restrained with the utmost difficulty an impulse to run. But after walking a hundred yards and hearing no challenge, I knew that . . . I was at large in Pretoria.

The next problem was even greater. He was in a city that was in the center of enemy territory. The closest British outpost was 300 miles to the east. The people who lived between Pretoria and the outpost were Boers, who spoke Dutch, a language totally foreign to Churchill. In his pocket, he had only £75 and four chocolate bars.

His race to safety, Churchill decided, would best be made by following the Delagoa Bay Railway; it ran directly to Portuguese East Africa. Using the cover of night, Churchill made his way to what he thought—hoped—was the proper set of railroad tracks. He trudged along them, being careful to detour around stations and bridges, all of which were manned with Boer guards. After an hour of walking, he heard the sound of a train behind him and saw its beacon light as it bore down on him.

The flaring lights drew swiftly near. The rattle became a roar. The dark mass hung for a second above me. The engine-driver silhouetted against his furnace glow, the black profile of the engine, the clouds of steam—rushed past. Then I hurled myself on the trucks [freight cars], clutched at something, missed, clutched again, missed again, grasped some sort of handhold, was swung off my feet.... It was a goods train, and the trucks were full of sacks—soft sacks covered with coal-dust. They were in fact bags filled with empty coal bags going back to their colliery. I crawled on top and burrowed in among them.

Churchill stayed in hiding on the train until just before dawn. Then he decided to get off rather than risk a station-stop in the daylight. Someone might even unload the freight car that he was riding in, he feared. So he leaped from the train and spent the long daylight hours hiding in a field. He planned to hop another train that night, exit it before daybreak, and continue that routine until he was back with his fellow Britishers.

That night, however, no trains chugged up the track. He waited and waited and finally began walking. By this time, however, he had begun to feel hungry and weakened by the lack of exercise in prison. He suspected that he might not be able to make it all the way to Portuguese East Africa without some help—certainly he was going to have to get some food.

After walking for a while he could see several fires in the distance and thought they might be the campfires of some Kaffirs (South African tribespeople). He decided to seek their help, aware that they had little liking for the Boers. The fires came, however, not from a tribal village but from the furnaces of a coal mine. Weak and exhausted, Churchill walked toward the glowing lights. Several houses, all dark now in the late hours of the night, were clustered near the entrance to the coal mine. In desperation, he knocked on the door of the largest house.

A man armed with a revolver answered the door, looked curiously at the bedraggled young man, and told him to step inside. The man lit a gas lamp and spoke to Churchill in both Dutch and English. What did he want, the man asked. Young Winston told him a trumped-up story, which the man clearly did not believe. Churchill shook his head and said, "I think I had better tell you the truth."

"I think you had."

Churchill then told him who he was and how he had escaped.

The man, staring coldly at him in the glow of the lamp, said, "Thank God you have come here! It is the only house for twenty miles where you would not have been handed over. We are all British here, and we will see you through."

He then explained that word of the escape had been spread all over the land and that there was a reward offered for Churchill's capture "dead or alive." Churchill learned later that the man was the manager of the Transvaal Collieries and had emigrated to South Africa from England some years before. His sympathies still lingered with Britain.

The man hid Churchill in one of the mines for several days until young Winston regained his strength. He then smuggled him aboard a train that carried him to Lourenço Marques in Portuguese East Africa; from there Churchill went by steamer to Durban, where he was welcomed with fanfare and applause.

Hannah Senesh, Woman with a Mission

A comrade-in-arms who parachuted with Hannah Senesh behind German lines into Yugoslavia during World War II, Reuven Dafne once explained to a journalist (as translated by Marta Cohn in the preface to *Hannah Senesh: Her Life and Diary*):

> We parachutists were not supermen—nor superwomen. . . . We were small, frail, inexperienced, romantic people with all the shortcomings of the average person. None of us was unique, excepting perhaps Hannah. She was different . . . a spiritual girl guided almost by mysticism. . . . She was fearless, dauntless, stubborn. Despite her extraordinary intelligence and prescience, she was a kind of tomboy—a poet tomboy—which sounds rather odd, I know. A girl who dreamed of being a heroine—and who was a heroine.

Hannah Senesh was 22 years old on March 13, 1944, when she donned a parachute and a helmet, slung a rifle over her shoulder, and climbed aboard the British air force plane that would carry her to occupied Yugoslavia. She was a slender girl whose dark complexion, soft features, and warm smile made her quite attractive. Despite the fact that she was outfitted for battle, she looked far too fragile for the dangerous, perhaps suicidal, mission she was undertaking. A woman, a Jew, a commando with only three months' training, she was on a personal mission to make her way into Hungary, warn the one million Jews there of the fate the Nazis had planned for them, and organize their escape.

Young Hannah, the daughter of a respected and well-to-do journalist and playwright, was born in Budapest, Hungary, on July 17, 1921. Her father had died when she was only six years old, and she and her brother were raised by their mother, Catherine. A brilliant student with an effervescent personality and a vivid streak of romanticism, she intermittently kept a diary and wrote poetry from the time she was 13 until her death. Her writings, all of which have been preserved, provide a keen insight into this most remarkable young woman.

At the age of 18, Hannah emigrated to Palestine and arrived there alone in 1939, just as the war was breaking out in Europe. From the Nahalal Agricultural School where she was enrolled, she wrote to her mother in Budapest:

> I am in Nahalal, in Eretz.
>
> I am home. The being "home" does not refer to school. After all, I have been here only two days and haven't become part of the regular life yet. But the entire country's atmosphere, the people—all of them so friendly—one feels as if one had always lived here. And in a way this is true, since after all I've always lived among Jews, but not among such free, industrious, calm, and, I think, contented Jews. I know I still see things idealistically, and I know there will be difficult days.

How difficult, Hannah Senesh at 18 could never imagine. But in the next few years, she would come face to face with the horror of war and would wage her own personal battle against it.

Hannah learned about agriculture in Palestine and did all the various chores associated with the farms and the orchards of the country and eventually settled into a kibbutz near Haifa. During the same time, she followed closely the events of the war and the ever-increasing stories about the criminal treatment of the Jews in Europe.

By mid-1942, the thought of what she could do to help in the war effort had become almost an obsession. She felt she had to do something positive, something effective. In January 1943, she determined just what it was and inscribed it in her diary:

> I've had a shattering week. I was suddenly struck by the idea of going to Hungary. I feel I must be there during these days in order to help organize youth emigration and also to get my mother out. Although I'm quite aware how absurd the idea is, it still seems both feasible and necessary to me, so I'll get to work on it and carry it through.

Coincidentally, the British air force at about the same time was organizing in Palestine a unique force of infiltrators. It intended to assemble and train teams of Jewish commandos to be dropped behind enemy lines in Europe. Palestine was chosen as the assembly point because Jews from all European countries were there. Teams of Jewish commandos—each team familiar with its own country's customs and fluent in its language—would be smuggled into their native countries. There they would join with and organize the partisans and resistance forces. The primary goal would be to find Allied airmen who were shot down and help them get back to friendly territory. Secondarily, the infiltrators would set up escape routes for Jews and sabotage in whatever way they could the Nazi efforts to destroy the Jewish population.

Hannah heard about the clandestine project and volunteered. The British planned to use males only for this hazardous operation but then decided to include a few females, since they would be less conspicuous. Hannah was interviewed by a joint panel of British officers and Jewish officials and was accepted. But it wasn't until December 1943 that her training for the mission got under way.

She wrote to her brother, who was also in Palestine, on Christmas Day:

> Day after tomorrow, I am starting something new. Perhaps it's madness. Perhaps it's fantastic. Perhaps it's dangerous. Perhaps one in a hundred or one in a thousand pays with his life; perhaps with less than his life, perhaps with more.

Hannah would have less than three months to learn how to use rifles, handguns, knives, and explosives; practice hand-to-hand combat; learn how to read a map and navigate by the stars; become familiar with undercover tactics—and, of course, how to parachute from an airplane.

There were 32 members of this elite force—29 men and three women. (Only one of the women besides Hannah, however, would actually parachute behind enemy lines. Chaviva Reik would land in Czechoslovakia but eventually would be captured and summarily executed by the Germans.) Hannah, totally absorbed with the importance of her mission, worked hard during the training sessions. In January 1944, when the last phase of her training had begun, Hannah wrote in her diary: "This week I leave for Egypt. I'm a soldier."

The team designated to enter Hungary was composed of five young men (the eldest man was 24 years old) and Hannah. But because Hungary had become overrun with German troops, it was decided that Hannah's group would parachute into Yugoslavia instead. This was a very unhappy turn of events for Hannah and her personal mission, and she was quite vocal in her disagreement with the British. Her deepest wish was to aid *her* country and *her* people and especially her mother. A compromise was finally reached; some members of the group would be allowed to infiltrate into Hungary after first working with the partisans in Yugoslavia.

Hannah and three other members of her team—Reuven Dafne, Yonah Rosen, and Abba Berdichev—boarded the British troop plane at Brindisi, Italy, on the night of March 13. The other two commandos, Yoel Palgi and Peretz Goldstein, would link up with them later in Yugoslavia.

The plane flew across the Adriatic Sea and soon was circling over the drop zone. First, parcels of supplies and equipment for the partisans were dropped, and then the team's most precious item, a radio transmitter, floated to earth under the billows of a black parachute.

Reuven Dafne and Hannah were the first to leap from the plane. Dafne observed later:

> I'll never forget the moment I made that jump. Hannah standing by, so slim, her face wreathed in a hugh smile, her expression calm, happy, thumbs up—her favorite victory sign. I jumped . . . and she was right behind me. A few moments later, we were on the soil of Yugoslavia.

It did not take long for this special group to make contact with the partisan army. The partisans were well organized by this time and in fact controlled the mountains of Yugoslavia. During the next two months, Hannah's team moved with the partisans through the country. They took part in battle skirmishes; rescued airmen who had been shot down and arranged for them to be smuggled out of the country; and sabotaged German communications—all while deftly avoiding the German patrols.

The partisans, however, had little concern with the mission that most obsessed Hannah—the opening of escape routes in Hungary that would lead to Palestine. Hannah never lost sight of that key objective, however, and it grew dramatically in importance when her team received word of the mass movements of Hungarian Jews to destinations that were then unknown but were reported to be camps where Jews were systematically exterminated. Reportedly, a calculated program was being carried out by SS Lieutenant Colonel Adolf Eichmann to destroy the entire Jewish population of Hungary.

The life of a soldier and a resistance fighter in enemy territory, compounded with the gloom of the news of what was happening in Hungary, took its toll on Hannah. As Yoel Palgi later explained: "Her eyes no longer sparkled. She was cold, sharp, her reasoning now razor-edged; she no longer trusted strangers."

Hannah had been the undisputed leader of the team; she was the person who would talk and argue with the partisan leaders and who never lost sight of the objectives. She alone continually urged the institution of the secondary purpose. Hannah, however, became increasingly impatient. As she told Yoel Palgi:

> We are the only ones who can possibly help. We don't have the right to think of our own safety. We don't have the right to hesitate. Even if the chances of our success are minuscule, we must go. If we don't go for fear of our lives, a million Jews will surely be massacred.

And they did go—three of them anyway. Hannah, Yoel Palgi, and Peretz Goldstein were to enter Hungary, while the others were chosen to stay to carry out the team's primary mission in Yugoslavia.

The three who would enter Hungary agreed that they should do it separately. The borders were heavily patrolled by German troops, and the roads, the cities, and even the towns and the villages were filled with enemy soldiers. Infiltrating individually, they felt, would broaden the odds of one of them getting in and carrying out the mission. Budapest would be their goal, and they made plans to meet at an appointed time on a specified date at the main synagogue in that city.

Hannah, toting the radio transmitter and escorted by a few partisans who agreed to go with her to the vicinity of the border, set out for Hungary. Near the border, they met three refugees who had just come from the opposite direction. They were fleeing the Germans and said that Hungary was now in a state of siege and that a massive operation of rounding up all Hungarian Jews was indeed under way. Of the three, two were Jews—named Kallos and Fleischmann—and the other was a Frenchman, Jacques Tissandier, who had been a prisoner of war. When the partisans refused to provide Hannah with a guide into Hungary, the three refugees decided to go with her, back into the hell-hole from which they had just fled. On June 9, 1944, the group managed to sneak across the border and, with a map, a compass, and the stars for guidance, struck out for Budapest.

They swam the Drava River and in the morning came upon a Hungarian village. From their vantage point in the woods nearby, however, they could not tell if any Germans were in the town. They decided that only two of them would reconnoiter the village. Hannah and the Frenchman would wait with the radio transmitter in the woods.

The two young Jewish men were routinely stopped in the village by the Hungarian police. Their papers appeared to be in order, but the Hun-garians decided to take them to the police station for some additional questioning. They were not searched or handcuffed or inhibited in any other way, but as they walked, Kallos, for some bizarre, inexplicable reason, pulled a gun from his pocket, shot himself in the head, fell down, and died in the street.

Kallos and Fleischmann were carrying guns, and Kallos had in his pocket the earphones for the radio transmitter. The Hungarians immediately turned the matter over to the Germans. A Hungarian farmer then came forward to tell the Germans that he believed there were others; he had seen all of them together in the woods earlier in the morning. A company of more than 200 German soldiers began to systematically search the woods. It was not long before they found Hannah and the Frenchman and, buried not far away, the radio transmitter.

Yoel Palgi would wait in vain at the synagogue in Budapest. Hannah would never join him there. The Germans took her into custody, questioned her, and tortured her in an effort to learn the radio code that they knew she must have. It was important to them because with it they could send false or misleading military and intelligence information to the Allies. But she would not tell them, even though she was tormented physically and psychologically. The code they wanted was contained in a book of poetry that Hannah had left on the train on her way to Budapest, and she did not know it from memory.

Then Hannah was taken to Budapest. It was not how she had dreamed she would enter the city—in handcuffs and under the guard of a Gestapo agent. She was tortured, debased, and beaten at the Horthy Miklos Street Military Prison, but Hannah couldn't give them any information.

This did not, of course, prevent them from trying. And on the morning of June 17, 1944, Catherine Senesh, the yellow star of Jewry on her faded dress, was taken from her home and brought down to the prison on Horthy Miklos Street. There she was questioned at some length about herself and her two children. She answered all their questions and told them confidently that both her children were safe in Palestine. She was disturbed by the amount of questioning, especially about Hannah, but finally she was told it was over. She had not dared to ask why she had been brought there.

Then her interrogator said, "One last question—where do you *really* think your daughter is?"

"In Palestine, as I said."

He shook his head. "No. She's in the next room."

A few moments later, Hannah and her mother met for the first time since the young woman had left for Palestine in 1939. Catherine Senesh later described the shocking moment:

I felt as if the floor were giving way under me and clutched the edge of the table frantically with both hands. My eyes closed, and in a matter of seconds I felt everything—hope, faith, trust, the very meaning of life, everything I had ever believed in—collapse like a child's house of cards. I was completely shattered, physically and spiritually.

The door opened. I turned my back to the table, my body rigid. Four men led her in. Had I not known she was coming, perhaps in that first moment I would not have recognized the Hannah of five years ago. Her once soft, wavy hair hung in a filthy tangle; her ravaged face reflected untold suffering; her large, expressive eyes were blackened; and there were ugly welts on her cheeks and neck. That was my first glimpse of her.

It did not, of course, change anything. Hannah had nothing to tell them, no matter what the threats to her or her mother. Hannah was taken back to her cell. Her mother was subsequently interned in the same prison. So was her fellow-commando Yoel Palgi, who finally had been arrested on a street in Budapest. On occasion, Hannah and Yoel were allowed to talk to each other, lamenting the failure of the mission and discussing the disillusionment they both felt but expressing hope for their own freedom and for an end to the horrors in Hungary and elsewhere in Europe.

In September, through coincidence, Hannah and Yoel Palgi were placed in the same van to be taken to different prisons. At the Conti Street prison, Hannah was taken off the van while Palgi watched and later remembered, "As the van moved off, she put down her bag and gave us an encouraging thumbs-up sign.... It was the last time I saw her."

Hannah Senesh was tried by a military tribunal in Budapest on October 28, 1944. But very little is known of the trial, which was held in secrecy. She was found guilty of treason. On November 7, Hannah was taken to the prison courtyard, tied to a wooden post, and executed by a firing squad.

Reuven Dafne and Yoel Palgi, as well as Hannah's mother, Catherine Senesh, survived the war. Peretz Goldstein, the other team member to infiltrate Hungary, was arrested and later died at a concentration camp in Germany. In 1951, Hannah Senesh's remains were brought to Israel, where she was buried with full military honors.

Capturing the U-505

One of the most daring and dramatic events on the high seas during World War II, or in any conflict for that matter, was the capture intact of a German U-boat, the 505, and its subsequent tow to American shores. The following article tells the full story of this amazing naval deed. It is reprinted from the booklet "The Story of the U-505," published by Chicago's Museum of Science and Industry, where the boat is on permanent exhibition.

On June 12, 1940, the Deutsche Werft laid the keel of another *Unterseeboot* in its Hamburg shipyard. There was nothing special about this particular U-boat—nothing to set it apart from similar submarines already in service or being produced in other German shipyards. . . .

Yet this particular submarine was destined for a special fate. . . .

August 26, 1941, was the U-boat's first important date—the day it was commissioned as the U-505. As the newly assigned commander received the U-505's staff [flagstaff] and Wimpel [commissioning pennant], the members of the crew stood at attention on the trim deck, and Vice-Admiral Wolf, commanding officer

for the Hamburg naval district, delivered the traditional address.

Afterward, he and other guests inspected the submarine and left their names and congratulatory wishes on the pages of the U-505's guest book.

Under the heading, lettered carefully in German script, *Wir Fahren Gegen England* ("We sail against England"), the guests inscribed their greetings and good wishes.

Admiral Wolf wrote, "Always lucky in your trips—hail and victory."

. . . Colonel Rohrbeck, who wrote that he had seen submarine service in World War I, wished for "a good journey and rich booty." Another well-wisher penned the hope that the U-505 would always show its face to the enemy. Someone else set down the well-known Latin phrase *ad astra per aspera* ("to the stars through difficulties"). The officers of the U-505's first crews were also listed:

Commandant–Captain Lieutenant Loewe
Chief Engineer–Captain Lieutenant Foester
1st Watch Officer–Ober Lieutenant S. G. Nollan
2nd Watch Officer–Lieutenant F. G. Stolzenburg

Next came a bit of doggerel verse, paraphrased from an old German nursery rhyme, composed by various members of the crew, anticipating future successes for the U-505. It read about like this:

Ten proud British freighters sailing in a line,
Along came U-505 and left only
  nine;
Nine proud British freighters
  heading for their pier,
Then came U-505 and made one
  disappear;
Eight proud British freighters
  outlined against the heaven,
U-505 shot one torpedo, and then
  there were but seven;
Seven proud British freighters
  loaded to their "sticks,"
U-505 attacked again, and that
  left only six;
Six proud British freighters making for the shore,
The last ship fell behind a bit—it
  isn't any more;
Five proud British freighters just
  a short way from home,

Along came a torpedo—it hadn't
  far to roam;
Four proud British freighters in
  the periscope were plain,
Two torpedoes left their tubes—
  two ships were cut in twain;
Two proud British freighters,
  their journeys almost done,
The "Lion" fired once again, and
  that left only one;
One proud British freighter got
  to Northmouth then,
But the English newspapers still
  reported ten.

The moral of this story is don't believe everything you read in the English newspapers.

The reference to the lion in the next to the last verse was a reference to the name of their commander, Loewe, which is also the German word for lion.

Although this bit of doggerel was somewhat premature for a U-boat that had yet to make its maiden voyage, it indicates the high morale that the new crew had—and which no doubt reflected the success German submarines were having in the Atlantic shipping lanes. For example, in one particularly successful week in spring, the U-boats had accounted for 148,000 tons of vital shipping.

Following the commissioning celebration, the U-505's crew [was] given three days of special instructions, and then the U-boat proceeded on its first orders—through the Wilhelm canal to the large naval base at Kiel for an intensive period of training.

The next four months were devoted to the various aspects of submarine warfare and undersea operations. There were torpedo and gunnery practice, diving and evasive exercises, and tactical maneuvers with the 25th U-Boat Flotilla in Danzig [Gdansk, Poland]. Each crew member not only knew his own special functions and responsibilities but had to be familiar with the entire operation of the boat, for in each man's hands rested the possibility of fatal error in crisis.

Following an outfitting at Stettin [Szczeci, Poland], the U-505 now made her maiden voyage, from Kiel to Lorient on the French coast, where a few final adjustments were made and additional war supplies taken aboard.

The first real war assignment for the U-505 was off Freetown on the coast of French West Africa from February 11 to May 7, 1942. In this undertaking, the U-505 sank four ships totaling 26,000 British Registered Tons. Here is the roster:

March 5—English
   freighter *(Benmohr)*   6,000 B.R.T.
March 6—English
   tanker (no name)   8,000 B.R.T.
April 3—American
   freighter *(West Irmo)*   6,000 B.R.T.
April 4—Dutch
   freighter *(Alphacca)*   6,000 B.R.T.

From June 7 to August 25, the U-505 was assigned to the Caribbean, where she sank another 14,700 tons of shipping:

June 28—American
   freighter (Robin
   Hood type)   6,900 B.R.T.
June 29—American
   freighter (Thomas
   McKean)   7,400 B.R.T.

July 27—Columbia
   sailboat *(Roma)*   400 B.R.T

The U-505 then broke off because of the ill health of the commander and returned home.

The next entry in the U-505's scrapbook is by Captain Loewe, who was detached from his command on September 5 [1942]. He wrote:

> I wish for the U-505 under my successor, Captain Lieutenant Zscheck, and for the future always a happy journey, success, and good homecoming. May the good star that has led the boat until now watch over it in the future. The U-505 shall remain ever in my thoughts, for I will always remember the crew and boat of my first command.

October 4 saw the U-505 back in service again, this time assigned to Trinidad. Three days after sinking an unknown freighter of 5,500 tons on November 7, the U-505 was attacked from the air, and a bomb scored a direct hit. Heavily damaged, the U-505 headed home.

While repairs were being made, the entire crew got a two-week rest period and went to Bad Wiessee, a famous German resort area. Many of their families joined them there.

There remains only one more entry in the U-505's unofficial diary, this dated December 29, 1943. It reads as follows:

> In August of this year, the torpedo boat T-25 rescued a large part of the crew of the U-106 about 13 degrees West.
> On December 28, 1943, the

crew of the U-505, of the same flotilla as the U-106 and almost on the same spot, rescued a part of the crew of the T-25.

With waving flags in a battle with heavy and light English cruisers, the T-25 was sunk.

We are grateful to our rescuers of the U-505 and for all their comradeship and are thankful for the good luck that makes it possible for us to face the enemy again very soon on a new boat.

May we soon overcome the enemy.

For this, we wish the U-505 much war luck and at all times a happy homecoming.

Signed by the Corvette
Commander

Although no more entries were made in the U-505's scrapbook, a former member of the crew has supplied the rest of the story:

I came aboard the boat in February 1943, after it had been bombed by an American plane in the Caribbean Sea near the Orinoco River. The boat was very badly damaged, and it took us weeks and weeks to get it repaired. Finally, we were able to start again, but when we tried to dive deeper than [about 590 feet], something broke again, and we had to get back to the harbor for repairs.

And so we tried it about three or four times, but we were always followed by misfortune. The U-505 had been very successful before the bomb had hit it, but now something like a curse lay over the boat.

Finally, everything seemed to be all right again. We left the harbor of Lorient in June, I think it was, bound for the southern Atlantic, but we did not get very far. Near the coast of Spain, we met a British destroyer, got depth charged, and had to get back again because we were losing oil. The whole crew, including the captain, was upset about our constant misfortune, but we couldn't help it.

In October, we started again, and this time we were lucky and got out of the "Biscaya" [Bay of Biscay] (the hell of the U-boats). I think we were near the Azores when it happened. We were about 200 feet under the surface when a ship crossed our course. The captain brought the boat up to periscope depth in order to have a look.

But the destroyer, or whatever it was, came back again and dropped five or six depth charges, which exploded quite near us and shook us like peas in a can. Everything was out of control, and the enemy attacked again with high speed. Everybody on the U-505 knew that would be the end.

But now a miracle happened. The destroyer was in the best position to blow us to pieces with depth charges, and we all were expecting them, our nerves strained to the utmost. But there came no more.

Again the boat had to be repaired, but this time we also got a new electric engine. This time, we started on Christmas under the command of the new captain, Ober Lieutenant Lange. While we were going through the Biscaya, we received an order by radio to change our course. German and British destroyers had been engaged in an encounter, and we were to help the men who had lost their ships and were swimming in the icy cold water. During two nights, we picked up 36 men and saved their lives—that made about 100 men altogether in the small boat. I slept during this time behind the periscope in the tower, twisting my legs around it like a snake. Well, anyway, we managed to get them all safely back to the next harbor, which was Brest.

From Brest, we started about two months later on our last voyage.

We left Brest in February 1944, bound for the Gold Coast of Africa, and this time we were lucky; we got through the Biscaya without any interruption and proceeded down the coast of Africa until we came to Monrovia (Liberia). Here, we stopped and looked into the harbor. But there were no ships, so we kept on.

We were very careful then, as we didn't want to be detected by radar. So we submerged during the day and emerged only at night for a few hours. Our operating area was along the Gold Coast, and we spent about four weeks there. We tracked about three or four steamers, but they had too much speed, and we were unable to get them. Finally, we

turned back again, hoping to catch at least one or two on the way home.

But this time, they caught us. . . .

In the middle of May 1944, U.S. Navy Task Group 22.3, known as a "hunter-killer" group, sailed from Norfolk, Virginia, to look for submarines.

The task group was commanded by Captain Daniel V. Gallery, U.S. Navy, later a rear admiral, and comprised the escort carrier *Guadalcanal* and five destroyer escorts under Commander F. S. Hall, U.S. Navy; the *Pillsbury, Pope, Flaherty, Chatelain,* and the *Jenks.* Their destination was a known U-boat rendezvous area near the Canary Islands.

Although the primary mission of the group was to find and destroy enemy submarines, Captain Gallery had long considered the possibilities of a daring plan—to capture a U-boat intact. Such a prize would be of inestimable value to the Allies, not because of the U-boat itself but because of the equipment and documents it might yield. Standard tactics in dealing with U-boats called for sinking them as expeditiously and efficiently as depth charges, bombs, and armor-piercing ammunition could accomplish. But Gallery reasoned that if the U-boat could be forced to the surface, it might be possible to get some men aboard her under certain conditions. Since such an opportunity had seemed possible with a U-boat previously brought to the surface and sunk, he decided to prepare for it.

As the task group proceeded, a boarding party was organized aboard each ship and rehearsed in a role that few ever expected to materialize.

After cruising south along the West African coast, the task group headed north for Casablanca. About 150 miles off the coast of Cape Blanco, Africa (latitude 21 degrees 30 minutes north and longitude 19 degrees 20 minutes west), they encountered the U-505.

It was Sunday, June 4, at 1109 hours, when the *Chatelain* reported sonar contact on an object 800 yards away on her starboard bow. Although sonar contacts are frequent and do not always mean submarines, the *Chatelain* turned toward the object immediately and prepared to attack.

But in the brief moments required to identify the contact definitely as a submarine, the *Chatelain* had come so close that her depth charges would not sink fast enough to intercept the U-boat. So she held her fire and opened the range to set up the attack. Turning back, she closed and fired her "hedgehog" (ahead-thrown depth charges that explode on contact only) battery. Regaining sonar contact after a momentary loss due to the short range, the *Chatelain* passed beyond the submarine and swung around toward it to make a second attack with depth charges.

When the *Chatelain's* first contact had been evaluated as a U-boat, the *Guadalcanal* had sent two Wildcat fighter planes over to have a look; and now as the *Chatelain* heeled over in her tight turn, the planes sighted the submerged U-boat and fired their machine guns into the water to mark the submarine's position.

The *Chatelain* steadied up on her bearing and moved in swiftly for the kill. A full pattern of depth charges, set for a 60-foot target, exploded in the water around the U-boat. As their detonations threw geysers of spray into the air, a large oil slick spread on the water, and the fighter planes overhead radioed jubilantly, "You struck oil! Sub is surfacing."

Just 6½ minutes after the *Chatelain's* first attack, the U-boat was on the surface, a wounded but still formidable enemy.

Gallery's plan for capturing her alive now moved into its first phase. As the submarine broke the surface only 700 yards away from the *Chatelain*, the escort opened fire with all guns that would bear and swept the U-boat's decks. The *Pillsbury* and *Jenks*, which had also closed in, and the two Wildcats overhead also added to the intense barrage that was directed not at sinking the U-boat, but at keeping its crew from manning its deck guns. For that reason, the guns had been loaded with anti-personnel rather than armor-piercing ammunition.

Believing that his U-boat had been mortally damaged by the *Chatelain's* depth charges and sinking was imminent, the commanding officer of the U-505 had brought his ship to the surface to permit the crew to escape. As the partially submerged U-505 circled to the right, because of a jammed rudder, at a speed near seven knots on her electric motors, the crew went over the side.

Seeing the U-boat turning toward him, the commanding officer of the *Chatelain* quickly fired a single torpedo at the submarine in order to forestall what appeared to be an attack. The torpedo passed ahead of the U-505, which now appeared to be completely abandoned. The "cease fire" was now given, and the *Pillsbury's* boarding party was ordered away. The *Chatelain* and the *Jenks* meanwhile began to pick up the U-boat's crew.

When Lieutenant Albert L. David, U.S. Navy, and his eight-man boarding party caught up to the still-circling sub, they found only one man topside, and he was dead—the only fatality.

The lieutenant and his party now tumbled quickly down the hatch from the conning tower.

Their hurried examination found the U-boat completely deserted. But there was water in the control room and more coming in through an open eight-inch sea strainer. Engineer's Mate Zenon B. Lukosius found the cover lying nearby and, quickly putting it into place, secured it. In their haste to abandon ship, this was the only valve the Germans had opened, and this one only partially.

Meanwhile, under the direction of Lieutenant David, the other men, not knowing how long the submarine might remain afloat, were snatching the code book and whatever documents they could find and passing them up topside to be put into the motor whaleboat. The engine room was checked, and a hasty search was made for booby traps.

The sub's motors were now stopped, but as she lost way the U-505 settled dangerously low in the water. So the motors were hastily set to full speed ahead again. But time was fast running out, as the sub was operating on her batteries, which were already low.

The *Pillsbury* came alongside to use its main pumps to get out the water that threatened to sink the U-505. Both ships were turning in tight circles to the right on diverging radii. When one of the lines holding them together parted under the strain, the U-505's bow hydroplane slashed the thin side plates of the *Pillsbury*, flooding two forward compartments and forcing it to haul away to make emergency repairs.

The *Guadalcanal's* boarding party, under Commander Earl Trosino, U.S. Naval Reserves, had now arrived on the sub, and temporary salvage measures were completed. In order to keep her afloat, she would have to be towed. So the *Guadalcanal* stood in to take up the tow, and as the carrier took up the slack in the line, the U-505's engines were again cut. A cheer went up as the submarine sluggishly rose when the *Guadalcanal* picked up speed.

As the task group formed up and headed with [its] still partly submerged prize for Dakar, the nearest friendly port on the African coast, orders were received to proceed to Bermuda instead.

For Dakar was full of spies, and the German high command would shortly have learned of the U-505's capture. To keep the secret, the *Guadalcanal* started on the 1,700 miles to Bermuda with hardly enough fuel for the trip.

After three days of towing the still partially submerged U-boat, the fleet tug *Abnaki* arrived to take over the tow and the tanker *Kennebec* to provide the much-needed fuel.

On June 19, the U-505 was brought into Port Royal Bay, Bermuda.

It was one of the most valued prizes of the war, for the U-505 gave the Allies the secret to the radio code used by the Germans in directing their U-boat operations.

Two days after the U-505 was captured, Allied troops landed on the beaches of Normandy. The importance of providing a continuous flow of reinforcements, food, and supplies safe from the menace of the U-boats was more vital than ever, once Allied forces had been committed to the mainland of Europe.

Another prize found on the U-505 were several torpedoes of a new type—a formidable weapon in undersea warfare.

For this heroic capture of an enemy war vessel on the high seas, Task Group 22.3 received the Presidential Unit Citation.

In addition, the following received individual awards: Lieutenant (junior grade) Albert L. David, Congressional Medal of Honor; Commander Earl Trosino (Springfield,

Pennsylvania), Legion of Merit; Stanley E. Wdowiak (Maspeth, Long Island, New York), Navy Cross; Arthur W. Knispel (Newark, New Jersey), Navy Cross. The Silver Star was awarded to the following: Zenon B. Lukosius (Chicago, Illinois), Gordon F. Hohne (Worcester, Massachusetts), Chester A. Mocarski (Cleveland, Ohio), William R. Riendeau (Providence, Rhode Island), Philip N. Trusheim (Montrose, Colorado), George W. Jacobson, Jr. (Portland, Oregon), Wayne M. Pickels (St. Louis, Missouri).

Today, the U-505 resides at the Museum of Science and Industry in Chicago, Illinois, and as an exhibit is open to the public. In 1954, the U-505 was first towed up the Atlantic Ocean from the navy yard at Portsmouth, New Hampshire, where it had been dry-docked, then down the St. Lawrence River, through Lake Ontario, Lake Erie, Lake Huron, and Lake Michigan, and then was hauled 800 feet overland to its berth outside the museum.

A Devastating Submarine Attack

This dramatic first-person account of one of the most successful submarine operations in U.S. naval history provides a unique behind-the-scenes view of a submarine attack. Told by Richard H. O'Kane (Rear Admiral, USN, Retired), the boat's captain in 1944, it is one memorable segment in the wartime cruise of the U.S.S. Tang.

The Tang saw only a brief nine months of duty during World War II, but in that time it became one of the most destructive attack boats in U.S. naval history. Only one submarine sank more ships than the 24 the Tang sent to the bottom (the U.S.S. Tautog with 26).

O'Kane and his crew also rescued 22 American flyers who had been shot down in the Pacific. For its combat accomplishments, the Tang received two Presidential Unit Citations (only three other ships in the U.S. Navy have ever been so honored), and its skipper, then Commander O'Kane, won the Congressional Medal of Honor, three Navy Crosses, and three Silver Stars among his many other combat decorations.

The following action took place in the Formosa Strait during October 1944. The Tang happened on a Japanese convoy consisting of five tankers and freighters and five escort vessels, penetrated it, and wrought incredible devastation in a brief ten-minute skirmish, sinking five of the Japanese transport ships and then escaping unscathed.

Admiral O'Kane's narrative is reprinted from his book Clear the Bridge! The War Patrols of the U.S.S. Tang.

We moved north at a modest two-engine speed so as not to churn up a luminous wake. The remainder of the evening watch was uneventful topside, and the first movie in some days played all the way through below. For all appearance, *Tang* could be on a peacetime interisland cruise. An encouraging report came down from Ed [radar officer Lieutenant Edward Beaumont], but we'd continue our run out of the strait and give the radar a shakedown all its own. We had done this for our torpedoes off Honshu, and now Ed and his gang deserved the same.

The midwatch relieved with Larry [engineering officer Lieutenant Laurence Savadkin], the senior officer. I'd hate to lose him as an engineering officer, but he should be fleeting up to exec; someone would get a gold mine. These thoughts were interrupted by his report that they were firing off the revamped SJ [surface-search radar]. There was no "Fixit Book" in *Tang*, and these men had spent more hours than any

others in staying with their gear until it worked. I flipped on the eavesdropping switch to hear the results, and in the background came [radar operator Floyd M.] Caverly's unmistakable report of good sea return. Switching off the Voycall, I considered a change in the night orders but decided to stick with the original plan to clear the strait. The decision was barely firm when the duty chief's messenger literally burst into my cabin.

"We've got a convoy, Captain!" he almost shouted, and then added to the official report in his enthusiasm, "The chief says it's the best one since the Yellow Sea."

. . . I raced aft and up the ladder to the conning tower. Caverly had reported the cluster of blops as an island group at 14,000 yards after the very first sweep of the SJ.

No such islands, other than the Pescadores, lie in the strait, and Larry's turning south to put the convoy on our quarter as soon as the range was shown to be closing was absolutely correct. We'd need time to think this one over, and not just the minutes that would be available had we continued to close the enemy. Fortune had not been with us since the first two attacks, for the carrier possibility might well have resulted in an attack, and surely no warship had ever given more than *Tang* in her effort to chase down a cruiser. But in each case, so unlike our last patrol, we still had the torpedoes, and this convoy offered another chance to really hurt the enemy.

We had two options. One would be to stay with the enemy for an always successful, as far as *Tang* was concerned, crack-of-dawn submerged attack. With a split salvo we could sink two ships and, if luck were on our side, possibly a third. The other would be night surface firing, though I shuddered at the thought of another penetration between trailing escorts. That might not be necessary, however, for the best count from Caverly had been ten ships, half of them probably escorts based on the height of their pips on the A-scope, or five escorts compared to the 12 south of Nagasaki. This night, time was on our side, too, for the convoy had no nearby port, and a night surface attack, which could be deliberate and devastating, would not preclude an additional submerged attack at dawn.

A smaller pip moving swiftly from the convoy directly toward our position, now 12,000 yards on the enemy's bow, was to make the decision for me. It was now 0050, only 20 minutes after the initial contact, and two more engines pulled us away,

but not before the enemy patrol had closed half the distance. She then turned back, according to our plot, and was proceeding on a parallel but opposite course to that of the main body. . . .

We turned to follow her, and the Bells of St. Mary's chimed for the sixth time on this patrol. First things first, and [steward Howard M.] Walker preceded those coming up to their battle stations with my cup of coffee. He was fast indeed if the general alarm had turned him out of his bunk. Then I remembered the chief's messenger proceeding on forward. If Walker had a standing call every time I was called, it would account for his promptness in many things. . . . I'd have to ask [Chief William] Ballinger—but on further thought, why inquire about a good thing and maybe spoil it.

The patrol had slowed, and we moved inside 5,000 yards for a good observation. Her narrow though tall silhouette positively marked her as an escort but larger than any we had previously encountered, perhaps close to the size of our DEs [destroyer escorts]. Our business was not with her, and we came right 30 degrees so we could close the convoy and cross its bow. It was still a probing operation to size up the enemy and thus see how we could best attack. The SJ screen showed three ships in column flanked by two other large ships, one to port and the other to starboard. Four small pips, presumed to be escorts, surrounded the convoy. The fifth, which we had just observed, would probably make up a five-ship circular screen.

The frequent zigs, placing one or the other of the forward flanking escorts in the lead, made it impossible to tell from the SJ just what position if any had been left uncovered by the patrol that we had followed back halfway to the convoy. But finding out was our immediate task, and we would do so with the eyes the good Lord gave us, albeit with an assist from our 7 × 50 binoculars.

The range to the main body closed quickly with our combined speeds, and we came right to pass broadside to the enemy while still outside of possible visual sighting. Now with the convoy on our port quarter, we slowed to let the range close as we slid silently across its van. [First Class Boatswain's Mate William "Boats"] Leibold and [Chief Quartermaster Sidney] Jones were to starboard and port as I marked bearings on the after TBT [target bearing transmitter], and I felt the best of eyes and experience were searching out the enemy. The silhouettes loomed big as the range closed below 4,000 yards, and those ships in the center showed little freeboard. This and their protected position marked them as tankers, targets of highest priority among Japanese merchantmen and second only to capital ships of the Imperial Navy.

They would receive our first salvo, split as necessary; but moving *Tang* into firing position undetected offered a problem. A possible solution appeared with a report from Frank [torpedo fire control officer Lieutenant Frank Springer] during our second pass across the enemy's van. Larry, on the true plot, had the convoy now steaming on its base course of 210, and the fifth member of the screen was indeed absent from her leading position while making the precautionary sweep. If she continued around the convoy she would be gone for an hour. There was our hole, dead astern of *Tang* at a range just under 3,000 yards.

Rather than present a broadside silhouette in turning, we stopped and let the convoy overtake us. The range dropped quickly, now 2,300 yards, and the ships took on sharp outlines, all appearing big and black. The situation was developing more quickly than it had with the convoy in the East China Sea, and we had little time for apprehension. At the moment the enemy was zigging, and we zigged too, arriving at the new course by an angle on the bow. If any of the ships could see us, they did not challenge our presence, but for the moment we had to go ahead at convoy speed or lose our selected slot between the port freighter and the tankers.

Frank would report when the convoy was again on or near its base course, and in the meantime Boats had another chance to maneuver with the enemy. On the next three legs of the enemy's zig plan, we moved closer to the major ships till it was my estimate that we occupied the position of the wayward escort, and we now identified the starboard flanking ship as a transport. Frank reported all tubes ready and outer doors open, and then on the next zig that the enemy was close to the base course. Plot was surely correct, for our position was right on an extended line drawn between the tankers and the freighter.

"All stop." The ships came on quickly.

"Port ahead two-thirds, starboard back two-thirds." *Tang* twisted right for near zero gyro angles on the tankers and to get her stern in position for a subsequent attack on the freighter. It was our standard maneuver, but the first time for ships in two columns.

Our bow was nicely ahead of the leading tanker, and shifting the screws for a moment stopped our swing. The three lumbering ships were coming by on a modest line of bearing, slightly disadvantageous to us since only the after half of the second tanker protruded beyond the leader. Tankers were not sunk by hits in their forward section, however, and this vulnerable stern would be all that we needed.

To assist plot, I had been marking bearings on each of the three ships; Caverly would be supplying the corresponding radar range. Then came Frank's warning of ten degrees to go. All bearings up to firing would now be on the leading tanker's stack. I marked but two.

"Everything checks below. Any time now, Captain."

"Constant bearing—mark!" The cross hairs rested on her superstructure.

"Set!" came immediately. Her squat stack was coming on.

"Fire!"

"Constant bearing—mark!" The wire was on her after well deck.

"Set!" Her after superstructure was coming on.

"Fire!" We shifted targets in trying to get all torpedoes on their way before the first would hit, perhaps impossible, for the range on the leading ship was 300 yards.

The third torpedo went to the stack of the second tanker at a range of 500 yards. The fourth sped to the stack of the trailing oiler at 800 yards; the fifth, to the forward edge of her after superstructure, was delayed a few seconds by the first two detonations.

John [Lieutenant John Heubeck], Leibold, and the lookouts would have to vouch for the other detonations, as I was racing to the after TBT, where Jones was keeping an eye on the freighter. She was still coming on in spite of the detonations beyond our bow and the eerie light of oil fires, which surely must make us stand out in silhouette. Perhaps she figured that the torpedoes had come in from the starboard flank and that the tankers had in fact formed a protective barrier for her. Between TBT bearings, Jones checked forward for me and was gone but seconds.

"They all hit as we aimed 'em, Captain. They're afire and sinking."

No one could have asked for a better report, but I did not have time to acknowledge, as Frank had asked for one more bearing. I gave a "Mark!" on the freighter's stack; her bow was about to cross our stern. Impatient, I called, "Constant bearing—mark!" with the reticle ahead of her midships superstructure, but Leibold literally collared me, physically dragging me forward. I would not have left the TBT otherwise.

The transport on the other side of

the tankers had spotted us in the glow of the fires and, like a monstrous destroyer, was coming in to ram. She was close; there would not be time to dive, and never had flank speed been rung up twice with greater urgency. Frank must have phoned maneuvering about the emergency, for the black smoke that poured from our overloaded diesels rivaled a destroyer's smoke screen. The transport continued to hold the upper hand, however, with her bow becoming more menacing by the second.

I would doubt that more amperes had ever poured through the armatures of a submarine's four main motors; the fields limiting the current were near zero, for the props had now driven *Tang's* bridge across the transport's bow. But she was dangerously close, inside 100 yards and still headed to strike us near amidships. The enemy now added to our precarious situation with a fusillade, apparently of anything that would shoot. The gunfire was cracking overhead as if we were in the butts at a rifle range pulling and marking targets.

At her 16 knots the transport would strike us in another 30 seconds. We had gained a little more, and in calculated desperation I ordered, "Left full rudder." At least the blow would be oblique, perhaps glancing, and there would be ballast tanks and frames to crumple before her bow could slice to our pressure hull. For the moment we were protected from the transport's gunfire by the extreme down-angle; a rifleman standing on her deck would have to lean out and shoot down. But more important, our stern's swing to starboard was fast, now accelerating as if it were the end man on a snap-the-whip, as indeed it was, for a submarine pivots well forward.

Unbelievably, *Tang* was alongside the transport. If we had been mooring to a submarine tender it would have been a one-bell landing, passing the lines over by hand, but not at our combined speeds of 40 knots. In seconds, with the transport's continued swing and *Tang* pulling away, the gunfire now above us could be brought to bear. I yelled, "Clear the bridge!" sounded two blasts, and counted seven men precede me down the hatch. Out of habit, I took a glance aft to be sure nobody was being left behind. What I saw changed my mind about diving. "Hold her up! Hold her up!" I shouted. . . .

About a ship's length astern, the transport was continuing to turn in an attempt to avoid the freighter, which had apparently been coming in to ram us also. Collision was imminent; the freighter would strike the transport's stern. I yelled, "Stand by aft!" and marked three consecutive bearings for a speed check before Frank's call, "Set below." The two ships stretched from quarter to quarter; I marked a single constant bearing on their middle, nearly dead astern, and Larry directed the spread of four torpedoes with the TDC [torpedo data computer] along their dual length. . . .

The four fish left in a seeming single salvo. Small arms fire dropped astern, and larger calibers had obviously lost us in the night. I called for John, Jones, and Leibold, for there were PCs [patrol craft] on our port bow and beam and a larger DE about 1,000 yards on our starboard quarter with a zero angle; *Tang* was far from being out of the woods. To put the DE astern we headed for the PC on our port bow. The Mark 18-1 torpedoes commenced hitting, four tremendous explosions in rapid sequence, and Jones called the results, the freighter going down almost instantly bow first and the transport hanging with a 30-degree up-angle.

For some reason the PC ahead turned left, probably to assist the last stricken ship, and *Tang* pulled steadily away from the pursuing DE, perhaps catching her with one boiler on the line. When we had opened the range to 4,500, she gave up the chase, and our radar tracked her back toward the scene of the transport. The battle stations lookouts now came topside since diving was not imminent. We followed the DE, however, for the bow of the transport still showed on radar and then became visible through our 7 × 50s as the range neared 6,000 yards. Suddenly a violent explosion lighted the skies for a moment, and then the transport's bow disappeared from sight and the radar screen. The detonation set off a gun duel between the DE and other escort vessels, who seemed to be firing at random, sometimes at each other and then out into the night. Their confusion was understandably complete.

In this particular attack, the Tang was credited with sinking one large freighter (7,500 tons), three large tankers (30,000 tons each), and one large transport (7,500 tons).

As happens so often in war, however, the story of the Tang does not have a happy ending. Later that month, while attacking another Japanese convoy in the Formosa Strait, the Tang fired its last torpedo, a faulty one, which curved around full tilt and, ironically, hit the Tang and sank it. Of the 87 men on board, only nine survived, among them Commander O'Kane; they were picked from the sea by the Japanese and held prisoner until the war ended.

A One-Man Army

The story of Staff Sergeant Andrew Miller's exploits for two weeks during the Allied march on Germany in November 1944 is not merely one of heroism and uncommon fearlessness. It is the saga of a virtual one-man attack force.

Sergeant Miller was born in Manitowoc, Wisconsin, on the shores of Lake Michigan. He joined the U.S. Army in the town of Two Rivers a few miles north of there and was serving with Company G, 377th Infantry, Ninety-fifth Infantry Division, when he bravely faced a series of events that threatened to claim his life and the lives of his men.

On November 16, Company G, moving through the province of Lorraine, was approaching the eastern border of France, when in the town of Woippy, Sergeant Miller and the rifle squad he was leading were suddenly pinned down by a crossfire of enemy machine guns. He ordered his men to remain under cover and then went forward alone. The bursts from one machine gun were coming from inside a building. He sidled up to the door and crashed through it, surprising the five members of the German gun crew. Sergeant Miller took all of them prisoner and then went after the second machine gun. Still by himself, he got close enough to lob several hand grenades, killing two Germans, wounding three others, and taking prisoner the remaining two, who were uninjured.

The following day, just outside the city of Metz, another battle raged. The Germans had the edge, and Allied tanks began to withdraw under heavy fire. Sergeant Miller's platoon began to move back as well—all but Sergeant Miller, that is. He remained with a rifle and an automatic rifle to take on a German machine-gun nest that was blocking the withdrawal of the entire platoon. He succeeded in knocking it out and then held the position until the men in his squad had regrouped and were able to rejoin him.

Two days later, as the Allied forces pressed on toward Germany, Sergeant Miller led an attack on a German-occupied barracks. Pinned down by fire from the building, he told his men to cover him while he crawled to one of the windows in the barracks and climbed through it. A few moments later, he reappeared at the window, pitched out six rifles, and waved his men toward the building. One by one, they raced to the window and joined him inside, along with the six now-disarmed Germans whom he was holding at bay. Sergeant Miller then led his men through the building, and by the time they had scoured it, a total of 75 Germans had been taken prisoner.

One of the prisoners told Sergeant Miller that other Germans hiding out in a building nearby were ready to surrender but were being prevented from doing so by a contingent of Gestapo officers. Miller quickly left with three of his men and ran a gauntlet of machine-gun fire to the building. Then his men boosted him up and through an open window, and upon clambering into the room, he came face to face with one of the Gestapo agents and the barrel of his Luger. Miller did not drop his own rifle but began talking immediately. The German understood English, and the sergeant was able to convince him of the hopelessness of the German situation there. The Germans might be able to kill him, he said, but they could not save themselves from the army outside. The Gestapo officer talked with several of his comrades, and they agreed to give up the fight and were taken prisoner along with the other Germans in that building.

Early the next morning, on November 20, Miller's platoon was again under heavy fire from a strategically placed machine gun. Miller, setting out by himself, grabbed a bazooka and started up a stairway on the outside of a nearby building, hoping he could get high enough to fire down on the enemy gun emplacement. But he soon realized that the only place high enough was the roof of the building. Although that position would expose him to a voluminous amount of direct enemy fire, he climbed there anyway. Walking quickly out into the open, he appeared oblivious to the enemy fire that turned on him and coolly aimed the bazooka and sent a rocket into the heart of the German gun emplacement, blowing apart both the machine gun and its operators.

The next day, Sergeant Miller volunteered to go out alone on a scouting patrol. And when his men caught up with him, they found him standing by a destroyed German machine-gun bunker, with 12 dejected German prisoners sitting before him.

Then on November 29, Company G climbed a hill overlooking Kerprichemmersdorf, Germany. Suddenly, heavy enemy fire opened up, and the entire company, with Sergeant Miller's squad at the rear, was pinned down. Miller got into a crouch and began to move forward, motioning for his men to follow. Together they ran past the forward element of Company G and hit the dirt, got up and moved forward, and then hit the dirt again. One by one, the other squads in the company began to follow them while Miller continued to lead his men forward. The barrage of gunfire was incredible, and the smoke, dust, and debris caused by the grenades and the light artillery set up an àlmost impenetrable fog. But Company G overran the German position, and the battle ended. In the middle of what had been the German defensive line, however, Staff Sergeant Andrew Miller now lay dead, his unbelievable one-man war finally at an end.

A Military Hanging

This true story from the annals of World War II tells the ordeal of a young German U-boatman when the submarine on which he was serving was attacked and sunk in the Atlantic. He survived, only to go on to a much more bizarre fate. The story is reprinted here from Martial Justice, The Last Mass Execution in the United States.

The city of Chemnitz is in the hill country of East Germany, not far from Dresden and less than 30 miles from the Czechoslovakian border. After World War II, its name was changed to Karl-Marx-Stadt, but it remains an odd mixture of picturesque old castles and bustling modern industry, with a population of more than 250,000. In the days before the war, Chemnitz was a good place to live; jobs were relatively plentiful, and the standard of living was more than adequate. It was in this atmosphere that Werner Drechsler grew up, a good-looking little boy with a long, rectangular face whose most salient feature was a large pair of soft, almost sad, blue eyes. He lived in a modest but pleasant home at Number 1 Sebastian Bach Strasse and could walk to the nearby public school, which he first started attending in the autumn of 1928.

In school, he was a better-than-average student, a likable boy with a quick smile and a somewhat devilish disposition. He stayed in the public school system for ten years, graduating in 1937, after experiencing the radical changes that were brought about in his training as Hitler began to intrude in the education of German youth. In effect, his early interest in history and the arts changed to interest in the more practical subjects of an industrial state. In the public school, he had picked up a smattering of both French and English—more French than English—and probably would not have been diverted into a technical school if the times had been different. But Germany was mobilizing, and the emphasis was strictly on the useful and critical trades, so Werner Drechsler went to trade school to become a mechanic. He attended the school for one year, and then in the summer of 1938, as a 16-year-old boy, began his apprenticeship. He worked for about 2½ years in Chemnitz before joining the navy in 1941.

Drechsler volunteered for U-boat service and was sent to Kiel for advanced submarine training. His first assignment was to the crew of the U-118, which, even though it was a U-boat, was not a fighting sub but rather a sub supply boat and minelayer, sometimes referred to as a "milch cow." The U-118 was still under construction when Drechsler arrived at Kiel. It was a large boat, 1,600 tons, assigned to join the 12th Flotilla, which was headquartered at the German naval base in Bordeaux, France. Drechsler became intimately acquainted with the boat while it was undergoing its last stages of construction and he was moving through the final days of his training. He was present at the dock as the last touch was added before launching— the painting of the boat's emblem on the conning tower: the coat of arms of the city of Bad Gastein, Austria. And on December 8, 1941, the day after Pearl Harbor and three days before the United States officially declared war on Germany, the U-118 was commissioned.

The U-118 had been placed under the command of Korvettenkapitän Werner Czygan, who was relatively old at 38 for a U-boat command. Although this was Czygan's first U-boat command, he was truly an old salt who had seen quite a bit of the German navy from many different bridges, including the old battleship *Schleswig-Holstein*. Czygan was from the North Sea port city of Wilhelmshafen, but because of the heavy bombings of that city, he had moved his wife and daughter the length of the country to the mountain resort town of Berchtesgaden on the Austrian border. He was a strict commander, but his men were very fond of him, probably because he made it exceptionally clear at the outset that their welfare was his prime concern. Werner Drechsler especially liked Czygan and had nothing but good things to say about him. The one officer Drechsler did not like, and in this opinion he was in tune with most of the other crew members, was Kapitänleutnant Felix Müller, the boat's first engineering officer. Drechsler came to refer to him disdainfully as "Felix the Strong" because of his harsh, bullying tactics.

Czygan took the U-118 out of Kiel for its U-boat acceptance commission trial runs between December 10 and 20 and then granted the crew leave for the Christmas holidays. Werner Drechsler went home to Chemnitz, enthusiastic and proud of his assignment; he was 19, and this was to be the last Christmas he would spend with his family before going to war. Drechsler reported back to Kiel shortly after New Year's Day, and the U-118 finally put out to sea on January 6 [1942]. The boat traveled on the surface eastward, heading for Danzig, Poland; and it was a treacherous and tricky cruise through the bitter cold and rapidly forming ice in the Baltic Sea. Czygan, however, brought the U-118 safely into the Gulf of Danzig the next day and tied up next to a German cruiser, on which Drechsler and the other members of the crew were berthed in roomy and relative comfort. Diving trials were held the fol-

lowing day, but the ice had gotten so thick that the U-118 had to be led back to port by an icebreaker. After docking his ship, Czygan knew that [he and his crew] would not be going anywhere in the near future, at least until the ice began to break up.

Drechsler lived aboard the cruiser for the next 2½ months but worked and trained daily on the U-118. Life was pleasant, food was good, and the war was a long way away. But finally on March 29, the U-118 slowly steered a course out of the harbor behind an icebreaker and made its way to the Hela Peninsula. For most of the next two months, the U-118 stayed in the Baltic Sea, conducting various tactical exercises and drills. One of the exercises Werner Drechsler was most excited about was the test firing of the torpedoes. Even though it was not a fighting U-boat as such, the U-118 carried a load of torpedoes and would be constantly on the alert to use them if the opportunity ever presented itself, and among Drechsler's duties was that of a torpedo man.

Eventually, the U-118 sailed out of the Baltic Sea, following the now well-worn submarine lane up through the Kattegat, down to the North Sea, and out into the North Atlantic. The first two war cruises of the U-118 were principally to supply other submarines operating in the mid-Atlantic. During the cruises, Drechsler worked hard and maintained a good rapport with the rest of the crew. He held up his end of the work and was accepted even by the more experienced U-boatmen as a good submariner.

One member of the crew, Herman

Polowzyk, was from occupied Poland. He had, surprisingly, been drafted into the U-boat service, a fact that was later interpreted by the U. S. naval intelligence authorities as a strong indication that Admiral Karl Doenitz was having difficulty in finding volunteers for his elite but now highly hazardous underwater service. Because Polowzyk was not a German, he was not fully accepted into the innermost confidences and camaraderie of the crew. Not that he was isolated; that just could not be on a submarine, where each man was important as an individual for his own duties, and all the men were forced together into an uncommonly close environment. But Polowzyk was ignored as much as possible, and he was indeed aware that his crew mates looked on him as a Pole, not a German [and therefore an interloper of sorts].

Two men on the submarine, however, went out of their way to be friendly with Polowzyk. One was Korvettenkapitän Czygan, who on occasion would personally invite the young seaman to his quarters for a game of chess—an effort to keep Polowzyk's morale up and to make him feel that he was accepted as part of the crew and probably as an example to the other men of the boat. The other person to befriend Polowzyk, even though it was in a somewhat guarded way, was Werner Drechsler, perhaps because Drechsler did not share the Third Reich's racial and nationalistic attitudes and hence did not feel any strong alienation from people other than those born and raised in Germany. In another way, Drechsler felt sorry for Polowzyk, whose vanquished country was now in ruins and who had made the large decision to allow himself to be conscripted into the navy of the conqueror. But whatever the extent of Drechsler's reasons, they were, at least at that time, appreciated by Herman Polowzyk.

[On December 7, 1942,] at the end of the second war cruise of the U-118, Werner Drechsler had his first terrifyingly close encounter with death. The last U-boat had been supplied, and Czygan was preparing to take his submarine back to port. He took the boat under, but as [the U-118 was] submerging, [it] began to tilt, stern first, and descend, almost sliding, backward, deeper and deeper. The consistently increasing angle of inclination reached a full 55 degrees. Czygan ordered the entire crew to move to the bow of the boat in a desperate attempt to alter the angle of descent, but by this time the angle was too steep for any of the men to move forward. Everything that was not battened down came crashing to the floor and then clattered toward the boat's stern. Drechsler and Polowzyk, who were in the stern section, looked at each other in horror. The depth gauge registered [623 feet]. For a chilling moment, every man on the submarine, with the possible exception of Czygan, thought that there was no way that they could be saved and that any moment the pressure would crush their boat like a paper cup, and they would be spilled out to a watery grave.

The engineering officer, Felix Müller, "Felix the Strong," gave way to panic, and screamed wildly at Czygan, "What shall I do?"

"Blow the tanks!" Czygan screamed back at him.

Müller momentarily regained some of his composure and managed to blow the tanks but in his frenetic state neglected to close one of the diving tanks at the bow of the boat. Czygan again shouted at the engineering officer, who reacted automatically and was able to rectify his almost fatal mistake. The submarine then began to surge rapidly upward at the same steep angle that it had been descending. When it broke the surface, its bow leaped right out of the water and then slapped down violently on the water's surface. Drechsler's eyes were laden with fright, and there was an awkward silence for a few seconds before he and the rest of the shaken crew realized that they were now safe. They found the cause of their near-fatal accident. During their last supply transfer, one of the negative buoyancy tank valves had become clogged with debris that prevented it from being closed while they were submerging. It was quickly remedied, and the U-118 was safely back on its way to port.

On the following day, December 8, 1942, the crew held a dual celebration. It was the first anniversary of the ship's commissioning, and [the men] had all survived the previous day's dilemma. Czygan ordered a special meal to be served, replete with beer to drink and cake for dessert. Drechsler even proposed a toast at his table; he was very happy to be alive and on his way back to safer waters.

Their destination was Lorient, France, an Atlantic coastal town where German subs put in for repairs. When they arrived, however, they found that the concrete shelters built to protect U-boats while they were docked were not large enough for the U-118. Czygan was forced to tie up next to them [which left his U-boat vulnerable to an air attack]. The U-118 stayed there for three weeks until the routine overhaul was completed, and Czygan's constant apprehensiveness about the nakedness of his boat was finally relieved.

The U-118 embarked on its third war cruise on January 26 [1943], leaving Lorient for the dangerous waters [of the Strait of Gibraltar]. As soon as [the boat was] under way, Czygan informed the crew that they would be traveling submerged most of the time and that their mission was to be the very dangerous one of laying mines in the strait itself. On February 5, Czygan brought the U-118 to rest on the bottom of the sea between Casablanca and Tangier to wait for weather suitable for the intricate job of minelaying in obviously hostile waters. The boat remained submerged for two days, and [the men's] mild excitement about their mission began to give way to a distinct fear for their lives. Drechsler was already having deeply disturbing thoughts, not only about his decision to volunteer for the U-boat service but also about the war in general and Hitler in particular. He did not, however, let his feelings be known to his fellow crew members. In any case, as they began their mission, Drechsler and the rest of the crew were too busy to think about anything other than successfully carrying it out. Eventually, their mission accomplished, the crew and the U-118 returned to port.

The fourth and final war cruise of the U-118 was also a minelaying mission—this time in the vicinity of the Azores. Part of the morning of June 12 [1943], a beautifully clear day with the sun bright in the sky and angled off the sub's bow, Werner Drechsler was on deck with several other crew members, sunbathing. Shortly before noon, they went below for lunch, leaving on deck the four men on bridge watch. No more than two minutes after Drechsler had closed the conning tower hatch, however, one of the bridge watch suddenly screamed, "Planes, planes," and sounded the alarm.

Seemingly from out of the core of the sun, two [U.S.] airplanes were streaking directly for them. The four men ran to the U-boat's gun, but the planes' machine guns were already zeroed in and strafing the deck. Three of the men fell seriously wounded as Czygan threw open the hatch and rushed on deck. The planes were already circling for another attack. He immediately gave the order to submerge and held the hatch open as the one uninjured man on deck, Werner Reinl, dragged the other three men to relative if only temporary safety. Reinl pushed the last man into the submarine and then jumped in himself, closing the hatch

only seconds before the water rushed over the diving U-boat. Below, it was absolute chaos.

When the boat had reached a depth of about [115 feet], the first depth charges hit and exploded near the stern. The damage was considerable, and the submarine began to angle downward, stern first. More depth charges hit, and the U-boat's motors went dead, the electrical steering failed, and the hydroplanes and rudder were wrenched loose. Czygan gave the order to surface and fight it out with the planes. But as [the men] flung open the hatch and started for the guns, they were astounded to see not two but nine planes circling overhead. The planes dove to the attack, and the gunnery submariners never made it to the guns; they were cut down in their tracks by machine-gun fire. Others tried to reach the guns but with no better luck. Czygan was on deck and wounded, blood streaming from a vicious gash in his leg. Werner Drechsler was still below, but then one of the motors suddenly exploded and burst into flames. Drechsler watched helplessly and in horror as the young seaman tending it turned into a screaming sheet of flame and crumpled to the floor. And then Drechsler clambered out onto the deck.

A depth charge exploded just forward of the conning tower, and the submarine began to break in two. A fragment from the explosion tore into the side of Drechsler's neck; at almost the same moment, a bullet ripped into his right knee. He collapsed on the deck. Czygan gave the order to abandon ship, and Drechsler half-dragged himself and half-crawled to the edge and plunged into the water. He was able to swim with difficulty and did not look back at the sinking submarine. If he had, he would have seen his captain, Werner Czygan, kneeling on the forward deck, covered now with blood from several wounds, as the boat went under in a dazzling fountain of spray and debris.

Drechsler managed to stay afloat and watched in fear as one of the attacking planes swooped down at the men struggling in the water, but instead of opening fire, it dropped a life raft and then streaked off into the sky. Two of the survivors helped Drechsler into the raft, and then he helped pull in two other seamen, who were also seriously wounded, one of whom was obviously dying. About an hour later, the survivors were picked up by the destroyer U.S.S. *Osmond Ingram*. Of the 58 men [who] had been aboard the U-118, only 17 were alive when the *Ingram* arrived on the scene, and the most seriously wounded sailor died shortly after being lifted onto the destroyer.

Werner Drechsler was taken directly to the ship's sick bay. His right knee was operated on at sea by the ship's doctor, and he remained in bed for most of the eight-day voyage to Norfolk, Virginia. The day of [the ship's] arrival in the United States, he rejoined the other prisoners, but he could walk only with great difficulty and a good amount of pain. At Norfolk, he was helped off the ship by his friend from Poland, Herman Polowzyk, and led to a waiting ambulance. Drechsler and the other wounded prisoner were taken to the naval base hospital; the other 14 prisoners were shipped directly to Fort Meade, Maryland, for interrogation. It was the last time Werner Drechsler would see his crew mates until he finally caught up with them nine months later. Drechsler was hospitalized for the next nine days, and so it was not until June 30 that he was finally transferred to Fort Meade and the interrogation center. When he arrived there, the other survivors of his crew had already gone on to other POW camps.

Werner Drechsler remained at Fort Meade for almost nine months, during which time he helped U.S. Navy officers when they interrogated German U-boatmen who had been taken prisoner. When the officers felt that he was of no further use, Drechsler was turned over to the U.S. Army to be placed in another prisoner of war camp. On June 12, 1944, Drechsler was sent to the camp at Papago Park, Arizona, mainly housing U-boat prisoners of war. During his six hours there, a kangaroo court was held by the other Germans in the compound and Drechsler was found guilty of betraying Germany, beaten, and then hung in one of the shower rooms. Seven German prisoners of war were eventually accused of murdering Drechsler. They were tried by the U.S. court martial, sentenced to death, and then hung at Fort Leavenworth, Kansas, on August 25, 1945. It was the largest single execution for a crime in the history of the United States.

On Guadalcanal with Carlson's Raiders

In 1942, Major Evans F. Carlson received permission to form a new unit, in the Second Raider Battalion, in the U.S. Marine Corps. Carlson's Raiders, as it was to become known, would prove to be one of the most successful and famous commando-type outfits of World War II.

Its members, all seasoned Marines, were carefully selected, highly trained, and rigidly disciplined for the tremendous rigors of jungle warfare and behind-the-lines combat. They were trained in Hawaii for the most perilous raids in the Pacific theater of operations—in-and-out surprise assaults on Japanese-held strongholds as well as extended behind-the-lines operations in such notorious battles as Guadalcanal and Bougainville.

One of the 900 men who served with Carlson's Raiders was Corporal Arthur D. Gardner. In November 1942, he participated in an incredible month-long foray with the Raiders behind Japanese lines on the island of Guadalcanal. During the operations, the Raiders moved over 150 miles, raiding the Japanese on a daily basis. When it was finally over, Carlson's Raiders had killed more than 700 of the enemy and lost only 17 of their own. Corporal Gardner kept a brief diary of one of the most amazing exploits in U.S. Marine legend. The portions reproduced here first appeared in Soldier of Fortune magazine.

Nov. 8—Arrived at Guadalcanal about daybreak and were unloaded before noon. Some of us are on outposts along the river. There are crocodiles in this river.

Nov. 9—Loaded us in tank lighters and moved several miles up the coast. Set up a command-post bivouac. We have about 50 native guides with us to carry supplies and extra ammunition.

Nov. 10—Started out about 0700 and advanced about ten miles. Rugged going. We had to ford three rivers: the Bevande, Tine, and Balesuma. Set up a new bivouac here. We now have about 200 natives with us.

Nov. 12—Moved forward at daylight. The Japs had moved out during the night. We lost five men yesterday and buried them where they fell.

Nov. 13—We followed the Japs to the next river, the Asa Mona, and attacked them on both flanks. They are dug in, so we dropped back and called for 7th Marines' artillery to soften them up.

Nov. 14—Lost five more men yesterday. We escorted about 100 natives to the beach for more needed supplies—especially ammunition.

Nov. 15—Rested all day. Dug wild potatoes, gathered red peppers, killed two tree lizards, and made a stew. The lizards are green, about a foot long, and the meat is something like white meat from chicken—if you have a good imagination. Had a "gung-ho" meeting. We are going into the interior to harass the Japanese in every way we can. We will take no prisoners under any circumstances. Any Raider caught stealing from another Raider will be executed without exception.

Nov. 16—Moved our base about three miles. Ran into occasional scattered Japs separated from their companies. Killed several of them. Lots of dead Japs lying around. We are bivouacked in a native village.

Nov. 17—On combat patrol. Lots of dead Japs; some knocked out by artillery. I found one alive but wounded, and I shot him. He watched me with his eyes all the while. We ran into a bunch of cattle and shot eight of them. We had to send a runner back to the command post for natives to pack it [the meat] in.

Nov. 18—We escorted a group of natives to the beach, where the 7th Marines are based and brought back rice, tea, hardtack, and ammunition.

Nov. 19—Carlson told our doctors to survey everyone not in A-1 condition. About 70 weeded out today.

Nov. 20—Guarding the supplies here now. We have outposts in trees all day and listening posts all night. Mosquitoes are terrible here. Impossible to sleep.

Nov. 21—Company headquarters joined us and set up their TBX, so now we have communication. They sent about 50 natives to pack supplies so we can move out, but that isn't enough for what we have to pack. So we are waiting for further word.

Nov. 22—More natives showed up, and we moved about four miles to the next river, the Toni. Set up bivouac.

Nov. 23—Moved about nine miles and made a new bivouac. Very rugged here with thick brush, vines, thorn stringers that we call "wait-a-minute vines," and a thick overhead that prevents the sun from ever getting to the floor. There is a small creek nearby.

Nov. 24—Had a combat patrol about six miles up the river. We were on the alert for Japs but didn't contact any. However, found lots of fresh sign[s] and also one well-used trail that they have been using.

Nov. 25—On alert but rested some. About 40 men surveyed out and sent back to the beach.

Nov. 26—The doctors spend all day examining Marines to determine how good a shape they are in. Only the best can stay. Fifty or 60 were sent back today. One of our jobs in the interior will be to locate a 75 mm gun the Japs have there and put it out of action. They have been shelling Henderson Field with it.

Nov. 27—Moved up the river straight inland for about nine miles. Sent out native scouts, and there are several thousand Japanese close by. Can't build fires, so we don't eat tonight.

Nov. 28—Went on combat patrol up an ungodly steep hill and located the East-West Trail on top of the ridge. Found where they had the 75 mm set up, but they have moved it.

Ran into several Japs who were startled to see us. I killed two and believe we killed about a dozen altogether.

Nov. 29—We are down to about 136 men and honed to what you might call a razor's edge. We moved about two miles [farther] upstream. We have Japs on all sides of us now and are moving with utmost caution.

Nov. 30—We crossed a ridge so steep we used ropes to get over the top. Found the 75 mm we have been looking for and also two 37 mm guns and destroyed all three. We crossed the East-West Trail, dropped into the upper Lunga River, and ran into several hundred Japs. It started to rain and came down in bucketfuls. We killed 40 or 50 Japs, and the rest escaped across the river. Finally quit raining about dark, and we are bivouacked on a small stream. We decided to build fires and take our chances.

Dec. 1—Discovered this morning that we camped about 70 yards from a battalion of Japs all night. We surprised them at daylight and completely disorganized them. We killed at least 200, and the rest escaped across the river and into the jungle. Blackie was killed by a Jap sniper. We buried him here in this place. We make a cross for his head and covered it with tin from hardtack containers. Planes came over and dropped us bags of rice and some five-gallon tins of hardtack. They were so low the chutes didn't have time to open, and we were out on our hands and knees picking up rice a grain at a time. The hardtack was not much more than crumbs.

Dec. 2—We formed a guard unit and accompanied our doctors while they made an inspection of Japanese medicines and supplies. Jap bodies are stinking really bad now. We buried two that were close to our sleeping area. Rain came down like a waterfall all afternoon.

Dec. 3—We moved about two miles down the river and split into two groups. Some continued on down the Lunga River toward the beach, and the rest of us climbed a Japanese trail up a steep ridge. Near the top, we ran into two Jap machine-gun nests and a number of Jap snipers and riflemen. Took us 1½ hours to wipe them out. . . . Someone came around asking for water for the wounded, but no one has any.

Dec. 4—Camped last night without grub, fires, or water. Moved out this morning and over the first ridge contacted a large number of Japs dug in on a fringe of jungle overlooking a grassy plain. They surprised us when they first opened fire, but we deployed and outmaneuvered them and killed them all in about three hours. We lost three men last night and three more this morning, besides wounded. Lieutenant Miller died today.

Dec. 5—We marched 27 miles yesterday. We haven't eaten or had water for two days. We marched clear across Henderson Field. It is bigger than I had realized. Adams had a hand grenade in his back pocket, and the pin worked out, and it exploded you know where. He was hurt pretty bad. The natives built another stretcher and packed him along with our other wounded. Goodbye, Guadalcanal.

Above: Six of the crew of
Kon-Tiki (Thor Heyerdahl
third from left) at the start
of their epochal trans-
Pacific voyage in 1947.
Thor Heyerdahl **Left:** Thirty
years later, on the reed
boat *Tigris*, Heyerdahl
navigated more than 4,000
miles in the Persian Gulf
and Arabian Sea. *Carlo Mauri*

Left: Johann Ludwig Burckhardt, a young Swiss, disguised himself as an Arab in 1809 to try to gain entrance to the forbidden city of Timbuktu. *Library of Congress* **Below:** The death of Captain James Cook at the hands of Hawaiian natives is shown in a 1788 print. *Library of Congress*

Grainger delin et sculp.

The Death of Captain Cook by the Natives of Owhyhee.

Right: Jean François de la Pérouse sailed the length and breadth of the Pacific Ocean on expeditions for King Louis XVI of France and finally, like Captain Cook, ran afoul of hostile natives. *Library of Congress* **Below:** Another ill-fated explorer, Henry Hudson, in 1611 was set adrift by his mutinous crew on the bay that was to bear his name. *Library of Congress*

Above: Hugh Clapperton (left) of Scotland discovered Lake Chad in 1823 but died en route to Timbuktu. *Library of Congress* German scientist Ludwig Leichhardt (right) also met with misadventure, disappearing on an 1848 trek across Australia. *Library of Congress* **Below:** Salomon Andrée of Sweden and crew depart by balloon for the North Pole. *Library of Congress*

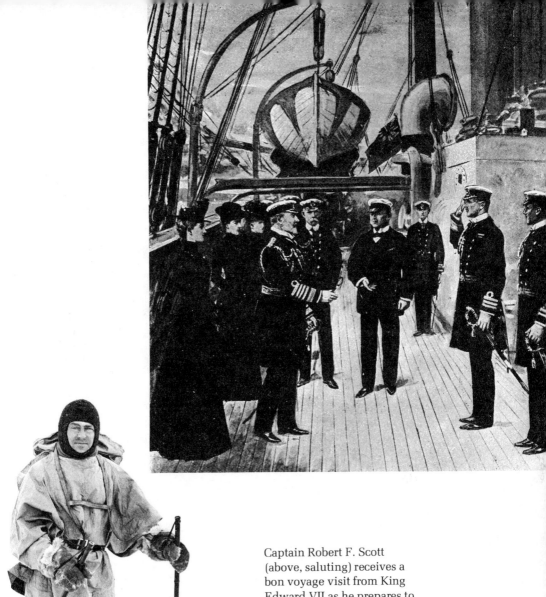

Captain Robert F. Scott
(above, saluting) receives a
bon voyage visit from King
Edward VII as he prepares to
embark on his first Antarctic
expedition (1901–1904).
Library of Congress Scott, shown
at left in Antarctica on his
second expedition, reached
the South Pole in January
1912 only to find that Roald
Amundsen of Norway had
beaten him there by a month.
Tragically, Scott and his
companions died on the
return trip. *Library of Congress*

Above: William H. Carney (left) was the first black to earn a Congressional Medal of Honor, in the Civil War. *Library of Congress* Colonel Edward Hatch (right) led a unit of Grierson's Raiders that destroyed a vital Rebel rail line. *Library of Congress* **Below:** In the Great Locomotive Chase, Confederate soldiers pursue the hijacked train. *The Story of American Heroism*

Grierson's Raiders, above, parade triumphantly through Baton Rouge in 1863. *Library of Congress* A Boer War correspondent in 1899, young Winston Churchill, at right, became famous as the result of his capture by the Boers and his subsequent escape. *Library of Congress*

An American crew (above) mans
the captured German submarine
U-505. *U.S. Navy* Captain Daniel
V. Gallery (left), who
masterminded the operation,
stands atop the conning tower of
the U-boat. *U.S. Navy*

Above: Captured U-118 sailor Werner Drechsler (left), later killed by
fellow German prisoners who believed he had informed on them. *U.S. Navy*
Below: The U-118 takes a depth charge as the crew begins to flee. *U.S. Navy*

Above: France, 1944—American troops enter battle-scarred Metz during the push in which "One-Man Army" Sergeant Andrew Miller captured scores of Germans, killed many, and gave his own life. *U.S. Army* **Below:** Vietnam, 1966—Guns at the ready, U.S. troops advance across a rice paddy. *U.S. Army*

Captain Lewis L. Millett, right, gained fame and a Medal of Honor by leading the last American bayonet charge, in February 1951, during the Korean War. *Stars and Stripes* Below, Kachin guerrilla fighters in Burma, led by OSS agent Vincent Curl, follow a jungle stream. *101 Association Archives*

Above: Rudolph Roessler (left, wearing hat) obtained information that helped the Russian Army turn the tide of World War II. *Wide World Photos* French-born English resident Violette Szabo (right) became a parachute commando to avenge her husband's death. *Photoworld* **Below:** Nazi war criminal Adolf Eichmann stands trial in Israel after his capture in Argentina. *Photoworld*

The Last Bayonet Charge

To those who knew him, Captain Lewis L. Millett was the best knife-fighter and the most deft bayonet-wielder in the U.S. Army. He brought his exceptional skills to the Korean conflict in the early 1950s. At a time when nuclear weapons were being stockpiled and the war was being fought with jet aircraft, rockets, missiles, fast-moving tanks, and a variety of sophisticated long-range and automatic weapons, the day of the bayonet seemed to be over. Yet there was one last, illustrious moment in the history of combat for this unique weapon.

It came about under the command of Captain Millett, on a cold hillside in South Korea in February 1951, earning for him the Congressional Medal of Honor. None other than S. L. A. Marshall, America's foremost military historian, personally wrote the following citation:

Captain Millett, Company E, distinguished himself by conspicuous gallantry and intrepidity above and beyond the call of duty in action. . . . Captain Millett ordered the Third Platoon forward, placed himself at the head of it, and with fixed bayonet, led the assault up the fire-swept hill. . . . Despite vicious opposing fire, the whirlwind hand-to-hand combat assault carried to the crest of the hill. His dauntless leadership and personal courage so inspired his men that they stormed into the hostile position and used their bayonets with such lethal effect

that the enemy fled in wild disorder. . . . The superb leadership, conspicuous courage, and consummate devotion to duty demonstrated by Captain Millett were directly responsible for the successful accomplishment of a hazardous mission and reflect the highest credit on himself and the heroic traditions of the military service.

Captain Millett was no newcomer to battle when he arrived in Korea in 1950. In World War II, he had fought as a private at the Kasserine Pass, where the U.S. armed forces first faced General Rommel's Afrika Korps. At one point during the battle, he took charge of a 50-caliber machine gun on the flatbed of a truck and shot down a German ME-109 fighter plane. Later, under a fusillade of small-arms fire and an artillery barrage, he rescued one army ammo truck and drove it to safety. Then he went back for another truck and repeated the feat. For these acts of heroism, he was awarded the Silver Star.

Lewis Millett moved right along with the advancing U.S. troops. In Italy, he was promoted to corporal at Salerno and to sergeant at Cassino. His battlefield commission followed shortly thereafter.

Near the end of the war, he received another major military honor, the Bronze Star. His platoon had been surrounded, and so he moved forward alone. Then he called in artillery fire on his own position and in the chaos guided his men to the safety of American lines.

It was a bitterly cold December day in 1950 when Captain Millett's jeep pulled into the Twenty-seventh Infantry's compound just north of Seoul. It was on a ridge overlooking the Imjin River. He had come to take command of Company E, or Easy Company, as it was called.

Captain Millett was a tall, rangy, steel-faced young man, sporting a reddish handlebar mustache in a time long before such things were popular and wearing a close-cropped crew cut under his fatigue cap. In basic fatigues, but with grenades hung from his shoulder straps, a sheathed bayonet hooked to his cartridge belt, with an M-1 in one hand and an army duffel bag in the other, he looked like a warrior.

Millett had taken commando training in England prior to World War II, and he prided himself in his proficiency in the deadly science of knife-fighting. It did not take Easy Company's men long to learn that he was indeed a hardened combat veteran. And Company E itself was no ordinary group of GIs, having received a Presidential Unit Citation for its heroic defense of a strategic hill early in 1950.

A journalist, Ed Hyde, later wrote about Easy Company and the man whom Captain Millett had to follow:

[Easy Company was] fighting a rear-guard action while the Eighth Army retreated before a massive Communist onslaught. . . . Captain Reginald B. Desiderio . . . raced Easy Company to the top of a strategic hill overlooking the Eighth Army escape route. The breathless GIs dug in just in time to repulse an attack by 5,000 screaming Chinese who stormed the heights. Easy Company's machine guns, grenades, rifle fire, and mortars mowed down the Reds by the hundreds as they charged again and again. . . .

Scrambling from foxhole to foxhole, Desiderio told his men to hang on. "Just until the first light, until dawn," he shouted. . . . From his experience in China in World War II, Desiderio knew that the Chinese Communist soldiers were great night fighters who usually shunned broad frontal daylight assaults.

An hour after midnight, a bullet punched into the CO's shoulder, slamming him to the ground. But he continued to make his rounds. Later, two more bullets spun him around, one in each thigh. He continued to crawl from position to position. Still later, a mortar burst kicked him in the back with two fragments. An hour before dawn, a bullet clipped his left knee. Spurning medical aid, the Easy Company CO kept crawling . . . still encouraging his men to hold out.

A final attack ended with the appearance of the first gray streak of dawn. Despite six wounds, Desiderio rallied the 120 survivors of what started out as a 220-man rifle company. Just then, a last mortar shell landed in the shell crater he used for a CP. Easy's exec officer, a young West Pointer, crawled over to the fatally wounded captain's limp figure. Easy Company's CO died in the arms of his exec. "Captain," the young lieutenant sobbed, "it's first light, and we're still holding on."

A very tough act to follow.

Millett knew that Easy Company's soldiers were good, proven fighters; he also knew they would have to remain that way if they were going to survive in the hell-hole of Korea. They would have to stay in top physical condition and would have to hone their fighting skills.

When Millett joined the company, only a few of the men had been issued bayonets. And none of them had given much thought to using them; they had in fact been given only a scant introduction to bayonet fighting in basic training, which was now far back in their battle-worn memories. Soon, however, the men were clipping the gleaming steel blades into their M-1s each day and training hour after hour in how to lethally wield them against an enemy. Captain Millett did not know whether his men would ever need to use a bayonet—certainly just about every other officer in the war had forgotten about bayonet attacks. But he wanted his men to be prepared if the time ever did come.

And it did.

The Twenty-seventh Infantry, including Easy Company, was moving in to liberate the Korean capital city of Seoul. It was February 1951, and the fighting was bitter all the way. It was hill after bloody hill—the story infantrymen would tell over and over in the years to come. Easy Company ended up pinned down near the foot of one of these hills, a steady, heavy barrage of fire coming from Communist positions above. The North Koreans were well entrenched in foxholes, with at least six machine guns and two artillery pieces to defend the hill.

Captain Millett called in an artillery barrage of his own and then moved his men under its cover to the foot of the hill. They were pinned down there with no place to go but up. Millett called for another artillery barrage and asked, in addition, for a raking of the enemy's battle lines with machine-gun fire. When the pyrotechnics began, he shouted to his men, "Fix bayonets." They all suddenly realized that it was not an obsolete weapon; they were in fact going into hand-to-hand combat with it.

Millett led the charge up the hill, and the enemy never even saw the Americans coming. They were preoccupied with the heavy fire, and when it stopped they were suddenly astounded to see American soldiers pouring into their foxholes, slashing and stabbing and rifle butting. The fighting was intense, and the Americans were vastly outnumbered, but their unorthodox battle tactic sent panic through the enemy. The North Koreans suddenly became disorganized—some fled, others just stared in disbelief, and some fought back. But it was soon over. The hill belonged to Easy Company, and when the casualties were counted, there were 57 enemy soldiers whose cause of death would be listed as the result of "bayonet wounds." No one knows how many other enemy soldiers had hobbled off nursing serious wounds.

It was only one step, one skirmish, in the Korean War for Captain Millett, but he received the Congressional Medal of Honor for the valor of his action there that winter day. He also received orders shortly afterward never to lead such an attack again. As far as the army was concerned, apparently, the last bayonet attack had been led.

Beyond the Call of Duty

The Congressional Medal of Honor, the highest military award for bravery that can be given to an individual in the U.S. armed forces, was established by a Joint Resolution of Congress on July 12, 1862.

The criteria for awarding the Congressional Medal of Honor are subjective, but basically they include conspicuous gallantry, the risk of life, intrepidity, self-sacrifice, and exceptional bravery far beyond the normal call of duty.

Since its inception, the medal had been awarded to many individuals in the army, the navy, the marines, and the air force. It has been awarded in the following wars, conflicts, and campaigns:

Civil War
Indian Campaigns
Korean Campaign (1871)
War with Spain (1898)
Philippine Insurrection
Boxer Rebellion
Philippine Conflict (1911)
Mexican (Vera Cruz) Campaign
Haitian Campaign (1915)

Dominican Campaign
World War I
Haitian Campaign (1919)
Nicaraguan Campaign (1928)
World War II
Korean War
Vietnam War

The brief stories here are a random sampling of the brave deeds that men in war achieved to be honored with the medal.

The Civil War

William H. Carney, a sergeant in the Union Army, had the unique distinction of being the first black to perform a heroic act for which the Congressional Medal of Honor was awarded. He is one of 20 blacks who received the award for meritorious deeds performed during the Civil War (16 from the Army and four from the Navy).

Sergeant Carney earned his medal July 18, 1863, at the battle for Fort Wagner in South Carolina. The Confederate fort, which protected the harbor of Charleston, was under attack by Union forces and, as the Medal of Honor citation states: "When the color sergeant was shot down, this soldier [Carney] grasped the flag, led the way to the parapet, and planted the colors thereon. When the troops fell back he brought off the flag, under a fierce fire in which he was twice severely wounded." Although the Union Army was unsuccessful that day at Fort Wagner, Sergeant Carney's actions were noted and a report of them was forwarded to the Department of the Army in Washington, D.C., for special commendation.

Sergeant Carney, who had been born in Norfolk, Virginia, but joined the Union Army at New Bedford, Massachusetts, was a member of Company C, Fifty-fourth Massachusetts Colored Infantry, when he performed his brave act. The medal, however, was not formally bestowed on him until 37 years later, on May 23, 1900. As a result, he was not the first black to receive the Congressional Medal of Honor. That distinction goes to Union sailor Robert Blake, a former slave, who received the medal for "outstanding gallantry" when his ship, the U.S.S. *Marblehead*, a steam gunboat, was attacked in the Stono River about nine miles south of Charleston, South Carolina. He received his Congressional Medal of Honor on April 16, 1864.

The Philippine Insurrection

Near the confluence of the Cadacan and Sohoton rivers in the Philippines, the enemy was deployed along the top of a row of cliffs made of soft volcanic rock, like pumice, in a defensive line that was considered impregnable. Footing was treacherous, and the task of scaling the sheer walls, honeycombed with caves, was considered practically impossible. Worse, atop the cliffs were platforms loaded with tons of boulders held by cables made of vines, ready to be dropped at a moment's notice on an enemy that might appear below.

The fortifications had taken three years to construct and were fully manned on November 17, 1901, when U.S. Marine Colonel Hiram I. Bearss led his troops up the Sohoton River for a sneak attack. The Marines first laid down a heavy blanket of rifle and small-artillery fire, and then Colonel Bearss led his unit to the side of the cliffs. There, with the aid of bamboo ladders, his unit managed to climb to the top of the cliffs, destroy the fortifications there, and capture or drive off the remaining insurgents. He was rewarded by Congress for his "courage, intelligence, discrimination and zeal" in leading the operation.

World War I

On September 28, 1918, at St. Hubert's Pavilion, in Boureuilles, France, First Lieutenant Dwite H. Schaffner and his men were pinned down by heavy fire at both flanks, especially from a machine gun on one of them. Lieutenant Schaffner made three reconnaissance missions alone to get within hand grenade range of the machine gun. On his third trek, he did come within throwing range and with two grenades destroyed the

The Highest Awards for Military Valor

Belgium
Decoration Militaire and *Croix de Guerre*—The *Decoration Militaire* (awarded since 1902) and the *Croix de Guerre* (awarded since 1915) are both of the highest order. They are awarded for "acts of courage and distinguished service."

Canada
Canada Medal—Established in 1943, the *Canada Medal* is given for "meritorious service above and beyond the faithful performance of duties."

France
Médaille Militaire—Instituted in 1852, the *Médaille Militaire* is awarded only for the most "distinguished conduct in action." (The *Legion of Honor*, founded by Napoleon Bonaparte in 1802, is principally an order, not a medal or decoration, although it is accompanied by an official ribbon.)

Germany
Iron Cross—Instituted in Prussia in 1813, the *Iron Cross* has been the supreme award for military valor from the War of Liberation of that year through World War II.

Great Britain
Victoria Cross—Created in 1856 at the request of Queen Victoria, the *Victoria Cross* is awarded for "some signal act of valor." The "signal act" must be of the highest order of bravery.

gun and its crew. He then returned safely to his men.

Another enemy detachment moved up, however, and counterattacked, surrounding the lieutenant's unit. In fierce trench fighting, Lieutenant Schaffner managed to break through the enemy's lines and shot a German captain with his pistol. Then he dragged the wounded officer back to his own company's trench, where he was able to elicit valuable information about the attacking force from the man. Lieutenant Schaffner then held his position for five hours, even though he was surrounded on three sides, until reinforcements arrived. He was cited for his "bravery, contempt of danger ... gallant soldierly conduct, and leadership."

World War II
First Lieutenant Edward S. Michael was at the controls of his B-17 bomber over Germany on April 11, 1944, when a swarm of Luftwaffe fighter

India

Param Vir Chakra—Established shortly after India gained independence in 1947, the *Param Vir Chakra* is awarded for "outstanding bravery in the face of the enemy."

Italy

Medal for Military Valor—Initiated in 1833, the *Medal for Military Valor* is awarded for "high acts of bravery and sacrifice in the line of military duty."

Japan

Kinshi Kunsho—Instituted in 1891, the *Kinshi Kunsho* was a symbol of the highest echelon of valor and gallantry in battle. It was abolished after World War II, in 1945.

Poland

Order Virtuti Militari—First awarded in the late 1700s, the *Order Virtuti Militari* is given for the "most meritorious acts in the field of battle."

Soviet Union

The Order of Glory—This order is awarded for valor in battle to members of all branches of the military. (The *Order of Victory*, however, is the highest award for senior officers.)

United States

Congressional Medal of Honor—Established in 1861 for the U.S. Navy and in 1862 for the U.S. Army, the *Congressional Medal of Honor* is awarded for "conspicuous gallantry and intrepidity at the risk of life above and beyond the call of duty."

---

planes appeared from out of nowhere. They broke through the Allied fighter escort and swooped to attack Lieutenant Michael's plane. Their machine guns and cannons ablaze, they swiftly riddled the U.S. bomber. One cannon shell exploded in the cockpit, wounding the copilot and Lieutenant Michael and destroying most of the instruments and controls of the airplane. The bomb bay was in flames from another direct hit, and smoke was now billowing through the aircraft. The B-17, reeling from the attack and now descending uncontrollably, was forced out of formation. Lieutenant Michael, however, was able to level it off. The fire in the bomb bay, he learned, was nearing some incendiary bombs, and when the emergency lever to release them failed, he gave the order to bail out.

Seven crewmen leaped from the plane and floated to the earth under their parachutes. Only Lieutenant

Michael, the bombardier, and the co-pilot remained on board, the bombardier manning the navigator's machine gun and shooting at the attacking German fighter planes. Lieutenant Michael ordered the bombardier to bail out, but the bombardier found that his parachute had been torn apart by cannon fragments during the attack. Lieutenant Michael then realized he could not abandon the airplane without abandoning the bombardier and the wounded co-pilot. So he turned the plane toward France, trying to make it back to friendlier territory. The attack, which continued for a total of 45 minutes, was relentless, but he managed to keep the crippled bomber in the air and finally flew into a cloud bank, eluding their pursuers.

Lieutenant Michael passed out from loss of blood shortly afterward, and the copilot took over. But as they passed across the English Channel, the lieutenant regained consciousness and took over the controls. And despite the fact that the plane's undercarriage was totally useless, the bomb-bay doors were jammed open, the incendiary bombs were still precariously housed there, most of the instruments were inoperable, and the plane's flaps would not work, Lieutenant Michael managed to land the plane without further injury to the three men aboard it.

Korean War

Frank N. Mitchell was a first lieutenant in the U.S. Marines in November 1950, the commander of a rifle platoon in Company A, First Battalion, Seventh Marines, First Marine Division, operating near Hansan-ni, Korea.

On a routine patrol through a thickly wooded, snow-covered area, his platoon was suddenly attacked by a much larger enemy force. A blistering rain of fire from enemy rifles and automatic weapons was unleashed on them, and Lieutenant Mitchell dashed to the front of his platoon. He grabbed an automatic rifle from one of his wounded men, and at almost point-blank range, he fired into the enemy positions until he was out of ammunition. Then he dropped to the ground and began lobbing hand grenades until he ran out of them. His actions not only destroyed or wounded many of the attacking force but also enabled his own men to regroup and set up an effective defense.

Lieutenant Mitchell, wounded now from enemy gunfire, rejoined his men and then led an assault on the enemy position. After frantic hand-to-hand combat, the enemy withdrew, and Mitchell then led a search party to locate and evacuate his own wounded. The enemy soon returned in force and encircled Mitchell's platoon. With those who could not walk being toted on litters, he guided his men back through enemy lines. Just before they reached the safety of their own lines, however, Lieutenant Mitchell fell in a spray of rifle fire as he stood alone covering his men's withdrawal.

Vietnam War

Lewis Albanese was born in Venice, Italy, in 1946, but 20 years later, he was a U.S. citizen and a private (first class) in Company B, Fifth Battalion (Airmobile), Seventh Cavalry, First Cavalry Division, deployed in Vietnam. In December 1966, his platoon was moving cautiously through dense jungle terrain when suddenly sniper fire, seemingly coming from everywhere, pinned the men down. Then automatic weapons opened up, and the sniper ambush suddenly became a full-scale attack. Private Albanese was ordered to guard the platoon's left flank. As he gazed out at the jungle, he saw the flash of an enemy gun, keyed in on it, and crawled toward it. There he found a well-concealed ditch and leaped into it to surprise the sniper, whom he then bayoneted to death.

He could now hear rifle fire and the booming reports of automatic weapons down a line from the ditch, stretching along his platoon's left flank. He realized that it was not just an ordinary ditch but a carefully camouflaged series of trenches and tunnels. Albanese quickly moved down the complex of passageways, encountering enemy soldiers along the way. He managed to kill six of them before running out of ammunition. Then he dispatched two more in hand-to-hand combat before he himself was killed. His courageous, unsolicited action enabled his platoon to move forward and to counterattack and destroy the tunnel complex of the enemy.

Spies and Other Secret Warriors

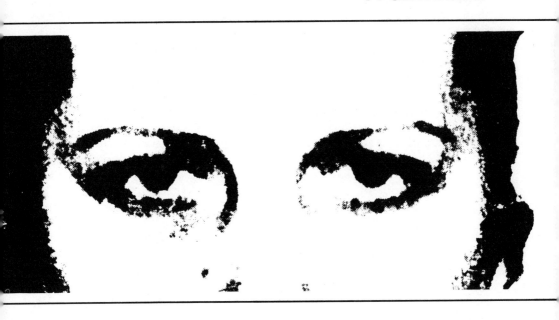

Capturing Adolf Eichmann

In the dusky twilight of March 21, 1960, Ricardo Klement stepped from a bus in a sparsely populated residential area on the outskirts of Buenos Aires. A slight, balding, middle-aged man, wearing heavy-rimmed glasses, he walked briskly, a small bouquet of flowers clutched in his right hand. At Garibaldi Street—a desolate street with only a single run-down house and a smaller cottage next to it—he turned the corner, and when he started up the walk to the house, the door opened and a stout woman stepped onto the porch to greet him. Smiling, she took the flowers. They embraced warmly but then were interrupted by a boy about five or six years old, apparently dressed up for some kind of celebration, who came running through the doorway, jumping with excitement at the sight of the man and the woman together. Klement reached over and patted him pleasantly on the shoulder, and then all three went inside the house.

The agent on surveillance detail noted it all from his well-hidden post.

Later that evening, in another part of the city, Yosef Kenet, senior investigator in the Israeli Secret Services, said to several people seated around a table, "*He* is back. And *he* is back to celebrate *his* twenty-fifth anniversary." Kenet pulled from a large dossier a single sheet of paper. "They were married March twenty-first, nineteen thirty-five—Adolf and Vera Eichmann."

The house on Garibaldi Street had been carefully watched for several weeks. The man who was now inside it had returned home the day before from a temporary job in the town of Tucumán, about 1,000 miles from Buenos Aires. Kenet had said earlier that if he was the man Kenet believed him to be, he surely would return home for his silver wedding anniversary. And he had—he even brought flowers for the occasion.

"The description fits him perfectly," Kenet said. "Everything points to the fact. I am certain now *he* is Adolf Eichmann."

"But the others in Tel Aviv want a photograph of him," one of the young men at the table said. "To be absolutely sure."

"We will get one."

•   •   •

The dossier that Kenet carried with him almost constantly now had been started shortly after World War II and had grown considerably since 1957, the year that the Israeli Secret Services had received a highly reliable tip that Adolf Eichmann—the key administrator of the Nazi program to exterminate the Jewish people, the man who oversaw the execution of millions of Jews—was living and apparently working in Buenos Aires.

Isser Harel, the chief of the Israeli Secret Services, took the matter all the way to Prime Minister David Ben-Gurion, who agreed that an investigation would be a top priority item. If Eichmann were really there, the Israeli leader went on to say, undercover agents would be instructed to apprehend him and bring him back to Israel to stand trial for his crimes.

Soon, agents began to travel in and out of Argentina, following leads and making contacts until finally the case began to take shape. It was first learned that the Eichmann family was indeed living somewhere in Argentina under the name of Klement. Then two of Eichmann's older sons were located, both found to be living away from the family and holding jobs in Buenos Aires. The youngest boy, only six years old, they heard, was living with his mother and father. Finally, the residence of Ricardo Klement was traced to a house on Chacabuco Street, in Olivos, a suburb of Buenos Aires. By the time the agents were able to pinpoint the house, however, the Klements had moved away, predictably leaving no forwarding address. It was not until December 1959, through surveillance of the older sons, that the agents were able to track down the new Eichmann residence on Garibaldi Street. But he was not there, they learned; he was on a temporary assignment out of town.

As Yosef Kenet had predicted, however, Ricardo Klement would return home to celebrate the wedding anniversary of Vera and Adolf Eichmann.

. . .

The camera was housed inside a briefcase, specially designed so that the telephoto lens would not be seen by the person being photographed, nor would the small shutter button under the photographer's finger on top of the briefcase be visible. It would require just a slight pressure from the finger, and silently the camera would snap the picture.

On Saturday, April 2, two weeks after his return to Buenos Aires, Klement was still at the house on Garibaldi Street. He had been kept under constant surveillance, and the Israelis now presumed his temporary, out-of-town assignment was over.

The next afternoon, a young man loitered at the bus stop near Garibaldi Street until he saw Klement emerge from the house and step into the garden. Then the young man, briefcase in hand, walked up the street. When he reached the house, Klement was talking with one of his older sons, who had come out after him. They both turned to look at the young man approaching them. He was swarthy, appeared very South American, and asked in fluent Spanish if they knew if any of the houses in the area were for sale. Klement said no, but his son said he had heard that the cottage next door might be. The young man nodded, thanked them, cut across Klement's yard, and then knocked at the cottage door. Klement and his son stared after him for a moment but then went back to their conversation. The young man spoke to the woman who had answered the door and then left and walked back up the street to the bus stop.

Two days later, Yosef Kenet picked up the processed film at a photo shop in downtown Buenos

Aires, looked at the results, and almost shouted with joy at the clear, sharp images of the face of Ricardo Klement. Before the week was over Kenet was aboard a jet on his way back to Tel Aviv.

In Israel, he went directly to Isser Harel, who, after seeing the evidence, had pulled from the Israeli Secret Services' file a small portfolio of pictures taken of Adolf Eichmann two decades earlier. He then ordered extensive lab tests to be taken, so that both of them could be certain, or at least as certain as they could be, that the man in the photographs brought back by Kenet was the same SS lieutenant colonel for whom they had been searching for so long. After every fragment of information regarding the identification was studied in detail, Isser Harel and Kenet stared at each other and then nodded in agreement—Ricardo Klement *was* Adolf Eichmann.

The Israelis were left with two choices. First, the legal route—they could work through the Argentine government and request the extradition of Eichmann to Israel to be tried for crimes against the Jewish people. But experience reminded them that this method would probably have an effect directly counter to their purpose. Someone would tip off Eichmann, and he would once again disappear into the friendly darkness of South America. The alternative was illegal—simply kidnap him and spirit him out of Argentina. There would be, they believed, somewhat of a hue and cry about the method, not only from officials in Argentina but in other nations as well, but, they reasoned, it would be brief and less than heartfelt. After all, who would want to be known as an ardent defender of such a heinous criminal as Adolf Eichmann? That was the reasoning Isser Harel and ultimately Israeli Prime Minister David Ben-Gurion accepted. So it was agreed that they would attempt to capture Adolf Eichmann themselves.

But so many things could go wrong and so much had to be precisely planned. The Israelis first agreed that Eichmann or his relatives or his acquaintances must never suspect anything; and no Argentine official, no matter how friendly, could be let in on the plot. They also knew that the abduction would have to be executed as deftly as it was planned, conducted in absolute secrecy, and carried out so swiftly that the peripatetic Eichmann would not have time to move to another hiding place.

Isser Harel, in Tel Aviv, set the plan in motion, gathering together a team of professionals. All together, more than 30 agents would be directly involved. Among them was Shalom Dani, an expert forger who would handle all the documents and papers that would be necessary to get the agents in and out of Argentina and who also would produce the papers that would be used to smuggle Eichmann himself out. A doctor who was added to the team would keep Eichmann drugged to incapacitation without harming or killing him in the process and also would handle any of the agents' health problems. The others were highly trained, fully trusted secret agents.

The operation would have two

major phases—kidnapping Klement and then smuggling him out of the country. The latter seemed the more difficult of the two, but then coincidentally the Israelis received an official invitation from the government of Argentina, inviting the state of Israel to celebrate the 150th anniversary of Argentina's independence. Delegations from countries throughout the world were being asked to take part in the festivities—a perfect opportunity to bring an Israeli plane into the airport at Buenos Aires, Isser Harel concluded. (El Al did not have regularly scheduled service to the Argentine capital in those days.) It would not be at all out of the ordinary for the Israeli delegation to arrive aboard a charter flight, which would then fly back to Israel. All Harel and his agents would have to do would be to work out a plan to get Eichmann aboard that return flight. The celebration was planned to begin on May 20, 1960. Israeli officials responded that they would be most happy to attend.

In Europe, meanwhile, an Israeli agent set up a small travel agency to handle the airline arrangements for the agents, who inconspicuously would be entering Argentina. Holding various passports and visas, they would travel individually from various cities in European countries, arrive on a staggered basis, and then take lodging in different hotels in Buenos Aires.

The first Israeli agent to enter the Argentine capital arrived on April 22. After spending a few days in a hotel, he rented an apartment and began to cache supplies for the others, who would begin to filter in there. On April 25, Yosef Kenet returned to Argentina, and on May 1 Isser Harel himself arrived, traveling under a false name. Within the next few days, all members of the operation safely entered Argentina, and then the home of Ricardo Klement was put under continual surveillance.

Cars were rented, meetings held, assignments given, and a search was begun for a "safe house" where Klement could be taken for interrogation and safely held until he was put aboard the El Al plane. There too he would be physically examined to gain further proof of his real identity.

Klement, since his return from the temporary assignment, apparently had gone back to work in Buenos Aires. He would leave home each morning, the agents observed, and would return each evening on a bus that arrived at 7:40 P.M. His uniform schedule was a surprising but welcome boon to the Israelis. They had no way of knowing, however, whether it would last or come quickly to an end, Klement suddenly leaving the city again for some reason or other.

The El Al plane was scheduled to arrive in Argentina on May 19 and take off two days later for the return trip to Israel. However, the agents were already undergoing the preparations necessary for the kidnapping of Klement on May 11, the date set by Isser Harel. They would then have to keep their captive under wraps for about ten days, until the El Al flight departed for home. But they could not, Harel felt, hold off the first phase of the operation any longer without risking the loss of Eichmann or the exposure of their plot.

The plan called for the use of two autos and seven men—a quick hit, Klement being grabbed and carried off in the dark as he walked from the bus to his house, and a fast escape. In charge of the abduction itself was agent Gabi Eldad, a senior intelligence officer highly respected for his daring and resourcefulness.

The evening of May 11 was cold and raw (May is an early winter month in the Southern Hemisphere), and the clouds that night made it even darker. At precisely 7:35 P.M., two cars pulled up to the corner of Route 202, the street the bus traveled, and Garibaldi Street. One car stopped on Route 202 on the far side of the street Klement would turn onto, its hood pointing down Route 202 to the bus stop a little more than 300 feet away. The other car turned onto Garibaldi Street and stopped at the curb just past the corner; two men got out and opened the hood to study some fictitious engine problem. Still in that car was Yosef Kenet, behind the wheel, and Gabi Eldad, sitting on the floor in the backseat and peering out the window at the bus stop, illuminated by a streetlamp. The corner where the Israelis' two cars were parked, however, had no streetlamp, so that someone coming from the bus stop would not see the cars until he was almost on top of them.

The two men looking curiously at the supposed engine trouble under the hood of the car parked on Garibaldi Street were startled suddenly by a voice behind them. A young man on a bicycle wanted to know if he could be of any help. It was 7:39 P.M., one minute before the bus was due. They assured him that they had everything under control, breathing a sigh of relief as he pedaled off into the darkness.

Moments later, the bus pulled into the halo of light up the street and stopped at the curb. A few passengers got off, but Ricardo Klement was not one of them. Five minutes later, another bus arrived—he was not on that one either. At 7:55 P.M., a third bus stopped but still no Ricardo Klement. The agents were worried now. Had he somehow learned of their plot? Had he left the city? Had he simply decided not to come home that night?

Since the agents had agreed beforehand that they would not stay at the corner after 8:00 P.M. for fear of attracting attention, thereby destroying any possibility for an ambush another night, one of the agents in the car parked on Route 202 got out at 8:01 P.M. and started to walk over to the other car to discuss with the men what they were to do. Before he got more than a few yards, however, another bus pulled up to the stop, and a single man stepped off and began walking up the street toward him. The man was out of the glow of the streetlamp, so that the agent could not identify him. To be safe, the agent moved quickly and silently back to his car. Those at the car on Garibaldi Street also saw the man but could not make out who he was either.

As the dark figure reached the corner of Garibaldi Street, the headlights in the car parked across the street on Route 202 suddenly came on, catching the figure full in their light for a moment or two, and then the car began to move away from the curb. In that instant, the men at the car on Garibaldi Street saw clearly that the figure was Ricardo Klement.

Klement paid no attention to the car pulling out and turned away from it onto Garibaldi Street. For just a moment, he saw the other car with its hood up, and then suddenly someone was tackling him, and both he and his assailant went sprawling to the ground. Klement shrieked loudly in the night, but a hand quickly covered his mouth, other hands grabbed at his legs and arms, and suddenly he was being carried and then shoved into the backseat of the car. From the floor, amid the feet and legs of three other men, he heard the hood being slammed shut and then someone jumping into the front seat on the passenger side and that door slamming. Suddenly the car was moving away, past his house, quiet and undisturbed, the occupants inside unaware of the swift but fierce drama that had just taken place. Hands now reached down and handcuffed Klement, blindfolded him, and stuffed a gag in his mouth.

•   •   •

Fifty minutes after Klement had been knocked to the ground on Garibaldi Street, the car pulled up to the entrance of a villa, where a man threw open the gates, and the car was driven into a garage. Klement was then carried into the house, taken to an austere room, and shackled by one leg to a bed.

His false teeth were removed and his mouth was searched for a cyanide capsule; his clothes were taken and his body examined. Kenet then lifted Klement's arm to look at his armpit, where SS officers customarily had their blood types tattooed. All he found now, however, was a scar.

Then Kenet began the interrogation. "What was your serial number in the National Socialist Party?"

Klement was nervous, shaken, but he answered clearly, "889895."

"What is your name?"

"Ricardo Klement."

"Your real name?"

"Otto Heninger."

There was a long silence. Klement, his eyes still covered, could not see his interrogator.

"All right," Kenet said. "Were your SS numbers 45326 and 63752?"

Klement hesitated, understanding now who his captors were, what the situation really was. "Yes," he said.

"And your real name is?"

"Adolf Eichmann."

Isser Harel cabled a coded message back to Israel—they had their man. Phase one was over.

As the days passed, Eichmann was kept under 24-hour guard. No word of his disappearance surfaced anywhere. As Harel had assumed, Eichmann's wife was reluctant to go to the police. Although the authorities would treat the matter as an ordinary disappearance—husbands ran off every day and many came back— they would ask questions and conduct an investigation. Neither Eichmann nor his wife would want that kind of attention. And she would certainly not want to risk the implication that he was kidnapped, because the police would want to know the motive of the kidnappers. On the other hand, she could be thinking that perhaps he had disappeared of his own volition, suddenly suspecting something and fleeing, and would be contacting her when it was safe again. So the Klement family stayed clear of the authorities.

On May 19, the El Al airliner's wheels skidded onto the runway at the Buenos Aires airport and then taxied slowly up to a receiving area near the terminal, where the Argentines greeted it with pageantry and protocol. A band played; a red carpet was stretched out on the tarmac; and dignitaries from both countries were there to welcome the delegates. And word of its arrival was accepted with great sighs of relief by those manning the safe house not far away.

Security at the airport had been tightened because of the various government officials who were arriving from all over the world to attend the anniversary celebration; there were even special military checkpoints to monitor who got onto the airport grounds. These precautionary measures surely would contribute to the hazards of phase two, the agents agreed, but the airliner still remained their best avenue of escape.

The El Al plane was moved to the Argentine national airline's maintenance area and moored on an apron there until takeoff the following night. Most of the crew, including several new agents posing as crew members, went into the city.

The next evening, the actual crew members were gathered together in the airport hotel and were told that they would be taking a passenger in the guise of an ill crewman back to Israel. His identity could not be revealed because great national security was involved, and secrecy must be maintained at all costs. Then they were told to go to the plane and prepare for its flight back to Israel.

At 11:00 P.M., two autos drove through the main entrance to the airport, turned onto the road that led to the El Al plane, and then were stopped by an Argentine sentry at the entrance to the maintenance area. In the first car, there was a boisterous group of crewmen, happy and friendly, obviously back from being out on the town. In the second car were the ones who perhaps had partied *too* much—three of them were asleep in the backseat. The sentry examined the drivers' identification papers, glanced at the others, who were wearing crewmen's uniforms, and then waved all of them through, never suspecting that the crewman asleep in the middle of the backseat of the second car was a drugged Adolf Eichmann and that on one side of him was an Israeli doctor and on the other an Israeli Secret Services agent. The cars pulled up near the plane, and the crew members clambered out and helped their ill comrade up the steps into the plane, depositing him in one of the seats near the front of the aircraft.

Moments later, the engines fired, and the aircraft taxied to a holding area near the runway. There was now another agonizing wait, not ten days, as it had been at the safe house, but only 45 minutes; yet those agents watching from inside the terminal and those aboard the plane found it equally as excruciating. Finally at 12:05 A.M. on May 21, the tower granted takeoff clearance, and the plane roared down the runway and soon was lost in the darkness of the Argentine night.

In Jerusalem, on the morning of May 23, 1960, rumors were floating around the Knesset, the Israeli parliament, that the prime minister was going to make an important announcement. At 4:00 P.M., the parliament members and the Israeli cabinet gathered in the Knesset and watched as David Ben-Gurion took the floor and said solemnly but proudly:

> A short time ago, one of the greatest of Nazi criminals was found by the Israeli Secret Services—Adolf Eichmann, who was responsible, together with the Nazi leaders, for what they called the Final Solution to the Jewish Problem—that is, the extermination of six million Jews of Europe.
>
> Adolf Eichmann is already under arrest in Israel, and he will shortly be brought to trial in Israel under the Nazis and Nazi Collaborators Law of 1950.

In April 1961, Eichmann went on trial in Israel before a special court of three judges and pleaded innocent. In December of that year, he was found guilty of 12 counts of murder and crimes against the Jewish people, as well as of three lesser counts of membership in a hostile organization, and was sentenced to death. On May 31, 1962, Adolf Eichmann was hanged. His last words before the execution was carried out: "Long live Germany. Long live Argentina. Long live Austria. These are the countries with which I have been most closely associated, and I shall not forget them. I greet my wife, my family, my friends. I had to obey the rules of war and my flag."

Ten Modern Masters of Intrigue

Espionage is referred to as a game by some and as an art by others, and most agree it surely is one of the most dramatic and adventuresome of human activities. But it can be a dirty business and often a deadly one. Practiced in an arena of perpetual danger, where there are no rules nor any standard procedures, and populated with minds that run from the precisely mathematical to the wildly imaginative, it is a bizarre world of plot and counterplot, of ruse and chicanery, of theft and blackmail, persuasive charm and cold-blooded violence.

For the agent, the milieu is obscurity, the day-to-day life one of secrecy, subterfuge, and uncommon self-reliance. The motivation and rewards vary as widely as the personalities of those men and women who choose espionage as a way of life or are coerced into it. Only a rare few have achieved notoriety—Mata Hari, the Rosenbergs, Herbert ("I Led Three Lives") Philbrick. The vast majority have never had their stories told; many of them were killed while they practiced their trade, and others simply retired from the business with no intention of betraying the secrets they swore never to reveal. Yet there are always stories of spies and their intrigues that do come to light. Here are ten modern-day but not-so-well-known agents whose exploits vividly illuminate the high drama of the business of espionage.

Oleg Penkovskiy

Greville Wynne, an English businessman, arrived at the Peking Restaurant in Moscow for a dinner meeting on the evening of July 5, 1962, but the person he was to meet had not arrived yet. So Wynne went back outside to wait for him, and as he strolled back and forth under the arc of a streetlamp, he noticed that two men across the street appeared to be watching him. Finally, after about ten minutes, his dinner companion came up the street, glanced at the two men, and then walked right past Wynne, without even a word of greeting, and into the restaurant. Wynne, knowing something was awry, lightly stepped into the restaurant himself. Inside, the man turned to him and said quickly, "I think you're being watched. Wait a moment and then follow me out of here."

Wynne did as he was told, following the man out of the restaurant and into the darkness up the street. But then, in the next block, the man disappeared from sight, turning into the courtyard of a building. Wynne quickened his pace, being interrupted shortly afterward by a hushed voice from the shadows. Wynne turned into the courtyard, and the dark figure said, "You're being followed. You've got to get out of the country quickly. Go to the airport early enough for the first flight out tomorrow. I'll try to be there to help you."

Wynne left without a word and again noticed the two men on the way back to his hotel. His companion, furious at the surveillance, waited for a few moments to calm himself and then went home. He was Colonel Oleg Penkovskiy, a senior officer in the GRU, the Soviet Union's Chief Intelligence Directorate, and he knew that those who were tailing his friend were operatives of the rival Russian agency the KGB, the Committee of State Security. Penkovskiy was furious because it was *officially* known that he was using Wynne for Soviet intelligence purposes.

Greville Wynne was booked on a flight to London for the next afternoon, but he was at the Moscow airport before 6:00 A.M. Not too much later, Penkovskiy approached him— the first flight out was to Copenhagen at 9:00 A.M., Penkovskiy said. They quickly walked to the ticket counter to get Wynne on that flight, but there were problems, the ticket agent said, when he looked at Wynne's ticket and passport. Penkovskiy interceded, identifying himself, and by showing his impressive credentials, he was able to override the objections of the agent as well as of his supervisor, thereby securing passage for Wynne.

Later, Penkovskiy lodged a strong complaint with his own superiors and the KGB regarding surveillance, ranting how it was interfering with, perhaps destroying, his efforts. Everyone agreed, it seemed, that the surveillance was counterproductive, and the KGB agreed not to resume it.

The KGB, however, was not really interested in Greville Wynne. Wynne had been investigated thoroughly by the KGB, and it could not find the slightest link to any foreign intelligence agency. He was and had been for a long time simply an active businessman involved in the international trade of heavy equipment. The KGB was actually interested in Penkovskiy. Despite his brilliant record in the Soviet army during World War II, his respectable tour of duty in embassy service, his unblemished career in intelligence work, and his authoritative position in the GRU, certain members of the KGB hierarchy were having some doubts about him. They had by chance learned that Penkovskiy's father was a White Russian who fought against the revolution, a fact that tainted Penkovskiy's background in the eyes of the KGB. Then too Penkovskiy's cover—representing the Soviet Union among the trade delegations—and his extensive travel abroad and contact with Western businessmen afforded him an all-too-easy opportunity to deal in the black market. So the KGB was investigating Penkovskiy, and following Wynne was only part of that operation.

The irony, however, was that Penkovskiy was totally unaffected by either his father's background or his own opportunity to profit in the black market. On the other hand, for 16 months, Oleg Penkovskiy, with his great access to Soviet top-secret material and information, had been working as an espionage agent for the United States and Britain. He had been passing along vital information about Soviet intelligence operations and agents; about millitary plans, weapons, and preparedness; and about highly sensitive diplomatic and political documents. For the full 16 months, he had been collecting the information, transcribing it, photographing documents, and passing it all to the West through businessman Wynne as well as other contacts in British and American embassies and various other secret agents. Some of the information would end up in the hands of President John F. Kennedy in 1962. It would prove influential in the president's decision to invoke a naval and air quarantine of Cuba and to face down the Soviet ships that were bringing missiles and other military equipment to that island.

Penkovskiy's action at the airport in Moscow only bred further suspicion and stirred the KGB to greater efforts in checking him out. The agency now was becoming convinced that he was trading in black market items with the West, and that Wynne was a principal contact. Soon the KGB began to uncover further evidence of Penkovskiy's double-dealings, eventually finding all the tools of the espionage trade in a hidden drawer in his desk at home.

Penkovskiy was arrested on October 22, 1962. Ten days later, Greville Wynne, who was in Budapest, Hungary, on, at least this time, legitimate business, was kidnapped by Soviet agents and carried off to the Soviet Union. There both were charged with espionage, tried, and convicted. Penkovskiy was sentenced to death, and Wynne to eight years in prison. Wynne was released in 1964 and went back to England. Penkovskiy, according to the Soviet Union, was executed on May 16, 1963. Many believe, however, that he was not executed but instead was kept alive for purposes known only in the darker halls of the KGB or the GRU.

Ruth Kuehn

The story is told that Ruth Kuehn as a teenager in Berlin had a torrid if brief affair with Joseph Goebbels, the Third Reich's minister of propaganda and one of the most powerful men in Hitler's Germany. As the scandal began to surface, to the embarrassment of the minister, she and her family were hastily sent to Japan.

Whether there is any truth to the story is still questionable. There is also the story that Ruth's stepfather, Dr. Bernard Kuehn, was a member of the Gestapo, reporting directly to Heinrich Himmler, and another that he belonged to Reinhard Heydrich's SD (at that time, the SS Security Service), working in the foreign intelligence division, a unit in competition rather than cooperation with the Abwehr. Those rumors were never adequately corroborated either, but what is a fact is that the Kuehns went to Japan in 1935 as a somewhat struggling middle-class family and within months moved to Hawaii as a handsomely affluent one.

Dr. Kuehn was a professor of anthropology, he claimed, and a man of obviously independent wealth. He bought an elegant home in Honolulu and quickly melded his family into the highest echelon of island society. His wife, Friedl, moved with ease among the wives of U.S. naval officers and those of wealthy planters and merchants. His stepdaughter, Ruth, 18 years old, was a beautiful girl, who became an almost instant attraction to the young American naval officers at Pearl Harbor. Hans, his son, only six years old then, was friendly and liked by everyone.

Whether the Kuehns were initially sent to Hawaii to spy for the Germans or for the Japanese is not known. As it turned out, however, they ended up working for both countries, and Ruth became the principal agent in the arrangement. Her place in any espionage Hall of Fame was secured by her role in America's largest military disaster, Japan's surprise attack on Pearl Harbor on December 7, 1941.

By 1939, the Kuehn family was well entrenched in Hawaii. Besides an opulent villa, the family also had purchased a beach house on Oahu's Lanikai Bay. With all the fashionable American ladies on the island in those days, the Kuehns decided to open a posh beauty salon and promoted it well among their friends—and Ruth herself added the personal touch, always, it seemed, meandering through, talking to the ladies being coiffed and listening to the stories of the comings and goings of their husbands and the ships they were on. At the same time, the professor and his young son often took strolls together down by the naval yards to look at the great ships docked there. No one seemed to suspect that all the while the Kuehns were collecting information and relaying it by secret couriers and radio transmitters to both Germany and Japan.

For most of 1941, America was not a participant in the war, but most informed sources in Germany and Japan strongly suspected that it would enter soon. As the year wore on and plans for attacking Pearl Harbor were being formulated in the war rooms of Tokyo, the existence of Ruth Kuehn and her reports took on a new significance.

For their intelligence work, the Kuehns had been receiving a great deal of money by 1941 standards, especially since their operation was basically a routine one. But their cover was far from good, suspicious in fact if anyone had ever taken a close look. They were German, having emigrated from their fatherland by way of Japan, and the inflow of money was substantial for a professor who apparently had no other source of income besides his wife's beauty shop. Ruth was more than casually curious about military affairs, her dates would remember later, and she was almost unduly nosey, as the officers' wives who frequented her beauty salon would recall. And for all the dangers, Ruth was excessively bold: She would meet not too discreetly with the Japanese vice-consul general and

even communicate directly with a Japanese submarine by using signal lights from the dormer window of the family beach house that looked out on the ocean waters.

By November 1941, Ruth Kuehn knew something very big was afoot. Her Japanese contacts now asked for daily reports of ship movements at Pearl Harbor; they wanted to know how and precisely where those in port were docked and what the state of military readiness was at the naval base and any other shred of intelligence she might be able to pick up.

Then on December 6, Ruth met with the Japanese vice-consul general, who told her that her correspondence by signal to the Japanese submarine now must be carried out on a continuing basis for the next 24 hours and that she and her family should be prepared to be evacuated from the island the next morning. It had been arranged, he explained, that the consular corps and the Kuehn family would motorboat to the submarine she had been communicating with and the sub would bring them all back to Japan. The war, he said, was about to begin.

Ruth Kuehn sent her messages through the night, and indeed the next morning the war did begin for the United States. As bombers roared over Hawaii and the devastation of the Pacific fleet was under way, those at the Japanese consulate scurried to destroy all intelligence material, codes, and other sensitive paperwork, but they were not quick enough. Hawaiian police and the FBI descended on the consulate and placed all the employees under arrest. They put out the smoldering fires and found that most of the intelligence material was intact, including some very incriminating evidence regarding the work of the Kuehns.

Authorities arrived at the Kuehn beach house as Ruth and her family, packed and ready to go, sat awaiting their consular friends. They were taken into custody, and the Japanese submarine presumably made its way home alone.

Dr. Kuehn, in an effort to save his family, claimed he was the only spy involved. But the evidence pointed the other way. (Ruth admitted later that in fact she was the chief operative.) Dr. Kuehn was sentenced to death after a court-martial in 1942, but that was commuted to a prison term. He was ordered deported to West Germany in 1946, but was reluctant to return, instead emigrating voluntarily to Argentina, in 1948. Ruth Kuehn and her mother were incarcerated by the United States until the war was over, when they were returned to Germany.

Hermann Lang and "Tramp"

In the year 1938, before the atom bomb, the jet fighter plane, and the combat rocket, America's "number one secret weapon," much publicized but closely guarded, was the most revolutionary bombsight of the age, developed by Carl L. Norden, then a civilian employee of the Navy, and Captain Frederick L. Entwistle of the Navy Bureau of Ordnance, and manufactured by the C. L. Norden Company at its plant on Long Island, New York. The Norden bombsight incorporated a unique gyrostabilized automatic pilot, which enabled bombers to stay level and fly in tight formation during bombing runs, allowing them to hit specific targets with greater precision than had been possible before. No one in the world wanted that instrument more than the German Luftwaffe as the Third Reich was gearing up for war. And no one was making more of an effort to steal the secret than Admiral Wilhelm Canaris, the chief of the Abwehr, Germany's central intelligence agency.

Admiral Canaris and Germany were successful in their quest to obtain the Norden bombsight. But the information did not come by way of a professional spy, nor through an intricate espionage plot, but rather it was received as a gift from a man who simply handed them the blueprints and refused to take anything in exchange for his generosity.

The man was Hermann Lang. In 1938, he lived with his wife and daughter in a middle-class apartment in Glendale, Queens, New York. In 1923, however, he had lived in Germany and had marched with Adolf Hitler in the famous Beer Hall Putsch in Munich that year. Lang had later immigrated to the United States and became a naturalized citizen. By 1938 he was working as an assembly inspector at the Norden engineering plant, where the bombsight was being made.

Lang was aware of the importance of the instrument and decided without any outside influence that his fatherland should have it. Because of his job, he had access to various blueprints from time to time, and one evening he managed to sneak two of them home with him. He copied them line for line and then returned the originals the next day. Through friends at a German-American bar in New York, he made contact with an Abwehr agent, who sent the duplicates to Germany. As time went on, Lang was able to copy other blueprints, and finally German engineers had enough information to construct their own version of the super-secret Norden bombsight.

The members of the German intelligence community were so pleased with Lang and his unsolicited contribution that they invited him and his wife to Germany shortly after the last of the duplicate plans had been received. There he met with Admiral Canaris himself and was even entertained by Hermann Goering, the supreme commander of the Luftwaffe and soon to be the marshal of the Third Reich. Canaris suggested that perhaps Lang should remain in Germany for his own safety, but the technician-turned-agent decided to return to America.

Back in America in 1940, Lang was contacted by a new Abwehr agent, a man whose American passport carried the name William G. Sawyer. The man also was known as William G. Sebold, but his real name was Wilhelm Debowski. He had lived in America for a number of years under the name Sebold and had worked at the Consolidated Aircraft Company in San Diego. In 1939 he returned to Germany to visit his family. The war broke out in Europe while he was there, and he was con-

tacted about returning to the United States as an operative for the Abwehr. He declined, but then the Gestapo reminded him of his past criminal record, and so he agreed to go along with the plan. The Abwehr trained him for several months and then gave him a forged passport so he could return to New York City to set up an office as a cover and to rig a radio transmitter out on Long Island. He was also given the names of four key agents he could contact in the area—among them Hermann Lang.

Sawyer (or Sebold or Debowski) took on the code name Tramp and soon began to radio a vast amount of intelligence information to a receiving station in Hamburg, Germany. The communication continued for 16 months, and the Germans were delighted with the cornucopia of data they were receiving from Tramp in America.

Hermann Lang was invited to meet with Tramp in the New York office and in the course of their conversation told him point-blank that he was the man who had stolen the secret of the Norden bombsight. But he also told the FBI, because two government agents were secretly recording the conversation in the next room. They were there at the express invitation of Tramp, because Sawyer/Sebold/Debowski, never having any great desire to be an Abwehr agent, had related the Abwehr's proposal to the American consulate during his recruitment by the Germans. U.S. intelligence officials advised him to go along with the plan but to work for them, thereby becoming a double agent. He agreed, and when Tramp arrived in the United States, he was greeted warmly by the FBI and quickly went about his task of subterfuge.

In June of 1941, Lang and other German espionage agents were arrested and brought to trial. Tramp was the surprise witness, providing the testimony that was the principal source for their convictions. Lang, sentenced to 14 years in prison, was sent to the penitentiary at Fort Leavenworth, Kansas. He was released in August 1950 and sent back to West Germany.

Major William Martin

Major William Martin, of the British Royal Marines and a military intelligence courier, was instrumental in the success of the Allied landings in Sicily in 1943. He was the central figure in an imaginative espionage plot known as Operation Mincemeat. The strange thing about Major Martin, however, was that he was not a member of any intelligence or espionage community, nor was he a member of the British armed forces, nor was he even a human being for that matter. Major William Martin was nothing more than an unidentified cadaver with a totally fabricated identity.

After North Africa fell, it was obvious that the Allied armies would soon try to invade Europe. The most likely landing point was Sicily, a fact known not only by the Allies but by the Germans and the Italians, which certainly cut down its desirability. So British intelligence decided the best way to handle the situation was not to change the location of the invasion but rather to mislead the German high command into believing that the landing would take place elsewhere.

That's when Major William Martin came into being. Somewhere in the cellars of the British intelligence establishment in London his existence was concocted as part of an elaborate plot.

Major Martin, a specialist in landing-craft operations, would carry orders assigning him to the assault forces being formed in North Africa for the coming invasion. He also would have ancillary orders for stops to deliver various pieces of military intelligence—in effect to serve as a courier on the way to his assignment, something that was not really out of the ordinary in World War II.

In his bag of secret documents would be a highly sensitive communication to General Sir Harold Alexander, the British army commander in Tunisia. It would clearly imply that the coming invasion was to be focused on the southern coast of Greece and secondarily on the island of Sardinia. Sicily was to serve only as the site of a diversionary operation. There would also be a cover letter regarding Major Martin as a courier, written by Lord Louis Mountbatten himself, whose wartime titles included Commander of the Royal Marines. Major Martin's plane, however, would crash in the Atlantic, off the coast of Spain; and his body would wash up on shore, with the briefcase containing all the classified documents secured in the traditional manner to it.

The creation of Major Martin involved first the appropriation of a body—and it had to be just the right one. It had to belong to a young man who was in his thirties, who had died of pneumonia (a postmortem would have to show that the major had died of water in his lungs, as if he had drowned), and who had been dead for eight days (to coincide with the dates of the papers he carried and later with a leaked intelligence report about a plane that went down on that specific day).

A carefully documented identity was also arranged for Major Martin, and all the necessary papers, orders, and personal ID's were forged. He even carried a picture of his girl friend and the last letter she had written him before he flew off to war.

A search turned up an appropriate body for Major Martin, found in a small English town and buried just a few days earlier. It was exhumed and conscripted into the service of the British Royal Marines. The major's locked briefcase was chained to the belt of his uniform in official courier style. Then Major Martin was placed in a coffinlike container and packed in dry ice. In mid-April 1943, the major set out for Spain not in an airplane, but in the bowels of the British submarine *Seraph*.

On April 30, the boat surfaced about a mile off the southern coast of Spain, not far from the Portuguese border. In the dead of night, several sailors emerged from the conning tower with the coffin and took the body from it. They put a Mae West life jacket on Major Martin, lifted the body over the side, then watched as the major was picked up by the tide and carried toward shore.

The choice of Spain had been a calculated one. It was not too overt, at least it would not be to German eyes and minds, but at the same time it would be in the direct flight path of a Britisher who had left his homeland for the Mediterranean theater of operations. And it was crawling with German agents to whom the native Spaniards would regularly report. The British felt sure that the body, or certainly the courier's briefcase, would be discovered by the Spanish and discreetly turned over to the German operatives.

And that is exactly what happened. Three days after Major Martin's body slid from the submarine into the Atlantic swells, the British attaché in Madrid was informed by Spanish authorities that the body of a British marine officer had been discovered by some local fishermen. Papers on the body identified him as a Major William Martin. He cabled the news to London; it was a routine transcription of information.

But it ceased to be routine when London began to send him classified inquiries regarding a briefcase and its contents that might have accompanied the body. Instructed to discreetly question the Spanish authorities on the matter, the attaché (who knew nothing about the plot) found that there was indeed a briefcase, and the Spanish authorities said they would turn it over to him soon. He received it within a few days, and then he sent it back to England—exactly as he had received it, as per his instructions.

In London, the contents of the
(continued on page 166)

The Ten Greatest Spies of All Time
By William E. Colby, former Director, Central Intelligence Agency

The test of the "greatest" should be the importance of the contribution of the spy, not his degree of derring-do. Thus, despite the sensational aspects of the lives of Mata Hari or Colonel Rudolf Abel, who was discovered in a photographic establishment in Brooklyn living under an assumed identity, neither can be said to have accomplished very much. In terms of their contributions to modern intelligence, my list is as follows:

1. William J. Donovan
World War I hero, close friend of President Franklin Roosevelt, world traveler, and scholar. He was asked by Roosevelt to form America's World War II intelligence agency (the Office of Strategic Services), and he made one of the major innovations in intelligence, considering scholarly study as the central feature of modern intelligence. He directed widespread espionage and guerrilla operations, but never lost his focus on the real purpose of intelligence, to inform our government of all the factors affecting the world situation, not just to steal secrets.

2. Reginald V. Jones
A one-man British science and technology intelligence wizard. During World War II, he used the techniques of radio, radar, and other technology to mislead German bombers and to frustrate their operations, and opened the tradition of the spy service to the contributions of science.

3. William F. Friedman
America's foremost cryptanalyst, who almost singlehandedly maintained our code-breaking capabilities between the two world wars, and built them up for World War II, making a major contribution to our defeat of Japanese naval power.

4. Richard Sorge
Trained in the Soviet Union, he returned to his native Germany and then went to Japan, where he penetrated the German Embassy in Tokyo to the extent that he was totally informed of exchanges between Germany and Japan in the early 1940s. His greatest contribution, and frustration, was a warning to Stalin of Hitler's imminent attack on the USSR, which Stalin ignored.

5. Julius and Ethel Rosenberg
Executed for their espionage, but not before they had passed important secrets of America's new nuclear capability to their Soviet masters, they enabled the Soviet Union to leapfrog many years in its development of nuclear weapons.

6. Kim Philby

Recruited by the Soviets in the 1930s, he served in a succession of high British intelligence posts for over 20 years, reporting amply to the Soviets on such matters as American and British intelligence cooperation during the years of the Cold War. Unmasked before he almost became the chief of British intelligence, he fled to the Soviet Union, where he still resides.

7. Oleg Penkovskiy

Colonel on the Soviet General Staff, frustrated with the brutal cynicism of the Soviet regime, he contacted British and American intelligence and served as an active spy for a number of years before he was unmasked and executed. His contribution to our understanding of Soviet military matters was very important during the 1960s and is still relevant in many respects.

8. Clarence "Kelly" Johnson

One of America's foremost aerodynamics engineers. As designer of the famous U-2 aircraft in the Lockheed "skunk works," he revolutionized intelligence by making it possible to overfly the Soviet Union and bring home photographs of important targets accessible in no other way. His early efforts have been successively improved by later aircraft and, of course, today's satellite photography.

9. Arthur Lundahl

Head of CIA's photographic interpretation center, his skill in organizing photographic interpretation literally saved the nation when he identified shapes on a field in Cuba in 1962 as Soviet offensive nuclear missiles in the process of being erected.

10. Edward Lansdale

The prototype of the "ugly American" (a complimentary term in the novelized version of his life), whose political imagination and warm empathy with Southeast Asian leaders and peoples helped democratic alternatives to emerge between corrupt colonialists and ruthless terrorists. His assistance to President Ramón Magsaysay in the Philippines and nationalist President Ngo Dinh Diem in Vietnam were of critical importance to American policy in those areas.

This brief listing would be incomplete without tribute to the corps of scholars, engineers, and intelligence officers who constitute America's intelligence community, engaged in the broad collection and analysis of all the aspects of the world around us—political, economic, sociological, psychological, and cultural—to produce better understanding of the threats and opportunities our nation faces. No single spy, however heroic or effective, could match their constant contribution.

briefcase were carefully examined. The letters had been intricately rigged so that the lab technicians in London would be able to tell if the envelopes had been opened. Every piece of mail in the briefcase had been steamed open and carefully resealed, they quickly determined. Now the British simply had to hope that the act was done by the Germans or at least that the contents had been disseminated to them.

As history would later show, the information held in the single envelope addressed to General Alexander not only went through German intelligence in Spain and Abwehr headquarters in Berlin but was placed in the hands of Adolf Hitler himself. The letter was a key factor in guiding Hitler to rebuke his advisers and to move most of his forces to defend Sardinia and the Greek coast, leaving only a token group to handle the Allies' "diversionary" action in Sicily.

British intelligence officers were able to gloat over one of the finest military hoaxes to be carried off since the Greeks of legend crawled into the giant horse outside the walls of ancient Troy.

George Blake

The story of George Blake sounds more like one scripted in Hollywood's motion picture colony than enacted in the real world. He was born George Behar of Spanish, Turkish, Dutch, and Jewish heritage in Rotterdam in 1922; educated in Cairo; at 18 years old, stranded in wartorn, German-occupied Europe; quickly converted to an active member of the Dutch underground resistance; and was arrested by the Gestapo but engineered his own escape and made it to England. There at 20 years of age and a master of four languages (English, Dutch, German, and French), he was enlisted into the ranks of British Naval Intelligence, serving for a while in postwar Hamburg, West Germany, until he was transferred to the Foreign Office in 1947. But that position was a real surprise, not so much because of his youthful age, 25, but because he was the first non-British-born person to be hired into the Foreign Office at a staff level—and British-born of British-born parents was a definite requirement at the time.

Blake first studied and mastered the Russian language and then was assigned as vice-consul to the British embassy in Seoul, South Korea. When war broke out on the Korean peninsula and the capital fell in June 1950, he was arrested and taken to a prisoner of war camp in North Korea. There Blake was subjected to intense questioning, Communist indoctrination programs, and the full spectrum of threats, tantalizing inducements, and other ploys to get him to join the Communist cause.

Some say it was here amid the desolation and the brainwashing that George Blake was converted to Communism. Others say that he withstood it, even duped his Communist interrogators. Still others say that Blake not only survived the ordeal but also brought his chief antagonist, a Soviet major, over to his side (later the major did defect to the United States).

Whatever happened there is still unknown, but upon his return to

England after the cease-fire in 1953, he was welcomed back as a hero, a young man who had been unjustly incarcerated and abused but had proven himself a loyal subject impervious to the enemy's tactics.

He resumed his career in government service, this time joining the super-secret MI-6 bureau of British military intelligence. After some training, he was sent to West Berlin as a spy. Here the story becomes murky, filled with mystery and paradox. It is known for certain, however, that Blake carried out the role of a British agent. He interrogated defectors; set up contacts with friendly agents in East Berlin; and channeled intelligence information back to his superiors in London. At the same time, he acted as a double agent, funneling sensitive and secret information to agents of the Soviet Union. It is known that various Free World agents in East Berlin were exposed and disposed of as a result of the information he provided to the Soviets.

Yet some maintain to this day that he was acting as a triple agent—in a carefully orchestrated scheme, British agent Blake was purposely compromised so as to become a double agent for the Soviets but in actuality was taken into their confidence so that he could guide false or misleading information into their hands.

The answers to what George Blake actually was up to and to whom he truly had granted his allegiance are not definite, the facts of the case shrouded in mystery to this day.

Blake's role as a double agent was first uncovered by another double agent, Horst Eitner, who betrayed Blake after being arrested by West German authorities for giving information to the Soviets. Then Colonel Michal Goleniewski, a high-ranking intelligence officer from Communist Poland, defected to the Free World and provided a list of agents, including the name George Blake, known to be working for the Soviets.

At the time, Blake was no longer stationed in East Berlin; he had been transferred to Beirut, Lebanon. He was recalled from that post; brought back to England and placed under arrest; charged with several counts of espionage under the Official Secrets Act; and brought to trial. He confessed to the charges, was found guilty and sentenced to 42 years in prison. He served five years but then escaped.

The story has never had an adequate ending, many of the questions remaining unanswered. How could a foreign-born person attain such a sensitive level in the British intelligence system? Why would he freely return to England after news of his identification as a double agent had already been spread through intelligence channels? Why was he able to escape so easily and disappear so effectively?

No one has ever reasonably answered those questions. Some say that George Blake, clever as always, escaped from prison with the help of the KGB and was smuggled into the Soviet Union, where he now lives. There is evidence to support that theory. Others speculate that he stayed in prison to fulfill the "plausible" story in his game with the Soviets but then was allowed to escape, and now a wealthy man with a new identity, he resides somewhere in the British Commonwealth or the United States. But then, as George Blake's double life as a spy had clearly shown, nothing is ever perfectly defined in the world of espionage and intelligence.

Velvalee Dickinson

If ever a person looked like she should be the proprietor of a quaint doll shop, it was Velvalee Dickinson. At 50 years old, not quite five feet tall, weighing less than 100 pounds, with gray hair and spectacles, she was the epitome of the local toy shop owner. But neither she nor her small store, located in New York City, was ordinary by any standards. The shop was overflowing with the most fashionable handmade dolls of the day as well as rare and antique items for the serious collector—among Velvalee's clientele were movie stars, other celebrities, and people of wealth. And Velvalee . . . well, her story is a unique one.

Her story was approaching its climax one day late in 1943. The diminutive lady quickly walked out of her doll shop one afternoon in autumn, waved down a taxicab, and told the driver to take her to Gimbel's department store on 34th Street. Velvalee looked around nervously several times from the backseat of the cab but could see only the cars, the trucks, and the other cabs that glutted the New York streets. Inside Gimbel's, she wove a strange and fast-paced path up and down the escalators, through the crowds of midday shoppers, and finally into the basement of the store. With a quick glance over her shoulder, she darted through the store's direct entrance to a subway station. Several train transfers later, she ended up in Penn Station and, carrying only a purse, purchased a ticket to Philadelphia. On arriving in that city, she immediately bought some clothes and luggage and then made arrangements for the continuation of her trip to Portland, Oregon.

For all the looking over her shoulder that she did, Velvalee never saw the team of FBI agents who followed her through Gimbel's, to Philadelphia, all the way to Portland, and finally back to New York.

The FBI had become interested in Velvalee Dickinson shortly after Mary Wallace of Springfield, Ohio, received in the mail a letter addressed to Señora Inez Lopez de Molinali in Buenos Aires. It was delivered to Mrs. Wallace because the envelope bore her name and return address and was marked "return to sender." But Mary Wallace had never written the letter, although when she read it, she was surprised to find mention of things that were personal to her. And the basis of the letter had to do with dolls and the collection of them, which was in fact a hobby of hers.

Confused by the contents and upset that someone for some strange reason was using her name, she brought the letter to the attention of the postal authorities (it was a time of war and postal censorship). They found nothing extraordinary about the letter other than the fact it was written in a silly, somewhat meaningless sort of way but as a matter of routine forwarded it to the FBI. There an agent became suspicious, thinking perhaps it expressed a code of some sort, so he passed it on to the bureau's cryptanalysts. The first reaction was that the letter was a code but a crude and amateurish one.

The FBI alerted the postal authorities to put a stop on any letters going to or coming back from Señora Inez Lopez de Molinali. Soon the FBI had several others—written in the same inane way with vague references to dolls—that had been returned to different senders in the United States. A quick check showed that none of the return-addressees had sent the letters, but they all had an interest in collecting dolls and had recently dealt with Velvalee Dickinson in her New York shop.

The FBI immediately ran an exhaustive security check on Velvalee Dickinson's background and found that she had been born Velvalee Blucher in 1893, grew up in California, was well-educated, and eventually married a man by the name of Lee Dickinson. The couple had lived comfortably on the West Coast but moved to New York in 1937. There Velvalee found a job at Bloomingdale's, in the doll department, but not too long afterward left to open her own store.

Of more concern to the FBI, however, was the fact that during the 1930s Velvalee and her husband were exceptionally active in the Japanese-American community in California. Among their closest friends were members of the Japanese consulate in San Francisco as well as a wide variety of Japanese businessmen. The Dickinsons even lived in a Japanese colony outside San Francisco before they moved to New York.

The FBI intensified the investigation and determined that each letter addressed to Señora Inez Lopez de Molinali had been written on the same typewriter and posted from cities in which Velvalee was known to be on the particular date of mailing. With all the letters in hand, the crude code was easily broken—it was clear that the dolls were references to U.S. naval ships and their movements.

Meanwhile, Velvalee began to become suspicious of the men who suddenly seemed to have an interest in dolls and were forever browsing in her store. In addition, she had not heard anything in some time from her contact in Argentina. All of it combined to make her more than a little nervous. So she decided to get herself to Portland, where she hoped to meet with her only Japanese contact left in the United States. But when she got there, she found that he had disappeared.

Velvalee then returned to New York and tried to go about her business, but a few days after her return in January 1944, as she was opening her safe deposit box in a New York bank, she was startled by a team of FBI agents, who placed her under arrest. Velvalee Dickinson was charged with espionage and with violating postal censorship laws. The first charge was dropped, but she pleaded guilty to the lesser count and was sentenced to ten years in prison. Velvalee served part of her sentence and was released in April 1951.

Elyesa Bazna

The story of Elyesa Bazna, spy, is one of irony after irony. He had worked as a manservant for Albert Jenke, a member of the German foreign ministry in the late 1930s, and was believed to have lived for a while in the German embassy in Ankara, Turkey. Then during World War II, he secured work at the British embassy and was given lodging there, apparently without any check on his past. He became a very active spy, who passed vital intelligence secrets of the Allies to the Nazis. But for all its value, the information was not accepted as valid by the Germans and consequently was ignored in Berlin. For his services, however, Bazna was probably the highest paid spy in World War II, or history up to that time, receiving from the Germans somewhere in the vicinity of £300,000 (about $1,000,000 in 1944 U.S. currency). But as it turned out, all but a minuscule portion of it was in counterfeit notes that Bazna would never be able to cash.

Elyesa Bazna, born in Albania (although he claimed to be a Yugoslav), was 38 years old and living in Turkey in 1943 when he somehow landed his first job with the British embassy as a chauffeur. Soon, however, he insinuated himself into a higher position, personal valet to Sir Hugh Knotchbull-Hegessen, the British ambassador, with unrestricted access to his living quarters and his office. Among the first things Bazna did in his new position was to make wax impressions of the keys to the reinforced steel boxes where the ambassador kept all his classified information. In a matter of days, Bazna had his own personal set of keys, which he carried without trepidation in his pants pocket.

Bazna's next step was a brief visit to the German embassy, where his former employer, Albert Jenke, who had since become the Third Reich's first secretary at the embassy, referred him to the attaché responsible for intelligence matters, a man named L. C. Moyzisch. Bazna told Moyzisch that as the British ambassador's valet, he could deliver photographs of the most highly classified documents passing through the British embassy. He would give him the information, he said, because he hated the British. But he expected a lot of money for it, £20,000 to be precise.

Moyzisch suspected a scam but related the offer to Franz von Papen, the German ambassador. The possibility of it being genuine and the probability of it being a setup by British intelligence as well as the amount of money involved would warrant a decision at the highest level of government, von Papen reasoned, so he also sent a coded message to Joachim von Ribbentrop, the German foreign minister in Berlin. Three days later, von Papen received an okay and packets of fresh currency totaling £20,000. Von Papen then instructed Moyzisch to contact Bazna.

Bazna came to the German embassy and handed over two rolls of film—52 exposures. They were developed immediately, and in the words of Moyzisch:

> Here on my desk were the most carefully guarded secrets of the enemy, both political and military, and of incalculable value. These were no plant.... Out of the blue, there had dropped into

our laps the sort of papers a secret service agent might dream about for a lifetime. . . . Even at a glance, I could see that the valet's service to the Third Reich was unbelievably important.

The contract was cast on the spot. Bazna agreed to continue his espionage work—at exorbitant prices, £ 15,000 per roll of film—then left with his first bundle of counterfeit notes. Shortly afterward, Bazna was given the code name Cicero to be used in all future transactions.

In the foreign ministry, von Ribbentrop, however, did not share Moyzisch's estimation of the value of the documents. He was highly skeptical of their authenticity, and so for all practical purposes the information was disregarded. As new rolls of film flowed in, von Ribbentrop remained unchanged in his opinion. It was a great blunder, because during the year Cicero photographed secret documents and collected his pay, he provided such morsels as news of the formation of Operation Overlord, the Allies' second European invasion, scheduled to take place on the Normandy coast of France; transcriptions of top-level Allied conferences in Moscow, Casablanca, and Tehran; information on Turkey's intention to join the Allies and declare war on Germany; British codes and ciphers; and lists of Allied secret agents operating in Turkey.

Meanwhile, Bazna amassed his fortune, spending some of it on a secret life away from the British embassy but hoarding most of it for the war's end.

By mid-1944, however, the Allies knew there was a leak emanating from somewhere in the British embassy in Ankara. The Americans, the first to learn about it, informed the British, and security was tightened at the embassy. But the source was not discovered until an agent infiltrated the German embassy; ironically, she was placed as a secretary to attaché Moyzisch. She managed to trace the connection to the ever-obliging British ambassador's valet, Elyesa Bazna, and then suddenly fled the embassy. Moyzisch, now knowing that the entire Cicero operation was blown, managed to get word to Cicero, who quickly fled the country. Moyzisch himself was ordered back to Berlin, but before he could return, Turkey had entered the war, and he was interned for the remainder of it.

Elyesa Bazna learned of the Nazi's double-dealing when he tried to cash in his worthless fortune after the war. The counterfeit notes were confiscated and destroyed. For all the information he had given, which was never put to use, he had been paid royally with money he could never use.

Mathilde Carré

On a damp November morning in 1941, Mathilde Carré, a bewitching 33-year-old woman with sparkling, translucent green eyes, turned onto the Rue Cortot in the shadows of Montmartre's famous landmark, the Cathedral de Sacre-Coeur, walking briskly to her Paris apartment. But she never reached it. Abwehr agents in civilian clothes and two uniformed German soldiers stepped out from several doorways and placed her under arrest.

Wily, seductive, cunning, known as the Cat, her days as a spy against Germany were suddenly over. Mathilde Carré, once a bright teenager studying at the Sorbonne, later a young married woman, who, while living in Algeria, shared equally the affection of an impotent husband and the bed of a Muslim lover, was now in the clutches of the enemy.

Mathilde Carré abandoned her husband after the start of the war and made her way back to France, where she began a career in espionage after her country was occupied by the Germans.

In the city of Toulouse, in the south of France, she made the acquaintance of Roman Czerniawsky, a Polish air force officer, who had escaped from a German prisoner of war camp. The two of them contacted the few remaining members of the Deuxième Bureau, France's intelligence agency, and began to set up an espionage network. The operating center would be Paris, and so Mathilde Carré, under the code name Cat, and her Polish friend, now encoded as Armand, moved to the occupied capital. They recruited other agents and activated their secret radio transmitters. The web was strung. The subterranean organization took the name Interallié, "between allies."

It was a dangerous business. Paris was teeming with Gestapo and Abwehr agents, as well as French collaborationists. Summary executions were all too common. But Interallié flourished, and a continuing flow of important information was transmitted to the British intelligence community in London. And the Cat, so naturally sensual, proved to be as adept at spying as she was alluring to those she seduced to achieve her purposes.

Interallié lasted only one year, however, failing as a result of the work of a handsome and exceptionally effective Abwehr counterintelligence agent named Hugo Bleicher. He knew there was an enemy organization functioning well in Paris and worked assiduously until he finally penetrated it and traced its leadership to Armand at his headquarters in Montmartre. The Cat was not a suspect when Bleicher raided the Interallié's headquarters, but as Armand and his mistress-of-the-moment, Renée Borni, were being arrested, she turned, and with a long-pent-up jealousy and hatred, told the Germans of the existence of Armand's former lover, the Cat. After Mathilde Carré was arrested, Renée Borni stood before her and happily told the Germans that they had arrested the right party.

Mathilde Carré was thrown into a filthy prison cell in Paris and then brought before Hugo Bleicher the next day. He was gentle and charming with her, explaining that he wanted to secure her help in his work. In other words, he wanted her to become a double agent. When she did not respond, he told her simply that she had at that precise moment a choice to make—to work for the Germans or be executed summarily.

Mathilde Carré made her choice

and at the same time became Bleicher's mistress. The Abwehr then leaked word that Armand and several other Interallié agents had been captured but that the Cat had escaped. Then one by one during the next month, many of the remaining operatives of Interallié began to disappear, each being set up by Mathilde Carré. And no one ever suspected the Cat of her duplicity, not until an undercover agent from Britain smuggled himself into Paris and infiltrated the ever-diminishing ranks of Interallié. His code name was Lucas, and he was introduced to the Cat by a go-between, one whom the Abwehr had allowed to function to facilitate the Cat's work. Lucas also had his own network of agents in France, as the Cat learned, and informed Bleicher, who decided to have her play along with Lucas and possibly infiltrate that group as well.

But Bleicher's plan backfired because Lucas soon learned that the Cat had provided the false papers so that the go-between could escape. Evidence of her double-dealings continued to surface; Lucas now strongly suspected that Mathilde Carré might be a double agent. So when he had to return temporarily to London, he decided to take her with him. Bleicher told her to go because he did not realize that she was under suspicion.

After Lucas and the Cat arrived in England, Lucas told his superiors that he had become suspicious of the woman. British authorities quickly conducted clandestine investigations into the Cat's activities.

When Lucas returned to France,

he traveled alone. Back in Paris, he was arrested almost immediately by Bleicher. The full treachery of the Cat was now understood, and she was imprisoned in England until the end of the war.

In 1945, Mathilde Carré was returned to France, and after being held in custody for almost four years, she was tried and convicted of treason and sentenced to death. Her execution was never carried out, however; her sentence was commuted to a prison term, and in 1954 she was finally freed.

Rudolph Roessler

One of the great questions still unanswered from World War II is, Who was Rudolph Roessler's contact in Germany? The person who could supply such a large amount of top secret information, with its incredible accuracy must have had key access to the highest echelon of Adolf Hitler's military staff. Speculations have ranged all the way up to Martin Bormann, Hitler's personal secretary and one of the most powerful men in the Third Reich, but no proof has ever been offered.

Rudolph Roessler was a quiet, unassuming man, who wore heavy-rimmed glasses and made his home in Lucerne, Switzerland, during World War II. Born in Kaufbeuren, Germany, in 1897, he had been a loyal German having fought for his country in World War I, but with Hitler's rise to power, he quickly renounced his fatherland and in 1934 emigrated to Switzerland. There he took a post with a publishing company, and during the next five years, he was a journalist and an editor, specializing in anti-Nazi writings.

When the war broke out in 1939, Roessler took on a side job—he became a spy. The Swiss, even though their nation was neutral in the war, maintained a secret intelligence agency that was quite active in the gathering of crucial military information about both sides. And there was no question that the agent who was able to supply the best intelligence about Germany was Rudolph Roessler. He would acquire the information in his own mysterious way and then would meet with his Swiss contact at a cafe, and over a cup of coffee or glass of wine, he would simply pass it on to him. Later, after Germany turned against the Soviet Union, the information that Roessler was able to obtain so readily was suddenly dispersed well beyond the country's neutral borders.

In early 1941, Rudolph Roessler made the acquaintance of a Britisher by the name of Alexander Foote, somewhat of a soldier of fortune who also happened to be in the employ of the Soviet Union as its chief spy stationed in Switzerland. In his apartment in Lausanne, Foote had a transmitter over which he almost daily radioed his findings to Moscow. That year, he also began sending messages for Roessler, now encoded as Lucy.

A short while later, the quantity of communications from Lucy became so large that it necessitated the setting up of a system of radio transmitters direct from Switzerland to a contact at Soviet intelligence in Mos-

cow. After a while, the information that was being relayed was deemed to be of such a high level and so cogent that the Soviets began to suspect that it might be a sham—that Lucy was in fact a double agent planted there to feed them misleading information. They could not believe that he was able to gather secrets that legitimately would be known only in Hitler's headquarters or in his war rooms. Their investigation, however, proved only that Lucy was indeed the Soviet's man—he just happened to have the finest of sources.

Lucy proved his inestimable value to the Soviets in 1943. On March 30, the supreme staff of the Wehrmacht met in Berlin with Hitler and top members of his staff to discuss plans for a massive offensive against the Soviet Union. The surprise attack was to be concentrated in the area of Orel, Kursk, and Kharkov, about 250 miles south of Moscow. Two days later, on April 1, Lucy radioed the information to Lucerne, and in turn it was sent on to Moscow. Two weeks later, Hitler set the date for the attack, and Lucy forwarded that news to Moscow as well. When the date was postponed, that piece of information, too, was relayed to the Soviet high command, compliments of Lucy.

The attack was rescheduled for July 5, but before it could begin that day, one of the greatest concentrations of Soviet military might ever assembled for battle opened fire on the Germans, reversing the surprise. Thus began one of the greatest armored battles in history. It ended a week later, when Germany conceded defeat, pulling most of its Panzer units out of the battle and sending them to the south to protect the Greek and Italian shores from the Allies.

Rudolph Roessler continued his espionage work from Lucerne until he was arrested by the Swiss police in May 1944. Behind-the-scenes maneuvering by secret Swiss intelligence authorities who tried desperately to get him released without revealing their own intelligence-gathering operation finally led to Roessler's unconditional release four months later.

After the war, Roessler still served the Soviet Union, mainly through Communist Czechoslovakia, but now sent most of his intelligence data from West Germany. He was arrested in Switzerland in 1953, charged with espionage, and sentenced to one year in prison.

Rudolph Roessler died in 1958 and was buried in a cemetery outside Lucerne, not far from where he carried out with such virtuosity his role as a spy. And when he died, he left the world not only without having revealed the name of his highly placed informant, but without having revealed how the information had been relayed to him.

Violette Szabo

In the more romantic vision of espionage work, the black parachute is as commonplace as the trench coat, the microdot, and the radio transmitter hidden in a dusty attic. But it is not merely the product of an imaginative novelist. Many modern-day spies and saboteurs have used the black parachute as a vehicle to drop unnoticed behind enemy lines on many moonless nights. As romantic as it seems, that kind of infiltration and masquerade is among the most hazardous of espionage activities. Violette Szabo's tragic fate testifies to that fact.

On three separate occasions during World War II she parachuted through the blackness of the night into Occupied France to gather military intelligence and set up liaisons with the French underground.

Born Violette Bushell in Paris in 1921, she later moved with her family to London, and by the time she was a teenager, Violette had acquired fluency in both French and English. She was only 19 when she married Etienne Szabo, who, as an officer in the Free French Army, was stationed in London. Two years later, in 1942, a daughter was born to them, but unfortunately Etienne would never see her because that same year he was killed at the battle of El Alamein in the Egyptian desert.

Violette, who had always expressed a desire to join the war effort, now had her part defined. She offered fluency in the French language, youth, beauty, resourcefulness, and dedication—excellent requisites for work in Britain's ultrasecret Special Operations Executive, a hand-selected group of infiltrative agents trained to work behind German lines.

Violette, code-named Louise, was a 22-year-old widow and mother when she first leaped from an airplane over the fields of rural France.

There, she and veteran agent Philip Liewer gathered information for the coming D day invasion and searched for those agents who had lost radio contact with Allied headquarters. Several weeks later, they returned to England by plane from one of the hidden airfields in the French countryside.

Soon afterward, she once again parachuted into France, her second sojourn amid the enemy being a bit more harrowing. An underground agent who she had been led to trust went directly to the Gestapo with the story of her activity, but fortunately she learned of the treachery before the Germans could apprehend her, and Violette quickly moved her base of operations to another section of France. She was in fact arrested once on this mission but only on the suspicions of local Vichy authorities. They turned her over to the SS, who could find no fault with her story or her papers, and so she was released. Then she carefully made her way back to England.

It was her third trip to France that proved to be the fateful one. It was shortly after D day, June 6, 1944, and Violette, along with other agents, was parachuted in well behind the ever-changing battle lines. Her job this time was to work closely with the established underground, gathering information for the advancing troops and aiding them by various methods of sabotage.

Everything was going well until one sultry afternoon in August, when she and several other agents were holed up in a house that they had set up as an operational center. Suddenly two armored cars appeared on the street, and plain-clothes Gestapo and uniformed SS soldiers poured out of them and surrounded the house. Once again, Violette Szabo had been betrayed—an informant had led the Germans to their hideout. And this time she would not be able to talk her way out of it, since the house abounded with evidence of undercover work as well as arms and materials for sabotage.

She was arrested and taken to Paris for intensive interrogation, and although it is said she was brutally tortured, Violette gave the Germans no information. Finally, as the autumn in Paris came to an end, she was herded onto a train with hundreds of other prisoners bound for the concentration camps in the East. Violette was sent to Ravensbrueck, a facility for female prisoners in the province of Mecklenburg, north of Berlin, and the site of some of the most vile Nazi medical experiments.

Violette Szabo was never put on trial but simply imprisoned in the German death camp. In the spring of 1945, as the Allied armies were surging into a collapsed Germany, just a few weeks before the war's end, Violette Szabo was taken out of her squalid barracks, marched to a wall of the prison, and shot to death. She was awarded posthumously the George Cross, Britain's highest civilian honor.

Memoirs of an Ex-Spy

Because former spies do not often talk about their activities, this is a unique account of how an agent got into the business and what it is really like. The article was written by Ted Allbeury, a former British counterintelligence officer (and author of five espionage novels), and is reprinted by permission of Workman Publishing Company from Murder Ink *by Dilys Wynn (copyright © 1977).*

Harry Truman, when asked what it was like to be president, said, "It's great for the first two minutes." Similarly with being a spy, except you're never actually a spy, because in the business the word is never used. Inside MI-5 and MI-6 you're an intelligence officer or a counterintelligence officer, and if you live on the west bank of the Potomac and normally turn left at Langley where the sign says "Bureau of Public Roads," you're called an agent.

Way back, you would have been recruited in your second year at Oxford or Cambridge. Your membership in the university's Communist party would have been written off as growing pains, provided you could drop a Latin tag in the right place—which meant that the intelligence services, like Homer, nodded from time to time and that would sometimes lead to keen cricketers ending their days boozing in Moscow and getting the test match results four days late.

World War II let poor boys become four-star generals and ruined this Olde Worlde sanctuary. If you wanted men who could speak Estonian and who knew the difference between Lombardo and Ellington, you had to cast your net much wider.

And there were those who didn't wait for the net but swam inside, waving their Union Jacks. I was one of those.

How did I get into this elite? There could be only one way—the personal columns of the London Times. The advert asked for linguists, and my interview took place at the back of a barber's shop in Trafalgar Square. They tested my French and German, and I swore my one ambition was to lie in the rain in wet ditches. Officers with penetrating eyes were anxious to know whether I liked my father better than my mother, and others asked what I could see in various inkblots. Photographs were flashed on a screen, and ten or so of us likely lads had to describe what they represented. Rumor had it that what we said would be utterly revealing of our minds. With this daunting prologue, it was little wonder that an otherwise normal young man was driven to describe a naked couple on a bed as a "nurse tending a wounded man." We also underwent the usual medical checks, with our urine examined for Communist infiltration. The officers running the battery of tests fell into two distinct groups: The seniors were cast in the mold of C. Aubrey Smith; the juniors were young captains with short hair-cuts and an air of already knowing every skeleton in our closets. When it was all over, they said, "We'll check carefully on your background. Don't ring us."

A week later, I was a full-fledged member of the Intelligence Corps, inducted by an archetypal colonel, who told me my background had been researched with diligence and I was joining a fine club. "Bring," he said affably, "your sports car, your golf clubs, everything." That was my first moment of doubt. Somebody had got my background all wrong, diligent look-see or not. I had just bought my first second-hand bicycle for $2.00 and had only once sat in a car; I didn't own golf clubs; I barely owned a jacket.

Regardless, I reported to the Intelligence Corps depot at what previously had been a theological college in Winchester. Here I hobnobbed with professors of French and German who could write theses on trade unions in the Middle Ages but couldn't ask a girl out for coffee. On our second day, a Sunday, which even in the Intelligence Corps follows Saturday and the Saturday night dance, the professors and I were detailed to clean up the abandoned prophylactic devices as our introduction to security work. This led to much quoting of Rabelais and Juvenal.

We were taught very advanced map-reading and then abandoned in the night in fields of cows to find our way home. We tailed "suspects" through the busy streets of South-ampton and found it gave us time to make dates with the girls in Woolworth's. We learned how to strip and reassemble a whole range of weapons—blindfolded, of course. We were given extensive instruction on the organization of the military machine, which subsequently proved useful for knowing how to indent for rations and services you were not entitled to. Several weeks were devoted to a rough-riding course on motorcycles, and our egos inflated when we learned ours would always be tuned to give us more speed than those of the military police. (Some of us later forgot that the additional weight of a girl on the pillion would eliminate this advantage.)

The badge of the Intelligence Corps was the red-and-white roses of Lancaster and York entwined in a laurel wreath. Referred to by our envious contemporaries in the other services as a "pansy resting on its laurels," it added luster to our nickname "the eunuchs" (there were no privates in the Intelligence Corps).

In Scotland, our trainers were ex-Shanghai policemen, who spent two months borrowing my body to show more delicate frames how to severely injure or, if necessary, kill the enemy. "Okay, lofty, you," they said, pointing a finger at me when no one volunteered for these exercises. I was a tall lad, alas.

At various points, members of the Class of '40 dropped off the production line. The nervous would go as interrogators at prisoner of war camps; the mathematicians and chess players went to the cryptography setup at Bletchley Park. The cream of the dregs that were left would go on to aggravate the king's enemies and on occasion his friends.

When you read spy thrillers about that daring MI-5 man doing his stuff in Berlin, just quietly ask for your money back. MI-5 only operates in the United Kingdom. And even though it's responsible for internal security, MI-5 doesn't even arrest naughty boys in the UK. The Special Branch does the dirty work for them. Besides, now it's called DI-5.

MI-6 is responsible for counterespionage and espionage, and it's now DI-6, sometimes referred to as SIS, the Secret Intelligence Service. If you land up in that camp, your pay will be tax-free to prevent even the Inland Revenue from putting two and two together. One finds SIS boys in all the old, familiar places: journalism, Rolls-Royce franchises, banking, oil companies, language schools, and departments of history at universities. They're recognizable by their charm and fondness for Jamieson Ten Year Old. In later life, they take up religion, in the style of Malcolm Muggeridge, and grow roses in Britain's equivalent of the Bermuda Triangle—the borders of Sussex and Kent.

Intelligence work, like computery, has its own vocabulary, and you can date an alumnus of the theological college fairly accurately. There's a touch of the Scott Fitzgerald about wartime alumni, with echoes of Adlai Stevenson. Today's boys are definitely more Daniel Patrick, with a shade of Haldeman if under stress. But there are still some consistently used words:

Debriefing consists of a man with cold blue eyes listening to your side of the story when you return from an operation. It's a mixture of explaining why you're still alive and why you had to stay at the most expensive hotel in Berlin.

A *safe house* is where you go to be briefed or to rest or to escape the bad guys.

Dead-letter drop is the place where you leave messages in code on the secrets of IBM's latest software (like you used to leave the girl friend love letters in the geranium pot because her mother wouldn't let you on the premises).

The *cutout* is the man who keeps your identity from field operators.

Blown means that the elaborate cover story your directorate wrote to protect you has been exposed. I was "blown" by a dear old lady in Scotland. She was telling fortunes at a party and told the whole assembly exactly what I was up to. I was withdrawn, as they say, to Scottish Command HQ, and I often wonder what happened to that old lady.

Turned is what happens to operators who get caught and start trembling before they're even asked their name, rank, and number. We did this to most of the German espionage agents in the UK during the war. They then got to live in luxury apartments in St. James's Street with the most beautiful "ladies" we could find. In return, we held their hands on their Morse keys when they sent their news back to Berlin. It went on for years, and there were several of us who wished it could've happened to us.

In Occupied Germany, we cooperated with the American CIC [Counterintelligence Corps]. On the grounds of security, however, both intelligence organizations kept just a little bit of information back. I well remember a joint operation in which 40 plainclothes operatives had to find a central information clearing point that would not arouse suspicion if visited frequently by large numbers of men. The CIC had theirs, we had ours, and neither would confide its place to the other. Halfway through the morning of the roundup, I had to deal with an angry city mayor, who complained bitterly that British and American civilians, all speaking frightfully bad German, were monopolizing the only public men's lavatory in town. Great spy minds had thought alike once again.

What makes a good intelligence agent? He certainly won't be a James Bond type—arrogant, pseudosophisticated, and mentally ill-equipped. Bond wouldn't get past the first selection filter. If pressed to give an opinion as to what made me suitable material, I should unhesitatingly attribute it to the fact that since my father died when I was a baby, I was brought up by a posse of women and some of their intuition rubbed off on me. As an intelligence officer, this combination of innate male cunning and feminine intuition served me well. The war my father fought in was to make "a land fit for heroes to

live in." My own war aim was to make "a land fit for cowards to live in." Heroes are for the Marines; only the well-tuned coward can survive in the world of espionage.

I've heard it said that once a spook, always a spook, but my own career doesn't bear this out. I left the counterintelligence business several years after the war, and although I've been contacted two or three times since, it was only to give advice. One reason for declining to stay on was an inclination on my part to quit the poker game while I still had my winnings; the other was a growing dislike of what I was doing. This was not from some high moral standpoint, nor a feeling that it should not be done, but that I personally had done it long enough. Playing games against the Italians was fun, but against the Germans it was solid, serious stuff—with venom in it on both sides. I was beginning to know too much about people and politics, and I needed a period of innocence.

Unfortunately, it's not quite that easy to reclaim. You can't be an experienced intelligence officer one day and an innocent civilian the next. The training, the experience, just won't go away. One of the earliest pieces of training is that everybody tells lies and you have to dig holes for people to fall in so you can find out as soon as possible in what area they're lying. In civilian life, you go on doing this. You don't always like the results, and neither do your victims. Little bells ring and red lights flash, because not only do you know when people are telling lies but you know they're going to before they know it themselves. It takes about three years before you're halfway back to normal. . . .

There's a club in London that I belong to called the Special Forces Club, and there you can see mild men who now sell insurance or wine who ended the war in Dachau or Belsen. There are schoolteachers who once calmly parachuted into the wet forests of the Dordogne. Unless we have another war, the club will soon close for lack of members, as we all head for our appointments in Samarra.

Behind Japanese Lines: Perils of a Guerrilla Fighter

One of the most incredible stories to come out of World War II was that of OSS Detachment 101, a special force whose members fought in the jungles of Burma, behind Japanese lines, from 1942 to 1945. With the aid of Kachin headhunters—Burmese natives loyal to the Allied forces and bitterly opposed to the Japanese—the men of Detachment 101 waged guerrilla warfare and collected and disseminated intelligence information in an atmosphere of constant peril.

Besides the ever-present danger of the Japanese army and those Burmese who had allied themselves with their conquerors, the men of 101 also had to do battle with the alien elements of the jungle and the tropics. It was a continual adventure, a seemingly endless trial of man's ability to combat the eccentricities and the inherent hazards of nature. The following excerpts offer some insight into what that adventure was for the OSS men of Detachment 101 during those three long years in the Burmese jungles. They are excerpted from the definitive book on that segment of American war history, Behind Japanese Lines *by Richard Dunlop, a member of the OSS whose reports are firsthand.*

As the men walked up the trail, streaming with sweat and itching with insect bites, they felt the prickly sensation that they were being observed by unseen eyes. Rounding a bend in the trail, they unexpectedly came upon three nearly naked Naga girls carrying baskets on their heads. Without a sound, the girls threw down the baskets and ran. There was the soft patter of bare feet on the path, and then silence. A slight breeze stirred the foliage by the trail, or was it a Naga spearman? The Burmese and the American were nowhere near the Inner Line, but the flight of the girls might well mean that the hard-to-understand Nagas were on the warpath.

"Call out and say we are friends," Eifler [101's commanding officer, Carl Eifler] told the agent.

"I don't speak their language."

"Well, damn it, say it in any language you can, then."

The agent gave him an agonized look, but he called out in Burmese and then in Hindi. Eifler shouted friendly greetings in Japanese. The silence was more profound, except for a coppersmith, which unaccountably began its song. Usually this bird began its "tong, tong, tong, tong" chant in the night, but here it was singing in the day. Perhaps the darkness and gloom of the jungle could account for the strange behavior, or perhaps instead the bird was not a bird at all, but rather a tribesman hidden among the giant ferns, signaling to other tribesmen who waited in ambush.

The two men moved ahead up the trail until they came out into a clearing. There in the middle of the open space three Naga men, naked except for loincloths, squatted on their heels around a cook fire. They paid no attention whatsoever to the strangers and made no response or motion as Eifler and the agent spoke to them in Burmese, Japanese, Hindi, and English and then vigorously pantomimed their friendly intentions. Still without any verbal response, one man at last reached into a woven bag which was tied around

his waist. He took out a tin can. The tin can contained a smaller tin can, which in turn contained still a smaller can. With deliberation he took can from within can, until from within the fifth can he drew out a piece of paper. He handed the paper to Eifler.

"The bearer of this note and his people wish to work for the U.S. Army," were the English words on the note. . . .

Six days later, as the American staff was sitting down to lunch, several Nagas strode out of the jungle carrying a basket woven of bamboo. Unsmiling and stolid, they put it down on the table amid the serving dishes. One of the Americans took off the lid. Within were the severed heads of [several] Japanese [infiltrators]. Gagging, the men dashed away from the lunch table. Carl Eifler remained seated. He calmly dug into his pocket, took out a fistful of silver rupees, and paid them to the Nagas. The Nagas clinked the rupees cheerfully in their hands, smiled at last, and slipped back into the jungle. . . .

•   •   •

Refugees fleeing through the Naga Hills to escape the catastrophe in Burma during the spring of 1942 fell easy prey to the tigers, who were numerous in the jungles. Many of the enormous striped cats developed a fondness for human flesh. It was so easy to come by and was so tender, particularly if the cat was growing old and his teeth were losing their strength. Then without warning the stream of easy kills ended, and only the hard-to-catch and difficult-to-kill

Nagas were left in the hills. In search of more toothsome prey, tigers invaded the Nazira tea gardens. There the lithesome girls who picked the tea proved easy to seize and just as easy on the palate. Even at their camp on the edge of the tea plantations, A Group could hear the jungle cats prowling close by each night.

There was a rash of tiger encounters as the 101 men went about their night duties. Ozzie Klein, newly arrived from the States, was driving in a jeep along the road that ran beside the tracks of the Bengal and Assam. Something huge and shadowy loped along the road ahead of him. "That's a cow," Klein told the man at his side.

Suddenly the "cow" leaped ten feet straight up in the air, snarled, and sprang away into the dark. Cecil Crafts, a communications man who was also a new member of the group, drove a jeep along the same road with a Kachin boy. A tiger sprang into the headlights. The Kachin pulled out his newly issued .45 and fired at the beast, which jumped over a high bank and was gone.

Ray Peers [wrote about] a frightening encounter with a tiger as he drove down the road from Mackeypore to Behubier.

The Assam Company had removed a steel bridge to smelt for war purposes . . . and had made a detour around it while [replacing it with] a wooden one. As I drove along in the jeep, my mind was far away on activities in Burma, and I paid scant attention to the reflections from the eyes of the small burrowing owls sitting on numerous fence posts. As I approached the bridge barrier, I could see a couple of reflections but figured them to be a couple of owls on the posts. As I came closer, the lights of the jeep outlined a large body with eyes shining. I thought it was just another water buffalo roaming the countryside. When I was about 30 feet away, he turned sideways, and there was the biggest tiger I had ever seen. I was without a gun of any kind on a built-up road where I couldn't turn around, back up, or go forward; I was completely at his mercy.

They say tigers rarely exceed 500 pounds, but this creature appeared ten feet high and must have weighed a ton. I could only think, "If he makes one false move, I am going to give the jeep full throttle and head right at him." Perhaps he was about as scared as I, because he flicked his tail a couple of times and strolled across the railroad track and into the tea garden. I waited briefly and had to follow right behind him to take the detour through the jungle.

When I reached my destination, I obtained a rifle to carry in the jeep on the return trip, but, of course, I saw no tiger.

The next day Peers met Harold Geach, the manager of the Mackeypore Tea Garden. He told him of his experience.

"Yes, you undoubtedly saw the Mackeypore tiger," said Geach. "He is a huge brute, and do you know, that fellow has killed five Europeans in the past ten years that I know of."

A tiger might kill a human being for a snack, but it was much more worth its while to kill a water buffalo or a cow, since then there would be a good meat supply for several meals. One night a tiger jumped into the pen at the Lahksmijhan Tea Garden and stunned manager Ted Healy's prize Brahma bull with a sweep of its paw. Throwing the hapless 1,500-pound beast on its back, it seized it in its mouth and jumped over a four-foot fence, dragging the bull off into the jungle to eat the carcass at its convenience. . . .

Ted Healy had scarcely gotten over the loss of his bull when he strolled into the drawing room of his bungalow one night to get some cigarettes that he had left on the table. The lighter was in his bedroom so he went back to get it. As he came back into the drawing room, his dog rushed past him and pawed the rug, barking furiously, about six feet in front of the table. Healy snapped on the lights. Beneath the table, coiled and ready to strike, was a king cobra, nine feet long and four inches around. It had come in through an open window.

Carl Eifler and John Coughlin discovered that Charlie Ashfield also had some cobra residents. One day Ashfield's dog circled a stack of old lumber until the men gingerly joined in pulling the pile apart. Down at the bottom, nesting securely away from prying eyes, was a family of cobras. Three of them were seven to eight feet long, and some younger ones were each two to three feet. At the sight of all the deadly, writhing snakes the men felt a cold chill in their insides.

The ones in Charlie's house were common hooded cobras, which in their maturity reach a length of nine to ten feet, but their bite was just as venomous as that of the more terrifying Hamadryad or king cobra, which can grow to be 20 feet long. One king cobra, 20 feet long or so, regularly sunned itself on the road close to 101 headquarters.

"He'd feel our jeep coming and plunge over a five-foot wire fence and disappear," said Ray Peers. "We never could get close enough for a shot."

• • •

Once a thousand people had lived in the valley to which Peter Lutken now came. He stood on a high ridge and looked across the green jungles to the mountains on the far side. Where had all the people gone? Why had they gone away? The Kachins had a strange answer.

"It is because of the weretigers, duwa [leader]," said the jaiwa [soothsayer].

The other Kachins nodded their heads. They refused to enter the valley. It was one thing to fight the Japanese, but it was another thing to enter the domain of the magic tigers. No bullet or spear could wound them.

"A Kachin hunting party went in the valley," the jaiwa said. "It was only a week ago, and the men sat around their fire in the night. Suddenly several tigers attacked out of the jungle. One jumped over the fire, seized a hunter by his waist, and escaped. The hunters fired at him, but their bullets could not harm him.

"A Japanese patrol passed through the valley only ten days ago," continued the jaiwa. "In the middle of the valley they camped on a river bank. That night the tigers attacked the camp and ate all of the Japanese."

Lutken's Kachins built their campfires on the high ridge overlooking the valley, but they would not agree to cross the valley in the morning. Other 101 men have thought that perhaps they were haunted by ancestral fears of the giant tigers of the Burma jungles and imagined that weretigers existed. After Peter Lutken entered the valley, and after I too had an experience with a tiger at Sinlumkaba that same year, neither of us will ever be certain.

My tiger came in the night. I was sleeping in a stone rest house built by the British at Sinlumkaba, high in the mountains close to the Chinese border. The heavy wooden door of the house was closed, but the catch had long since been broken off, and it would not fasten. Sometimes in the night a gust of wind blowing through the valley would push the door open. We slept with our feet to the door. On my right was Mike, the Hindu radio operator who had walked into Sinlumkaba with me, and on my left was Ngai Tawng. We'd been playing cards late by candlelight, and I had won, which was not the rule. It was surprising how rapidly Kachins, even a youngster

like Ngai Tawng, could learn to play winning cards. I slept soundly.

"Dick!"

Mike was shaking me awake.

"What's the matter with you?" I growled.

"Dick! Wake up, there's a tiger outside the door!"

I listened. Something was scratching at the door.

"You're crazy. It's just a dog."

"No, it's a tiger. That's his claws."

Ngai Tawng slept peacefully. I sleepily reasoned that if there was indeed a tiger outside, a Kachin boy was more likely to know it than a pudgy Indian who had been born and raised in Calcutta. Mike insisted.

"Get your carbine," he said. "It is a tiger!"

"Mike, damn it all, go back to sleep. Last night you had an attack of malaria and kept us awake most of the night, and now you've got an attack of the tigers."

Despite Mike, I went back to sleep. In the morning we went to the door and opened it. There were enormous pugs to show where a tiger had indeed come up [to] the house, encircled it, paused at the door, and scratched his claws against it. With the slightest pressure, he could easily have opened the door and in one or two bounds been upon us. Even in the morning light I felt an involuntary shiver, but I was not nearly so frightened as Ngai Tawng. He stared at the tracks, his eyes round.

"Duwa Dick," he said in a shaking voice. "The tiger has five toes."

"Does it matter how many toes a tiger has?" I said. "I know people who have cats with five and even six toes."

"Duwa Dick," he said. "Only a weretiger has five toes, same as a man has five fingers."

I could see that the boy was very frightened for the first time since he had joined us. I put my arm around his shoulders.

"Don't worry," I assured him. "The tiger won't be back tonight."

"That is so," he said. "If he wanted one of us, he could have had us last night. He won't bother us again." . . .

"Some villages are well known for their weretigers," [the jaiwa] said. "There is said to be one near Sinlumkaba, to the east and closer to the Chinese border. You have to know the right spells to turn into a weretiger, and those people know the spells. My village also has men who know the spells."

"How do you turn into a weretiger?" I asked.

Whenever a jaiwa tells a legend of his people, sings one of the old ballads, or speaks of magic lore, he sucks in air through a puckered mouth as if he is fanning his imagination with his own breath. He alters his voice to speak in a reedy whisper. The jaiwa spoke in this soothsayer's voice.

"You must take off all your clothing so that you are naked before the night spirit. The clothing should be rolled into a neat bundle. Then you must throw yourself naked on the ground. You roll from side to side as a tiger rolls in its ecstasy, and you say the incantations. As you roll, your body lengthens, and your head flattens and changes its place in rela-

tion to your shoulders so that it is as a tiger's head. A tail appears from your tailbone, and your legs and arms turn to paws. Your nails grow into claws, and your body grows stronger and furrier and striped until you are a tiger. When you speak, you growl, and when you shout, you roar."

The strange voice and the strange words filled me with dread, for the thought came to me that perhaps this very jaiwa could turn himself into a tiger. The thought had occurred to Ngai Tawng too, and he spoke to the jaiwa in a very respectful, almost pleading voice.

"How can a weretiger become a man again?"

"The tiger goes about his business of killing and devouring his prey. He may seek vengeance on a villager who has become his enemy. He may seek the flesh of a woman. He may devour his own wife or his daughter, but he often prefers to enjoy instead the firm flesh of a young boy."

The jaiwa stopped to look almost hungrily at Ngai Tawng, who hunkered down farther on his heels with a stricken look on his face.

"A tiger may roam for many miles, and he may be away from his village for weeks, but at last he comes back to where he has left his clothing. When he sees the clothing lying on the ground, he may then turn back into a man. He rolls and stretches and grows smaller and once again takes on his human form. He puts his clothing back on and returns to his village."

Lutken, sitting in his camp with the Kachins and looking down on the valley that the Kachins said was infested with weretigers, knew that there was something down there in the dark that had frightened his brave Kachins. He called the duwa to him. According to his maps, the valley was 42 miles across.

"Will you cross the valley if we make the entire trip between dawn and sunset?" he asked. "I promise you that we will not camp in the valley or be in it when the night comes."

Even with Lutken's reassurances the duwa was not at all happy about telling the men that they must cross the valley. The fires were kept high all that night. The men jammed close together about the fire to sleep.

"I slept in a hammock," Lutken recalls. "Usually I slept by myself, but that night the Kachins jostled one another to sleep beneath me."

At first light, the company ate breakfast in haste.

"I've never eaten so fast," Lutken says. "I've never walked so fast or so far as when crossing that valley either. There was not a sound or a single clank of equipment as we went down the trail that led down into the valley. I got a foreboding feeling. The valley was dark with a canopy of giant trees, and the cover along the trail was, nevertheless, thick. It was muddy."

At noon the hurrying Kachins reached the river that flowed through the heart of the valley. It was clear that there, beneath a large banyan tree, the Japanese patrol had camped. The supplies and equipment of the patrol were scattered about as if a violent storm had struck. There were struggle marks, but no signs of the soldiers. Everywhere were enormous tiger pugs. Some-

body had carved "TIGER" in English on the trunk of the trees. "Run, don't camp here" was carved beneath it in smaller letters. Nearby on the trunk a similar warning was cut into the bark in Burmese script.

"I guess the Japanese couldn't read either English or Burmese," Lutken told me.

The Kachins glanced at the havoc about them and forded the stream without a moment's pause. They ran on up the trail with Lutken, for once, puffing along behind them. They did not even pause when they passed by a half-eaten Japanese soldier decomposing by the trail. Lutken didn't pause either. Terror chased after the fleeing men. They did not stop running until they were well up on the mountain on the far side of the valley. They kept moving, glancing fearfully behind them. Finally at midnight, when they were well out of the valley, the hypenlas [soldiers] stopped their flight and collapsed in exhaustion. Even then they started up from their sleep to look in terror back down the trail toward the valley of the weretigers.

．　．　．

"If you are bitten by one of them, better kiss your wife good-bye, because that is about all you will have time for," the planters told the Americans.

They were warning the OSS men about the krait, a tiny, wiggling shoelace of a reptile that was so deadly its venom usually brought about death within 20 minutes. If the bite was in a particularly vulnerable place a victim might die in two minutes. The krait was called the "widow snake," the "kiss of death," or the "shoe snake" because it crept into a man's shoes at night and waited, snug and happy, for him to slip his foot inside in the morning. It also was called the "door snake" because it was fond of dozing atop a door ledge. When the door was slammed, the sleeping krait tumbled down onto the shoulders of an unsuspecting person below.

"The krait is not a vicious snake," said Ray Peers, always accurate even when it came to poisonous reptiles. "He bites only in self-defense. If he is stepped on, or rolled on in a sleeping bag, he may strike. We had the most difficulty with them in our shoes. Everyone got in the habit of banging their shoes on the floor a couple of times before putting them on in the morning. There were about eight of us sleeping in one large room, and during one week, three kraits were found in our shoes."

The men had screened in an open space beneath one of the bungalows to provide more space. One night Bob Aitken and Ray Peers were working late in the enclosed space when they heard something pushing at the screen door.

"See what it is," suggested Peers, his mind on the training plans laid out on the table in front of him.

"We have a caller all right," said Aitken when he stepped to the door. "Look for yourself."

Peers joined his friend. A krait of nightmarish size was outside lunging against the screen. Instead of the pencil-like snake that they had expected a krait to be, it was an enormous, banded reptile, six feet long. In a way, the black and yellow creature was beautiful, but it also was deadly. The snake had the two men at its mercy. There was only one door leading out of the enclosure, and once a man stepped through this he had to walk down a dark passageway. In the gloom the snake could strike him at any time.

There was a screened window on the far side of the room. Peers knocked it out and climbed through the aperture. He stole up the stairs into the bungalow, returned with a shotgun, and stationed himself in a hall that crossed the one in which the snake lurked. Fortunately, Aitken had a flashlight. The snake had disappeared from the doorway, but now that Peers was in position, he carefully opened the screen door and began a wary advance. His flashlight stabbed into the gloom. There was the snake! It was coiled and ready to strike. Aitken was slow and patient. He must not goad the krait into an attack. The snake was just as slow. As it uncoiled and slid indolently along the floor away from him, Aitken kept it in the beam of his flashlight.

Peers, waiting at the cross hall, saw the patch of light advance beyond the corner of the wall. Then the snake poked its head into view. It glided forward. Peers pulled the trigger. At the shotgun's roar, 101 men sleeping in the bungalow above leaped out of their beds, snatched up their weapons, and came running. They found that the blast from Peers's weapon had blown about a foot off the front of the snake, still writhing in its death agony. At least, the 101 men agreed, a banded krait had the advantage of being too big to crawl into a man's shoe.

Operation Gunnerside

The pilot had been informed by weather control that the sky would be clear above the North Sea but cloudy over the mountains of south-central Norway on the night of March 28, 1942. Perfect, the crew agreed, as its unmarked, four-motor RAF plane carried its lone passenger to his destination in a remote area of Telemark province, some 60 miles west of Oslo.

Above that desolate, rugged splash of land, the drone of the propeller-driven engines came first. Then the airplane itself, only a vague, dark silhouette, emerged from the clouds, and while it made a sweeping circle over the mountainous terrain, a panel door slid open, and a single figure tumbled out into the night, quickly being jolted erect as his parachute filled with air. The figure, dressed totally in black even to a ski mask, and the black parachute blended invisibly with the darkness as he floated to earth. The airplane continued its bank but now began to ascend into the clouds for the journey back to England.

The man in black landed safely, appearing in sudden, stark contrast to the virgin white snow. He quickly rolled his parachute, grabbed his other gear, and headed for the protection of the trees not far away. There, in the bitter Scandinavian cold and the awesome stillness of the mountains, he peeled off his jump suit and hid it along with the parachute, put on his skis and pack, and headed down the mountain.

One of the greatest sabotage efforts in history had just begun.

"Gunnerside" was the code name of the super-secret project. The brainchild of a group of British and American intelligence officers, it would be carried out by a crack team of Norwegian espionage agents. Allied intelligence, by early 1942, had located the plant where the Germans were producing heavy water, an ingredient necessary for the nuclear experiments they were conducting in an effort to develop an atom bomb. Sources had determined that the location was somewhere within a Norsk Hydro factory compound in an isolated area of Telemark province. The man who parachuted in that frigid March night was a Norwegian agent who had fled his homeland almost two years earlier, when the Germans moved in to occupy Norway. Now he was back to lay the groundwork for Gunnerside. He would verify the exact site where the heavy water was being produced, determine the German defense facilities there, and gather as much other intelligence material as he could.

For 11 months, the Norwegian agent clandestinely radioed his findings back to England. There, all the intelligence was evaluated and disseminated, and the next phase of the operation was being formulated. Models of the plant were built in England, and detailed architectural renderings of the building complex were created. Norwegian agents practiced the assault that they would one day attempt, learning how to face any emergency or contingency that might arise in such a hostile battleground, and how and where to place the demolition charges. By February 1943, they were ready, or at least as ready as they could ever be, for such a daring adventure. By the end of that month, they had been smuggled into Norway, along with all the equipment, arms, munitions, and other supplies they would need.

The staging area was a mountain hut, about a three-hour journey on skis and by foot to the Norsk Hydro factory. There were two separate groups. One was the demolition team, the other was called the covering party—one to lay the explosives, the other to protect the first group while it was doing it.

Only 15 German soldiers were assigned to guard Norsk Hydro, the agent had reported. He also determined that at night, only two Germans were on guard duty at any given time and that the guard duty changed every two hours. There were a number of Norwegian guards too, but they were concentrated inside the factory buildings and would probably cause little interference, their sympathies not residing with the army that occupied their country.

The operation was set for the night of February 27, 1943, weather and all other factors permitting. The agent in charge of the demolition team, referred to simply as X, was in command. He gave the order as darkness fell that night—the operation was on. The two teams set out for their target, skiing most of the way but traveling the last mile or two on foot. It was a quiet night, with good cloud cover making it protectively dark.

Less than a mile from the plant, as the groups were walking along the plowed side of a road approaching the Vaaer bridge, a small stone structure that spanned a frozen river, a pair of headlights reached out around a curve on the other side of the road. The highly trained saboteurs reacted instantly and scattered down the river bank before the vehicle and its driver came around the bend. One bus rumbled over the bridge, then another, carrying workers up to another plant in the town of Rjukan. The men then climbed back up to the road, and brushing the snow from their uniforms, they moved on, aware that if it weren't for a few seconds' warning and the fortunate proximity of the bridge, the operation would have been blown.

The two German guards were normally posted at the front and rear entrances to the factory compound. A tall chicken wire fence topped with barbed wire ringed the entire complex. The Gunnerside leader planned to enter through a railroad gate, which was effectively concealed from both German guard posts.

About one-third mile from the factory, in a copse of trees, the Norwegians cached their skis and discussed last-minute instructions. The factory was in view, although it appeared to the men as a dark outline against the snow and the sky, because as a precaution against air raids all the windows had been painted black and there were no lights outside the buildings. But even though it looked deserted, the hum of the machinery inside could be heard clearly by the saboteurs. They waited in this last outpost until 12:20 A.M., when one of the men who had crept up near the front gate returned to the group and told X that the guard had been changed and everything inside the compound appeared to be quiet.

At exactly 12:30 A.M., the two teams moved into place about 100 yards from the railroad gate. One member of the covering team crouched and ran toward the gate. Armed with a powerful pair of wire cutters, he made three or four cuts, sending sharp cracking sounds into the night; fortunately, these were lost in the noise from the factory. He then raised the cutting shears in the air and dropped them, giving the signal to move out—the gates were open.

The men in the covering party, one armed with a machine gun and one with a .45 strapped to his waist, led the way. The demolition team was directly behind them. Inside the gate, the covering party veered quickly to the left to take up defensive positions around the German barracks, while the demolition party headed straight for the factory building, whose cellar housed the heavy-water facility. As X and the three other members of the demolition team reached the cellar door, down a flight of stairs from ground level, they paused for any alien sound but heard nothing out of the ordinary. The door was securely locked and its heavy metal plating and bolting rendered it impossible for them to break

it open. The four men moved quickly back up the stairs to try the door at ground level, but it too was bolted.

They would have to use the cable tunnel, which they knew was there and accessible from the outside; at least that was what the intelligence reports said. X and one member of the team began to search for it, while the other two left to find another door on a different side of the building. Finally, X found the tunnel, and he and his compatriot crawled along the pipes and conduits into the building. They found a trapdoor that X calculated would open into a room adjacent to the heavy-water facility in the cellar. Sidling up to the inner door and then bursting into the heavy-water room, they totally surprised the Norwegian guard, who stared wide-eyed with fright at the two men pointing machine guns at him. He quickly surrendered his rifle.

X then began to lay demolition charges around the tanks and machinery, just as he had practiced in England. With only three left to be planted, however, a window pane shattered above them, the glass crashing to the floor. X grabbed for his machine gun, but his partner had already turned his weapon to the window, only to find one of the other members of the demolition team staring back at him. Not being able to get in any other way, he and his partner in desperation decided to break the window. Now they stood frozen, waiting for a fusillade to erupt as the Germans came pouring out of their barracks or as the guards at the two gates came running to see what had happened. But nothing disturbed the humming of the machines, which continued to dominate the night.

Quickly, X laid the last three charges; he and his partner lit the fuses; and then he turned to the unarmed guard, who was still gaping at him. "Get the hell out of here!" he said. They all raced from the building and were not more than 20 yards away when the first blast rocked the compound, followed by a string of ear-shattering concussions that shook the ground underfoot.

The guards at the gates left their posts, and lights came on in the German barracks, but by the time the first German reached the smoking building, the demolition team, along with the covering party, was already through the railroad gates. And by the time the Germans figured out just what had happened, the Norse saboteurs were skiing to the west to a secret rendezvous, where they would be picked up and flown out of Norway.

Operation Gunnerside was a key element in derailing the German efforts to create an atom bomb. Without the success of Operation Gunnerside and subsequent clandestine actions, Hitler's war machine might have developed weaponry that could have altered the course of the war and world history.

On the Land
and in the Mountains

An Interview with Sir Edmund Hillary

The title of world's most famous mountain climber belongs justifiably to Sir Edmund Hillary, who along with Sherpa Tenzing Norgay became the first to conquer Mount Everest, a feat accomplished at 11:30 A.M. on May 29, 1953. Besides being the first to scale the world's tallest mountain, Hillary was the first man after Captain Robert F. Scott to reach the South Pole overland, on January 4, 1958. His entire life has been one of adventurous expeditions and scientific exploration. He has searched the Himalaya mountains for the yeti, or abominable snowman; become the first to make the 180-mile ascent of the Sun Kosi River from the Indian border to Katmandu; and most recently was the first to lead a 1,500-mile jet-boat excursion from the mouth of the Ganges through some of the most treacherous white-water rapids in the world to the river's source high on the icy slopes of the Himalayan mountain Akash Parbat.

Sir Edmund Hillary, born in Auckland, New Zealand, in 1919, is by experience a mountaineer, explorer, conservationist, river-runner, author, apiarist, and great friend to the people of the Himalayas. Over the years he has helped build scores of schools, roads, hospitals, and airfields for the people of Nepal. An inveterate adventurer, he is also a true romantic; in his own words: "I was always too restless and life was a constant battle against boredom. . . . I have had the world lie beneath my clumsy boots and seen the red sun slip over the horizon after the dark Antarctic winter. I have had more than my share of excitement, beauty, laughter, and friendship."

R. W.: With the wide range of adventurous things you've undertaken—Mount Everest, the yeti expedition, Antarctica, island exploring during the war—what was the most memorable adventure of your life?

HILLARY: I find that very hard to answer. I suppose as far as the world is concerned, the ascent of Everest was the major achievement. But I've found that more or less every adventure I've undertaken is the most important at that time. I've certainly had just as many exciting moments and just as great a sense of success in other adventures as I did on Mount Everest.

R. W.: Has anyone else to your knowledge been to the two most remote places on earth—Mount Everest and the South Pole?

HILLARY: Not to my knowledge, but that doesn't say that some haven't. There are quite a few people who have climbed Mount Everest, and it's by all means possible that at least one of them would have been to the South Pole as well.

R. W.: Are there still any remote places you have a desire to go to?

HILLARY: There are dozens of exotic places, I suppose, that would be exciting. The opportunity of my ever visiting them might be just as remote as time goes by. But there are certainly corners of the globe that have been relatively unexplored that I would still love to get to.

R. W.: In all your various adventures, what do you think is the single most dangerous or fearsome?

HILLARY: Once again I find that difficult to answer. If you've been at it as long as I have, inevitably you've been involved in dozens of occasions where there's been a possibility of disaster. I think perhaps that's one of the major attractions of adventuring—periodically you do have somewhat traumatic experiences. I think this adds something to the whole adventure thing. It's a stimulating factor—fear is a stimulator—and as long as you can overcome your fear, I think it certainly means at the conclusion of the expedition that it's given you a greater sense of satisfaction.

R. W.: You mentioned in your book, *Nothing Venture, Nothing Win*, that fear accompanied you on many of your adventures. Can you tell me a little more about this kind of fear? How does it affect you?

HILLARY: Well, I'm quite a fearful person. I wouldn't say I'm cowardly or anything like that—in the sense of running away from fear—but I'm certainly very much aware of things that are dangerous and try and take good care to see that I can overcome the problems and the fear of them. I do feel very strongly that one of the great motivations of explorers and adventurers is this question of fear. You know you hear of people who say they are completely lacking in fear. Well, there may be a few of them around, but I think in general someone who says that is usually kidding himself.

R. W.: You almost lost your life in the Pacific in World War II—in a boating accident. Have you ever had as close a call with death?

HILLARY: Yes, I think I have on a number of occasions—in the Himalayas. I've had to be taken off the mountain. I've fallen down crevasses and been involved in avalanches, which could have been fatal. It's happened on more than one occasion. And I think this is all once again part of the challenge really. You have a basic knowledge of mountaineering, but you need a reasonably quick reaction to escape from danger. That's very important.

R. W.: What would you characterize as the five most challenging mountains in the world to climb? Is that a reasonable question?

HILLARY: It's a difficult one because it depends on many things. A mountain like Everest, for instance, has certain characteristics—it's very big, and the problems of altitude are very great, and then it does depend considerably upon the actual route you climb. Many mountains can be climbed rather easily by, say, the standard route, but they may be extremely difficult by a more demanding route. So I would have great difficulty in picking out just five mountains. There are simply hundreds of mountains that by the difficult route are extremely hard to climb. Then too there's always the weather factor. A mountain that may be quite straightforward if the weather is adequate can be a real death trap under bad weather conditions.

R. W.: Wasn't Makalu one mountain that you had particular trouble with?

HILLARY: We certainly had our problems on Makalu, but I think that the standard route that we successfully ascended on one occasion would not be regarded as one of the most formidable routes on that mountain, and certainly not in the Himalayas. There are other routes that have been climbed on Makalu now, the west ridge, for instance, climbed by the French—a magnificent climb and a very difficult one.

R. W.: What did you feel when you first laid eyes on Mount Everest?

HILLARY: It was very exciting actually. I think the first time I really saw Mount Everest was from down on the India-Nepal border, at a place called Birātnagar. This was when we were going into Everest on the reconnaissance in 1951. It was a very clear morning, and we could see on the horizon a big mountain far off but looming up. The local people assured us that was Mount Everest. I really don't know whether it was or not, but it was certainly an impressive-looking peak. As we traveled across country, we finally got up into the Khumbu Valley and climbed up toward Namche [Bazar], and then we had our first really good view of Everest, and it certainly was impressive. There was a long tail of windblown snow trailing out from the summit, and that certainly was a very exciting moment.

R. W.: I'm sure you've been asked this question a thousand times, but could you tell me how you felt when you finally reached the summit of Everest?

HILLARY: I think in many ways perhaps my reaction was less ecstatic than people might think. We were tired—we had been coming a long way, and then we had this constant concern about the descent from the mountain. And this aspect tended to reduce a lot of our excitement in reaching the summit. But I did have sort of a deep sense of satisfaction, and I can remember it very clearly. I had this feeling of surprise that here was Ed Hillary at the top of Mount Everest. People had been trying to climb it for a long time. And it almost seemed surprising that it should be me, finally, who was standing there on the summit.

R. W.: You had first anticipated going with Eric Shipton, but then that was changed, wasn't it?

HILLARY: Eric Shipton was initially to be the leader of the 1953 Everest expedition. But there were some disagreements in London on this, and finally John Hunt took over the leadership. He was a very competent leader too.

R. W.: What were the things you most feared in the ascent of Mount Everest? What would be the greatest dangers in climbing a mountain like that?

HILLARY: I think probably in many ways the most dangerous place is the icefall, which is relatively low down the mountain, going from about seventeen thousand up to nineteen thousand feet. The major dangers are that it's under constant movement and it's got massive crevasses and ice pinnacles that come tumbling down periodically. On quite a number of occasions, we would come up our route in the morning and find the route peppered with chunks of ice, which had come from the breaking down of ice pinnacles. Many people have lost their lives on the icefall in the ascents. Then once you get above the icefall, the climbing was just hard work and demanding, and life gets pretty miserable at high altitudes, no doubt about that. But the actual, technical side of it wasn't too terrible. In the final summit ridge,

the south summit to the top, there was a step in the ridge that we knew would be something of a problem and that has proved to be reasonably demanding for all the expeditions that actually climbed the mountain. In actual fact, they call it the "Hillary step" these days, and it is one of the more difficult stretches on the climb.

R. W.: If you had miscalculated the oxygen or had to use up more than anticipated, would you have been able to get back down?

HILLARY: Oh, I think we would have. You must remember that we, as first up there, had a limited knowledge of what effect lack of oxygen would have on us at those altitudes. We didn't know, so we took a lot of precautions. Physiologists back then indicated that if we ran out of oxygen at twenty thousand feet that there was a very grave danger we would collapse and die. We know now this is not true—in actual fact, the body can resist the lack of oxygen for quite an extensive period of time. If it were too long, however, you would certainly suffer brain damage from the lack of oxygen. But in general, we had oxygen—sufficient oxygen, shall we say—certainly all that was allowable, we carried with us. We did in fact run out of oxygen before we got back down to the south col, but at least we had enough to get down there.

R. W.: When you went in search of the abominable snowman, or the yeti, as it's called, did you feel that there was much more than a remote chance that it really existed?

HILLARY: No, I didn't actually. I had grave doubts about the existence of the abominable snowman. But there was a lot of evidence that seemed to indicate that something was milling around up there. I didn't have any reasonable explanations to say that it didn't exist. In effect, our expedition wasn't an expedition to go off to find the abominable snowman. It was an expedition to examine all the evidence and try to assess whether or not the creature actually did exist. I think this was an advantage we had over other expeditions that had in a sense committed to try and *find* the abominable snowman. We wanted to find out whether there was one. And it was a very interesting experience. We found tracks in the snow that the local people said were the tracks of the abominable snowman, and we found out how these particular tracks had been formed. They were made by the tracks of the Himalayan fox, and the sun had shone down on the snow and melted these tracks, and they'd run together—and they did look like giant footprints, there's no question about it. But by following these tracks and going into an area where the snowslide was lying away from the sun, where it wasn't getting melted, instead of the giant footprints, suddenly there would be a group of footprints of the Himalayan fox,

showing that this was the animal that had created them. Then we looked at all the other evidence, the stories from the lamas in the monasteries—we interviewed all the lamas in the area—and although they claimed to believe in the existence of this creature, the fact remains that none of them claimed personally to have seen one. It was always Lama Bill Jones over in the next valley who had seen one. Then we saw Lama Bill Jones, and he said it was Lama Tom Smith, and so on. It sort of went around from one to the other, and we weren't able to find one lama who personally claimed to have seen it. We came to the conclusion in the end that the creature was essentially mythological. I'd be delighted to be proven wrong, but I have a feeling that this is not the case.

R. W.: Did you have any contingency plans, in case you did in fact come upon one, to capture or photograph it?

HILLARY: Oh, yes, we did indeed. We had some of these guns that shoot drugs that would put the animal to sleep. We had every intention of having a thorough survey of the creature made and even bringing the animal back to the Western world to be examined. It would have been a fascinating experience to have discovered this creature. There are animals in the Himalayas that are certainly very uncommon. The Tibetan blue bear, for instance, is a very rare animal. And on occasions, I'm sure it has been sighted on the

Nepalese side of the border, seen by Sherpas and quite possibly mistaken for the traditional yeti.

R. W.: You had one of the skins of the blue bear scientifically analyzed, didn't you?

HILLARY: Yes, we did. We had claimed one of the skins of the blue bear and brought it to Chicago, where we had it examined by the Chicago Natural History Museum. There are a number of blue bear skins in various museums around the world. But it still is a very rare animal. And certainly even for the Sherpas, it would be quite uncommon to see one, and if they did see one, one could understand their taking it for the abominable snowman.

R. W.: Do you feel that the North American sasquatch, the creature called bigfoot, belongs in the same realm of mythology as the yeti?

HILLARY: I'm rather inclined to think so, because people have been looking for it for so long, and there are such an awful lot of people in the United States. It seems difficult to believe that more evidence wouldn't have been obtained of this creature by now. Perhaps something does exist, but the story has been around for so long and so little real evidence has been produced that I have the feeling that it once again is a bit of mythology.

R. W.: In Antarctica, you endured some tremendously low temperatures. How would you describe that kind of cold, say, to a person who's only experienced the cold of the middle latitudes?

HILLARY: Well, although we had very cold temperatures—minus sixty-five and that—we were very well equipped. On the other hand, even though we were traveling to the South Pole, we didn't have any heating in our tractors. But we had very warm down clothing. Most of the time, we didn't suffer too severely from the cold. I think having good equipment makes all the difference, of course.

R. W.: How in fact did you dress?

HILLARY: We had a wide variety of things. Close to the skin we had these string singlets, you know, these open-weave singlets that allow the circulation of the air. And then we had woolen undershirts and woolen shirts. Also we had woolen sweaters. And then on the outside, there would be a dacron jacket and then finally a large heavy down jacket, which was also windproof.

R. W.: Were there any special precautions that had to be taken because of the cold or any extraordinary measures because of the severity of the climate? I remember a friend of mine telling me that when he was up in Fairbanks, Alaska, that you could not run in the severe cold because your lungs would freeze.

HILLARY: It's always been believed that at temperatures below minus forty, you shouldn't run your dog teams because they would get frostbitten lungs and you yourself, if you ran around at those temperatures, could be affected the same way. We in fact didn't find this to be true. We ran our dogs at minus forty and below, and certainly they didn't come to any harm. And we ourselves were out driving our tractors in temperatures down to minus sixty, and I wouldn't say we suffered any major discomfort from it. It was, of course, pretty chilly at times, but I don't think we got any serious effect on our lungs. Possibly, under certain circumstances, this could occur if you were really exerting yourself strenuously in these very cold temperatures.

R. W.: Were there any especially fear-producing instances on that expedition?

HILLARY: There were. One reason was that it was a very long-term expedition, a matter of many months traveling south to the Pole, and we traveled through many crevasse areas. Driving tractors through crevasse areas is a rather uncomfortable sort of business. The weight of a tractor, of course, will break through a bridge over a crevasse, and on quite a number of occasions, we had this happen to us. We had tractors sink down in a crevasse. We had large bars welded on the front to lengthen the tractors, and we pulled behind heavy troughs with large loads on them, so that generally speaking the tractors wouldn't go down very far. Then with the light tractors that we were using, we roped them together so that all the tractors were

joined together. If one went down it would be held up by the very strong ropes to the other tractors. This proved highly advantageous on a number of occasions. But it was a constant worry. There's no question that as one was driving along, one never really knew at any moment if you might break through into a crevasse. This meant that literally for months, we were under constant tension, and it became wearing.

R. W.: Did you encounter any interesting forms of wildlife down there?

HILLARY: Not on the polar plateau. The polar plateau is devoid of wildlife. I don't even remember seeing any birds of any type. But around the coastal areas of Antarctica, there is a vast amount of wildlife—seals, penguins, and quite an extensive variety of birds. The coastal area of Antarctica is actually very beautiful. Although there isn't a variety of color, there is a tremendous variation in the blues and greens of the ice and of the water, the white of the snow, and the black shades of the rocks. It's very attractive indeed.

R. W.: When you finally reached the South Pole, was there any special feeling that you might have experienced, say, similar to the kind of thing you felt on Mount Everest, or was it just a relief?

HILLARY: It was a relief, of course. But we had a very considerable sense of satisfaction on reaching the South Pole. We'd been worried. One of the reasons was that

our navigating over the polar plateau involved the use of sextants
and watching the sun. My sextant
was acting up, the actual bubble
enlarging and bumping against
the sides, and so we doubted the
accuracy of our observations. It
was a very good moment indeed
when we saw a flag that had been
planted by the American Pole station and knew that we had been
and were on the right track and
were able to check into the South
Pole quite safely.

R. W.: What would you consider today to be some of the great challenges for an adventurer?

HILLARY: I think that the more grandiose challenges have largely
been met—the poles have been
reached, and the summits of most
of the great mountains have been
conquered. I think the challenges
that the young climber and explorer now are meeting are a little
different. What they're doing is
more technique—their technical
competence, greater than ours,
and the much more sophisticated
equipment, which they know
how to use, open new horizons.
The trend is not so much more the
reaching of a summit today by the
most obvious route, which was
certainly our objective, but it is to
climb the mountain on a difficult
route. And in attempting a mountain on a difficult route, you get,
even though you've got all the
more sophisticated equipment,
the same challenge out of it that
we did out of just reaching the
summit. The young mountaineers are becoming extremely

competent technically and have
very good equipment; therefore,
they are looking toward harder
and harder objectives.

R. W.: One last question—you, I have
read, have been doing a lot of
work for the people in the
Himalayas, the Sherpas, in terms
of helping to establish hospitals
and schools. Could you tell me a
little bit about that?

HILLARY: It all really developed from
the fact that in the 1950s, I became extremely friendly with the
Sherpa people. The Sherpas
worked for us on expeditions carrying loads up to considerable altitudes. They're very hardy,
cheerful people, and it's very easy
to like them. But when you go
down into their villages, you find
that life is pretty tough there, and
certainly in those days they
lacked many of the things that we
consider an ordinary part of our
life. There were no schools and
there was a complete lack of medical treatment for any disease. So
after I spent a number of years in
the Himalayas, the thought struck
me that instead of just talking
about the problems the Sherpas
had, it would be a good idea to actually do something for them.
And so with this motivation, to
try and do something positive,
substantial for the Sherpas, I was
able to organize a project with
some financial assistance. And
we went in and we built the first
school in the Khumbu area. It was
the Khumbu School. This was really the start of quite a long-term
and reasonably extensive assis-

tance program. Other villagers approached me and said the Khumbu School is very nice, and we would like a school too. I would always ask them what they were prepared to contribute to the construction. They didn't have money, but they had the strength of their hands and the ability to work, and so we got regular free labor for the construction of the schools. Over the years, we built seventeen of these little schools out in the mountains and two hospitals and three airfields and a number of bridges and water pipelines. I really feel that this has been a cooperative effort between ourselves and the Sherpas, and I personally found it, I must admit, the most satisfying activity I've ever undertaken.

Mountain Charley

In the mid-1800s, when the American West was still young and raw, frontiersmen, mountainmen, gunfighters, trappers, traders, Indian scouts, bandits, and merely wayfarers roamed its vast and often hostile land, drifting through its trading posts, mining camps, and cow towns. One of the most colorful and unique characters in the panorama of the Wild West was Mountain Charley, who survived two face-to-face gunfights and an Indian attack, worked on a riverboat and on the railroad, then as a miner, a saloonkeeper, a gold prospector, a wagon master, and a mule trader. And afterward, Mountain Charley wrote about those adventures, privately publishing an autobiography in Iowa in 1861. It was entitled simply *Mountain Charley: An Autobiography Comprising a Period of Thirteen Years Life in the States, California, and Pike's Peak.* The key to Charley's uniqueness, however, is revealed in a subtitle that was added much later, when the autobiography was reissued by the University of Oklahoma Press in 1968: *The Adventures of Mrs. E. J. Guerin, Who Was Thirteen Years in Male Attire.*

Mountain Charley, who dressed and lived as a man, became a legend in the American West, leading a life that was one long saga of melodrama and adventure. It began in the early 1830s, when she was born the illegitimate child of Miss Anna Baldwin of New York, who, while visiting Baton Rouge, had made the acquaintance of a French planter by the name of Henry Vereau. That liaison, according to Mountain Charley's autobiography, "soon ripened into a warm attachment, as honorable on his side as it was devoted on hers. And yet at one unlucky moment in their intercourse, passion had usurped the domain of affection." Vereau departed while Miss Baldwin was pregnant, and so she married the manager of a nearby plantation, her husband being described as a "drunken, worthless vagabond." Vereau returned shortly afterward, but hastily departed again on learning of Miss Baldwin's marriage.

Mountain Charley lived on a Louisiana plantation for the first five years of her life and then was sent to a boarding school in New Orleans. She remained there until she was 12 years old but then eloped with a Mississippi riverboat captain, who brought her to St. Louis.

She had a son shortly after, then a daughter, and at the age of 15 became a widow, her husband gunned down on the riverboat by a disgruntled mate named Jamieson. Her happy family life ruined, she lived with a growing obsession to avenge her husband's murder. But as a woman in the mid-19th century, she would not find that very easy. In fact, it would be practically impossible to earn a living and travel freely while tracking down the villain Jamieson. For a man, she thought, it would not be so difficult. So she cut her hair short, changed her garb, practiced male mannerisms, toned her naturally husky voice, put her children in the care of the Sisters of Charity, and left her home as a man—or a boy, still being only 15.

The first job Mountain Charley landed was as a cabin boy on a steamer that plied the Mississippi River between St. Louis and New Orleans, just ten years before Mark Twain began his apprenticeship on a similar riverboat. For four years, she worked on the river, always inquiring in the towns and riverfront saloons she visited if anyone knew of Jamieson or his whereabouts, and once each month discarding her

male togs and dressing as a proper young lady to visit her two children.

In the spring of 1854, Mountain Charley left the river and took a job as a brakeman on the Illinois Central Railroad. It was here that her true sex was first suspected. A conductor who she worked for thought that his brakeman might be a young lady, so he conspired with another man to get the young railroad worker drunk, strip away her clothes to determine her true sex, and if his suspicions were correct, he and his friend would take their sexual pleasures with her. Mountain Charley fortunately learned of the plot and fled, thus ending a budding eight-month career on the railroad.

One evening shortly afterward, Mountain Charley was sitting in the lobby of the King's Hotel in St. Louis and overheard a group of men talking nearby about a poker game planned for that night. Mountain Charley was almost startled out of her chair when she heard one of the men called by his last name, Jamieson. She turned quickly and stared at him; the description she had carried in her mind for the past five years fit the man perfectly. Later, she followed Jamieson to a club and watched as he played poker into the night. When the game was finally over and he left alone, she followed and eventually overtook him. Jamieson thought he had been stopped by a youngster for some ordinary reason. The "youngster," however, quickly told him who she was and drew a revolver. Jamieson grabbed for his gun, and they fired almost simultaneously. Both shots missed their marks, but they fired again.

Mountain Charley was shot in the leg. She fell down but then managed to drag herself to an alley. Meanwhile, Jamieson, clutching his wounded arm close to his chest, dashed around the nearest corner.

The next morning, Mountain Charley awoke in a stranger's house, having been carried there the night before by a few persons who happened to pass by the alley and find her lying there, unconscious. It took Mountain Charley a while to fully recover from the gunshot wound in her leg, but once back on her feet, she again donned men's clothes. This time, Mountain Charley signed on with a wagon train headed for California, leaving St. Louis in the spring of 1855 with 60 men (actually 59), a six-mule team, 50 oxen, ten cows, and 15 saddle horses. The group would average only about 15 miles a day on a six-month journey to the Northwest, passing over the mountains in Wyoming and then across the steaming deserts of Utah and Nevada. This trip, like those taken by many other ambitious settlers who were striking out for the West, was arduous, filled with danger and often disappointment, and sometimes death. Mountain Charley kept a diary that tells the story of her epic wagon train journey across the country, giving a sharp taste of what those who made the trek saw and experienced.

June 3—[In Nebraska] Water fine ... antelopes plenty. The plains are full of emigrants, many of whom are returning ... to the states [the settled lands in the East and Midwest] .... Met today some trappers and hunters with a team laden with buffalo robes and furs.... Saw for the first time that curious little animal, the prairie dog.... No Indians to be seen, although much talked of. They do not visit much the line of emigration....

June 4—In camp today and were passed by over 100 emigrant teams.... Hear and see wolves in great quantities.

June 5—See no buffalo yet, as it is too early in the season, although later, as we learn, thousands make their appearance.... Learn that the reason why we see no Indians is because the government agents have forbidden them to visit the line of emigration. Traveling very unpleasant as clouds of dust roll up from the trains.... On the Platte [River] bottom we find gold wherever we dig for it, but not in quantities that would indicate profitable working....

June 7—Crossed today the North Fork of the Platte. The ford is wide but shallow. Twenty teams crossed at one time, and there were at least 100 teams in sight from either bank. Eight miles from this ford, we came across an Indian village of some 200 lodges and 500 inhabitants. The chief called together some of his people and demanded of us some presents, which were given. They do not understand English but make themselves very well understood by the use of signs. There is apparently a good deal of aristocracy among them—some being handsomely dressed, others ragged and poor. . . . Made 16 miles today.

June 8—The plains are white with the bones of buffalo, upon the skulls of which are written the names of many passing companies.

June 12—Cloudy and cold. Hunters are out in every direction and are so thick they have driven the game all away from the line of emigration. . . .

June 13—One wagon broke down and had to leave it. Are encamped . . . in sight of Chimney Rock [near Bayard, Nebraska] spoken of by [Brevet-Captain John C.] Frémont. . . .

June 14—Are near Chimney Rock . . . probably 200 feet high; broad at the base; and for the last 100 feet of its height, it does not appear to be over 15 feet thick. We are within 15 miles of a place known as Scott's Bluffs [near Gering, Nebraska]. . . .

June 16 and 17—Very warm—passed a solitary grave. One of four brothers was today drowned in the Platte, near our camp. Many large trains pass us.

June 18— . . . Crossed the Laramie [fork], a swift stream, three feet in depth and 100 yards in width and camped within two miles of Fort Laramie [Wyoming]. . . . All kinds of goods are offered for sale at Fort Laramie.

June 20— . . . Along here are distributed thousands of dollars' worth of property. I saw left along the road here eight broken-down wagons and an almost infinite quantity of beans, flour, stoves, cheese, kegs of nails, spades, shovels, racks, log chains, water kegs, barrels, and in short every kind of property used in an emigrant's outfit. . . . There were also many worn-out mules and horses that had been turned out to die. Found about 11 o'clock a spring of pure cold water—a luxury that can be appreciated only by those who come upon one after being hours parched with dust. Saw two graves, one that of an infant. . . .

June 21— . . . Regretted that I had not provided myself with goggles, as the road is so constantly traveled that the dust became a most serious nuisance. One yoke of cattle became so footsore that they were unserviceable, and we were obliged to drive them behind the wagon. . . . Wild sage grows very abundantly. . . . We also found along here numberless insects resembling grasshoppers without wings.

June 22— . . . The high, rocky, and clayey hills present in many instances the appearances of grotesque cities. This afternoon we entered a region volcanic in character. We pass through deep hollows surrounded on all sides by huge masses of rocks, evidently piled high in their present position during some convulsion of nature. The earth is of a color red as brick.

June 24— . . . A man was drowned this morning in attempting to cross the Platte on horseback. Thirty men are reported to have lost their lives there

First Woman to Conquer Everest

On May 16, 1975, a diminutive Japanese housewife and mountain climber, Junko Tabei, became the first woman ever to reach the top of Mount Everest. Along with Sherpa guide Ang Tsering, she reached the 29,028-foot summit of the world's tallest mountain by scaling the South Col–South-East Ridge.

Tabei, who lives in Fukushima, capital of Fukushima Prefecture on the Japanese island of Honshū, was part of the Japanese Ladies Expedition, a group of 15 women mountaineers who were sponsored by a Tokyo newspaper and television syndicate. Only 4 feet 11 inches tall and 94 pounds, Tabei had been climbing mountains since she was nine years old, and had earlier conquered the 26,504-foot summit of Annapurna, the 11th-tallest Himalayan peak and one of the world's most coveted mountaineering achievements. She had also climbed just about every mountain in Japan as she built toward her historic assault on Everest.

The ascension of Everest by Tabei and her group took a full month. Tabei, the other six climbers, and six of their Sherpa guides were injured in a sudden avalanche at about 25,000 feet. After having oxygen administered for two days, Tabei and several of her companions recovered sufficiently to forge on, but only Junko Tabei made it to the top. As she said later, however: "I was the only one to make it, but not because I was the best climber. It was only because I was in the best condition physically. But the others were a part of it, reaching the summit. If even one climber reaches the summit from a good team, then it means that the whole group has succeeded in reaching the top."

Later that same year, another woman conquered Mount Everest, a Tibetan named Phantog, but the treasure of being first will always belong to Junko Tabei of Japan.

---

this year, it being unusually high.

June 26—Start early and after traveling ten miles reach a ferry kept by the Mormons. They charge us $3 per wagon for taking us over. They have a large store of goods at this place, for which they charge most exorbitant prices—however, they were very polite and kind to us.

June 28—Today we leave the Platte. . . . We pass over a barren, sterile country, destitute of water. Saw the alkali springs and streams, which are fatal to cattle. . . .

June 30—Leave early this morning and reach Sweetwater River in the evening, near Independence Rock [Natrona County, Wyoming]. . . . Five miles from it is the Devil's Gate, at which point the Sweetwater has cut through a ridge of rocks. . . . The walls upon each side are perpendicular. From here mountains rise upon mountains till they seem to meet the sky, forming a scenery of the most majestic and beautiful character. Upon Independence Rock are cut and written the names of thousands of emigrants, and my own was added to the rest.

July 2—Air very impure, owing to the large number of dead cattle along the route. . . . Here, for the first time, we saw the sage hen. . . . Game plenty, seemingly not fearful of the presence of man. This proceeds from the fact that along here, emigrants are more anxious to care for their teams than to secure game. Pasture very poor. . . . Everyone we meet has got the blues—many have lost their all or nearly all. . . . Picked up two women who had inhumanly been left to starve by some train in advance and took them along to cook and thus work their passage through.

July 4—Very cold—the water in one of the vessels was found frozen an inch thick at sunrise. . . . Slight fall of snow. . . . We are now on the trail of the Snake Indians, but they have not as yet visited us. . . . Crossing Wind River Mountains [Fremont County, Wyoming]. . . .

July 5— . . . Here I shot an antelope—my first essay at killing game with a rifle. I found at first the carrying of a heavy piece rather awkward but in the present instance acquitted myself so well

the company said I did well for a green boy of 18.

July 7— . . . Here we met three men who stated that they had got lost from their train and had been 36 hours without food. They had killed, they said, the first day plenty of game, but it made them wretchedly sick to eat it without salt. Fed them and they left. . . . Today we reach snow. . . . We passed an immense bank some ten or 12 feet in depth. . . .

These are most of the direct excerpts from the diary that Mountain Charley included in her autobiography; the rest was told in narrative form. The wagon train crossed the Continental Divide in Wyoming, and on the way the party met two Indians from California, who "gave us some interesting news from the land of gold." By July 21, Mountain Charley had reached the Bear River, in northern Utah, where she saw her first grizzly bear, which one of the party killed: "One of those terrible monsters . . . it weighed some 1,200 pounds and had a foot whose breadth was six inches." Mountain Charley also came upon "another characteristic of the country, and that was a dead Indian in the fork of a tree. His body had been wrapped in a buffalo robe and placed there to prevent his being devoured by wolves."

During the next five weeks, the wagon train passed by many of the West's natural features: the Great Salt Lake, sulfur deposits, boiling springs, and an extinct volcano. The group met with a tribe of Panock Indians, "a tribe of hunters"; dealt with

Indian traders; and watched the seemingly endless traffic of hopeful settlers heading west and the disillusioned ones passing on their way back east.

On September 1, the party started on the trek across the Nevada desert to California:

> Not the most pleasant portion of our journey. Many of our cattle died on the way.... In crossing, we came to the Boiling Springs, of which there is nearly 100.... The thermometer in the water in some cases indicated 160 degrees [Fahrenheit]. It was warm enough to make tolerable good coffee, and we were also enabled to "do up" some washing without the trouble of making a fire. We saw many cases of destitution along the road.... All along were the carcasses of cattle, and at intervals a rudely rounded hillock would show where slept some unfortunate whose search for wealth had ceased forever. One day I had ridden somewhat in advance of our train, when in passing a rude tent, my attention was attracted to it by a faint moaning. I rode up and dismounted, when I was shocked to find within, a woman lying on some dirty blankets and, by her, two little children. All were emaciated to the last degree.... The woman could scarcely find strength to inform me of her trouble, but she managed in the faintest of tones to tell me that several days before, her husband had gone on to find feeding ground, and their team had died the day he left. He had intended to return in two or three days at farthest.... He had now been gone a week, and she had not tasted food in four days. As soon as our train came up, we relieved them and took them in one of our wagons. Not many miles distant we came across the body of a man who had evidently died from fatigue and inanition. The woman recognized it with a faint but agonizing shriek....

Finally, in October, the party moved into what is today the state of California, having traveled continuously since May. Mountain Charley left the wagon train along the banks of the Feather River to mine for gold in the remarkably beautiful Feather River Canyon. But the work was hard, the life lonely, and the return for the effort not worthwhile. So after three months, Mountain Charley, now totally on her own and low on money, moved to the city of Sacramento to find steady work. There she seized quickly on a perfect opportunity for an aspiring young man in the Old West—a job as barkeeper in one of Sacramento's many saloons, the salary $100 a month.

Mountain Charley managed to save enough money to buy a partnership in the saloon and eight months later sold her share at a profit. She then entered the mule-trading business, a lucrative one in the early history of California, and once again made a profit with its sale. Now financially secure—she had sold her business for $2,500 and made an investment in supplying provisions by mule pack to the mountains—Mountain Charley returned to St. Louis to visit her children, donning women's clothing as soon as she reached the city. But a few months later, California called again.

Almost two years from the start of her first trip to California, Mountain Charley, no longer a greenhorn, was signed as the wagon master of a train that included 15 men (14 actually), a number of mules and horses, and a drove of cattle. Like the first trek, it was tough going all the way—and a little more dangerous. Along the Humbolt River in Nevada:

> One night we were attacked by a prowling band of Snake Indians. We repulsed them after some sharp fighting, in which I took part by shooting one Indian and stabbing another. We had one man killed and several wounded, besides which they shot one of our mules and run off some two or three others. I received a severe wound in the arm, which disabled it for a time. Three of the Indians were killed, and they left and we saw no more of them.

In California, Mountain Charley took up ranching, and business boomed. With that and the mule-packing business, which she still owned, Mountain Charley did well but was always looking for a new venture. Eventually, she added fur trading to her string of businesses. Then came Pikes Peak gold fever.

Mountain Charley went to Pikes Peak, in what is today Colorado, in the spring of 1859 and began prospecting for gold. Her luck, however, was not much better than it had been at Feather River when she first came to the West. So after about three months Mountain Charley opened a combination bakery and saloon near Pikes Peak and once again met with financial success. She sold out, however, because of ill health and moved to Denver, where after a short recuperation, she once again got back into business, this time renting out the "Mountain Boys Saloon." And it was here in the gold fever days of Pikes Peak that the sobriquet "Mountain Charley" was given to the colorful character who had started out as a girl-boy but who had now become a successful young woman-man.

It was also near Pikes Peak, however, that Mountain Charley's masquerade finally would come to an end. She was riding on a mule in the mountains outside Denver one day in the spring of 1860 when she saw in the distance a man approaching her on another mule. The two riders drew closer together, their eyes warily on each other, until finally Mountain Charley found that:

> I was face to face with—Jamieson. He recognized me at the same moment, and his hand went after his revolver almost that instant mine did. I was a second too quick for him, for my shot tumbled him from his mule just as his ball whistled harmlessly by my head. . . . I emptied my revolver upon him as he lay and should have done the same with its mate had not two hunters at that moment come upon the ground and

prevented any further consummation of my designs.

Jamieson, however, did not die there on the trail. The hunters carried him to safety and eventually he recovered enough to travel to New Orleans. But shortly after his arrival there, he died of yellow fever.

Although Jamieson had spread the story of Mountain Charley's true sex before he left for New Orleans, she continued in the guise of a man, returning to saloonkeeping in Central City. In late 1860, with the word that Jamieson was now truly dead, Mountain Charley finally permanently shed her male attire and married H. L. Guerin, a barkeeper who was working for her at the time. The newlyweds then moved to the Midwest, where Mountain Charley wrote her amazing autobiography.

A Lonely Odyssey to the North Pole

It was April 29, 1978, and the man standing alone on the barren, glistening white landscape was smiling despite the rages of the icy winds and the shocking cold. He was Naomi Uemura, a 37-year-old Japanese adventurer, who had just reached the single spot on Earth where all directions point south. And he was smiling because he had become the *first* human being to successfully make a solo trip to the North Pole.

Uemura's lonely, frigid odyssey had begun 55 days earlier, 476 miles to the south. With 17 sled dogs and an oak sled handcrafted for him in Eskimo tradition, which when loaded weighed 1,000 pounds, Uemura struck out from Cape Columbia on the northern coast of Ellesmere Island, in the northernmost of Canada's Northwest Territories. What lay ahead was a journey with a grim variety of hazards, not the least being the Arctic cold: the temperature on the day he departed was −49 degrees Fahrenheit. There was also the mat-

ter of terrain—a vast, rough stretch of ice and impacted snow. As Uemura afterward wrote: "It is a terrible region, seemingly without a flat surface . . . an endless maze of ice boulders. . . . Often I must hack a passage through solid ice with an iron bar so that the dogs can scramble through." Besides the ice ridges and other obstacles, there were the "leads," the lanes of open water between ice floes that he would have to maneuver across, sometimes using floating ice blocks as rafts. And he was indeed aware that no one survives a dip in the freezing waters of the Arctic Ocean—even if the person manages to get back out—because the air temperature is so abysmally cold.

The ordeal would not, however, be a novel experience for Naomi Uemura. He was an experienced adventurer, who, as reported in *National Geographic* magazine, had "scaled the highest peaks in North America, South America, and Africa; rafted [3,600 miles] down the Amazon; and mushed more than [7,200 miles] from Greenland to Alaska—the longest solo dogsled trip on record. He [had] also climbed Mount Everest with the first Japanese expedition to reach the summit [1970]."

For this new adventure, he had chosen the fashions of the Eskimo— polar bearskin pants, a caribou-fur-hooded parka, and sealskin boots. Food would consist of pemmican, caribou meat, seal meat, whale oil, biscuits, coffee, and tea, as well as commercial dog food for the hardy creatures who would pull his sled to the North Pole.

It had been arranged that as Uemura progressed he would have new supplies airlifted to him at various checkpoints along the way. Five drops were planned. But the first, as it turned out, was needed earlier than anticipated.

Bedded down inside his tent on the fourth night, Uemura was awakened when the sudden yapping of his dogs broke the Arctic silence. "There are few creatures a sled dog instinctively fears," Uemura noted. "One is man, another is the polar bear." The frenzied dogs quickly ate through their tethers and fled across the ice, and as their noise diminished another replaced it, the heavy plodding and grunting of one of the world's most devastating carnivores.

Uemura, separated from the polar bear by only the nylon of his tent, could hear the bear as it rummaged through his supplies, munching on the frozen seal meat, lapping at the whale blubber, smashing some things, flinging others out onto the ice pack. Then there was silence, followed shortly by the unmistakable sound of cloth ripping as the bear pawed at his tent. Uemura had a rifle not far away, but it was not loaded and was therefore worthless. So he lay there, motionless and breathless, aware of how close he was to a most horrifying death. The huge bear poked his head through the shredded tent, sniffed loudly, and nudged the dead-still Uemura in the back. Then, for some unaccountable reason, the huge creature turned and padded off into the night. Uemura quickly loaded his rifle, then radioed for new supplies and rounded up his dogs. Hedonistic curs that they were, the dogs had forgotten the menace that had terrorized them minutes earlier and were now preoccupied with a bitch in their midst who was in heat. Uemura knew that the polar bear, virtually the only land animal known to track a human being for food, would be back when he was hungry again. This time, to survive, Uemura would have to shoot the bear, and he was worried about the rifle operating properly in the extreme cold. As a precaution, he soaked the firing mechanism in kerosine. The bear did come back the next day, and Uemura was waiting for him. At 164 feet Uemura had the animal in the cross hairs of the telescopic lens of his high-powered rifle, and dropped him with a single shot. The astounded and critically injured bear managed to get back up, but began to retreat from the strange, inexplicable horror he had just encountered. Uemura fired again and the bear finally fell dead on the ice.

Uemura, freshly equipped from the supply plane, which had ski runners so that it could land on the ice pack, set out again. As he maneuvered his dogs and sled from ice floe to ice floe, he came close several times to taking a deadly plunge into the waters of the Arctic Ocean. Once he unhitched his dogs and used the 14-foot sled as a bridge across a ten-foot lead, sent the dogs across the sled, clambered over it himself, then hitched up the dogs and dragged the sled to the new ice island and continued on his way.

The brutal cold was relentless, the routines incredibly arduous—12- to 16-hour days, constantly fighting the inhospitable terrain, forging on slowly but steadily. "I eat as the dogs do—once a day at the end of travel, and always uncooked meat," he wrote later, explaining that he did not really have the time to cook and that if he did the vapor from the boiling water would crystallize on the tent wall, creating a continual ice storm.

Uemura plotted his own position along his route, but his calculations were confirmed using a unique tracking system—a small, battery-powered transmitter attached to Uemura's sled automatically signaled the U.S. meteorological research satellite, Nimbus 6, in orbit around both Poles. The fix was transmitted to his base camp on the Arctic Ocean and radioed from there to Uemura. On a good day he covered as much as 36 miles, other days less than two. Gradually he drew closer and closer, and finally Naomi Uemura arrived at his destination. With the sextant he had used to plot his course over the preceding 55 days, he determined he now stood at the very top of the world, his body a slight extension of the Earth's axis.

Because of atmospheric interference, Uemura was unable to check with his base camp to make sure that his readings agreed with those of Nimbus 6. But the pilot of the supply airplane, which now came to take him back to civilization, verified with its instruments that Uemura had indeed reached the North Pole. Never before had anyone made a similar journey alone and survived to tell about it.

A Transglobal Expedition

With an uncharacteristic lack of British reticence, the two Englishmen, the 1980s heirs to the great British tradition of exploration and adventure, described their expedition as "earth's last great journey." The two men were Sir Ranulph Twisleton-Wykeham-Fiennes and Charles Burton, both in their late 30s, and the exploit they were talking about was the grueling Transglobe Expedition, as it was formally named, that would take them three full years to complete.

What they set out to accomplish had never been done before—to circle the planet Earth by following a north-south meridian, crossing both the South and North Poles in the process. It was, in their view, one of the last great adventure challenges on earth, and it would require Herculean effort, an incredible mix of outdoor skills, and a logistical plan and operation that would probably raise eyebrows at the Royal Navy.

Sir Ranulph Fiennes, the expedition leader, was far from a novice at adventurous undertakings. He had embarked on three major expeditions in the preceding decade: The first was a 1969 jaunt up the White Nile, from mouth to source, by Hovercraft. It was followed by a trek onto the Jostedalsbreen Glacier in Norway in 1970. The next year, Fiennes led a party on a 1,500-mile Canadian voyage over nine rivers and more than 100 stretches of white water to the Headless Valley in remote British Columbia.

The Transglobe Expedition was, however, the most elaborate of all. In its course it would incorporate a large ship, the *Benjamin Bowring*, an airplane, Land Rovers, snowmobiles, motorized boats, sleds, skis, even "pontoon boots" (resembling small kayaks and used to walk on the arctic slush), as well as plain-and-simple leg power. The cost of the three-year trek, underwritten by a group of 800 British and American companies, would be approximately $20 million.

Fiennes and Burton launched their transglobal trek from Greenwich, England on September 2, 1979. The route of the expedition would take them through the land masses of Europe, Africa, Antarctica, Australia, North America, and the Arctic Ice Cap; across the Pacific, the Arctic, and the Atlantic oceans; and through such weather extremes as the broiling heat of the Sahara Desert, as hot as 120 degrees Fahrenheit,

and the cold climes of the Arctic and the Antarctic, with temperatures as low as −60 degrees Fahrenheit and windchill factors even lower.

After leaving Greenwich, the two adventurers headed for Algiers, in North Africa. There, the first rugged leg of the journey actually began. With the aid of a pair of Land Rovers, they set out across the great Sahara Desert, crossing the breadth of Algeria, Mali, and Upper Volta, all the way down to the Ivory Coast capital of Abidjan, a journey of about 2,500 miles over some of the earth's most torrid and forbidding terrain.

From Abidjan the expedition, ferried by the *Benjamin Bowring*, sailed to Cape Town, South Africa, where outfitting began for the difficult journey across the continent of Antarctica. The group (Fiennes's wife, Lady Virginia, and another adventurer, Oliver Shepard, had joined the pair) had to bed down at Fimbulisen on the Antarctic coast to wait out the intense winter. They lived in cardboard huts for eight months because it would have been impossible to cross the great ice cap at the bottom of the world at that time of year. But when winter passed, Fiennes and Burton, with Shepard acting as mechanic, set out on snowmobiles, hauling their supplies on sleds. Lady Virginia stayed at the Antarctic base to operate the radio. The expedition moved from one coast to the other, a journey of 2,200 miles, in 78 days, the fastest man had ever traversed the continent of Antarctica.

The *Benjamin Bowring* took Fiennes and Burton to Australia, the United States, and on up the coast of North America to the western entry to the Northwest Passage. They then set out in smaller boats to cover the 3,000 miles to Ellesmere Island. From there, it was over the polar ice cap to the North Pole.

The expedition almost came to a tragic end in March 1982, as the two British adventurers were traversing the Arctic wasteland. Their snowmobile, laden with all their supplies, broke through a patch of weak ice and sank into the Arctic Ocean. Fiennes and Burton managed to get to the safety of solid ice, but had come

26 Historic Mountaineering Firsts

Different mountains pose different problems for those who attempt to scale them. Some are awesome in height, such as Everest; others have icy or mixed terrains; and still others have a sheer mountain face, such as the Eiger or El Capitan. The following mountains were selected because, for one reason or another, they are difficult to climb, making their conquest historic mountaineering events.

Mountain	Location	Height in Feet	First Scaled
Everest	Nepal/Tibet	29,028	1953
Godwin Austen (K2)	Kashmir	28,250	1954
Kanchenjunga	Nepal/Sikkim	28,208	1955
Lhotse I	Nepal/Tibet	27,923	1956
Makalu	Nepal/Tibet	27,824	1955
Nānga Parbat	Pakistan	26,660	1953
Communism Peak	Soviet Union	24,590	1933
Lenin Peak	Soviet Union	23,406	1928
Aconcagua	Argentina	22,831	1897
Chimborazo	Ecuador	20,561	1880
McKinley (South Peak)	United States	20,320	1913
Logan	Canada	19,850	1925
Kilimanjaro	Tanzania	19,340	1889
Popocatepetl	Mexico	17,887	c. 1520
Kenya	Kenya	17,058	1899
Vinson Massif	Antarctica	16,864	1966
Mont Blanc	France/Italy	15,771	1786
Matterhorn	Switzerland	14,692	1865
Whitney	United States	14,494	1873
Rainier	United States	14,410	1870
Pikes Peak	United States	14,110	1820
Eiger	Switzerland	13,036	1858
Fuji	Japan	12,388	c. 700
Cook	New Zealand	12,349	1894
El Capitan	United States	7,569	1962
Eiger (North Face)	Switzerland	6,600	1932

frighteningly close to accompanying their snowmobile to the bottom of the frigid Arctic waters. Gone was their tent, food, fuel, navigation equipment, and other supplies. All that remained was a single sleeping bag and a section of tarpaulin to help them fend off the Arctic winds and a temperature of −15 degrees Fahrenheit. The next day, however, their plight was discovered when they were located by the pilot of the escort plane assisting in the expedition. Shortly afterward, an Arctic bush pilot landed his Twin Otter airplane on the ice near them and unloaded a fresh set of supplies, and the two again took up their transglobal trek.

Despite the difficulties and hazards they faced, the pair managed to make the 518-mile crossing from the Canadian coast to the North Pole in a record 46 days, and arrived at 2:00 A.M. Greenwich Mean Time, April 11, 1982. Then it was a race across ice, snow, and stretches of open water to the western edge of the Arctic Ocean, where small motorized boats took them to Spitsbergen, Norway. There they boarded the *Benjamin Bowring* for the trip home.

Britain's Prince Charles joined the adventurers on August 29, 1982, as they sailed up the Thames to dock in Greenwich. "Gloriously and refreshingly mad," is how the prince once described Fiennes and Burton. Their 35,000-mile odyssey was "an extraordinary feat," said the prince. "The only problem is, what on earth is Sir Ranulph Fiennes going to do next?"

Crossing Greenland on Skis

It is a bleak, treacherous journey across Greenland's vast ice cap. About 23 degrees south of the North Pole, in the vicinity of the Arctic Circle, the east-west crossing may be as short as 350 miles. Farther north, the distance is 800 miles, but no human has been known to try that route on foot, snowshoes, or skis. It is a journey across a great sea of inland ice, in most places thousands of feet thick, covered with a thin veneer of glacial snow and riddled with deep crevasses. The more than 708,000 square miles of ice covers the entire interior of the island, burying valleys and mountains far beneath its surface, making it by far the largest glacier in the Northern Hemisphere. Here, on this barren, ice-carpeted surface held in by coastal mountains, the winter temperatures can easily drop to −85 degrees Fahrenheit.

The first crossing of this great plain of ice was made in 1888 by Norwegian explorer Fridtjof Nansen. Along with five companions, he traveled from east to west at approximately 64 degrees north latitude, several degrees below the Arctic Circle, accomplishing the feat in 43 days. The expedition journeyed on skis and hauled sledges, narrow, lightweight sleds that Nansen had designed for the Arctic trek.

In 1980, the world record was set for the swiftest crossing of the great Greenland ice sheet. Eight young American cross-country skiers—four men and four women—from Minnesota made a 375-mile crossing in 35 days. The expedition followed a southerly route never before traveled by man, authenticated by the National Museum of Greenland.

The goal of the Americans, as stated afterward by 28-year-old expedition leader Paul Erickson, was to cross the island in 30 days. But the trek was hampered by weather that was generally more severe than anticipated, including several fierce Arctic storms, and by terrain that was more difficult than expected.

"The last four days were the most difficult," Erickson said. "They were spent entirely on ice crevasses, which made it impossible to ski." But Erickson and his companions walked it, having tied their skis to their sleds, which they sometimes hauled and sometimes carried through waist-deep icy water, and bettered the previous record of 38 days, which was set by a Scottish expedition in 1965.

Six Fantastic Himalayan Treks

Exploration in mountainous regions has become a popular pastime and can be an adventure-filled, educational experience. Among the most interesting trips are those offered by Himalaya, a trekking and wilderness expedition group headquartered in San Francisco, California. Here's how Himalaya describes some of its exotic excursions to the top of the world.

Baltistan-Hunza
Deep within the vast Karakoram Range, we will travel by plane, jeep, and foot to serpentine glaciers, deep river gorges, and medieval castles and villages within the ancient kingdoms of Hunza and Baltistan.

This adventure begins with a spectacular flight to the oasis town of Skārdu, once a citadel of Balti kings. We will jeep to Khapalu on the Shyok River. Zuks (rafts of inflated goatskin) will ferry us to the trail head and the beginning of the ten-day walk to a glacial basin beneath the ice-crested cornices of Saltoro Kangri (25,400 feet). Here, unchanged by modern civilization, the hamlet of Khorkundus lies within a crescent formed by the Saltoro Kangri Massif. Its Balti shepherds retain a traditional way of life, their bobbed hair worn beneath homespun acorn-shaped caps (nathing). Passing a clear waterfall that plummets in rainbow mists from the vertical walls of Saltoro, we will ascend onto the ice of Sherpikang Glacier.

En route to the Astor Valley, we will cross the Deosai Plains, a rolling, grass-tufted plateau reminiscent of Tibet, with vistas from Kashmir to

Nānga Parbat (26,660 feet). We will descend the Astor Valley to the Indus River and on to the bustling bazaars of Gilgit. Beyond lies fabled Hunza—inspiration of James Hilton's *Lost Horizon*. This nearly vertical world of terraced gardens and orchards lies astride the main caravan route to ancient Cathay. The tranquil pace of life and simple diet—grain, fruit, nuts, and milk products—of the Hunza people have contributed to their good health and legendary longevity.

If conditions permit, we will drive into the Khunjerab Range bordering China, where we may see ibex, markhor [wild goats], and perhaps the elusive snow leopard.

Trans-Himalaya Trek
The great classic of Kashmir treks, this route encounters both the richness of Kashmir's alpine regions and the stark panoramas of Ladakh's lunar Zaskar Range. Beginning our 21-day trek on the slopes of the Pir Panjal, we hike across the Margan Pass (11,500 feet) into the untrameled Warwan Valley. Here, in rough-hewn timber houses, the people continue a centuries-old way of life. As we climb the valley, we will pass through the range of man's alpine habitation, reaching true wilderness at the foot of Bhoktol Glacier (14,500 feet). Following this serpentine river of black ice and rock to the crest of the Punjab Himalaya, we will emerge into the Suru Valley, under the towering peaks of Nun Kun, whose twin spires climb above 23,000 feet.

The barrier of the Punjab Himalaya deprives this land of the life-giving monsoon rains, but here and there the Balti people have created verdant oases in vivid contrast to the harsh surroundings. Terraced fields, guarded by tall poplars, are sustained by intricate canals carrying the waters of melting snows.

We will walk up the Suru River to Ringdom Gompa, a monastery, which marks the western border of a Buddhist world stretching eastward to Japan. Above Ringdom, we cross the Kanji-la (at 17,000 feet, the highest pass on our route) to the eastern margin of the Zaskar Range and the true "moonland" of Ladakh. All vegetation is left behind, but a riot of colors and shapes in rock turns the landscape into a kaleidoscopic fantasy, heightened by the incredibly clear air.

Returning to the realm of man at Budkharbhu, our jeeps will take us the last 60 miles to camp at Alchi. In the villages and monasteries of the Indus Valley, we will glimpse the art, culture, and religion of Tantric Buddhist Tibet before returning by jeep to our houseboats in the Vale of Kashmir.

Rolwaling—Everest—Island Peak Expedition
This is [the] grand tour of the highest mountain region in the world. Only those in excellent physical condition and willing to acquire basic mountaineering skills en route should consider this trip, since it involves two difficult passes above 17,500 feet.

Leaving the Kathmandu–Lhasa Road at Barabise, we will begin a 37-day expedition. We will first walk to the picturesque [Rolwaling] Valley, where the small Sherpa population is virtually cut off from its homeland in the Khumbu region by the 18,890-foot Tesi Lapcha Pass. As we cross this difficult pass, we will see world-famous Khumbu for the first time. Beyond Namche Bazar and Thyangboche Monastery, at the summer settlement of Gokyo, a spectacular panorama of Himalayan scenery will unfold.

From the Gokyo area, we will climb a 17,783-foot pass to reach the valley of Khumbu Glacier, at the very base of Mount Everest (29,028 feet). Climbing to Kala Patar ("black rock"), we will see the renowned view of Mount Everest most often pictured in books. Below, on the glacier, is the site of the base camp for all recent climbing expeditions, and above is the 1,500-foot-high jumbled mass of snow and ice that forms the notorious Khumbu icefall.

An optional two-day ascent of Island Peak (20,280 feet) [can be taken by those who possess] the necessary snow-climbing experience. Standing alone and surrounded by the fluted peaks of Nuptse, Lhotse, Ama Dablam, and Makalu, Island Peak is a short technical climb that provides one of the most outstanding experiences to be had in the Himalayas.

Annapurna Circuit Trek

Our 25-day trek will take us completely around the sprawling Annapurna Massif in north-central Nepal, through Hindu villages in subtropical lowlands, and past Buddhist monasteries on the fringes of the Tibetan plateau.

From Pokhara (3,000 feet), our trail follows the wide, fertile valley of the Marsyandi Khola, a river among groves of banyan, banana, and mango. The Hindu people live in prim houses of brick and thatch, cultivating rice on terraced hillsides.

Farther on, where the valley narrows and forks at the very base of magnificent Manaslu (26,760 feet), we will enter a wild gorge that leads to the remote northern margin of Annapurna. Medieval villages are separated by thick forests, cliffs, and plummeting waterfalls. The houses, clustered together like squat fortresses, protect their Buddhist inhabitants [today] from the fierce winds as [they once did from] the warlords of the past.

Beyond the stronghold of Manang (12,500 feet), with prayer flags snapping above every roof, we will climb steeply to the trip's high point of 17,770 feet, at the spectacular Thorong-la pass. Mighty Dhaulagiri lies to the west, unnamed giants to the south, and the endless plains of Mustang and Tibet to the north.

The first civilization we will encounter on the northern, rain-shadowed flank of Annapurna is the Hindu pilgrimage site of Muktinath, where ascetic holy men come to witness a miraculous fire that springs from the mountainside. Descending to Jomosom in the Kali Gandaki River gorge, we will join an ancient trade route between India and Tibet and follow it as the river carves a 17,500-foot chasm between the nearby summits of Annapurna I and Dhaulagiri.

At the whitewashed villages of Marpha and Tukche, we will visit Buddhist monasteries that brim with religious art and handscribed folios.

Upon reaching the bustling trading village of Tatopani, we will have returned from arid highland to subtropical vegetation and from Buddhist to Hindu culture.

Dolpo-Phoksumdo Trek

This is a rare and unusual outing to seldom-visited Dolpo, lying north of the Nepal Himalayas on the Tibetan plateau. Our trek will take us east from Jumla through magnificent alpine scenery skirting the southern ridges of Kanjiroba (23,105 feet). We will meet Tibetan drok-pa (nomads), now settled in a clustered village near a traditional Buddhist gompa (monastery). As we emerge from a pine-clad valley, we will see the roofs of Rimi village and its sentrylike wooden dhauliya (protector effigies).

The trail climbs toward the highest point of the trip at Kagmara-la (16,780 feet), and from the rock cairn at pass-top, we will gaze upon the sawtooth ridges of Kanjiroba and countless tall peaks.

Beyond the pass, we will walk into another world. This is the land of magical Bon Po, the pre-Buddhist religion of Tibet that survives today in only a few remote valleys. Its villages of Pungmo and Ringmo, whose houses are sturdily constructed of timber and stone, sit at the base of a precipitous spur leading to Kanjiroba. The villages support three sizable temples devoted to Bon Po, and their spirited people, although unused to outsiders, are most friendly and congenial.

Climbing past a thunderous waterfall, we will see the clear, turquoise blue of Phoksumdo Lake. From a base camp near the lake, [we] will have several days to explore the fringes of Dolpo, including its weathered Bon gompas, perhaps spotting some of the region's unique Himalayan wildlife. Beyond Crystal Mountain lies Inner Dolpo, described by Peter Matthiessen in his book The Snow Leopard. We will trace Matthiessen's route on our return through Rohagaon, Tibrikot, and over two low passes to Jumla.

Forbidden Kingdoms

This trip offers a potpourri of the culture and scenic beauties of Bhutan and Sikkim, the "forbidden kingdoms" of the Eastern Himalayas. We will combine brisk walks and exciting jeep rides with nights spent in comfortable camps or luxurious hotels.

By narrow-gauge train, we will wind slowly through jungled hills, tea plantations, and alpine forests to the fabled hill station of Darjeeling, perched on green slopes at the foot of Kanchenjunga (28,208 feet).

From here, we will drive to Gangtok, the capital city of Sikkim. After a short visit, we will begin a six-day walk through forests to the villages of the Lepchas (aboriginal inhabitants), pausing to inspect the art treasures of massive gompas. We will climb through alpine meadows to the snow line of Sinioluchu, which towers above at 22,595 feet. There, amidst serpentine glaciers, we will have excellent close-up views of Kanchenjunga.

Returning briefly to the jungles of Bengal, we will enjoy an early morning elephant ride in the Jaldapara Wildlife Sanctuary, with a chance of spotting tiger and the rare, one-horned Indian rhino.

Next, an exciting drive brings us to the lovely Paro Valley of Bhutan, where for 14 days we will explore the wonders of the Land of the Thunderbolt Dragon. On a six-day walk, we will see the traditional Bhutan, unspoiled by highways and other incursions of modern civilization. In addition, we will see the more familiar sights of Bhutan, with a short pony-trek to Taktsang Gompa (Tigers' Nest Monastery) and visits to major dzongs [fortified castles]. The pageantry of archery contests and religious festivals may coincide with our visit, and there [should] also be ample time for shopping in Thimbhu's festive bazaars.

Scaling Everest Alone

To reach the summit of Mount Everest, the world's tallest mountain, has been the goal of adventurers ever since Lieutenant Colonel C. K. Howard-Bury first attempted it back in 1921. Assaults by teams of professional mountain climbers followed, some with tragic results. It was, of course, finally conquered from Nepal in 1953 by Sir Edmund Hillary of New Zealand, and his Sherpa companion Tenzing Norgay. Other intrepid climbers followed with equal success. But Everest had never been scaled by just one person, completely alone, without porters, oxygen, radio, or supply relays, until a daring Italian mountaineer named Reinhold Messner accomplished the feat in 1980.

Alone, with all his supplies, including a tent, stove, sleeping bag, food, and climbing equipment, packed tightly into a rucksack (full, it weighed 33 pounds), Messner set out to scale the Tibetan side of Everest. Following the North Col–North-East Ridge route, after 2½ days he reached the summit—29,028 feet above sea level—at 3:20 P.M. on August 20, 1980.

Messner had been there two years earlier. Along with Austrian climber Peter Habeler, he had scaled the south face of the mountain. That ascent, however, involved a total of 11 climbers and 25 Sherpa porters. Its historic significance is that it was the first successful ascent of Everest without the aid of oxygen.

Born in the South Tirol, Italy, in 1944, Messner established his credentials as a mountain climber early. At the age of 26 he began challenging the Himalayas. In 1970, he successfully led an expedition to the top of Nanga Parbat (26,660 feet), but the climb had tragic consequences. His brother Gunther was killed during the descent, and Messner himself lost most of his toes as a result of frostbite. Undeterred, however, he went on to climb Manaslu (26,760 feet) alone in 1972; Gasherbrum I (26,470 feet) in 1975, with Peter Habeler; Nanga Parbat alone in 1978;

and the world's second-tallest mountain, K2, or Godwin Austen (28,250 feet), in 1979.

Messner's mountain-climbing career, and his life for that matter, were almost extinguished on his solo climb to the top of Mount Everest—only a few minutes after he began. Messner had set up his base camp at 21,320 feet. Departing in darkness at 5:00 A.M. on August 18, he had gone no more than 550 yards when a snow bridge over a crevasse gave way and he plummeted downward, bouncing from wall to wall. Miraculously, he landed on an ice ledge. As he later described it in *National Geographic* magazine:

> The snow platform that had halted my fall was no more than a meter square. I tried to illuminate the dark, empty space below [with his headlamp]. There seemed no end to it. I became acutely aware that if the platform collapsed beneath my weight, I would hurtle into the abyss. . . . Survival instincts surfaced. I quickly sought escape from the icy prison. A steep, narrow ramp angled up along the wall. With an ice ax in one hand and a ski pole in the other, I moved up the ramp, carefully balancing, kicking step after step in the ice, until I reached the lip of the crevasse.

Other hazards lay ahead. Messner risked dehydration in the treacherously thin air at that altitude, and lack of sufficient oxygen in his blood was a constant problem, sapping his strength, and affecting his judgment and other mental capacities in bizarre and dangerous ways. There were also winds that would gust at up to 50 miles per hour; soft, deep snow that under the circumstances was almost impossible to plod through; slick ice on steep inclines; the threats of avalanches or storms; and, of course, the total absence of anyone else upon whom to rely.

The first day Messner made good headway, ascending more than 4,000 feet. He pitched camp below the north ridge at about 25,585 feet, and ate some dried meat, biscuits, and cheese. He melted snow to mix with the dehydrated tomato soup, and to prepare Tibetan salt tea, then bedded down for the night.

The going was even more laborious the second day. Messner had to wade through knee-deep snow, the effort monumental in the thin air and worsening weather. With painful endurance he reached 27,000 feet.

The plan for the third day was to make a simple, unencumbered Alpine climb to the summit. All Messner took with him was his ice ax and a camera. Still, it was an agonizing ascension and Messner, hallucinating part of the time, bone-tired, and threatened by ominous clouds and high-altitude fog, thought from time to time that he might have to abandon his quest. But he kept on, for a time on his hands and knees, slogging away at the 2,000 feet he had to ascend. Finally it came into view—the highest point on earth. The site was unmistakable since the Chinese had anchored an aluminum tripod to the site in 1975, to mark the spot exactly. When he reached the summit, the mid-afternoon sun was hidden by clouds, dimming the magnificence of the scene. Messner was too exhausted to have enjoyed it even had the sun exploded on the great panoramic scene before him. He struggled through a few photographs to record his feat, rested briefly, and, after only 40 minutes at the top of Everest, began the perilous trek back down the mountain. In 3½ hours he reached the bivouac site of the night before, where he had left his food, tent, and other equipment, and virtually collapsed with fatigue. The next day he descended all the way to his base camp, reeling in like a drunken sailor and suffering from exhaustion and dehydration.

Afterward he wrote for *National Geographic*: "I still do not know how I managed to achieve the summit .... I don't think I could handle it again. I was at my limit." But he had, and in doing it, he forged forever the name of Reinhold Messner in the annals of mountain climbing.

Diary of a Himalayan Climb

Shisha Pangma is the Himalayan peak that Manfred Abelein, a member of the West German parliament, and his mountain-climbing team set out to conquer. It is one of the lesser-known peaks in the Tibetan Himalayas, even though it rises to a height of 26,287 feet.

The mountain's allure was that it had long been denied to European and American adventurers. Shisha Pangma was not conquered until 1964, when a team from China scaled it. Other groups had wanted to challenge it, but until 1980 no foreigners in the previous 30 years had ever been given permission by the Chinese government to attempt to climb it.

Manfred Abelein, however, managed to obtain that permission and then set out in early 1980 with a nine-man expedition to ascend mighty Shisha Pangma. He kept a diary from which the following excerpts, reprinted from Jet Tales: The Lufthansa Magazine, are taken.

March 18—Flight by Lufthansa from Munich to Frankfurt, and departure from there by scheduled flight bound for Hong Kong. ... Veritable mountains of luggage have to be handled, even though the bulk of the expedition's equipment had been shipped prior to departure.

Autographs, television, some fast newspaper interviews, two reporters from the mass-circulation tabloid *Bild*, women, children, representatives of various companies, rush: those were the fragmentary impressions just before takeoff. But finally the doors of the aircraft were locked behind us, and we experienced a feeling of uncertain relief. For the next three months, Germany, Europe, politics—nearly everything that happens in the world—will be left behind. At least, that's what I think. Ahead is the uncertainty of our coming adventure in Tibet.

March 26—We have determined that the process of physical adaptation—always a critical factor—from Beijing's altitude of [about 115 feet] above sea level, via Shengtu [about 1,148 feet] to Lhasa, which lies [about 12,304 feet] above the sea, should be accomplished in three days.

The Chinese take care that these days of acclimatization do not drag out excessively. They cater to our every whim. On the first day, we visit the old Tibetan temple in the center of Lhasa, the Jokhang. Although I had seen it last year, this time it is different. This happens to be one of the Three Days of Prayer, and several thousand Tibetans have come to the Jokhang to venerate their gods and to offer them gifts. Row on row, they prostrate themselves before the statues: as far away as the old tree that is said to be as old as the Jokhang itself, opposite the entrance gate, they fall to their faces in the dust. Never at any holy place have I seen such devotion and adherence to faith.

March 29—Since none of us encountered significant problems in adapting to Lhasa's altitude, we have set March 29 as our date of departure from Lhasa. Our convoy assembled outside our quarters. . . .

Just after breakfast we climbed into the cars, which had been loaded with our bulky equipment the day before, and with the first rays of sunshine we passed through the gates of the hostel on our way into the Kyitshu Valley. I was overcome by a strange sensation, a feeling of elation accompanied by apprehension—we had begun our journey into a momentous adventure.

April 1—After about an hour on the road, there was suddenly a clear view, between two brown mountains off in the distance, of the white peak of Shisha Pangma against the sky's clear blue backdrop. I suddenly felt as though I were one of those seafarers to whom the Flying Dutchman appears. A tingling sensation went up and down my spine. Just as suddenly as it appeared, the mountain was gone again. So that was the destination of our expedition.

•　　•　　•

How were we going to fare? The weather was perfect, and our convoy worked its way by stages upward across the rocky desert; the road had given out long before. In a wide sweeping circle we traveled below the hill-like glaciers that belong to the Shisha Pangma massif into the most beautiful and breathtaking amphitheater in this world of mountains.

We were encircled by glistening giants, all between [22,967 and 26,248 feet], which towered above endless stretches of meadows with countless yak and sheep herds. It seemed as though we had entered the sealed-off sanctuary of a god of the mountains. Now I understood the name Shisha Pangma, which translates as "crest above the meadows." The old name, Gosainthan, "place of the holy gods," was equally apt.

As though forming a huge bow,

there they were—the frigid, sharply edged Molamentshin, the elegant Risum, the Langtischiang, the powerful Kangpengtechi, and the overwhelming Shisha Pangma, as well as many nameless peaks. Everyone in the expedition was swept away by this vision.

. . .

April 10—The Zinti-Dacher-Sturm team, together with three Tibetan porters, has set up the first tent of Camp Number Two on the first big terrace of the Northwest Glacier. I enjoy a marvelous day of rest at the base camp. I have lost all sense of time, knowing neither the day of the week nor the date.

Days and nights flow into one another without delineation. For me, always hemmed in by appointments and schedules as though by a straitjacket, this is a completely novel experience. Even entries in the diary, which I jot down with increasing reluctance, do not alter this fact. I surrender without inhibition to this feeling of timelessness. It could be an automatic response to adapting to the new environment.

The nomads who live here with their herds and sometimes visit our camp may have a comparable understanding of this time factor. It is something of almost druglike quality, this dissolution of time.

The nature that surrounds us— the gigantic mountain, with its many changing faces; the glaciers, sometimes glistening, sometimes glowingly shrouded, sometimes somberly ice-cold; the harsh, unending expanse of the Tibetan highland pastures, with their sprinklings of occasional herds of yak and sheep; the distant blue lakes; the eternal everchanging sky—they all exert such a powerful influence as to pull the individual into their magic embrace.

It is like being in a spell, in which the individual and his singularity are dissolved and which smooths out the confrontation between individual and nature, reconciling contradictions. The circumferences of one's own life, with their duties and responsibilities, seem immeasurably distant in Europe, almost unreal.

A dispassionate sense of contentment takes hold. By stages, I have difficulty realizing that we are really here to climb the mountain. There are moments in which this undertaking—to scale the peak that towers over us—seems to me to be impossible, even senseless. It is enough to look at it, to contemplate, to lose oneself entirely.

April 16—Hard to believe, but we have been on the mountain and in camp for nearly four weeks. One day passes like another—in front of us, Shisha Pangma and its broad glacier valley; behind us, the unending expanses of the Tibetan West.

The mountain shows itself in a hundred different ways—sometimes forbidding, sometimes playfully gay, then radiant or somber. Then again, as on a warm spring day, when it is softly streaked by a warm sun or engulfed by the fierce gusts of a sudden storm, it almost bears a resemblance to some giant creature. But I no longer even look at it; the mountain and its appearance have become everyday facts of life for us.

April 22—Schaffert and I have spent the night in Camp Number Two. The other three German mountaineers, who were also up on the face of the mountain, stayed at Camp Number Three.

We experienced a terrible night. A wicked blizzard began around 8:00 P.M., accompanied by a thunderstorm. Lightning slashed the sky, thunder grumbled—something we had not expected at this altitude. For a while, the roar of the wind and the rattle of our tents kept us awake, but we were both so tired that we finally dropped off to sleep.

Neither the mountain nor the glacier chasms nor even the storm disturbed my slumber. I find it curious indeed that the mountain never touched my dreams, neither before nor during the expedition.

But at some point during that night, I awoke. I felt as though somebody was lying atop me; it was almost impossible to move. My one arm, though in the sleeping bag, was tightly wrapped around the food crate, which was in the middle of the tent, while the other was firmly wedged between the side of the tent and my own body.

It was only in stages that I finally comprehended the situation. The combined fury of the storm and the driving snow had bent and broken the pole supporting the roof of the tent. The tent lay on top of us, and newly fallen snow had jammed the tent sides down against our sleeping bags. Fortunately, the food crate occupied the middle of the tent, and since it was higher by some [eight inches] than our sleeping bags, it had

given us a bit of space. But I was so firmly squeezed into my sleeping bag that I had trouble freeing my arms in order to move one hand upward in search of the zipper ring over my head.

Finally, I succeeded in opening the sleeping bag and applying some upward pressure with one hand to the tent roof and then woke up Schaffert. He was in much the same condition as I. But we succeeded at last in getting one mountain boot on top of the food crate, thus expanding our breathing space by another [cubic inch or so]. After that we forced the roof up and reerected the broken metal pole, so that at least some of the snow that bore down on our tent could slide off sideways. Thus the immediate danger was averted.

With the help of a rope and another metal rod, we bridged the gap created by the earlier breach. Then we got the stove going to boil some tea. Eventually, the new day dawned, and I mused for a while about how the night might have ended. But then I shook off these thoughts.

April 25—Camp life and its routines were now sufficiently familiar. For boy scouts, under different circumstances, this might be a romantic affair. But after several weeks, camp life proves to be rather dreary. One literally lives with nature; the rising and setting sun determines the daily rhythm. Only occasionally do a few candles or a gas lantern prolong the day. As a rule, one spends 12 hours in the sleeping bag from dusk to dawn—that is, until the sun's rays touch the tent roofs, and one dares to creep out. Not that the bags are sufficient. One has to dress warmly before crawling into them, and the various individuals solve this problem in the oddest ways. A thin rubber sheet provides added protection from the ground's chill.

May 11—This was to be the day of decision. I have spent a relatively comfortable night under my oxygen mask. The night itself was fairly calm, the wind at bay.

As we prepared inside the tent for our ascent, it was still the dead of night. A faint rattling of the tent sides showed that the wind was gaining strength, which did not cause us any worry.... The wind is stronger still. The tent walls are beginning to whip back and forth. Then they snap and crack, as though we are in the middle of an artillery exchange. And still the winds gain force; I am afraid that the tent will be ripped apart. By and by, though, the day begins, but it is no day of sunshine. The wind reaches hurricane force.... A sense of paralyzing uncertainty hovered over all of us. Everyone knew in his heart that an ascent in this hurricane was not possible. But none wanted to be the first to begin the retreat.

At first, I too was uncertain what to do. But then my thoughts ran along these lines: I had the feeling my hands were suffering from the frost; one more day and another night at an altitude of [about 24,279 feet] would have weakened my physical condition. Under normal circumstances, one should not spend more than one night at this altitude, and I would have had to sleep with oxygen the following night as well. We had calculated that we would need two bottles of oxygen for the dash to the peak, so that made for three bottles. But only two were left. In an emergency, there would have been no reserve oxygen. And that is why I decided we should begin the descent....

Rock Climbing: An Interview with Dan Goodwin

Dan Goodwin, sometimes known as Spider Dan or Climber Dan because of his more publicized exploits in scaling the faces of major skyscrapers, like the Sears Tower and the John Hancock Building in Chicago, is in fact a very serious rock climber. This sport, one of the most difficult and demanding in all adventuredom, has gained international attention in recent years and is currently being considered for inclusion in the Olympic Games. Dan Goodwin is one of the sport's foremost practitioners, and has successfully scaled some of the world's most difficult mountain walls. He is an expert at free climbing, that is, climbing without the use of artificial equipment as

aids to the climb, just using hands and feet, muscle and determina-
tion, to conquer sheer-faced walls that rise straight up, and over-
hangs that appear unclimbable. Here, he tells about what this rug-
ged, dangerous sport is really like.

R. W.: How does rock climbing differ from mountain climbing in general?

GOODWIN: There's quite a difference. Mountain climbing, as most people know it, is simply climbing to the top of a mountain, and often by following the easiest way up. Certainly it can be challenging, but for the most part you follow the way of least resistance. Rock climbing is challenging the most difficult walls—those with sheer faces, roofs or overhangs, those kinds of things.

R. W.: Rock climbing is really a phase of mountain climbing, isn't it?

GOODWIN: Yes, at least it can be, but it's also a sport all its own. Climbers have always had to challenge these sheer rock walls; they would use the basic techniques, the regular climbing equipment, any means that they could to get to the top—use pitons, chocks, whatever, to get to the top. But in the last ten or fifteen years, climbers have taken it one step farther to eliminate the reliance on equipment, to just climb with hands and feet. In the past, say, five to ten years, climbers have been taking to what we call rock gymnastics. Climbers train with artificial climbs, simulating the real thing, and that's all they do, train every day, and they are very serious about the sport. The ath-letes are of such a quality now that when they are on the rock there are things that years ago they would question trying with equipment that are now being done with only their hands and feet.

R. W.: Tell me what a rock climb today is really like.

GOODWIN: Well, you pick out a sheer rock wall, one that may be slightly overhung, one you plan to climb using no equipment other than your hands and feet, wedging your fingers and toes into a crack, and climbing. You may be using equipment but it's only there to protect you if you fall. The technique and the strength required to go climb such an obstacle is almost unimaginable, mind-boggling, but it can be done. You have to be aware of the high stress factor as well as the difficulties and the use of your strength, and also there is a lot of pain. In order for your hands or fingers or toes to stick in a crack, there's going to be pain. You are wedging them in and there is counterforce. At the same time you experience a real fear about the difficulties—holding on with one hand while you put a piece of equipment in to protect you in case you fall, for example. As you do it, you are very aware of the risks, the consequences, of taking a long fall. Remember you're using the rope and other equipment not to climb up, but to save you if you fall. Sometimes you may fall thirty-five to forty feet and not blink an eye because it's part of the sport. You're on a rope, so you climb back up. But there's always the fear or worry about falling when you're not protected by the rope.

R. W.: Where were some of the most interesting rock climbs you've made?

GOODWIN: I've made quite a few climbs all over the country, on the east coast, the coast of Maine, out west. I like to go into an area that no one else has been to, has climbed in, that is. As far as climbs, the hardest climbs, well, I'd say Mickey's Beach in California is one, and another one I did was Separate Reality. It has a forty-foot roof [overhang], and the name really fits it because when you are on this roof you're upside-down with just your hands and feet wedged into a crack, and as you are going underneath the roof you have a drop of thousands of feet below you.

R. W.: You said "just your hands and feet," but you do have safety equipment while you're climbing on a roof?

GOODWIN: Yes, that is a definite requirement. You have a rope, but you have to put it together yourself as you climb. You put a piece in, and you may have to go another ten feet before you can put another piece in. It's not always

easy, but you have to have it. Without it you could be killed.

R. W.: How did you get started in rock climbing?

GOODWIN: I was brought up in the state of Maine. Years ago, I was hiking through the mountains, and I'd been into climbing mountains for some time, and I just thought it was time for a change, time to move ahead. The easier ways after a while seemed too simple so I was looking for harder ways, more challenging ways to climb a mountain. Then I realized that the trails I was hiking on weaved in and out of these massive rock walls, and I thought, my God, how fantastic that would be to climb one of them. The ultimate challenge. And as time went on I began reading about rock climbing, and I decided that I really wanted to do some of those climbs. I actually started climbing out in New York State.

R. W.: Did you ever climb El Capitan in California?

GOODWIN: Several times.

R. W.: That's certainly a well-known mountain for climbing, but is it very difficult as a rock climb?

GOODWIN: Yes, it is. It's probably one of the largest walls in the United States. It's three thousand feet, and usually takes several days to climb. The pictures that you see of people hanging in the hammocks, well, they're sleeping on the side of the mountain. They climb so long, then they have to rest—sleep—just like anybody else, but they have to fix their bed onto the side of the mountain.

R. W.: How long does one lie in a hammock? Do you spend the whole night there?

GOODWIN: Normally you'd climb from just before sunup until dark. When it's too dark to do anything else you'd set your hammock. You'd rig it to the mountain, then go to bed. The next morning you'd start climbing again.

R. W.: What about Grand Illusion? Isn't that one of the most difficult rock climbs?

GOODWIN: That's probably right now one of the most difficult climbs in the world. So far, only one person has done it—Tony Yaniro.

R. W.: Where is it exactly?

GOODWIN: In California, near Lake Tahoe.

R. W.: Have you tried it yet?

GOODWIN: Not yet, but I plan to in the next year. There are a number of climbs out there that are just spectacular. They are on my list.

R. W.: What makes Grand Illusion so difficult?

GOODWIN: There's a forty-foot roof, and the crack, its size, well it's very difficult and painful. You have to be in perfect condition. With Grand Illusion the jams are more difficult, more sustained, rather than jam your hands and fingers in there, you can only jam the tips of your fingers in some places, which obviously makes it more difficult.

R. W.: What's the height you actually ascend on a normal rock climb?

GOODWIN: Most normal rock climbing is on a pitch that may be from a hundred to a hundred and twenty feet. And on a rock wall you may have ten to fifteen pitches, a hundred and ten feet or more each. The majority of the difficult climbs are usually sixty to a hundred and twenty feet, and that may not sound like much, but when you're standing at the bottom trying to fit your hand into a crack and all you see is flat wall stretching up and maybe a roof jutting out, you know what an incredible challenge it is.

R. W.: How long would it take to ascend a one hundred-foot pitch?

GOODWIN: Depends on how difficult. I would say ten or fifteen minutes in most cases. But it would vary with each situation. That's why rock climbing is such an ever-challenging sport.

R. W.: How do you train for rock climbing?

GOODWIN: I do a tremendous number of pull-ups. I climb rope hand over hand. I also do a lot of running, leg work.

R. W.: Could you describe a rock climb up a one hundred-foot pitch? What would you do, step by step? What equipment would you have with you?

GOODWIN: There's just safety equipment. We used to use pitons but now we very rarely do. Most of the time climbers use chocks, or wedges, instead of pitons. What the item is, is basically an aluminum wedge with a wire or sometimes a nylon sling, and as you're climbing up with your hands and feet you put the wedge into a crack and you have a rope. It's just a harness system, you kind of climb into the equipment and then climb past it. There's a lot involved because if you don't place the equipment right, and then fall, the equipment is going to come out. And then it's all over. But basically to describe a climb is really just to say, "You climb." You find a crack to grab hold of, another for a foothold. You rig your safety equipment as you go, and you face each obstacle as it arises.

R. W.: What are some of the perils of rock climbing? Obviously, falling is the main one, but what are some of the other elements that might go against you?

GOODWIN: You've got the wind, sometimes cold weather. In hot weather moisture collects in the rocks, makes the rock slippery. So in the summertime you often see climbers using gymnastic chalk to absorb the moisture in the rock and on their skin. Also in warm weather, you sweat. You're trying to hold on to something and your fingertips may be very moist.

R. W.: What are some of the most frightening experiences you've had climbing rocks?

GOODWIN: I was on one climb in Red Rock Canyon outside of Las Vegas, a climb that they call Ixtlan. I remember, it was a new route. It was a face climb that was very, very difficult. I was using a crack and as I was climbing up the crack I found after a while I couldn't place any equipment into it. The crack was flaring out, nothing would stay. I couldn't go back down because it was too difficult, so I was facing a long haul upwards, not knowing if I could place equipment on up. I just kept pushing, pushing, pushing, and the next thing you know I was forty feet out from my last piece of equipment. That means I was facing an eighty-foot fall, which I knew was going to be a death fall if I fell. Farther on up I was facing a three-foot roof. As I was climbing it my feet were smeared against the wall and I found a hold at the very lip of the roof. It was about the size of a doorjamb, maybe only half an inch. But that was all, and when I cut loose I dragged up one arm to grab another hold and when I was in that position I realized I wasn't sure if I was going to be able to pull up over the lip because I couldn't see if there was anything above to grab onto. But there was.

R. W.: What's the farthest you've ever fallen?

GOODWIN: The farthest I've fallen was sixty-five feet, and I hit the ground. I was with a climbing friend of mine, it was in the winter, and we were trying to think of different ways to try to overcome the fear of falling. I would tie one end of a rope to the wall and the other end to me and jump off. I'd do it over and over again until I

Great Rock Climbs

The following is master mountaineer Dan Goodwin's list of 12 unique and ultimately demanding rock climbs in the United States. Because of their extraordinary difficulty, it is estimated that only about one percent of all the climbers in the world could successfully scale these sheer walls with their roofs and other obstacles. Goodwin has successfully scaled four, and plans to eventually conquer all of them.

Rock Climb *	Location
Mickey's Beach	Stinson Beach, California
Separate Reality	Yosemite Valley, California
Tales of Power	Yosemite Valley, California
Equinox	Joshua Tree National Monument, California
Grand Illusion	Sugarloaf, near Lake Tahoe, California-Nevada
Stone Cold Crazy	Lover's Leap, near Lake Tahoe, California-Nevada
Ixtlan	Red Rock Canyon, Nevada
Just an Illusion	Red Rock Canyon, Nevada
Super Crack of the Desert	Near Moab, Utah
Genesis	El Dorado Canyon, Colorado
Super Crack	Shawangunks, near New Paltz, New York
Kansas City	Shawangunks, near New Paltz, New York

*The name of a particular rock climb is given by the first person who climbs it.

wasn't afraid of the fall. It's practice. But this time it was raining and later snowing, and I jumped off, but we had miscalculated the length of the rope and I hit the ground. That was the longest I'd ever fallen and actually hit something.

R. W.: Is there something you feel inside that urges you to climb, that spurs you on?

GOODWIN: Always. It begins in training. You work yourself to the breaking point. You feel like you're going to be pumped out. Your arms feel like they're swollen, and your hands are being pushed even farther. So you make your workouts count, you go to the limit. I know I'm going to work out for two hours when I leave here. Solid, straight, and strenuous. No letup. I sometimes feel like I'm going to pass out halfway through, like I can't do it, the pain is so much. But since I'm doing it, so long as I know mentally that I'm not going to injure myself, I go on. It's just pain-bearing. If you talk to a lot of Olympic record-holders about the pain-bearing, they all have gone through it. They train so hard every day that they are at the breaking point, the threshold. It's part of the commitment.

R. W.: How is climbing a skyscraper different from rock climbing?

GOODWIN: Very different. And more difficult in a different kind of way. When you look at a "wall" like that of the Sears Tower, maybe fifteen hundred feet straight up . . . well, the wind howls just as it does in the mountains, you have the same weather—rain or snow or sleet. But when I looked at that wall, I thought, my God, to really be able to climb that building would be an extraordinary thing. I'd gone to the World Trade Center and it didn't seem as challenging to me, so I decided to climb the Sears because it offered a more difficult challenge than I had ever been offered before. It's different in that you're not using any of the same kind of equipment that you use in regular mountain climbing, and you have to rely on equipment as such, which also makes it very different from rock climbing—free ascent, that is. I had to devise, improvise, and make equipment to use. There was no book to go to, there was no one to ask how to do it. When you look at that building and compare you will find it's like climbing the outside of a very sheer wall. Your success depends then on what kind of equipment you will be using. I'd place a suction cup on a window, and all of a sudden it would slide. I'd reach out and clamp another one on, crank up, put another one on, and by the time I put the third one on the first one would come off. It was split-second timing sometimes. There are climbs done all over the country, all over the world, but of all the climbs I've heard done, I've yet to hear about one that was as difficult as the Sears or the Hancock. You have to remember, there were no safety devices or equipment. If I fell, I was risking a fall of hundreds of feet. All the way up I was risking death. It was just a step beyond.

R. W.: What interesting climbs do you look forward to in the future? What are your biggest challenges right now?

GOODWIN: I have a list of climbs all over the world. My hit list I call it. Here in the United States, the "Gunks," in upper New York State. I plan on traveling out west and climbing Phoenix, which is in Yosemite Valley, and Equinox in Southern California . . . I could go on and on and on. These climbs that I've mentioned are just a few. There are a dozen climbs in the world that are difficult, but they are just beautiful because you have to bring everything into play to conquer them— all your training, know-how, skill, determination. It's an ultimate individual challenge.

On the Water

Visiting the Bottom of the Ocean

On January 23, 1960, Project Nekton reached its climax. Jacques Piccard of France and Lieutenant Donald Walsh of the U.S. Navy descended in the bathyscaph Trieste into the Mariana Trench in the South Pacific, touching the ocean floor. The exact spot is known as the Challenger Deep, the deepest known part of the world's oceans, approximately 200 miles southwest of Guam.

After descending for almost five hours, the Trieste settled on the bottom, 35,820 feet below the ocean's surface, a distance of almost seven miles. There the bathyscaph withstood almost 200,000 tons of pressure (16,883 pounds per square inch), and the two men inside the amazing sphere became the first to view the ultimate depths of the sea. Jacques Piccard, leader of the diving expedition and the son of the inventor of the bathyscaph, August Piccard, coauthored an account of his experiences, Seven Miles Down: The Story of the Bathyscaph Trieste, from which the following passages are taken.

The sight that met my eyes when we boarded the wallowing bathyscaph was discouraging, to say the least. Broaching seas smothered her. The deck was a mess. Everything was awash. It was apparent at once that the tow from Guam had taken a terrific toll. [The Trieste was towed to the diving site by the U.S.S. Wandank and escorted by the U.S.S. Lewis; both navy ships would remain on the surface during the dive.]

A hasty inspection revealed that the surface telephone (used for topside communication after we were sealed in the sphere) had been carried away. The tachometer (the instrument that measured our diving rate) was badly damaged and inoperative. The vertical current meter was dangling by a few wires.

I was worried. [Giuseppe] Buono showed it. "So? Do we dive, signor?"

I asked myself that same question. Was it sheer madness to dive seven miles into the sea under such conditions?

I looked across the angry seas and saw that [Donald] Walsh was having a rough time getting seaborne from the Lewis in a motor whaleboat. He was on his way now. The whaleboat careened toward us. Walsh leaped aboard in good navy style. Walsh grabbed a stanchion, and the whaleboat peeled off to stand by.

Then he looked things over. He didn't like what he saw any better than I. He shook his head. "What do you think, Jacques?"

"I'll know better after I've checked below," I replied.

I swung into the conning tower, dropped down the ladder, and eeled through the door into the sphere. First I energized the electromagnets. All circuits were in order. I checked my watch. It was now 0800. The time factor was critical. If we were going to dive that day, we couldn't delay much longer. It was vital to accomplish the 14-mile round trip to the ocean floor and back before darkness.

If we didn't surface until after dark, we might not be spotted. According to my very careful calculations, we couldn't dive later than 0900 if we were to maintain a safe time margin. It is all very well for a man seeking adventure to take chances. I wasn't looking for adventure. I wanted a successful and uneventful operation. I wanted to leave nothing to chance.

Essentially things were in order. I made the decision. We would dive.

Topside they were waiting for my report. All I had to do was nod. Walsh signaled his agreement. Buono clambered aft to disconnect the towline. I removed the pins that hold the ballast mechanically. Once removed, the shot was held by the electromagnets alone. I could now jettison ballast at will by cutting the current.

Feverish activity on deck occupied final precious moments. Walsh had slipped below to check a new electric thermometer. I called to Buono to see if he was ready.

"E a posto tutto?"

"O kappa, signor." Buono nodded, using the Italian version of okay.

It was 0810—full morning now. I took one last look at the sea and sky. The *Wandank* was standing off a quarter mile away, rolling and pitching in the big swells. Still farther off was the *Lewis*, silhouetted against the heavy overcast. The tropical heat pressed down like a steamy blanket.

But there was no time for poetic contemplation. Quickly I gave Buono his last-minute instructions. Once we sealed the door, he would flood the sas [the entrance tunnel through the float to the observation gondola] and make final diving preparations. With communications from the sphere to topside out, we arranged a signal. If anything was amiss below, I would switch on the motor and rotate the topside propellers.

Buono clasped hands with me and then Walsh. He wished us *buona fortuna*.

"Grazie," I answered. "Arrivederci."

We swung closed the heavy steel door. We turned up the bolt that would seal us securely in our vault. The air was cool and dry in the sphere, thanks to the silica gel. But the seas were buffeting the float, swinging our little spherical cell to and fro. I had but one thing on my mind—to dive as quickly as possible into the serene depths.

I checked my watch. It was now 0815. Quickly I reviewed every essential detail. We were diving without some important instruments. I would have only my watch and my depth gauge with which to calculate our rate of descent. In a descent everything depends on buoyancy control—on conserving and expending ballast with a delicate and knowledgeable touch.

We had a total of 1,440 seconds of ballast; that is to say I could jettison 25 pounds of iron shot per second for a total of roughly 16 long tons. That amount of ballast would do it, with a lot to spare.

Through the after porthole I could see water flooding the antechamber. I opened the oxygen valves and checked the air purification system. We could expect to dive momentarily. Had our tachometer been operative, the very instant of descent would have been apparent. As it was, we simply had to wait to see the pressure gauge moving.

I wanted to log that instant. My eyes were on my watch. Suddenly at 0823 the rocking ceased, the sphere became calm. I glanced at the depth gauge. The needle was quivering.

We were on our way down. We were *entre deux eaux*, to use a French expression—"in mid-water." The *grande plongée* had begun. I looked over at Walsh. We both sighed in relief.

Slowly we settled to 340 feet. There at 0835 the descent was halted. In fact we were slowly bounced upward several yards. This, of course, was the main thermocline, the cold water of increased density resisting our penetration.

We took this opportunity to recheck our instruments. My usual diving procedure was to wait for the gasoline to cool sufficiently to push on through this obstruction. On this dive there was no time to lose if we were to surface before nightfall. I valved off some gasoline from the maneuvering tank.

Once again we began settling, but only briefly. Again, at 370 feet, we were bounced upward. I pushed the gasoline valving switch once more. At 420 feet and again at 515 feet, we were repulsed by the stubborn thermocline resistance. Never before

in all of my 65 dives had I encountered so many strong thermal barriers. The little ascents were caused by internal waves, which cause a constant rising and falling of the thermocline.

• • •

I did not know it then, of course, but another factor contributed to the slowness of our descent. The scaph refused to sink when Buono flooded the air tanks in the float. She was slightly light due to the high temperature of the gasoline. So he opened up the sas hatch once more, letting waves wash in, completely filling it with water. Split-second agility was then needed to seal the hatch and jump into the raft before the scaph sank. Normally some air is left in the sas; as we sink this air is compressed, adding weight to the *Trieste*. With this air pocket missing, we were almost neutrally buoyant, so that we came to rest on the slightest water density discontinuity.

• • •

Valuable time was consumed. At 0900 we had descended a mere 800 feet. There was a long way to go. Our average speed to this point was only four inches per second. At that snail's pace it would take more than 30 hours to complete our descent.

Now our sphere began to drop in earnest. We were through the sea's twilight zone. Beyond the port there was darkness, but not yet total blackness. Descending into the sea, the night comes slowly like a northern dusk.

At 1,000 feet I switched off the

cabin light for a careful look into the sea. A faint trace of light still seeped down from above. I could just barely see the outline of the after shot tub.

I turned the cabin light on again. I tested the forward beam that casts a cone of light into the sea. The probing beam picked up a familiar illusion, familiar to me at least. Formless plankton appeared like a snowfall, only streaming upward instead of downward.

As we plummeted, there was an illusion of great speed. And we *were* falling fast—more than three feet per second (the speed of an average elevator). This was just about our terminal velocity.

Walsh tried the UQC acoustic telephone. His effort to contact the *Wandank* had been unavailing. Now he made contact with the *Lewis*. This tenuous connection with the surface world is a pleasant diversion. Why, I don't know. We were now far beyond the reach of assistance.

I turned to my graphs. They were based on many hours of calculations and extrapolations especially from the previous 18,150-foot and 23,000-foot dives. My plan was to plummet the first 26,000 feet at a fast three feet per second. Then I would reduce speed to two feet per second and finally to one foot per second until we detected the bottom on our 600-foot range echo sounder. This, I knew, would give me time to discharge sufficient ballast to break our speed for landing.

I recalled a very real hazard. The charts had warned me that the bottom of the cleft into which we were plunging was a scant one mile in width. Oceanographers have little knowledge of the velocity of the abyssal drift. It was easily possible that we might collide with a wall of the trench—a chilling thought! I had to be extremely cautious.

. . . 0920—depth 2,400 feet. Outside, total blackness. We dimmed our cabin light, leaving only sufficient illumination to read our instruments. We wanted to dark-adapt our eyes for observation. We had entered the abyssal zone, the timeless world of eternal darkness. The water temperature had dropped abruptly when we had broken through the thermoclines. The chill was now penetrating the sphere. Both Walsh and I had been thoroughly soaked while preparing for the dive. Now it was time to change into dry clothing—no simple task in the restricted space of our cell, three feet across between the instruments and less than six feet high.

We broke out our first chocolate bars—the only food aboard. Walsh and I had a private joke about these "lunches." On the last dive I had provided lunch—Swiss Nestle' bars. This time Walsh offered to bring the lunch. He did—15 American Hershey bars.

. . . 0929—4,200 feet. A dribble of water entered around one of the cable lead-throughs. The small trickle meandered down the wall of the sphere into the bilge. This lead-through had always been perfectly sealed before.

. . . 0937—5,750 feet. A call from the *Wandank* on the UQC. The transmission was loud and clear. I was anxious to speak to Buono. It was important to know if the topside operation had gone off successfully. His musical Neapolitan voice came down to me through more than a mile of sea. "*Tutto bene, signor,*" Buono assured me. Yes, he had had time to secure the hatch to the sas. All was in order topside. There was no cause for worry. It was raining and squally on the surface. If anything, the weather was deteriorating. I signed off feeling completely detached from nature's vicissitudes in the world of the sun.

Now, as before, we were dropping down, down, down, at 200 feet per minute. I noted with relief that the first leak had stopped. Another now started. But this was an old friend from the previous dive. It started at around 18,000 feet and then sealed itself. It did, once again. The wax used in the watertight lead-throughs was apparently a little too old, so that it did not flow easily into some small crevices.

We continued to plunge. Black water rushed upward past us. Successively we overpassed the record depths that we had reached on preceding weeks. At 20,000 feet we were at the maximum depth of the normal Pacific sea floor. We were dropping into the open maw of the Mariana Trench, leaving the abyssal zone of the ocean and entering the hadal regions. Few bathyscaphs of the future need be designed for any depth greater than 20,000 feet. Only in trenches do we find the hadal depths. They comprise a mere one percent of the ocean floor.

Twenty-three thousand feet. This was a moment of special signifi-cance. The *Trieste*, Walsh, and I plummeted past the level of Dive 64. For the first time, man was descending so deep. For the fourth time the *Trieste* was carrying me into virgin depths: once in 1953, once in 1959, and now twice in 1960.

... 1124. The *Wandank* is talking to the *Lewis* on UQC. Then a call, barely audible, came through the still sea to us. By prearrangement, known to Walsh but unknown to me, we were to key tones on the UQC once out of voice range. An even number of tones meant good news; odd numbers indicated bad news. They had arranged a distress Mayday signal of five tones! Walsh transmitted a double signal meaning "all's well."

... 1130—27,000 feet, right on schedule. Already I had dropped six tons of ballast to keep our speed of descent from building up beyond three feet per second. It was time to further reduce our velocity, anticipating the approaching bottom.

... 1144—29,150 feet. Now we were as deep under the sea as Mount Everest is high above it. In the light cone the water was crystal clear—no "sea snow" and not the slightest trace of plankton. This was a vast emptiness beyond all comprehension. There was perhaps a mile of water still beneath us, but the possibility of collision with the trench wall was still on my mind. I pushed the ballast button, slowing us down to two feet per second—then to one foot per second, as decided before the dive.

... 1200—31,000 feet. I flipped on the echo sounder and sought for an echo to record on its 600-foot scale. No echo returned; the bottom presumably was still beyond 100 fathoms. Trying moments were ahead. We were venturing beyond the tested capabilities of the *Trieste*. On paper she could descend safely to ten miles and the sphere alone much more. I had confidence in those calculations. She was a complex of nuts and bolts, metal, plastic, and wire. But a dead thing? No. To me she was a living creature with a will to resist the seizing pressure. Above me, in the float, icy water was streaming in as the gasoline contracted, making the craft ever heavier and heavier. It was as if this icy water were coursing through my own veins.

The UQC was quiet now. The slow, silent descent was disturbed only by the hiss of oxygen escaping and the background hum of electronic instruments. I peered out the window looking for bottom—and then back to the echo sounder. But there is only water and more water. Perhaps the sounder wasn't working. On the last dive we were 120 feet from the bottom before we picked it up. But now I could see noise recording. It made a long smudge on the graph from the iron ballast just released from the tub. "Très bien, it is working fine."

Then an uneasy thought. What would the bottom be like? Clearly we were in the axis of the trench, and most probably we would miss the rocky walls. [Robert] Dietz, who was aboard the *Lewis*, had advised me that there was an outside chance that the bottom sediment would be a flocculent and unconsolidated "soup" of recently deposited turbidity current beds. Could we sink and disappear into this material before being aware that we had contacted the bottom? Russian scientists aboard the *Vityaz* reportedly had tried many times, unsuccessfully, to lower a camera and snap pictures in trenches. But each time blank negatives came up. It appeared that the camera had entered a thick, soupy bottom before finally being triggered.

On the other hand, Dietz had emphasized, the H.M.S. *Challenger* in 1951 had recovered a bottom sample not far distant from our diving site. It was diatomaceous ooze, composed almost entirely of siliceous remains of the tropical diatom *Ethmodiscus rex*. These diatoms live in the surface water, and their dead husks settle to the bottom. This would provide a firm bottom for landing. I could only hope that we would land on *Challenger* bottom.

... 1206—32,400 feet. A strong, muffled explosion! The sphere shook as though in a small earthquake. I caught Walsh's eye; he was watching me anxiously but calmly. "Have we touched bottom?" Walsh asked. "I do not believe so," I replied. We waited for something to happen. Nothing did. I wondered if the light case over the forward port had imploded. I tried to switch it on, and it didn't light up. This could be the trouble, but I wasn't satisfied. The noise we heard wasn't the high-pitched pop that had accompanied previous implosions. I studied the dials and switched off the UQC to silence the sphere. Still nothing happened. Our equilibrium seemed unaffected—we were not, apparently, losing gas. Our descent continued exactly as before. Without formal discussion we agreed to continue down.

Thirty-four thousand feet—no bottom ... 35,000 feet, only water and more water ... 36,000 feet, descending smoothly at 60 feet per minute. Now we were at the supposed depth of the Challenger Deep. Had we found a new hole or was our depth gauge in error? Then a wry thought—perhaps we'd missed the bottom!

... 1256—Walsh's eyes were glued to the echo sounder. I was watching alternately through the port and at the fathometer. Suddenly we saw black echoes on the graph. "There it is, Jacques! It looks like we have found it!" Yes, we had finally found it, just 42 fathoms down.

While I peered through the port preparing to touch down, Walsh called off the soundings. "Thirty-six fathoms, echo coming in weakly—thirty-two ... twenty-eight ... twenty-five ... twenty-four—now we are getting nice trace. Twenty-two fathoms—still going down—yes, this is it! Twenty ... eighteen ... fifteen ... ten—makes a nice trace now. Going right down. Six fathoms—we're slowing up, very slowly; we may come to a stop. You say you saw a small animal, possibly a red shrimp about one inch long? Wonderful, wonderful! Three fathoms—you can see the bottom through the port? Good—we've made it!"

The bottom appeared light and clear, a waste of snuff-colored ooze.

We were landing on a nice, flat bottom of firm diatomaceous ooze. Indifferent to the nearly 200,000 tons of pressure clamped on her metal sphere, the Trieste balanced herself delicately on the few pounds of guide rope that lay on the bottom, making token claim, in the name of science and humanity, to the ultimate depths in all our oceans—the Challenger Deep.

The depth gauge read 6,300 fathoms—37,800 feet. The time—1306 hours. . . .

And as we were settling this final fathom, I saw a wonderful thing. Lying on the bottom just beneath us was some type of flatfish, resembling a sole, about one foot long and six inches across. Even as I saw him, his two round eyes on top of his head spied us—a monster of steel—invading his silent realm. Eyes? Why should he have eyes? Merely to see phosphorescence? The floodlight that bathed him was the first real light ever to enter this hadal realm. Here in an instant was the answer that biologists had sought for decades. Could life exist in the greatest depths of the ocean? It could! And not only that—here apparently was a true, bony teleost fish, not a primitive ray or elasmobranch. Yes, a highly evolved vertebrate, in time's arrow very close to man himself.

Slowly, extremely slowly, this flatfish swam away. Moving along the bottom, partly in the ooze and partly in the water, he disappeared into his night. Slowly too—perhaps everything is slow at the bottom of the sea—Walsh and I shook hands.

Over Niagara in a Barrel

One of the most awesome natural wonders on the North American continent, Niagara Falls for a century has been an inland magnet to sightseers and honeymooners, as well as to a handful of daredevil thrill-seekers. Most people have gathered there to witness the nearly one million gallons of water that tumble over its 160-foot precipice every second. A few come for other reasons. Stunts involving the Falls have been attempted throughout the 1900s, and the body-wrenching plunge over Horseshoe Falls, on the Canadian side, has proven to be the most bizarre and also the deadliest.

Anna Edson Taylor, a widowed schoolteacher from Michigan, was the first person known to have negotiated the Falls and survived. On October 24, 1901, at the age of 42, Mrs. Taylor demurely stepped into a 165-pound oak barrel (which she had commissioned to match her weight), was pushed into the roiling river a mile above Horseshoe Falls, and was quickly swept over the drop.

For nearly 15 minutes, her 4½-foot barrel bobbed like a cork in the giant rollers at the base of the Falls until finally the sturdy craft floated to shore. Although she was a little woozy from the journey (she sustained facial cuts and a concussion), Annie Taylor emerged intact and then said: "Nobody ought ever to do that again."

Ten years later, an Englishman named Bobby Leach tried to duplicate the feat of the schoolteacher. Barely alive when he was pulled out of the barrel after hurtling over Horseshoe Falls, he spent six months in a hospital, then, somewhat later in New Zealand, he died from gangrene that resulted from his injuries. Another Englishman, Charles Stephens, disappeared over the Falls leaving behind only a severed arm to be recovered by would-be rescuers. A Greek bachelor, George Stathakis, also perished over the Falls, although a pet turtle traveling in the stuntman's barrel managed to survive the plunge.

In 1928, Jean Lussier, a French Canadian, went over in a large, specially designed rubber ball and escaped relatively unscathed. A New Yorker, Nathan Boya, specially constructed what he called a "Plunge-o-Sphere," and made the trip over the Falls. He lived, too, and for the stunt had to pay a $100 fine in the Niagara County, New York, courthouse.

Only one person has gone over the Falls *without* the benefit of a barrel or other survival vessel and lived. He was Roger Woodward, a seven-year-old boy who was swept over the Falls wearing only a life jacket, after a boating mishap in 1960.

Some say there is a hypnotic force in the constant roar of the oceanic volume of water crashing from the 160-foot free-fall into a rocky riverbed, that it is a force that beckons and challenges. One family that perhaps has felt this pull more strongly than others is the Hills, who have lived near the Falls for generations. One member of the family, Major Hill, was pulled unconscious from the river as his splintered, empty barrel was buffeted in the whirling waters at the foot of the Falls, perhaps proving how little he had learned from experience. Major Hill himself had pulled nearly 200 bodies out of the raging river (including several of the people mentioned here). Red Hill, Jr., from the same family, died trying to conquer Niagara in an elaborate collection of inner tubes.

Discovering precisely how many people have died trying to go over the Falls is complicated by the surprisingly large number of suicide victims whose bodies are discovered near the base of the Falls each year. Then again, in stunts such as this, the line between ultimate daredevilry and suicidal impulse becomes uncommonly fine.

A World Champion Hydroplane Racer

The craft are sleek, bulletlike constructions—combinations of fiberglass hulls and supercharged engines—that virtually explode across the water at speeds better than 100 miles an hour, trailing dazzling wakes (called rooster tails in boat-racing jargon) behind them. Hydroplanes, they're called, and their ancestry can be traced to the first nonsteam powerboat built in 1887 by Gottlieb Daimler, the German engineer better known perhaps for inventing the gasoline-powered engine.

From Daimler's efforts speedboats, P T boats, and finally hydroplanes evolved, the sport of racing them following soon after their invention. For example, speedboats were raced publicly in England as early as 1903 (the first motorboat race, the Harmsworth Cup Competition, over an 8-1/2-mile course, took place in Ireland on July 11, 1903). Today the top annual award for hydroplane racers in America is the Gold Cup. One of the sport's contemporary greats was Dean Chenoweth of Tallahassee, Florida, a four-time winner of the Gold Cup and holder of several world records. Chenoweth died July 31, 1982, when his hydroplane flipped during a practice run on the Columbia River near Pasco, Washington. In 1980, Chenoweth talked with the author about his sport, with its excitement and varied risks.

R.W.: What do you consider the most thrilling thing about hydroplane racing?

CHENOWETH: Competition and, I guess, the raw speed—that's it basically.

R.W.: That's what really drives you. What's the noise like when you're sitting in the cockpit of one of those boats?

CHENOWETH: Not bad, because we're not like the Indy driver. We're up front of the engine.

R.W.: But it's not really quiet.

CHENOWETH: Well, no. Naturally you hear the engine but in a very minor way compared, say, to what we used to hear when we were sitting behind it.

R.W.: Would you call hydroplane racing a profession, or your hobby, or is it more than that?

CHENOWETH: It's mainly a hobby. For a living I've got a beer distributorship in Florida, for Budweiser. That's why my boat is called Miss Budweiser. And, you know, it's kind of a two-fold purpose—being in the races, especially winning, gets me some kind of acclaim, and on the local and state levels, it helps business, for me and Budweiser.

R.W.: How fast do hydroplanes go?

CHENOWETH: In our competition setup, we usually hit about one hundred seventy-five miles per hour, maybe one hundred eighty, in the straightaway, although we have gone faster.

R.W.: How much horsepower does Miss Budweiser have?

CHENOWETH: Well, it probably packs about thirty-four hundred.

R.W.: Now maybe we could talk a little about the sport of hydroplane racing itself. When did it begin to become popular?

CHENOWETH: Let's see. It goes back to the time of Garfield Wood, and then Guy Lombardo, and the Miss Pepsi. How far exactly I really don't know, but I know it goes back probably into the late thirties or early forties. Those were the old flat-bottoms then. They could put out with some fast speed. But then they came out with what you called the three-point hydroplane. Let's see, I think it was Stanley Sayers's—his Slo-Mo-Shun was the first one to come on the scene, the first three-point hydroplane as we know it today, and the builder of it was Ted Jones—he was the first to actually design a three-point hydroplane.

R.W.: How have the engines in these boats changed over the years?

CHENOWETH: Not a whole lot, surprisingly. They have gotten more sophistication and more horsepower. When you think of it, hydroplanes are kind of like the Indy cars. You know, you bring them up to date. We actually started with an aircraft engine back in 1973, and hydroplanes still have aircraft engines today, like the Rolls-Merlin or the Rolls-Griffin.

R.W.: Are these jet engines that we're talking about?

CHENOWETH: No, not really. The first jet engine that actually was tried came about ten years ago. And now they came out this year with another jet engine, but in the first race in Tri-Cities, they had a kind of mishap when the boat went over backward and was completely destroyed.

R.W.: What type of engine does *Miss Budweiser* have?

CHENOWETH: We're running the Rolls-Griffin.

R.W.: And it has a prop that goes into the water?

CHENOWETH: Definitely. That is the one requirement that a hydroplane has to meet in order to come within the rules of unlimited hydroplane racing.

R.W.: What do you mean when you refer to hydroplane racing as "unlimited"?

CHENOWETH: The word "unlimited" means unlimited horsepower, that's all. And the boat must be propeller-driven. If it's a jet engine, it still must be propeller-driven.

R.W.: When did you first get involved in the sport?

CHENOWETH: Nineteen sixty-eight.

R.W.: What prompted you to take it up?

CHENOWETH: I'd driven limited inboards for years and I drove the little outboard hydroplanes and then I guess I just got lucky. There was the W. D. Gail Electrical Contracting Company up in Detroit, and it built the first unlimited I drove. I was a rookie, and one of its people called me up and asked me if I'd like a shot at it, and naturally any young guy coming up

through the ranks would be extremely happy to get a chance to drive it. And, of course, I said I would.

R.W.: Could you hazard a guess as to how many races you've entered over the years?

CHENOWETH: Boy. That's tough. In nineteen seventy-three I retired. That's when I got the Budweiser distributorship, and I didn't drive again until last year. And, let's see, I guess I raced in six last year, seven this year.

R.W.: Could you tell me how many you've won?

CHENOWETH: Seventeen—since I first started, that is.

R.W.: Could you tell me something about the actual race itself? Do hydroplanes race against each other or against a clock?

CHENOWETH: They race against each other.

R.W.: Are there unlimited numbers that might begin in a given race?

CHENOWETH: We can run only a maximum of six hydroplanes in any one race because of their size and speed.

R.W.: Six. Is that generally true all across the circuit?

CHENOWETH: Right. Because it's not that we don't have the facilities or the entrants; it's the idea that the boats are so big. They're actually fourteen-and-a-half feet wide, and you take six times fourteen or fifteen feet, you've got a pretty good amount of space. Plus you

(continued on page 253)

Above: Edmund Hillary (right) and Sherpa Tenzing Norgay ascend the Lhotse face of Everest during their 1953 conquest of the mountain. *British Information Service*

Right: A rock climber using no equipment, only his hands and feet, scales a rock wall. *John Yaworksy*

Opposite page:
Tenzing Norgay
astride a yak (top). Yak
rides are often among
the activities on
Himalayan treks. *Laurie
Engel* Greenland's vast
ice cap (bottom) was
traversed by eight
American cross-
country skiers in 1980.
U.S. Coast Guard **Right:** A
member of a 1980
American expedition
to the Punjab
Himalaya, shown here
at 19,000 feet on the
western face of Nun.
Craig Heimark **Below:** A
Kashmiri village in the
Warwan Valley, also in
the Punjab Himalaya.
Gordon Wiltsie

Above: Mel Fisher and family aboard their treasure-hunting ship. *United Press International* **Left:** The bathyscaph *Trieste* in 1960 descended nearly seven miles to the deepest known part of the ocean, in the South Pacific's Mariana Trench. *U.S. Navy*

Shane Acton and a Swiss companion (above) guide the sailboat *Super Shrimp* into harbor in Brisbane, Australia, after a 4½-year voyage from Britain. It took Acton another 3½ years to complete his circumnavigation of the globe. *United Press International* Dean Chenoweth (right) and his hydroplane racer, *Miss Budweiser* (below), in which he won four national championships. Chenoweth was killed in a racing accident as he made a bid for the world speed record in July 1982. *Hydroplanes, Inc.*

Above: Ice yacht (left) on the frozen surface of Lake Geneva, Wisconsin, at the turn of the century. *Courtesy Geneva Lake Area Chamber of Commerce* Rafters (right) shoot the rapids of the Bío-Bío River in Chile. *Sobek Expeditions* **Right:** In 1901 Anna Edson Taylor, a widowed schoolteacher, became the first person to go over Niagara Falls in a barrel and live. She was 42 at the time of the plunge. *Library of Congress*

On the Tatshenshini River in Alaska (above), rafters drift past icebergs calved from Saint Elias Mountains glaciers. *Sobek Expeditions* The first man to row alone across the Atlantic, John Fairfax of England (below) arrives in Florida in 1969 after a 180-day trip from the Canary Islands. *United Press International*

Left: Rubber rafts tied up in the gorge of the Zaskar River in India. *Sobek Expeditions*
Below: Adventuring vacationers run the rapids of a furious mountain river in the eastern United States. *Appalachian Wildwaters, Ltd.*

have to have x number of feet per lane extra, obviously, and then you know we run a two-and-a-half-mile course.

R.W.: Now is that an oval track?

CHENOWETH: Correct. It's just like the Indy, a two-and-a-half-mile oval.

R.W.: Do you have any special physical or mental training programs to keep you in shape for the sport?

CHENOWETH: I've kept in good shape for about ten years now. I run six to eight miles a day. You've got to be in good shape because you really do get some pretty good bumps and bruises, even broken ribs and shoulders. And it's just a very physically grueling activity and, of course, a real mental strain because of the speed and danger and the actual concentration in competition.

R.W.: What goes through your mind just before a big race?

CHENOWETH: Oh, naturally you think about who you're matched up against. You kind of plan your strategy as to who your competition is. You think about what they qualified at and how well they're running that particular racecourse and what they've done in the past. You really just try to size up all your competition.

R.W.: Is there a particular type of strategy that you come up with for each race?

CHENOWETH: Oh, yes. Again it depends on the racecourse—if it's a championship heat, how well the others are running that day and just different things like that.

R.W.: What might some of your strategy involve?

CHENOWETH: For instance, in all racecourses the inside of the track is the place to be, the inside lane. And in our sport we jockey for position there, so what goes through my mind before the final championship heat, you know, would be how I can establish my position and get by on the inside lane. You also consider how somebody else might maybe outmaneuver you. All these things really go through my mind, as to how I'm going to go into that final heat.

R.W.: You said you jockey for the inside lane? How does that work?

CHENOWETH: You make it for yourself. It's not established, I mean it's not given to you, you've got to get it yourself.

R.W.: You all come out from a starting position and then race for that area?

CHENOWETH: We go out on the racecourse like the stockcars and Indy cars. We go out at a certain specified time before the start of the race. But instead of being given positions, we're then allowed to jockey and get our positions.

R.W.: Are there other factors in a race—in bicycle racing, people consider drafting; or in horse racing, a jockey tries to be fast out of the gate or to hang back to make a move later. Are there plans or strategies like that in hydroplane racing?

CHENOWETH: Actually, top speed and acceleration are our two main things. And drafting, well, that's impossible because of that two-hundred-foot rooster tail coming out of the back of a hydroplane. It would blow your head off. So really we have to be extremely careful. There's no such thing as getting right in behind another boat. You've got to stay out of the actual backwash of the boat. You have to be two to three feet to the right of the rooster tail, off to the side.

R.W.: What kind of prize money is available today?

CHENOWETH: Each race is different. Usually the prize is anywhere from twenty to thirty thousand dollars.

R.W.: Is there a special national circuit for hydroplane racers?

CHENOWETH: Right. We run ten races a year in different locations.

R.W.: That's all in the United States. Is there a European circuit too?

CHENOWETH: They have a European circuit, but we don't go over. And they in turn don't come over here. It's too hard to ship the boats back and forth.

R.W.: Can you tell me how a race or a race strategy could be affected by weather and water conditions?

CHENOWETH: We have officials, like all forms of racing do, and they make the determinations. Water conditions play an important role. If the water is too rough, for instance, naturally the race is canceled for the day.

R.W.: Who specifically determines that?

CHENOWETH: The referee.

R.W.: How much of a wind would be necessary to scrub a race?

CHENOWETH: That depends on the location of the course. A thirty-mile-an-hour wind at Eldorado, Kansas, or Wichita, for example—the way those particular courses are set up, there's protection. The wind blows over the racecourse, and only the backstretch is mainly affected by it. But at Detroit the course is wide open and is vulnerable to the wind from any direction. So a thirty-mile-an-hour wind there would be impossible for a race. It all depends on where the racecourse is set. If there is protection from the winds, that's it. If a wind blows, you know, has the ability to blow right on the racecourse, probably a fifteen- to twenty-mile-an-hour wind would be enough to eliminate competition. If the wind is blowing across the racecourse rather than down the racecourse makes a big difference.

R.W.: How about the water conditions? Could you race on, say, a ten-inch chop?

CHENOWETH: A ten-inch chop? Oh, that's the greatest. What we can't race on is maybe a two- or three-foot chop. Oh, yeah, a ten-inch chop is ideal.

R.W.: Do you hold any world speed records?

CHENOWETH: Yes. We finished in Seattle with the fastest two-and-a-half-mile lap. It was one hundred thirty-eight miles per hour. We hold the world record for one lap. And last year we were going for the world record in Seattle for the straightaway record of two hundred one, and we ran about two hundred twenty when we were inside the trap, but we had a propeller break. We hit a very, very small object in the water, and the boat flipped over backward at two hundred twenty.

R.W.: Were you all right?

CHENOWETH: Well, I broke eight ribs, and I broke my pelvis.

R.W.: But you're back out on the water now?

CHENOWETH: Oh yeah, that was last October.

R.W.: How soon were you back out racing after the accident?

CHENOWETH: It happened in October, I was back in May, probably a six-month layoff.

R.W.: Did you have to do any special kind of mental psyching up to get back into the boat?

CHENOWETH: Not really, because, like I say, things happened so quick, and it's just part of the whole thing or can be part of it, I guess.

R.W.: What's the greatest danger in the water—floating objects?

CHENOWETH: No. It's usually something breaking down, not going right.

R.W.: Flipping over is probably the most sure way to get hurt?

CHENOWETH: You could say that.

R.W.: What was your most memorable race?

CHENOWETH: I'd have to say the Gold Cup in Madison.

R.W.: Could you describe the action in that?

CHENOWETH: We'd won every heat. Bill Muncey, one of hydroplane racing's all-time greats and a winner many times of the Gold Cup, had held a consecutive heat record of fifteen, and now we had won fourteen straight heats going into the Madison race. The way things happened, we started across the line last, came from behind, and won the final championship heat, won the Gold Cup, tied Muncey's world record of fifteen consecutive heat wins, and that was the most memorable of all my races.

R.W.: Was Bill Muncey in that competition?

CHENOWETH: Oh yeah.

R.W.: How many people had entered that?

CHENOWETH: I don't remember. They eliminate down to six as a final.

R.W.: You mentioned your accident last October. Is that the most serious accident you've ever had? How many others have you had?

CHENOWETH: Just one in August— and then another one in nineteen seventy.

R.W.: What happened in nineteen seventy?

CHENOWETH: The boat disintegrated, like it did in Seattle this year.

R.W.: Had it flipped over?

CHENOWETH: Yeah.

R.W.: What happens when it flips over? What can you do to protect yourself?

CHENOWETH: Nothing. You can't do anything. It happens so fast. You're going so fast. It just suddenly happens and is over.

R.W.: Have you witnessed other racers in serious accidents?

CHENOWETH: No, not really. The last couple of years, it's just been me.

R.W.: Let's see, since nineteen seventy you've had three accidents. Would that be considered a pretty safe track record or would you think that's more or less than normal for somebody active in hydroplane racing?

CHENOWETH: I guess it's about normal. But I've had two in the last year—that's a little on the heavy side.

R.W.: Did you ever have second thoughts about being involved in hydroplane racing?

CHENOWETH: No, not really.

R.W.: Not even after one of those bad accidents?

CHENOWETH: No.

R.W.: If I wanted to go out and build a boat similar to *Miss Budweiser*, how much would it cost?

CHENOWETH: The hull alone would probably run around a little over one hundred twenty-five thousand dollars.

R.W.: And how about the engine?

CHENOWETH: Well, it depends on what you're using, the type. It's easy to put a quarter of a million dollars into a boat, trailer, the whole thing—for a real winner, that is.

R.W.: What do you need to keep it in tip-top shape? Do you have a crew, just like an auto racer?

CHENOWETH: Yeah, just like the Indy—a crew chief and an excellent crew.

R.W.: How many people would be involved in the maintenance of a racing boat?

CHENOWETH: Four.

R.W.: And do they specialize?

CHENOWETH: Right. We, you know, design the specs on the boat. And they're specialists in taking care of the various aspects. It's exactly identical to the Indy people.

R.W.: How many racers would you estimate are active in the field today?

CHENOWETH: Probably twenty.

R.W.: What would you say to someone who is interested in starting out in the field?

CHENOWETH: The main thing is they have to have the financial backing, and a sponsor, just like the cars, racing cars.

R.W.: Are there sponsors out there available for new people, or is it pretty well saturated at this point?

CHENOWETH: No, I think the field is pretty well open. It just depends on what you've got to offer the sponsor.

R.W.: I often see TV coverage of these

races. Is there pretty good national coverage of the sport of hydroplane racing?

CHENOWETH: I'd say so. Recently every race has been televised, like Evansville, Indiana; Detroit; Seattle. All of the local networks televise the race or certain segments of it, and, you know, if there was anything outstanding, it would get on national TV.

R.W.: Well, it sounds like a very intriguing sport. Are there any to compare to it?

CHENOWETH: Not to my way of thinking.

The Bathtub Boat

Its official name was *Yankee Girl*, but the squat, dinghylike craft looked more like something someone would bathe in than sail, and therefore it was given the nickname the Bathtub Boat. Its skipper, Gerry Spiess, 39, was dubbed the Cockleshell Captain. But in 1979, despite its small size and unorthodox appearance, the *Yankee Girl* and its captain left an indelible mark on the story of sea adventure. The achievement: it set the record for being the smallest boat ever to cross the treacherous North Atlantic.

The record for crossing the much milder mid-Atlantic belongs to Hugo S. Vihlen of the United States, who, in 1968, sailed from Casablanca, Morocco, to Fort Lauderdale, Florida, on *The April Fool*, a skiff with a length of only 5 feet 11⅞ inches. That voyage took 85 days.

Spiess, an electronics worker from Minnesota, had designed the boat and then built it in his garage up in the Northland. It took him 3½ years. When it was finally finished, the *Yankee Girl* had these basic dimensions: ten feet long, 5½ feet wide, 14-foot mast, and a total weight of 1,800 pounds. Inside its coffinlike cabin was a six-foot bunk, VHF radiotelephone, shortwave radio, ham radio, and a compass. It also sported a four-horsepower outboard motor.

The adventuresome Spiess transported his nautical creation to Virginia Beach, Virginia, the site he had chosen to launch his historic sail. "To me, it was simply a personal challenge," he explained later, in that enigmatic way so well understood by adventurers of all types. His course would cross about 70 degrees latitude and 15 degrees longitude, and would take approximately two months, Spiess estimated, if everything went well.

Spiess set sail in the *Yankee Girl* on June 1, 1979, from America's Mid-Atlantic shore. By the end of the month he had reached the middle of the Atlantic Ocean, having weathered a major ocean storm where waves rose higher than the *Yankee Girl's* 14-foot mast, tossing the odd-shaped vessel about like a Ping-Pong ball, and almost swamping it several times. Spiess was able to stay aboard only because he was lashed to a life-line. Besides the storm, another major peril was the heavy traffic of large freighters and tankers plying their way across the Atlantic in the same sea lanes that Spiess was navigating. One came within 100 feet of the little craft, its captain oblivious to the tiny white shape in the ocean next to him.

The *Yankee Girl*, under Spiess's deft sailing, managed to maintain an average of 60 miles a day, reaching England after only 54 days. The Bathtub Boat, with its Cockleshell Captain, put in at Falmouth Harbor at Land's End on the southern coast of England, July 24, 1979.

(Spiess's record was eclipsed twice in August, 1982, first by Irishman Tom McClean in a 9-foot 9-inch craft, and then by American Bill Dunlop, who sailed for 78 days in a boat 9 feet 1 inch long.)

Rowing the Atlantic

Small sailboats have been skimming their way across the Atlantic Ocean since the mid-1800s, but it wasn't until 1966 that someone made the daring journey in a rowboat. Two Britishers, John Ridgway and Chay Blyth, hold that historic first. They rowed from Cape Cod, Massachusetts, to Inishmore, Ireland, in a 20-foot rowboat dubbed the *English Rose III*, completing their trip in 92 days.

That feat spurred rugged individualists to challenge the ocean alone in a rowboat. John Fairfax of England set out aboard the 22-foot *Britannia* in January 1969 from Las Palmas in the Canary Islands and rowed some 3,750 miles over a period of 180 days before he reached Fort Lauderdale, Florida. That long journey established him in *The Guinness Book of World Records* as the first person to row solo across the Atlantic from east to west.

That same year Tom McClean of Ireland launched his 20-foot rowboat, the *Super Silver*, from St. John's, Newfoundland, and manned the oars for 71 days before docking at Black Sod Bay, Ireland, to become the first person to row the Atlantic alone west to east.

In 1980, a Frenchman, Gerard d'Abouville, set out to row the Atlantic from west to east with the hope of doing it in less time than it took Tom McClean in 1969. But the winds and the rough seas ganged up against d'Abouville in his 18-foot rowboat, the *Captaine Cook*. He left Chatham, Massachusetts, early on July 11 and crossed the ocean with nothing but his own strength and skill and a pair of oars. It took him 72 days to reach Ushant, on the coast of France. Having traveled an estimated 3,230 miles, he claimed the record for the longest west to east solo crossing; and, having traveled at the remarkable rate of nearly 45 miles per day, d'Abouville had made the fastest solo west-east crossing of the Atlantic in a rowboat on record.

Shark Fishing

In recent years, shark fishing has become much more popular than it has ever been in the past. Perhaps it is because the thrill of the adventure became a subject of widespread interest as a result of the motion picture Jaws, or because word got around that shark was not a bad tasting fish, or because there are more fishing boats today specially equipped for shark fishing—or maybe for all three reasons. Nevertheless, it is both an exciting and strenuous sport. This article, written by Richard Whittingham, on what the experience is like, originally appeared in The Thrill Sports, by the editors of Consumer Guide.

In life a shark is a killing machine. Astoundingly vicious, the shark prowls the sea using hunting skills perfected over the millennia in a restless, relentless, merciless search for food. The drive is so intense that a shark must be feared even in death. Sharks that have been technically dead for as long as 30 minutes can, through some bizarre, instinctive muscular reaction, lash out at anything that approaches their mouths.

If you feel ready to deal with such a creature, you may want to try shark fishing. Alfred Dean tried it and made his way into the record books.

One day in April 1959 Dean went out to fish off the coast of South Australia. He brought home a 2,664-pound white shark. It measured 16 feet 10 inches from snout to tail and had a girth of 9½ feet. This may sound like the ultimate "fish" story, but it isn't. It is a true story about the man who caught the largest fish of any kind ever landed with rod and reel.

For its species, however, that was a mediocre fish. The great white shark, star of *Jaws* and legendary man-eater, can grow to a length of 36 feet or more and weigh in excess of 7,000 pounds. He has a reputation of being one of the most voracious eaters in the world. Stomachs of these monsters have yielded such odd items as tires, bailing buckets, and large hunks of wood; one even contained the entire carcass of a horse. Usually, however, the great white shark concentrates on tuna, sea lions, sea turtles, other large fish, and a wide assortment of bait offered by the more fearless of fishermen.

The great white is by no means the only shark fished today for sport. The International Game Fish Association lists five other shark species among the great game fish of the world: the mako, porbeagle, tiger, thresher, and blue. A woman has tied the record blue shark catch. There are many other species hunted as well. These fierce battlers—beautiful trophies—are currently fished in oceans all around the world: the hammerhead, lemon, bull, nurse, and sand sharks, as well as small ones, such as the black-tip or spinner.

The shark is feared and hated by human beings, but sharks are not fished simply because people want to destroy them. Sharks are great game fish. The sport of fishing for them—the craft of tracking and enticing them, the enormous struggle to land a big one, the satisfaction of bringing it in on rod and reel, and the trophy you have won by doing it— can be one of the most exhilarating of all sports.

The mako shark is sleek and fast, perhaps eight feet long and 600 pounds in weight, thoroughly unpredictable and inherently vicious. What might it be like to go after one of these formidable creatures?

You would travel to Florida, the Bahamas, the Virgin Islands, or southern California, where deep-sea fishing charters are available. You will want a charter unless you own a boat and the necessary equipment, can hire a crew, and know how to hunt shark and get your catch home.

You charter with someone who knows sharks and their habits and who is experienced at fishing for them. In keeping with the sinister nature of the beast, you probably will fish at night, often the best time to lure a large shark.

Your tackle is heavy for obvious reasons. You use a six-foot fiberglass rod, special for big-game fish. With it you use 600 yards of 80- to 130-pound test line on a 12/0 to 14/0 reel. The line has a 20-foot or longer leader of cable or wire that tests at least 250 pounds, because the shark can cut through ordinary line with his rough hide or with a swish of his powerful tail. At the end of the line is a 10/0 or 12/0 big-game hook. There is a big-game deck chair bolted to the deck of the boat and harness to aid you in the battle. You can be sure of one thing—if you hook a shark, it will be a battle.

To attract the shark you prepare an unappetizing (to you, not the shark) mixture of ground-up flesh called "chum." Chum often is made of seafood, including mackerel, herring, tuna, or squid. Some fishermen have other recipes with ingredients such as beef, horse meat, seal flesh, and the gory innards from almost any kind of land or sea animal. A meat grinder is carried on the boat specifically for the preparation of chum.

Using a method called chumming, you dump this rank mixture on the surface of the water. Your

World Record Sharks Caught by Rod and Reel

Species	Weight in Pounds	Caught Near	Date	Angler
Great White	2,664	Ceduna (S.A.), Australia	5/21/59	Alfred Dean
Tiger	1,780	Cherry Grove, South Carolina	6/14/64	Walter Maxwell
Mako	1,080	Montauk, New York	8/26/79	James Melanson
Thresher	739	Tutukaka, New Zealand	2/17/75	Brian Galvin
Hammerhead	703	Jacksonville Beach, Florida	7/5/75	H. B. Reasor
Porbeagle	465	Cornwall, England	7/23/76	Jorge Potier
Blue	437	Catherine Bay (N.S.W.), Australia	10/2/76	Peter Hyde

Source: International Game Fish Association

hook, baited with a whole fish, dangles 6 to 12 feet below the surface. As time passes, you continue to grind up and dump the chum overboard. It is quiet on the ocean. The only noise is the dull hum of the boat's engine as you slowly troll the water.

Suddenly a gentle nodding of the rod attracts your attention. A shark usually does not hit like a locomotive and run, even though it is capable of that. Your shark is toying with the bait, perhaps bumping it or ladling it around in his mouth. Line is coming off the reel, and the shark is moving, but you do not set the hook. It is too early. For another seemingly eternal minute, you continue to lose line. Then you engage the reel and jerk the rod; the hook is set; and all hell breaks loose. The line shrieks off the reel as the shark makes his run. Three hundred yards of it is ripped off before the shark dives, and then he tears off another 75 yards of it. Now you must turn the shark and regain some of that line. You reel, and the shark runs. You gain a few yards of line, and then you lose it. Then the incredible fish breaks the water and soars 15 feet above the surface, twisting to tear away from the hook. It is the scene that fishermen dream of. The battle goes on for an hour. You are straining, using all of the muscles in your back and arms. The shark is tiring, but so are you. Yet you are gaining ground. Two hours have gone by. The shark is brought in closer until it is alongside the boat. A crew member gaffs it. . . .

Your problems are not over. The

shark still must be dispatched, and it will not die easily. When it is lashed to the boat it can be beaten with a club, but this does not always work. It can be shot, but the IGFA does not approve of this method. It can be dragged backward through the water until it drowns. Everyone has his own method.

The shark may be dead, but you do not bring it on board. Remember what they say about dead sharks.

Running the Snake River

One of the most exciting rivers to run in all of America is the Snake. A winding, fast-flowing, deep river, it weaves through steep-walled canyons beneath the snow-capped peaks of awesome mountains, and rages through Hell's Canyon on the Idaho-Oregon border. Its white-water stretches are run by either raft or kayak, and the degree of difficulty ranges from intermediate to expert. The description of this exciting battle with the Snake is the account of Peter Wood, taken from his book Running the Rivers of North America.

The Snake is a white-water river, a young giant that bulls its way out of the heart of the Rocky Mountains toward the Pacific. Rising in Yellowstone National Park in Wyoming, the Snake draws early strength from snowmelt off the craggy heights of the Grand Tetons. It crosses the full width of Idaho in a lazy loop before turning north to form the boundary between that state and Oregon. The Upper Snake, in Grand Teton National Park, attracts thousands of river runners each year. But it is the Lower Snake, particularly the mile-deep canyon that separates the Wallowa Mountains of Oregon from the Seven Devils of Idaho, that concerns us here. . . .

Our first look at the river is disappointing. From Joseph, Oregon, we have descended by truck and microbus through forests of pine, spruce, and Douglas fir into the V-shaped valley of the Snake. We cross the river at Ox Bow Dam, more bridge than dam, as the water on either side stands roughly at the same level. Now as we follow a gravel road down the right bank, the river lies beside us placid and wide as three empty football fields and doing little more than reflecting the blue of the afternoon sky. The former riverbed was movingly portrayed by photographer Eliot Porter in his *Wildness Is the Preservation of the World* shortly before the sluice gates were closed. Now it lies hidden under more than 200 feet of water. Where the water laps at the steep hillside of gray rock and parched grasses, it is hard to discern any current.

At Hell's Canyon Dam the lake-like tranquility ends, as if cut with a knife. At the base of a 300-foot-high concrete wall, a froth of water bursts from the outflow of the generating plant. More dramatic, still, is a great plume of water that gushes from one of three gates at the top of the dam. Unseasonable summer rains have filled the reservoir, and Hell's Canyon Dam is dumping its excess.

The boatmen in our truck crow at the sight. The river will be fuller than usual, perhaps running at 30,000 [cubic feet per second], they think. Wild Sheep and Granite, the two major rapids that lie ahead, will be special challenges this run. As if eager to fulfill the boatmen's prophecies, the river charges away from the dam like a wild thing, frothing and dancing out of sight around a distant bend. But here the Snake becomes its old self again, lean and sinewy enough for someone with a good arm to hurl a rock across. The banks are rough talus slopes descending to a margin of water-worn boulders and bedrock. As we cross the top of the dam, the roar of river and rock rises to meet us. It is a sound that will echo in our ears for the next six days.

In a pelting thundershower we launch and load the boats we trailered with us. They belong to an outfit called Grand Canyon Dories, which runs commercial trips on the Colorado and a number of other western rivers, including the Snake. As a white-water craft the dory is still in the development stage. Our three boats represent three variations of flat-bottomed, double-ended fishing boats, the type that Spencer Tracy rowed on the Grand Banks in the movie *Captains Courageous*. River dories, designed for passengers rather than fish, are larger (18 feet) and wider abeam. They also have water-tight compartments for personal gear and equipment and to keep them afloat should they turn over. Like the houses of the Three Little Pigs, each of the Grand Canyon boats was built of a different material: wood, aluminum, and fiberglass.

Clarence Reese, 30, muscled like the Idaho state champion wrestler he once was and wearing his sun-bleached hair à la Prince Valiant, gathers his 13 charges together for a lecture on river safety. To escape the sudden downpour we crowd into the microbus. "It is not likely," Clarence tells us, "but boats do flip—turn over, that is. That's why every one of you has a life jacket. You don't have to wear it all the time (not true on nationally administered rivers, where to be caught in a boat without a life jacket on, even when the boat is beached, is to risk a fine).

"But when your boatman puts his on, you had better do the same, no matter how strong a swimmer you are. You can't swim in a river rapid anyway. Should a boat go over, above all, don't panic. You may come up under the boat. You'll know that's happened if you open your eyes and it's dark (nervous laughter). Reach up, feel for the rail, and move yourself to the side. Once out, stay on the upriver side of the boat. The worst danger you face is to be pinned between the boat and a rock. Stay with the boat. You may have to help the boatman right it."

•   •   •

At 3:00 P.M. we push off. The sun is out again but so low that it reaches into the canyon only in spots. We will get wet, we have been told, so most of us are wearing a minimum of clothing and our fat orange kapok life jackets, with collars designed to keep an unconscious person's head above water.

Forest Woods, Peter Bull, and I are seated in the bow of the *Stanislaus*, the aluminum boat named for the Stanislaus River in California. David Phillips and his blonde wife, Lore, occupy the stern seat. Between us sits our boatman, 24-year-old Jim Barton, bearded, wearing strong glasses, and gripping a pair of oars. Jim does not face aft, as is customary in most rowboats; in river dories the oarsman faces forward, toward the upswept bow. He can push the boat in that direction with a forward thrust of his arms, but when he pulls, really putting his back into it, the stroke propels the boat backward. For this the stern is also pointed. The arrangement means that the boatman can face the dangers—call them challenges, for we are all here to enjoy ourselves, are we not?—head on and pull away from them when need be. Rafts are rowed according to the same principle. The essential difference between rafts and dories is that the heavier dory, with its pointed bow, smashes through waves, while rafts ride up and over the top of them. Sometimes this means that the dory gets swamped and may capsize.

Rafts do not lose stability when they swamp, but sometimes they ride so high on a wave they are tipped over backward or, in some cases, bent double, making, in the vernacular of the river, a neoprene sandwich. There are advantages and disadvantages to each craft. Beauty, however, has never been an attribute of rafts. Dory men, a proud bunch, are condescending to raft jockeys, although to handle either craft requires a thorough understanding of white-water hydraulics.

This will be the 13th trip that Jim has made down the Snake; however, it is his first time in the aluminum *Stanislaus*. Now he spins the boat around twice in the current to get the feel of it. Spaced about 50 yards apart, the three boats sweep down through a few easy stretches of choppy water, clear of protruding boulders. The water is moving swiftly. A horseman would have to hold a steady trot to keep up. Where the canyon widens, sunlight suddenly pours in. Its warmth is welcome. Bow pointed downstream, Jim holds the *Stanislaus* at a 45-degree angle to the current. He meets the larger waves by swinging the bow into them, the way one turns into the wake left by a speedboat. But there is little that is regular or predictable about these waves, and sometimes one sloshes over the bow or rolls in amidships, dousing us. Then we take plastic buckets and bail. The water is warmer than the air. The long loop the Snake makes through southern Idaho kills the original glacial chill, and in the reservoir the water has been soaking up the sun all summer.

In the mountains around Joseph, it snowed the night before we set out, but here the river almost invites swimming.

Jim, seated in the middle of the *Stanislaus*, with his feet hooked under a stout wooden dowel for leverage, is letting the river do the work, rowing just enough to keep us in the current while swinging the bow this way and that to meet the oncoming waves—standing waves, really. It is we, borne on the current, that are oncoming.

On rivers the size of the Snake, most large rapids are the product of steep side streams that carry down with them the boulders and debris that obstruct the flow, creating drops, shoots, and fearsome holes. After about an hour on the river, we pass the mouth of Wild Sheep Creek and pull into an eddy. Ahead, the river seems to disappear, dropping from sight into a boil of turbulent water—Wild Sheep Rapids, Jim tells us. Our campsite, assigned by the U.S. Forest Service, lies beyond it around a bend. We beach the boats and climb the bank to have a look. Clarence tells us he has been accused by other parties of stopping to look these rapids over only to build the drama of the upcoming run. The truth is, every new water condition changes the shape of a rapid and the strategy for running it. Serious rapids, like Wild Sheep, biggest on the river, must be scouted, no matter how familiar a boatman is with the river.

So we survey Wild Sheep. Perched at a strategic spot on the big rocks above the river, we see it all.

No question, this does build drama. Three tongues of smooth water bend over the drop, hard to measure in real terms because the froth below the falls will not hold still. Six feet, perhaps? Not a very big drop, to be sure, but when one figures that 30,000 cubic feet of water, weighing 960 tons, is pouring over it every second, one begins to get a better handle on the enormous forces loose on a river like the Snake. The tongue of water farthest from us is aimed straight for a large rock buffeted by waves reflecting off a rock face on the Idaho shore. The middle tongue, the main stream, bends toward the perpendicular, scouring a deep hole in the river into which a great wave is constantly breaking. A boat or raft plunging into that hole would swamp immediately and be thrown backward by the wave. The same would happen to a swimmer. The hole is what river men call a "keeper," perhaps the single most dangerous phenomenon on big water. Keepers have been known to hold boats, rafts, and/or swimmers interminably. They cause the most drownings. Boatmen steer clear of holes like this one, which are too big to punch through.

The tongue nearest us appears to be the way to go. It points downriver between a mound of smooth water and a protruding boulder. The mound is the work of a large rock, clearly visible through the half-foot of water that pours over it on all sides, creating a nasty boil on the far side. This is a "sleeper." The danger of sleepers is that one may run into them. Boats will normally bounce over them but then come to grief in the froth at the bottom. A large raft, on the other hand, may actually hang up on a sleeper, bending around it like a fur piece on a matron's neck, and be pinned there. Sometimes the force of the current is so great that the raft cannot be pried loose, even by pulling with a rope from shore. In that case there is nothing to do but abandon ship and wait, sometimes for weeks, until the water level on the river changes.

"Our course," Clarence explains, "will be to shoot down this closest tongue of water between the sleeper and the rock that protrudes beyond it, skirt the big hole in the middle of the river, and meet the waves at the bottom of the drop head on." The first wave, really a breaking ridge of water reaching out from shore, will be the hardest. It is highest where the channel is deepest. We will want to miss that part if we can.

The tongue of smooth water and the breaking wave below it are basic elements of any rapid worth the name. The V-shaped tongue points downstream. When in doubt, and if you have not scouted ahead, the V indicates the way to go, providing it is pointing downstream. Vs pointing upstream represent a turbulence streaming backward from a protruding or nearly protruding rock. Beware Vs pointing upstream! The downstream V, on the other hand, usually signals the deepest water, while the waves curling in on either side of it spell trouble. What one must be mindful of is that the V does not lead to some other obstruction, as does the one farthest from us now, or that it does not drop so steeply that the water pouring down it piles up at the bottom, creating a dangerous hole and breaking wave.

Clarence takes his boat through first while the rest of us watch and take pictures from the riverbank. For a moment he hangs in limbo, sideways at the top of the V—then he slides down it, past the big hole, and is flung into a frightful jumble of waves. Pulling right now to miss the worst of the standing waves, bobbing up and down, he is safely through. Straining like a Trojan, he pulls left, driving his boat into an upstream eddy, which brings him back up to a point just below the first big drop. From there he and his passengers can watch us run the rapid and render assistance if needed.

The eddy, or countercurrent, is another basic element of stream flow. Technically an eddy is any discontinuity of flow. Eddies come in an infinite variety. Those that are useful flow upriver, usually along either bank, but also behind obstructions such as protruding boulders. When a river narrows, is obstructed, or the gradient increases, water accelerates. It gains momentum, and at the end of the obstruction or drop, it is moving faster than the configuration of the river at that point calls for. To compensate, water flows upstream to replace it. That is an eddy. An eddy fence is the boundary between two contrary currents. Crossing it can be as dangerous as entering a buffer zone between any two opposing forces.

Now it is our turn to run Wild Sheep. Jim stands in the middle of the boat to get a better look over the edge where the river disappears. His passengers scrutinize his face for signs of nervousness, any twist of the mouth or cast to the eye. Unfamiliar with this kind of water, we have no other way to judge the degree of danger we are facing. Jim shows no sign. We are reassured. And just in time, for we too are in the grip of the current—no turning back, no chance to pull for a friendly eddy. We slide quickly down between our Scylla and Charybdis, the sleeper and the opposite rock. I am surprised how long Jim holds the *Stanislaus* sideways. We sweep past the big hole. At the bottom Jim swings the boat to meet the wave. It towers over us. It crashes down on us. The *Stanislaus* swamps. But Jim seems to know what he is doing. Certainly we will push through. Then we turn over, rolling from starboard to port. I am sitting on the port side, and the boat comes down on me like a lid. By God, it is dark. In a confusion of foam, boat, and bodies, I start to work my way out and am struck on the back of the head. The blow is nothing compared to the confusion I feel. Then I am free, clinging to the overturned boat. But I am on the downriver side. Lore, wide-eyed, is next to me. We work our way around the boat. The life jacket holds me unaccustomedly high in the water. It is hard to swim. But now I have a chance to look around. All hands are accounted for, as we sweep and bob along in the water. It feels warm and rather pleasant. So this is what it is like to turn over in a big rapid.

Jim is fumbling with the painter, the rope attached to the *Stanislaus's* bow. Uncoiling it he leads it around the oarlock on the downriver side and throws it over the back of the boat, as if roping a huge turtle. He comes back to our side again and uses the rope to climb up on the overturned boat. I look past him down the river and understand his haste. Another stretch of nasty water lies ahead, with breaking waves and a few protruding rocks. I also notice that Jim still has his glasses on. They have no attachment around the back of his head. Clever fellow. Leaning his weight against the rope hitched to the downstream oarlock, Jim now tries to turn the boat over. Several of us clamber aboard to add our weight to the rope. Slowly the far gunnel rises. We grab it, and the boat flops right side up again. Jim is in like a monkey and helps pull the rest of us aboard, not an easy feat as our bulbous life jackets protrude and catch on the gunnel. Only one is left in the water—Peter Bull. But the next rapid is nearly on us. Jim has only one oar, the spare that had been lashed to the thwarts. Better than nothing to get through the rapids with but hardly adequate. Clarence's boat, having followed our travail, now bears down on us. A man in the bow holds out their spare oar. At the last second he gives it a heave. Not far enough. It goes into the river, but the momentum carries it to us. Jim slaps it into the oarlock and swings the boat around just as we enter rough water. Peter Bull is still hanging on astern. Two of us bail. The others sit shivering with excitement and cold. As soon as we have passed the new rapid, we haul Peter back on board and pull for shore. Granite Creek, our campsite, lies just ahead. Our first day on the Snake has disappointed no one.

Great Rivers to Run in the United States

The following are the principal rivers in the United States for rafting and adventurous canoeing and kayaking. The state or states where the currents and white water are best are listed. The degree of difficulty is scored as mild, intermediate, or difficult. (Difficult means the course, or part of it, should only be attempted by expert river-runners.)

East of the Mississippi River

River	Location	Degree of Difficulty
Allagash	Maine	Intermediate/Difficult
Ammonoosuc	New Hampshire	Intermediate/Difficult
Au Sable	Michigan	Mild
Bluestone	West Virginia	Mild/Intermediate
Buffalo	Arkansas	Intermediate
Carrabasset	Maine	Mild/Intermediate
Chattooga	North Carolina, South Carolina, Georgia	Mild/Intermediate
Cheat	West Virginia	Mild
Connecticut	New Hampshire, Vermont, Massachusetts, Connecticut	Intermediate/Difficult
Cumberland (South Fork)	Tennessee, Kentucky	Intermediate
Dead	Maine	Mild/Intermediate
Delaware	New York, Pennsylvania, New Jersey	Mild/Intermediate
Edisto	South Carolina	Mild
Flambeau	Wisconsin	Mild
Fox	Illinois	Mild
Gauley	West Virginia	Intermediate/Difficult
Hudson (Upper)	New York	Mild/Intermediate
Little Beaver	Ohio	Mild/Intermediate
Little Miami	Ohio	Intermediate
New	North Carolina, Virginia, West Virginia	Intermediate
Obed	Tennessee	Intermediate/Difficult

River	Location	Degree of Difficulty
Penobscot	Maine	Intermediate
Pere Marquette	Michigan	Mild
Peshtigo	Wisconsin	Intermediate
Pine Creek	Pennsylvania	Mild/Intermediate
Potomac	West Virginia	Mild
Raquette	New York	Mild/Intermediate
Saco	New Hampshire, Maine	Mild/Intermediate
St. Croix	Wisconsin, Minnesota	Mild
St. John	Maine	Mild
Shenandoah	Maryland, West Virginia	Mild/Intermediate
Sipsey	Alabama	Mild
Sugar Creek	Indiana	Mild
Suwannee	Georgia, Florida	Intermediate
West	Vermont	Intermediate/Difficult
Wolf	Wisconsin	Intermediate/Difficult
Youghiogheny	Pennsylvania, Maryland, West Virginia	Intermediate/Difficult

West of the Mississippi River

River	Location	Degree of Difficulty
American	California	Intermediate
Bruneau	Idaho, Nevada	Intermediate/Difficult
Clearwater	Idaho	Intermediate/Difficult
Colorado	Arizona, Nevada, California	Intermediate/Difficult
Dolores	Colorado, Utah	Intermediate
East Carson	California	Intermediate
Eel	California	Intermediate
Eleven Point	Missouri	Mild/Intermediate
Feather	California	Intermediate/Difficult
Flathead	Montana	Intermediate/Difficult
Gila	New Mexico	Intermediate
Green	Wyoming, Colorado, Utah	Intermediate/Difficult
Iowa	Minnesota, Iowa	Mild/Intermediate

(continued on next page)

River	Location	Degree of Difficulty
John Day	Oregon	Mild/Intermediate
Klamath	Oregon, California	Intermediate
Little White	South Dakota	Mild
Missouri (Upper)	Montana	Mild/Intermediate
Owyhee	Oregon	Intermediate
Rapid	Idaho	Intermediate
Rio Grande	Colorado, New Mexico, Texas	Intermediate/Difficult
Rogue	Oregon	Intermediate
Sacramento	California	Intermediate
Salmon (Middle Fork)	Idaho	Intermediate/Difficult
Salt	Arizona	Intermediate/Difficult
Selway	Idaho	Intermediate
Skagit	Washington	Intermediate
Snake	Wyoming, Idaho, Oregon	Intermediate/Difficult
Stanislaus	California	Intermediate
Tuolumne	California	Intermediate/Difficult
Yampa	Colorado, Utah	Intermediate
Yellowstone	Montana, Wyoming	Intermediate/Difficult

A Rafting Expert Picks the World's Most Exciting Rivers

Richard Bangs, born August 1950 in New Haven, Connecticut, is one of the world's foremost rafting experts and river guides. He has challenged the white water on every continent except Antarctica, and personally led rafting expeditions on all 20 rivers included here. To his river-running credits, he was the first adventurer to lead an expedition down the Omo River in Africa, the Euphrates in

*the Middle East, the Watut in New Guinea, the Bío-Bío in Chile, and
the Coruh in Turkey.*

*An intrepid explorer as well, Bangs founded Sobek Expeditions
in 1973 to offer professionally guided rafting trips on the world's
most challenging rivers, as well as a variety of tours to other forms
of high adventure, from trekking to mountain climbing. Through
Sobek today, which is headquartered in Angels Camp, California,
Bangs offers exotic expeditions in the continental United States,
Alaska, various areas of South America, Africa, New Guinea, New
Zealand, Hawaii, the Himalayas, Turkey, the Sinai desert, the Red
Sea, and the Galápagos Islands.*

*His extensive experience with rafting rivers uniquely qualifies
Bangs to name the world's greatest. A raftable river must meet some
special criteria to be among the world's best. A great rafting river
must have sufficient flow, a reasonably steep gradient (elevation
loss per mile), bearable weather, and a pristine environment. It
must also have an exceptional blend of the other qualities that
make a rafting experience unique: natural beauty, a fertile history,
unusual wildlife, and, of course, rousing rapids. Here, in Bangs's
opinion, are the 20 most exciting rivers in the world to raft.*

Five raftable rivers stand out, and another 15 close runners-up are worth brief mention.

The Omo (Ethiopia): The Omo is the champion and uncontested titleholder of great rafting rivers. No other river comes close to offering as much. Rapids, irrefutably, are the main reason for rafting, and the Omo has plenty. Great as they are, however, they stand backstage to the outstanding wildlife of southern Ethiopia: some 1,600 hippos, which create more obstacles than the rapids themselves (five have bitten passing rafts); over 200 crocodiles [on Bangs's first trip down the Omo a crocodile bit a chunk out of one of his boats]; thousands of monkeys and baboons; 400 species of birds; a profusion of fish, including Nile Perch weighing up to 200 pounds; and all the savan-na wildlife native to East Africa. Unusual people populate the Omo's banks, among them the Bodi and Mersi. And if this isn't enough, the Omo also has all the accoutrements of the best North American rivers—hot springs, water slides, broad beaches, spectacular tributary waterfalls, good weather, and awesome scenery.

The Bío-Bío (Chile): Although relatively unknown, the Bío-Bío has some of the best white water in the world. Rising from Lake Gualletue in the Sierra Nevada, on the eastern slopes of the Andes, it fumes and cascades over 150 crazy miles before it pauses at the town of Santa Barbara. Along the way, it burns through more than 100 of the finest rapids I have ever encountered. The infamous Lava Falls Rapids of the Colorado look like a rippling duck pond compared to the cataracts of the Bío-Bío. Navigating these rapids requires great technical skill, and when the water level is right (late January through March) all the rapids are runnable—if you're good enough. The river has other assets, too. It passes through the "Switzerland of South America," a raw and rugged land; its clear, clean water hosts brown and rainbow trout; the active, 10,000-foot Volcan Kallaque smokes and looms overhead; and scores of tributary waterfalls, some as high as 200 feet, drop into the main river. Perfect summer weather reigns there during our winter; and there are no snakes or mosquitos to be found.

The Tatshenshini (Canada-Alaska): This is an exception to the adage that rapids make a great river. There are rapids, and the average speed of the river is seven miles per hour, but its white water is intermediate at best. What makes the Tatshenshini special is its unbeatable scenery. Few rivers slice through a major mountain range—they either spring from its slopes or skirt it. But the "Tat" cuts its narrow course through the core of the rugged Saint Elias Mountains, a range that has more peaks over 14,500 feet than any other in North America. A glance can't begin to take in the panorama, crowned by Mount Fairweather at 15,300 feet. Even more spectacular are the glaciers. Rafters drift past more than 20 of these groaning, creeping rivers of ice and watch hotel-sized chunks calve off faces and fall into the river. One of the largest glaciers is the Alsek,

with its seven-mile-wide mouth. Rafters can hike up the tongues of glacial ice and maneuver through rapids beside dancing ice floes. The wildlife is among the richest in North America, with great concentrations of grizzly bears and bald eagles, as well as moose, mountain goats, black bears, and spawning salmon. At night, the aurora borealis keeps you company.

The Watut (Papua New Guinea): "Exotic" may be an overused word, but it fits New Guinea like a glove. It is a land of headhunters, with the highest mountains and thickest jungle in the Pacific, and one of the world's wildest waterways, the Watut. The rapids of this river hit like machine-gun fire, fast and furious. They're big, technical, and angry. All this in a haunting, mystical gorge, 3,000 feet deep, sheathed in jungle, draped with clouds, and filled with a kaleidoscope of tropical birds including parrots, cockatoos, lorikeets, and hornbills. This is the only white-water river I know where at a whim you can pluck ripe coconuts, mangoes, papayas, and bananas as you go along. Orchids and shimmering tributary waterfalls are equally abundant. Two villages poised on the banks of the Watut are inhabited by friendly and hospitable Melanesians, who no longer eat their enemies.

The Colorado (Arizona): An introduction to this river is hardly needed. Periodically embroiled in controversy over proposed dams and day allotments to private or commer-

The International Scale of River Difficulty

Rapids, or white-water areas, on a river are charted and classified by the degree of difficulty they pose for canoeists, kayakers, and rafters. Maps may contain the scale of difficulty of a rapids area, but if the temperature of the water is below 50 degrees Fahrenheit or if the river-running trip is an extended one in a wilderness area, it is appropriate to consider the run at a rating one class more difficult.

Class I—Slow current; few ripples and small waves; few or no obstructions.

Class II—Easy rapids; waves up to three feet; wide, clear channels that are obvious without scouting; some maneuvering required.

Class III—High, irregular waves, often capable of swamping an open canoe; narrow passages often requiring complex maneuvering; may require scouting from shore before attempting a run.

Class IV—Long, difficult rapids; constricted passages often requiring precise maneuvering in very turbulent waters; scouting from shore necessary; rescue difficult; not recommended for open canoes; covered canoes and kayaks should be able to Eskimo roll.

Class V—Extremely difficult; long and violent rapids; highly congested routes must be scouted from shore; rescue very difficult; Eskimo rolling a prerequisite; involves risk of life in the event of a mishap.

Class VI—A combination of the extreme difficulties of Class V and extremes of navigability; exceptionally dangerous; involves risk of life; only for teams of experts who have closely scouted and studied the rapids.

cial users, it is the most famous rafting river in the history of the sport. The best run in the United States, it is also the longest—close to 300 miles—and has the biggest and the greatest number of rapids. Purling through canyon corridors up to a mile deep, awash in desert textures and colors, the river unites rafters in a mystical communion with nature. And why not? With textbook-perfect stratifications telling the history of the earth, Indian ruins dating back a thousand years, sparkling side streams and waterfalls, and the grandeur of the grottos and cathedral-like canyons, seen from the bottom up, the Colorado takes rafters through an environment like no other.

• • •

And then there are these rivers, of somewhat lesser stature, but all of them offering great rafting experiences nonetheless:

The Indus, in Pakistan, was run only once, in 1956 by Bus and Don Hatch and film producer Otto Lang. They were making the film *Search for Adventure*—the first and only river rafting film in Cinerama. A big, chocolate-brown river with powerful waves, the Indus claimed the life of the film's lead actor when a 28-foot raft flipped.

The Gauley, in West Virginia, drops almost 100 feet per mile, which is quite a drop when you're on it. It's often pronounced "Golly," especially just before flipping.

The Ganges, in India, was initially run in 1976 by Lute Jerstad. It has big, wild water on the upper stretches and corpses on the lower—the dead [of India] are "buried" in the river itself.

The Orinoco, in Venezuela, was run for the first time in 1977 by Mike Jones of England. Upon completion of the trip, he announced that his party had successfully run "the world's biggest rapid." Flowing through thick jungle, the Orinoco is also called the "River of Diamonds" for the precious stones it has yielded to prospectors.

The Selway, in Idaho, is 70 percent rapids—the only river I know that is that intense.

The Usumacinta, on the border between Mexico and Guatemala, is distinguished by its Mayan ruins, jungle scenery, New World monkeys, and tropical birds.

The Blue Nile, in Ethiopia, is the Grand Canyon run of Africa. More rafters have drowned in the Blue Nile than in any other river.

The Sun Kosi, in Nepal, drains from the Himalayas and has a breathtaking backdrop.

The Thula Beri, also in Nepal, is a white wonder washing from the western Himalayas.

The Copper, in southern Alaska, is big and powerful, with glaciers, grizzlies, and huge mountains.

The Marañíon, of Peru, is worthwhile, if you can get through the portages at the top. The most fascinating of Amazon tributaries, it features great rapids, jungle gorges, and the Aguruna Indians.

The Mendoza, in Argentina, drains the eastern slopes of Aconcagua, the highest mountain in the western hemisphere at 22,831 feet. The big, nonstop rapids outdo the spectacular scenery.

The Tuolumne is California's gem—pure, pristine, and green. With a gradient of 60 feet per mile, it qualifies as one of the steepest runs around, and Clavey Falls ranks as one of the top runnable rapids in the world.

The Upper Youghiogheny, in West Virginia, is just a few miles upstream from the most popular whitewater area in the United States—the Pennsylvania "Yough" (rhymes with "gawk"). It drops 100 feet each mile. The first time we rafted it we flipped six times in 21 miles. The next time we "knew better": we capsized ten times.

The Motu, in New Zealand, is a crackling fast, shallow river that can only be run after a good rain—but when it flows, it's feisty. To top it off, the alpine scenery and trout fishing are nonpareil.

Around the World in Eight Years

In 1972 Shane Acton was a 25-year-old milkman in Cambridge, England, but one with an imagination and grandiose plans. He quit his job that year and used the £400 (about $1,000) he had in his savings account to buy and refurbish an 18-by-4-foot sailboat. He dubbed the boat the *Super Shrimp* and announced that he was going to sail the little craft not just on the ocean but all the way around the world.

When he set sail from his hometown that year, he had only £20 (about $50) in his pocket and a book on navigation that his sister had given him as a birthday present. He had no sailing experience whatsoever, no crew, only his ambition and his dream. Eight years later the *Super Shrimp*, with Acton, now 33, at the helm, sailed into the British resort of Walton-on-the-Naze in Essex County, having completed his incredible odyssey—traveling completely around the world by himself in a small sailboat that had been designed for weekend boating. From there he navigated up the east coast of England to the River Cam and on August 7, 1980, sailed into Cambridge to a ceremonious welcome home. *The Guinness Book of World Records* accepted the feat and entered the names of Shane Acton and *Super Shrimp* on one of its pages—crediting him with the record for the smallest boat ever to circumnavigate the world.

The journey of more than 30,000 miles had taken Acton to every continent except Antarctica and to 35 different countries. Along the way he took time out to work at a variety of jobs to pay for food and supplies. There were also tales of hurricanes; strange encounters with creatures of the sea and some on the lands where he put in; massive waves; and even a shipwreck that tried to claim the *Super Shrimp*.

Of his incredible feat, Acton shrugged and said, "I never thought it would take eight years."

A Little Sunken Treasure

On September 4, 1622, from the harbor at Havana, Cuba, 28 Spanish ships loaded with an array of riches acquired in the New World set sail for their mother country. Guarding the smaller ships were two heavily armed Spanish galleons, the *Nuestra Señora de Atocha* and the *Santa Margarita*, which carried their own caches of treasures to be taken back to the royal coffers in Spain.

Only two days out of port, however, and not far from the Marquesas Keys off the coast of Florida, the

A Grueling Swim

Diana Nyad, two days short of her 30th birthday, stepped from the surf at Juno Beach, Florida, August 20, 1979, after having swum 89 miles to become the first person ever to stroke her way through the Caribbean waters all the way from the Bahamas to the United States.

The grueling swim took 27 hours and 38 minutes through waters infested with a variety of stinging jellyfish, sharks, and barracuda. When it was over, her response to the question of how she felt was, "Like the F train in New York just ran over me."

Nyad, a marathon swimmer born in New York City but raised in Fort Lauderdale, Florida, had previously swum across Lake Ontario and had tried, unsuccessfully, to swim the 102 miles from Cuba to Key West, Florida.

ships sailed into the eye of a devastating hurricane. Eight ships were sunk, including the two galleons. The Nuestra Señora de Atocha alone took to the bottom of the ocean a treasure estimated at $100 million in present-day American dollars. A cargo list, which had been entered at Havana and preserved, described the particulars of the wealth in the hold of that ship—255,000 silver coins, 901 silver ingots, and 161 pieces of gold. The Santa Margarita, it was assumed, carried as much if not more.

As early as 1624 treasure hunters searched the shallow waters off the Florida keys and the southeastern coast of the peninsula for the wrecks and their booty, and throughout the centuries a number of the ships, or parts of them, have been found, paying rich dividends to the treasure hunters. But the Atocha and the Margarita remained a mystery, unraveled only recently by treasure seeker Mel Fisher, an American, who set out to find them in 1970.

Fisher founded a company called Treasure Salvors, Inc., in Key West, Florida, and announced his intention of locating the two lost galleons. Then a historian who was dispatched to Madrid to search through the Spanish Archives of the Indies for clues as to the precise location of the shipwrecks found reports from survivors on the other ships and a log indicating the course the fleet was to follow on its return trip to Spain. With this information, his salvage boat, the Virgalona, his divers—and his dreams—Fisher began the search itself.

It would not be an easy task. The galleons would not be found flawlessly intact, sitting on the bottom simply waiting for some diver to come down and swim about amid their holds and compartments. Over the years other storms, ocean currents, and the relentless movement and erosive forces of the sea undoubtedly would have broken up the ships and scattered their contents.

But luck was with Mel Fisher. In 1971 he found a part of the *Atocha* and with it a collection of artifacts and precious metals. The wreck site of the *Atocha*, Fisher estimated, covered an area of about 12 square miles, and most of the treasure was buried under the shifting sands and sediments of the ocean floor (as much as 20 feet deep). He was able to bring to the surface about $6 million worth of gold and silver, from ingots to coins to jewelry. Among the many artifacts were bronze cannons, musket balls, and a rare find, an astrolabe in perfect working condition.

In 1980 Fisher located the remains of the *Atocha's* sister ship, the *Margarita,* in shallow waters about 35 miles off the coast of Key West. This time his divers brought up a veritable jewel box, which contained an estimated $20 million worth of treasure. Among the riches were gold chains with 3/4-inch links, some as long as 11 feet; two giant silver ingot bars, each weighing approximately 80 pounds; many more thousands of silver coins. Period pieces, such as cannons, swords, crosses, plates, wine bottles, and knives, were also found at the site.

Mel Fisher has found, however, that finding treasure in modern times does not bring instant happiness and wealth. Four persons had died in the search for the *Atocha's* treasure, including Fisher's son Dirk and Dirk's wife, Angel. Mel Fisher has spent millions of dollars in the quest, he claims, and for the past ten years has been in and out of state and federal courts trying to establish his legal rights to the treasure. It was much easier in the early days of treasure hunting—once the hunter had found his treasure, he simply sold it to the highest bidder.

Wind-Surfing the Pacific

Eleven days and ten nights on a 750-mile journey, separated from a heaving, roiling Pacific Ocean only by a slender 13-foot-long surfboard—that is how the Baron Arnaud de Rosnay of France decided to spend part of his summer of 1980. In so doing, the French nobleman demolished the previous wind-surfing world record of 137 miles in 24 hours, which had been held by another Frenchman, Stephane Peyrone.

The surf-sail began from the island of Nuku Hiva, in French Polynesia, and ended on the atoll of Ahé, near de Rosnay's planned destination of Tahiti. Whether the records for distance and longevity will ever take their place in wind-surfing annals is doubtful, however, because de Rosnay made the journey unaccompanied. Usually, for such a dangerous adventure, an escort boat would follow, but he chose to sail alone.

Along the way, de Rosnay claims

his craft was attacked by sharks on five different occasions. There was, of course, no one to corroborate this, but shark bites were found in one of the flotation pontoons. Besides that, he also had to battle 12-foot waves and the scorching, tropical South Pacific sun.

Sleep posed the biggest problem according to de Rosnay, so he designed a special flotation device— actually an aluminum bar with flotation pontoons at each end that would be secured perpendicularly across the surfboard to turn it into a kind of trimaran. It would enable him to sleep on board without the surfboard capsizing or pitching him into the ocean. He also devised a watertight plastic cocoon on the surfboard into which he crawled each night. For food, he survived principally on nu-trition bars that had been developed by NASA for use among astronauts as well as on various other nibbles that included dates, macadamia nuts, and a variety of vitamin pills.

A champion surfer, de Rosnay had made an eight-hour surf-sail across the Bering Strait in 1979. In a wind-sail of a different nature, de Rosnay had also rigged up a land surfer to coast across the Sahara Desert, a feat he accomplished over a period of 12 days, also in 1979. He was no stranger to unusual journeys.

During his Pacific adventure, search planes and boats scoured the ocean for de Rosnay but could not locate him. He had been given up for dead when he finally glided up to the beach at Ahé. He was barely alive and, as one observer said, "he was too dehydrated to even cry."

British Columbia to Hawaii in a Canoe

The sunbathers, swimmers, and surfers at Waikiki Beach paid little attention to the sailing craft dubbed *Orenda* that rounded the bend at Diamond Head in the summer of 1978 and headed toward shore. From a distance, it looked like most other sailboats that cruise the blue Hawaiian waters, the sails fluttering from its 15- and 12-foot masts, but on close inspection it was an altogether different vessel. The *Orenda* was hardly a pleasure craft for leisurely sails among the islands; instead it was a hand-hewn, authentically replicated sailing canoe of the kind the Haida Indians of British Columbia, Canada, took to the sea about 1,500 years ago.

Its captain was Geordie Tocher, a sinewy, bearded, 50-year-old adventurer from the Canadian Northwest who was among other things a lumberjack, log cabin builder, wood sculptor, white-water rafter, scuba diver, sky diver, and airplane pilot. He had built the boat by hand, which took a full two years, outfitted it, and then set out to retrace the 4,500-mile voyage he believed the Haidas had made a century and a half earlier to settle in the Hawaiian Islands.

Tocher built the *Orenda* (an Iroquois Indian word for the spirit attuned to nature) in the fashion of the Haidas, carving it out of an enormous British Columbia Douglas fir. From a tree estimated to be 600 to 800 years old that once stood 300 feet tall and had a diameter of nine feet, he gouged out a one-piece canoe 40 feet long, then shaped two large spars to hold the craft's three sails, carved a rudder, and constructed a crude cabin. When finished, the *Orenda* weighed 3½ tons.

With a crew of two—Gerhard Kiessel, a 55-year-old baker and accomplished sailor who was to serve as navigator, and Karin Lind, 34, Tocher's girl friend and an anthropology instructor at Capilano College in Canada, Tocher launched his historic voyage from Vancouver Harbor. He took the *Orenda* down the west coast of North America. After two weeks on the ocean, they put in at Seattle, Washington, then continued down to Santa Cruz, California. That leg of the journey was a harrowing one, three weeks of almost continual storms with gale-force winds daily and 30- to 40-foot waves.

The boat weathered the inhospitable seas and weather, but Tocher suffered from severe dehydration and had to recuperate at Santa Cruz. There, Karin Lind forsook the trip and returned to Canada and the classroom. She was replaced on the crew by free-lance writer Richard Tomkies. When Tocher recovered, he guided the *Orenda* back into the Pacific and headed due west. It was a four-week sail, which writer Tomkies later described as "sheer terror interspersed with moments of boredom."

The voyage of the *Orenda* was actually Tocher's second attempt to cross the Pacific to Hawaii in a sailing canoe. The first was in 1971, in a boat hacked out of a 200-foot cedar tree he cut down himself in British Columbia. That boat, also called the *Orenda*, was 50 feet long and 4½ feet wide, and was destroyed on a reef about 30 miles north of San Francisco, California.

Geordie Tocher's second adventure on the Pacific was successful. Just as Thor Heyerdahl had done with his epic voyage from South America to Tahiti aboard the *Kon-Tiki*, Tocher had recreated what he believed was one of man's early and monumental migrations. Whether or not the Haida Indians of Canada had sailed similarly those 1,500 years ago and populated Hawaii is a moot point among scientists and historians, but Tocher at least proved that they could have done it. And the legends of the Hawaiian natives add some credence to his belief, claiming that their original homeland was a place where "the trees are without leaves for six months of the year and men ride the ocean in canoes."

The Longest Canoe Trip

It began in 1980, a planned 28,000-mile canoe trip weaving through the continental United States, Canada, and Alaska. The canoeists: two plumbers from Lansing, Michigan— Verlen Kruger and Steven Landick. Their goal: to rewrite the record books for long-distance canoeing.

The two adventurers put in at Red Rock, Montana, with two canoes, each 17 feet long and 28 inches wide, built by Kruger himself. The covering was lightweight but highly durable synthetic material, designed and tested to withstand extreme cold and saltwater. They took along an assortment of supplies, including canned goods and dried foods, but also planned to buy or forage for food as they went.

Following a variety of streams and the mighty Missouri River, Kruger and Landick paddled their way down through Bismark, North Dakota, and Minneapolis, Minnesota, until they reached St. Louis, Missouri. From St. Louis, they headed north on the Illinois River to Lake Michigan, traveled its length, then passed into Lake Huron, down through Lake Erie, and up through Lake Ontario. They canoed up the St. Lawrence Seaway all the way to its mouth at the Gulf of St. Lawrence, then passed between Newfoundland and Nova Scotia into the Atlantic Ocean.

The odyssey continued straight down the east coast of the United States, around the Florida peninsula, up the coast of the Gulf of Mexico, to the mouth of the Mississippi River. They paddled upriver all the way to Minnesota near the Mississippi's source, then branched off and continued into Canada. They passed through Manitoba and Alberta, into the Northwest Territories, and on past the Arctic Circle. At the Eskimo village of Tuktoyaktuk, on the coast of the Arctic Ocean's Beaufort Sea, near the northernmost point of northwest Canada, Kruger and his paddle-partner, Landick, headed west across Mackenzie Bay, the Yukon, and into northern Alaska. Heading south then, they made it as far as Glacier Bay National Monument, near Juneau, and the Alexander Archipelago in southeastern Alaska. There, the fierce Alaskan winter of 1981–1982 forced them to stop their trek.

The two canoeists had covered approximately 17,000 miles on streams, rivers, lakes, and two oceans when they finally had to put their paddles down.

But the journey was not over. The plan was to pick up where they had left off in Alaska in the spring of 1982. Kruger and Landick said they wanted to log an additional 11,000 miles by continuing down the west coasts of Canada and the United States, all the way around the peninsula of Baja California, and back up to the mouth of the Colorado River. They would then follow it through Arizona, Utah, Wyoming, the Dakotas, back into Canada, then down through Lake Superior, and finally through a system of tinier waterways to their hometown of Lansing, Michigan. When it was all over, they would have traveled about 28,000 miles by canoe, a distance greater than the equatorial girth of the planet Earth.

Sailing the Atlantic Without Instruments

In the spring of 1980, a sailor and former geography professor, Marvin Creamer, set sail on a novel oceanic cruise. His goal: to sail from Atlantic City, New Jersey, to Africa and back. The novelty: he would do it with no navigational instruments whatsoever, not even a compass.

Aboard his 39-foot cutter, the *Navstar*, Creamer and a crew of three set sail in April with only the stars and Creamer's theory of navigation to guide them. He called the method "latitude sailing." The key to it was in determining a known star at its zenith, which would then enable him to calculate the latitude at which he was sailing. Finding a given star at its zenith, Creamer pointed out, is accomplished with the help of the star Polaris, at least in the Northern Hemisphere. As he explained in an article in *Motor Boating and Sailing* magazine, January 1981, "All the stars go around Polaris counterclockwise, and . . . when an imaginary line is drawn from Polaris to the selected star, the star is at the meridian transit (zenith) when the line splits the hemisphere of the sky into two equal parts. This division into equal quarter-spheres lasts but a brief moment." Still, if carried off accurately, it would enable Creamer to determine his latitude within a quarter of a degree.

Creamer zeroed in on six different stars on his way to Africa—Cor Caroli, Vega, Hercules Alpha, Hercules Gamma, Arcturus, and Denobola. He reached Africa successfully, using his unique navigational technique, then turned around and sailed back. On the return voyage, however, he was putting his theory to a true pinpoint test. His destination was not the immense coast of Africa but instead the tiny island of Bermuda, about 570 miles off the coast of North Carolina and a mere speck in the vast waters of the Atlantic Ocean. He hit it perfectly on July 9. From there, Creamer guided the *Navstar* back to Atlantic City.

Although the stars were his primary source of navigation, there were other aids as well, according to Creamer. "Water color as seen by the eye and temperature felt by the hand offer locational hints," he said. "The presence of seaweed or marine animals suggests certain locations. The arrival on board of flies can tell the navigator he is close to land almost as surely as the sighting of a marked buoy."

The entire voyage covered 8,000 miles and took 92 days. Creamer and other scientists feel that his naviga-tional method can one day be of great help to shipwrecked sailors and pilots downed in the ocean who have only a life raft and usually the barest of navigational equipment.

Ice Yachting

Ice yachting is not one of the world's most commonly practiced sports, but it can be one of the most breathtaking. The lightweight, highly maneuverable craft skim across frozen lakes at speeds usually in the 60- to 80-miles-per-hour range. But they can go even faster than that. The world record, according to The Guinness Book of World Records, is 143 miles per hour, set by John D. Buckstaff on Lake Winnebago, Wisconsin, back in 1938—in a wind of 72 miles per hour. The account that follows, of a sail somewhat slower, was written by Dereck Williamson and appeared in Jack Andresen's Sailing on Ice.

Going more than 60 miles per hour in a sailboat is a lot of fun, if you don't mind the pieces of ice in your teeth.

You've also got to watch out for the old Christmas trees.

On Saturday, the sport of iceboating came to the reservoir, which is frozen over in some spots.

For the expert, it's an exciting, demanding, and often hairy sport.

For the novice, it's the same thing plus downright confusing. Like the Christmas trees.

"What are all the Christmas trees for?" I asked on Saturday morning, as guys wearing insulated boots and spiked ice creepers and insulated coveralls and face masks and helmets and goggles were taking a bunch of trees and boats from station wagons.

"We put them out there on the ice to mark the spots of open water," said a man in red coveralls with a shoulder patch that read "Don't Eat Yellow Snow."

As a newspaper reporter, I felt pretty silly. I mean, what a logical answer. And what a great way to make use of old Christmas trees!

The man in red had set the race-course—two flags about a mile and a half apart. The 17 slim racing craft now being assembled at the edge of the reservoir would sail around the flags three times. Four races were to be sailed, and similar events on Sunday would constitute a regatta.

One boat was coming in, fast. It wheeled around into the wind and the skipper, or pilot, or whatever you call somebody who runs an iceboat, pulled a lever and a sticklike thing scraped along the ice with a loud scraping sound and the boat stopped. The boat was named *Skidoo.*

A man wrapped up like a mummy climbed out, and ducked under the flapping sail. Somebody said it was Jack Andresen, Eastern Arrow Champion.

Arrow is the name of the boat, a two-place, 250-pound boat with about 70 square feet of sail area. Bigger than a DN and smaller than a Yankee and a Skeeter.

Jack invited me to go for a ride in his Arrow, and as we walked out on the ice he explained that water skiing used to be his thing, but that iceboating was his thing now.

"It's not a new sport; there are about, say, five thousand iceboats. The most popular, about three thousand of them, are the DNs, which are also the smallest. It's an Eastern Division race, and we're anxious to see how this reservoir is. It's the first time for iceboats here and it's nice and smooth. The wind is puffy though; it could be a real mast-breaker out there today."

Thus reassured, I climbed into the right side of the Arrow's cockpit.

I put on a pair of ski goggles, pulled my wool hat over my ears, and drew my parka hood over my wool hat. "Mmmmmm Mmmmmm Mmmmmmm," said Jack. I thought to myself, "this is going to be great; I can't even hear what he's saying. And I'm going out in an eighty-mile-an-hour iceboat with a guy who will be skirting patches of open water."

Jack climbed in beside me and I eased part of my left ear out of the wool. If he shouted Mayday I wanted to be the first to know. The boat started to move.

"Lean way back," he said, setting himself in a comfortable position and swinging a large wooden tiller to the left. The boat started to move in a graceful arc, to the right. "Some boats steer by foot pedals, and the larger Skeeters have a horizontal wheel under the deck," he said. "Keep your head down."

The boom swung across over my head, there was a snap of canvas.

From the skatelike runners, one on each side on sort of outriggers and a third in front used for steering, there came a hissing sound.

Suddenly, we were going very fast.

"We're just idling now, about fifteen to twenty miles an hour, 'til we get out of the cove," said Jack, doing things with the tiller. It crossed my mind that if this was idling, I would shortly be in some very serious trouble.

I had brought my camera along to take pictures of the boat under way. The camera was under my knees. It suddenly became clear to me that I wasn't going to take any pictures because I would be too busy just holding on.

The boat came out of the cove and headed down the vast frozen lake. Vast partly frozen lake, I remembered. Suddenly, it seemed like a giant hand grabbed the boat and shoved it skimming across the ice. The acceleration was breathtaking. Later, Jack said we had reached maybe a little over sixty, but when you're that close to the surface it seems like much, much faster. Tiny pieces of ice dashed against the lower part of my face. Now I knew why everybody wore full face masks.

I considered releasing my two-handed grip on the boat and putting one glove over my face. The boat whipped around and headed in another direction and I decided to hold on, and let my teeth bleed. "Here comes pressure ridge!" Jack shouted. I didn't know what I was supposed to do about it. Praying seemed appropriate.

We sped up on a long crack, and crossed it hsssss, crump, hsssss. The crack was just a bump. We tacked back and forth. Suddenly, the wind slowed.

"It's very puffy, and we'll probably have some runners up in the air today." He explained that sailing on just two of the three runners was ex-citing, but that "if it lifts up too high and then comes down with a bang you lose speed. There are ways to take advantage of the angle, though, and—WHOOPS! There are waves ahead!"

Waves meant open water right in front of us, and before I could even react to the information—like screaming or something—Jack had swung the tiller around and we were speeding back toward the cove.

"Gotta watch out for those places," he said, easily the understatement of the winter.

Maneuvering the boat up near the others in a series of deft tiller movements and adjustments of the main sheet (the rope that controls the sail's angle), Jack brought the iceboat to a stop without even using the brake.

I climbed out of *Skidoo*; I didn't know how to thank him. For one thing, my lips were frozen shut.

Above the Land

The Barnstormers

It was just after the end of World War I that the phenomenon known as barnstorming came to life to the wide-eyed amazement of Americans who were far more accustomed to watching birds cavort in the sky. Returning from the battlefields of Europe was a volatile mixture of thousands of dogfighting pilots and cheap, war-surplus aircraft. Soon America's skies were filled with heart-stopping, disaster-courting displays that were quickly dubbed barnstorming.

The former fighter pilots came back to the farms and cornfields of rural America, not to farm but, as one of them put it, "to scare hell out of the rubes and get paid for it." The sport, if it could be called that, flourished for only a decade until finally reduced to a very rare occurrence on the American scene by the economic hardships of the Great Depression. But while it lasted, this often maniacal exhibition of aerial derring-do produced some of the most bizarre events between man and airplane ever to occur in the sky.

Second Lieutenant Doug Davis was typical of the young flyers who found themselves out of a job when the armistice was signed back in 1918. He first considered selling insurance or going back to college, but such pedestrian pursuits seemed awfully pale after the danger-filled life of a wartime pilot, so Davis invested his life savings—$400—in a JN4D training plane, better known as a Jenny. He parked the Jenny at Chandler Race Track on the outskirts of Atlanta, Georgia, and propped a sign against the landing gear offering stunt-flying rides for $15 to $25. The curious and the thrill-seekers began to line up, and soon Davis had a thriving business going. Elsewhere in the United States others followed suit—some putting on shows, others taking the locals up to participate in the wild flights.

For barnstormers, the trick to turning a profit was to keep the overhead low and the flying time high. With no FAA inspectors looking over their shoulders, maintenance was only a sometime thing, usually undertaken only when it was absolutely necessary. In other words, if the plane wouldn't get the barnstormer off the ground, he had it fixed; if it would get off the ground, well, he had other things to worry about.

A classic example of how repairs were made in those days involves a young daredevil who later became a fully authenticated American folk hero, Charles Lindbergh. A number of years before "Lucky Lindy" took the Spirit of St. Louis across the Atlantic Ocean, he and a partner, en route to a town in southwest Texas, were forced to land on a cactus-covered mesa. The plane sustained some minor damage in landing but not enough to keep it from flying. Taking off in the field of desert-toughened cactus and sagebrush, however, was quite another story. Lindbergh and his cohort were going to have to hack out a runway. They could see a ranch house on a nearby ridge and went over to borrow some tools. In the sweltering heat they chopped out a takeoff strip, then cranked up their Jenny. But when they tried to take off, the landing gear did not clear the cactus barrier at the end of their too-short swath. The coup de grace was delivered by a giant Spanish dagger plant, which pierced the lower left wing, ripping the fabric covering and breaking the front spar. Now, if they were ever to get off the mesa with their plane, they needed not only a longer runway but also some fabric, adhesive, and other materials to repair their broken wing.

Near the ranch house there was a set of railroad tracks, so Lindy's friend camped by them until he was able to flag down a freight train and send for supplies. Lindbergh went back to hack out a longer airstrip. The next morning they had their adhesive, two pieces of crating board, nails, screws, glue, several balls of chalkline, and some muslin fabric. They borrowed a butcher's knife, needle and thread, and an ax from the rancher, and soon had the Jenny's wing mended. By noon they were airborne again.

Moving on was also an integral part of barnstorming. After a few days in one place, when the crowds began to dwindle, the flyer and his Jenny would have to leave for newer and more lucrative sites.

When the barnstormer arrived at a new town it wasn't enough to mere-ly land in some green pasture, prop up a sign, and wait for customers. He needed to promote his skills and product. At first it was simple; all he had to do was buzz the town. The clatter of the Jenny's untuned Curtiss OX5 engine and the rare sight of an airplane was often enough to lure the citizens from their plows, work-benches, or washboards to the out-skirts of town. Later, when there were hundreds of these flying gyp-sies making the circuits, it took a lot more. And that's when it really start-ed getting crazy.

At first a new gimmick might be something as sane as having a part-ner parachute from the plane. But it wasn't a giant leap from parachuting to other extravehicular activities, and soon every serious barnstormer had a fearless if not-so-sane compan-ion who crawled around the outside of the plane while it buzzed the town. This suicidal sidekick was known as a wing walker.

Wing walkers came in all forms, and some of the best were women. They stood on the wing; they hung from the wing; they walked, crawled, jumped, and danced on the wing. But perhaps the wing walker award for the weirdest would have to go to Wesley May for what he did above the canals of Venice, California, in 1920. Wesley wing-walked for Ivan R. Gates, a San Francisco used-car dealer who bankrolled what he called the Gates Flying Circus. To keep the public's attention, Gates constantly had to come up with new-er and more exciting promotional stunts. One day he announced that his intrepid airmen would keep a single Jenny aloft for 24 consecutive hours. Wing walker Wesley May was the key to the whole thing. As the crowd watched, the Jenny lazily circled the field. When its fuel was nearly depleted, another plane appeared—with Wesley on its wing. Strapped to his back was a five-gallon can of gasoline. The two planes would move to within a few feet of each other and Wesley would swing from his plane onto the wing of the fuel-thirsty Jenny, then crawl with his sloshing backpack to the center of the aircraft and pour the gas into the fuel tank.

After this exploit, there was no stopping Wesley. He eventually roller-skated on a wing, and bicycled on another. Wesley May took one too many chances, however, and was killed when he fell from the wing of an airplane during one of his shows.

Wesley May's fate was not unique. While there was a certain wild humor associated with barnstorming, it was more often than not black humor. In 1922, one out of every four barnstormers was involved in a serious crash. In fact, crashing was such a crowd pleaser that it was eventually made a part of most shows. (That's when the moviemakers discovered there were people who would do this kind of thing for money, and motion picture stunt flying was born.)

Dick Grace was a crash specialist. In one movie he was to crash a plane into a World War I battlefield crisscrossed with barbed wire that had been strung between two supposedly stout oak posts. For the stunt, however, a section of the posts was made of balsa wood and the "barbed wire" was string. That's where Grace was to "crash." When he made the run, however, his speed was a little high and he had to drop his wing and initiate the crash sooner than he had planned. He hit the real posts and the real barbed wire, the plane flipped over and a four-by-four-inch slab of oak ended up wedged between Grace's head and the back of the open cockpit. He survived, and said it was all in a day's work on the set.

Another barnstormer who performed as a movie stunt pilot was Hank Coffin. Coffin was employed to crash planes through barns or to clip off church steeples. Sometimes he would pluck distressed damsels from speeding freight trains or automobiles.

When the crowds stopped coming to the cow pastures, and Hollywood had all the footage of flaming crashes it could use, the federal government, with the 18th Amendment and prohibition, thoughtfully provided an alternate source of income for barnstorming veterans—rum-running. The Canadian and Mexican borders were hardly a barrier to the little planes, and they flew back and forth with their clinking cargo destined for the speakeasies of America.

For other burnt-out barnstormers who didn't have the disposition for the clandestine business of bootlegging, there was another career, also provided by the federal government—the job of airmail pilot. And it was as hazardous an occupation in those days as anything else in the world of aviation. As one writer put it: "If rube-buzzing, wing-walking, steeple-busting, and booze-lugging seem like crazy ways to make a buck, consider flying a war-surplus, open-cockpit biplane through a raging thunderstorm at night just to deliver a few bills and a Dear John letter a day earlier."

The U.S. Post Office had actually taken to wing six months before World War I ended, when it inaugurated regular service between New York and Washington, D. C. To accomplish it, the Post Office borrowed six Jennys and a matching set of lieutenants from the Army Air Corps.

Following the war, the Post Office pioneered the first transcontinental airmail route, generally following the old Pony Express trail, which wound through the passes of the Rocky Mountains and the Sierra Nevada. The planes selected for this new venture were American-built De Havilland DH4s, sturdy little single-place biplanes left over from the Great War. The first run sputtered across the continent from San Francisco, California, to Mineola, Long Island, New York, in 33 hours and 20 minutes on February 22–23, 1921.

By 1924 a series of landing fields was strung along the transcontinental route at 25-mile intervals. Every three miles an emergency strip was etched out, that is, assuming there was a level place to scratch clear a runway. This short span between landing spots tells the story of flying in the early days, when temperamental engines and the ever-present

threat of bad weather were very real flying factors.

J. D. Hill left Garden City, New Jersey, on his run one morning and soon found light showers turning into a torrential downpour. While below him in Pennsylvania 16 people drowned in the deluge, he managed to fly above it all. As he noted wryly in his trip report, "I suppose that I would have drowned too if it hadn't been for the fan on the front of my ship. My observation on this trip was that the DH [De Havilland] has too many wires for an airplane and not enough for a fishnet."

Another airmail barnstormer was forced by bad weather to land on a rocky ledge east of Salt Lake City, Utah. He slogged through heavy snow for 36 hours to reach a phone and report he was down. Then, when the weather cleared, he trekked back to the plane, chipped the frozen mailbag loose, and lugged it to town on foot.

One state west of there, Nevada, was the site of an even more heroic effort. Here the pilot became lost in a sudden fog as he crossed Saddle Pass, forcing him to skim along the treetops and then crash-land on a ridge. In the belly landing he dislocated his shoulder. Slinging the mailbag over his remaining good shoulder, the pilot-turned-hiker set off to find a post office. Struggling over the icy rocks he lost his footing and tumbled down a 1,000-foot slope. The impact at the bottom of the slide jarred his dislocated shoulder back into place. During all this he had tenaciously held onto the bag of mail. Eventually he scrambled out of the canyon, found a railroad track, and followed it to civilization.

Charles Lindbergh, who coaxed his Jenny off that mesa in Texas, was one of the barnstormers who took up airmail flying. His experience one dark foggy night over Chicago is another harrowing tale of this phase of daredevil flying. Unable to locate the landing field through a fog—the airport had the latest in navigational aids, two barrels of burning oil—Lindbergh circled until his engine sputtered, coughed, and died, leaving him in a dark, disconcerting silence. With resignation he adjusted his parachute, unbuckled his seat belt, stepped up onto the DH4's cowling, switched on his flashlight, and jumped. All he could do was hope; he had no idea what he was parachuting into. To make the descent even more interesting, the abandoned plane circled and made a ghostly pass at him. Lindbergh had no idea where he was. Was Lake Michigan beneath him? Or the top of some skyscraper? Or the roof of some soon-to-be startled citizen? Fortunately, he dropped into a cornfield. After gathering up his chute, Lindbergh followed a pair of ruts toward the main road. An approaching car caught him in its headlights and the driver, when he pulled alongside, yelled that he had nearly been hit by an airplane that crashed in a nearby field. Lindbergh said, "Yes, I know, I'm the pilot."

The Lofty World of Tightrope Walking

Only a special kind of person would try to catch the public eye by walking across a cable strung between two points high above the ground. Indeed, a great sense of balance is a prerequisite, and a kind of hellish abandon, an inherent quality of daring, a desire to hear the gasps of fear and amazement from the spectators below, a personality the diametric opposite of an acrophobiac.

Entertainers have been walking tightropes since the earliest days of circus entertainment, providing a source of amusement in ancient Rome and in Europe during the Dark Ages. At medieval fairs, they accompanied the jousters and the tilters.

Among the first to be identified by name, however, was Jacob Hall, a courtly young Englishman. Hall, who became known as the "rope dancer," lived in the middle of the 17th century and was acclaimed as a first-rate acrobat. Part of his act included walking the tightrope. Britishers who continually gathered to watch his performance must have been astonished by him, described as "being clever and alert in somersaults and flip-flaps, performing the former over naked rapiers and men's heads." It was said that he would somersault through a hoop and land lithely back on the rope. Besides these daring deeds, Hall was also reputed to be the first lover of the famed English actress Nell Gwyn (1650–1687), who later became mistress to Charles II of England. Whether Hall performed his feats before the wide-eyed, breathless audiences to impress Miss Gwyn or to satisfy his thirst for adventure will never be known.

Contemporary tightrope walkers have performed perhaps even more astonishingly, their feats earning world records. Philippe Petit of France was an impetuous 24-year-old when he made his mark on the world. On an August morning in 1974, he stepped out on a tightrope extended across the two towers of New York's World Trade Center, 1,350 feet above the street, with nothing whatsoever between himself and the concrete far below. With a balancing bar in hand, he walked across the cable; actually, he traveled back and forth, crossing it seven times, putting on a show that lasted 1¼ hours. *The Guinness Book of World Records* accepted his feat as "the tightrope walk over the highest drop."

However, his unauthorized performance also gained the attention of the New York City police. He was cited for criminal trespass, arrested, and forced to appear before a police psychiatrist.

The Guinness Book of World Records also accords a record to Henry Rochetain of France for remaining on a tightrope for a total of 185 days in 1973. The wire, strung 82 feet above a supermarket in St. Etienne, France, was 394 feet long. During his six-month stay on the wire, he walked approximately 310 miles on it, and the *Guinness* editors noted that "his ability to sleep on the wire left doctors puzzled."

But the true king of the tightrope walkers was a Frenchman who performed under the name Charles Blondin; his real name was Jean Francois Gravelet, but he preferred to be called the Prince of Manila or the Monarch of the Cable. He had been a tightrope walker for some years, then at the age of 35 he decided to attempt the ultimate. He would walk on a tightrope above Niagara Falls, from the United States to Canada.

It was July 30, 1859, and a cable made of tightly entwined hemp was stretched above the raging cascade of Niagara. The tightrope was on a slant—160 feet above the Falls and rising to 270 feet at the other end, across a distance of 1,100 feet.

More than 25,000 people arrived that day to watch Blondin's unprecedented feat—the "acme of acrobatics," as he called it. No one had ever before attempted such a dramatic act on the high wire. Vincent Starrett later described it in an article for the *Saturday Evening Post* (October 26, 1929):

His audience was waiting. Suddenly the air was torn with shouts and cheers. Blondin had appeared at the American end of the rope and was making his preparations. Now he was talking with those about him. He was making ready to step off. He was picking up his balance pole—a 50 pound burden—and placing his foot upon the rope. And now he was launched in space and had begun his journey toward the British province of Upper Canada.

Without hesitation, the performer proceeded briskly, almost casually, to the center of the cable. There he seated himself with great composure and glanced complacently about him at the thronging shores. He did not look down, it was reported. That was something he had trained himself never to do. After a few seconds he rose upright, strolled forward for some feet, and again stopped. This time he stretched himself at full length upon the rope, lying upon his back, his balance pole horizontally across his chest. Another moment of suspense; then a feat of appalling rashness. He turned a back somersault upon the rope, came upright upon his feet, and walking rapidly to his landing stage, arrived as cooly as if he had no more than alighted from a bus. In the pauses of the deafening shouts on either bank of the river, a Canadian band could be heard playing the "Marseillaise."

That was not the end of the show, however. As an encore, Blondin strolled back out on the rope, this time with a camera strapped to his back. Out above the Falls, he stopped, placed his balance bar on the tightrope, and then lashed it there. He took the camera from his back, balanced now totally on his own, and snapped a photo of the disbelieving crowd who stared up at him. He untied the balance pole and then walked back to the landing stage.

Still the show was not over. Blondin stepped back out on the cable. This time he was carrying a chair along with his balance bar. He walked carefully out above the waterfall, almost halfway back across the cable. There he stopped and carefully balanced the chair on two legs. Then he sat down on it, and in Vincent Starrett's words, "crossing his legs, gazed around him with magnificent unconcern." On the way back he stopped again and carefully placed the chair on the wire, but instead of sitting on it this time, he clambered up and stood on it.

And that ended the show. "Monsieur Blondin, still bland and smiling, came ashore at his original point of departure, and was seen to be no wise fatigued by his adventure."

A year later Charles Blondin made the same death-defying crossing of Niagara Falls, but this time he carried piggy-back his agent, a 135-pound, 31-year-old, who obviously had the greatest of faith in his client. And if that wasn't enough: "The same day, with immense pain to all beholders, and in spite of the [Prince of Wales's] injunction against 'anything extraordinary,' Blondin crossed the cable on stilts."

Charles Blondin, the Prince of Manila, the Monarch of the Cable, truly earned his lofty place in the world of aerial adventure.

The Pilot Who Wore Satin

It was 3:30 A. M., April 16, 1912, on a fogbound coast near Dover, England, when a darkly beautiful young woman stepped from her bed.

She dressed quickly, pulling on a lavender, one-piece satin flying suit, which was quickly becoming a trademark in her aviation exploits. Thirty minutes later she was walking briskly across a dark airfield toward a mist-shrouded shape. The young woman was Harriet Quimby, and the shape was a fragile-looking aircraft in which she planned to fly across the English Channel to France—the first woman ever to attempt that feat.

The airplane was on loan from Louis Bleriot, the famous French flyer and aircraft designer who three years earlier had become the first human being to fly the Channel. Harriet Quimby of New York had learned to fly in a similar single-winged aircraft, and the previous July had become the first American woman to qualify for a pilot's license.

Bleriot's aircraft was similar in appearance to the planes she had already flown, but it was in several important ways quite different. First of all, it was larger, with a more powerful engine, and secondly, the controls were arranged differently. Harriet felt the new plane would take some getting used to, so she had gone to France earlier to learn from its builder just how to fly it. Unfortunately, miserable weather hung over the coast of France for days, preventing her from making a single test flight. After waiting as long as she could, Harriet, fearing some other woman might preempt her bid for glory, had the Bleriot plane shipped to Dover. With the wind and weather conditions now just right she decided to challenge the treacherous Channel, even though she had never flown the plane before.

Gustav Hamel, who had previously flown the Bleriot across the stormy English Channel, was on hand at the Dover field to provide some assistance. His suggestions and last-minute instructions were welcomed and perhaps added the margin of confidence Harriet needed that cold, damp morning.

Harriet was prepared for the cold. Over her famous satin flying suit she wore a long wool coat, a raincoat, and a sealskin stole. "Even this did not satisfy my solicitous friends," she wrote later. "They handed me a large hot water bag, which Mr. Hamel insisted on tying to my waist like an enormous locket."

Hot water bag in place, goggles down, handshakes to the small group of well-wishers over, Harriet was ready to make history. "I felt impatient to realize this project on which I was determined, despite the protests of my friends. For the first time I flew a Bleriot monoplane. For the first time I was to fly by compass. For the first time I was to fly on the other side of the Atlantic. My anxiety was to get off quickly."

It was 5:30 A.M. when the plane

lifted from Dover Aerodrome into a partly cloudy sky, and headed toward an ominous fogbank that lay offshore. The engine, roaring away at 1,200 revolutions per minute, drowned out the cheers of the group that had gathered at the airfield to see Harriet off on her epic flight. Observers on the ground would soon lose sight of her, but Harriet later described the adventure.

In a moment I was in the air, climbing steadily in a long circle. I was up 1,500 feet within 30 seconds. From this high point of vantage my eyes lit at once on Dover Castle. It was half hidden in a fogbank. I felt that trouble was coming, but I made directly for the flagstaff of the castle, as I had promised the waiting *Mirror* [the London newspaper] photographers and the moving-picture men I should do.

In an instant I was beyond the cliffs and over the Channel. Far beneath I saw the *Mirror's* tug, with its stream of black smoke. It was trying to keep ahead of me, but I passed it in a jiffy. Then the quickening fog obscured my view. I could not see above, below, or ahead. I ascended to a height of 6,000 feet, hoping to escape the mist that enveloped me. It was bitter cold—the kind that chills to the bones. I recalled somewhat nervously Hamel's remark about the North Sea, but a glance at my compass reassured me that I was within my course. Failing to strike clear air, I determined to descend again. It was

then that I came near a mishap. The machine tilted to a steep angle, causing the gasoline to flood, and my engine began to misfire. I figured on pancaking down so as to strike the water with the plane in a floating position. But, greatly to my relief, the gasoline quickly burned out and my engine resumed an even purr. A glance at the watch on my wrist reminded me that I should be near the French coast, but Calais was out of sight. I could not see ahead of me or at all below. There was only one thing for me to do ... keep my eyes fixed on my compass.

My hands were covered with long Scotch woolen gloves which gave me good protection from the cold and fog; but the machine was wet and my face was so covered with dampness that I had to push my goggles up on my forehead. I could not see through them. I was traveling at over a mile a minute. The distance straight across from Dover to Calais is only 25 miles, and I knew that land must be in sight if I could only get below the fog and see it. So I dropped from an altitude of about 2,000 feet until I was half that height. The sunlight struck upon my face and my eyes lit upon the white and sandy shores of France. I felt happy, but could not find Calais. Being unfamiliar with the coastline, I could not locate myself. I determined to reconnoiter and come down to a height of about 500 feet and traverse the shore.

Meanwhile, the wind had risen and the currents were coming in billowy gusts. I flew a short distance inland to locate myself or find a good place on which to alight. It was all tilled land below me, and rather than tear up the farmers' fields I decided to drop down on the hard and sandy beach. I did so at once, making an easy landing. Then I jumped from my machine and was alone upon the shore. But it was only for a few moments. A crowd of fishermen—men, women, and children each carrying a pail of sand worms—came rushing from all directions toward me. They were chattering in French, of which I comprehended sufficient to discover that they knew I had crossed the Channel. These humble fisherfolk knew what had happened. They were congratulating themselves that the first woman to cross in an aeroplane had landed on their fishing beach.

Harriet had been in the air just over an hour and had landed 15 miles south and a little to the east of Calais, near the village of Hardelot.

Word would soon be wired around the world of Harriet Quimby's flight so as to grace the front pages of the world's newspapers. But it would not be headline news that day. Instead all that space would be reserved for a tragedy that eclipsed all other news—the sinking of the great luxury liner the *Titanic* (1,517

perished in the disaster). There was also another tragedy that day, much closer to Harriet Quimby—a young pilot attempted a Channel crossing the same day, but he got his directions confused, crashed, and was killed.

The *Titanic* disaster had dimmed Harriet's bid for international notoriety, but it did not slow her down. She continued her work as assistant editor and drama critic for the magazine *Leslie's Weekly,* and she wrote several articles about flying for other national publications. And she continued her sideline career as an aviator.

Three months after the Channel flight, back in Massachusetts, she took the pilot's seat in an even more powerful passenger-carrying Bleriot airplane. In the seat behind her was Bill Willard, promoter of the Harvard-Boston Aviation Meet. The goal of this flight was to break the world speed record in a round-trip flight from Squantum Air Field to the Boston Harbor Light and back.

It was late in the day on July 1, 1912, when Harriet raised her satin-clad arm in the traditional signal to pull the chocks. Soon after, the big Bleriot roared into the darkening sky. Rounding the Harbor Light there was no doubt they would break the record. As the plane neared the coast, however, something went wrong and the Bleriot suddenly lurched, sending Harriet and her passenger into a fatal dive to the earth 1,000 feet below. It was a tragic end for one of the most courageous pioneers in the history of flying.

Crossing the Atlantic by Balloon

Charles Lindbergh was the first to make a solo flight across the Atlantic Ocean, accomplishing that feat back in 1927 in the Ryan monoplane he had named the *Spirit of St. Louis*. To honor that historic flight, and following almost the same route as Lindbergh, three men set out in 1978 in the *Double Eagle II* to become the first adventurers ever to make a successful transatlantic crossing by balloon.

Ever since the Montgolfier brothers launched the first real hot-air balloon over the small town of Annonay, France, back in 1783, the dream of floating across the Atlantic Ocean has bewitched man. As early as 1873, a balloon called the *Daily Graphic*, captained by Washington Donaldson, was launched from a vacant lot in Brooklyn, New York, its goal Paris, France. The *Daily Graphic* traveled only 45 miles, however, and thumped to earth in New Canaan, Connecticut. Other balloon adventures followed. Early in 1978, aeronauts Don Cameron and Christopher Davey floated from Newfoundland to within 103 miles of the coast of France in their balloon *Zanussi* before a ripped gasbag forced them down into the sea.

Then came seasoned balloonists Ben Abruzzo and Maxie Anderson, and experienced pilot, navigator, and hang-gliding expert Larry Newman. Abruzzo and Anderson had first attempted the oceanic crossing in the *Double Eagle* in 1977, but a storm carried them far to the north and they were forced to ditch in the Arctic Circle just off the coast of Iceland. Now, on August 12, 1978, they were ready to try again. Their balloon, *Double Eagle II*, was designed in part by Ed Yost, who had set duration and distance records with his own transatlantic attempt in 1976. A mammoth gas envelope 11 stories tall, with an air capacity of 160,000 cubic feet, *Double Eagle II* was made of neoprene-coated nylon cloth. The upper portion, or orb, was sprayed with aluminum paint to reflect heat from the sun, and the bottom section was black to absorb heat from the earth and the atmosphere. The balloon carried a boat-shaped gondola that measured 8½ feet in length and six feet in width, and a hang glider, which was tethered to the gondola. (Larry Newman, a supreme optimist, had plans to dramatically soar to French soil on the hang glider.)

The gondola of *Double Eagle II* was jammed with equipment and supplies, a full 6,240 pounds' worth. Most of it would serve its function, then be used as ballast and dumped overboard in order to cause the balloon to ascend when that ballooning tactic was needed. Even the gondola itself could be used as ballast; if it came to such a dire emergency it could be jettisoned, leaving the three men to ride it out on the large ring at the base of the balloon.

Launch time was set for early evening, and as twilight descended over the farmlands around Presque Isle, Maine, great drafts of helium were being forced into the huge balloon, which when fully inflated looked like an inverted punching bag. Last-minute checks were made, the three men stood in the center of the gondola, the ropes tethering the craft to the ground were unleashed, and the balloon lifted gently into the sky, beginning an ascent that would eventually take *Double Eagle II* to an altitude of almost 25,000 feet. The balloon would average about 15 knots per hour and the journey was expected to take approximately six days.

In the clear night sky, the balloon passed over the U.S. border and drifted northeast across a splash of New Brunswick, Canada. By the next morning, *Double Eagle II* was over water, passing across the Gulf of St. Lawrence. The flight path was to be a great sweeping arc that would take the balloon as far north as 55 degrees latitude and then back down to Paris at 49 degrees latitude.

Storms, of course, are a major worry of balloonists. So is equipment damage. So are the unpredictability of the winds, the pressure systems, the updrafts and downdrafts. Navigability is limited because in many ways the balloonist is at the mercy of the whims of nature. The pilot can only move the balloon up or down in search of the most desirable wind currents. The rest is up to fortune and the Fates.

As the second night approached, so did the western shoreline of Newfoundland. All through that night, the balloon sailed slowly over the easternmost swath of North America. By midafternoon the following day, there was nothing but the Atlantic Ocean stretching out before them.

The balloonists faced both blistering sun and nighttime temperatures of nearly zero degrees Fahrenheit. The three men dressed in insulating layers to maintain body heat. And with the lack of breathable air at those heights, the three had to wear oxygen masks. Food was nothing special. Unlike the dried foods and beef jerky of the backpacker, or the specially prepared foods of the astronaut, the diverse menu brought along by the three balloonists included such items as Italian olives, sardines, lox, salami, nuts, and other ordinary staples, as well as a copious supply of fruit juices.

A Novel Flight

One of the most novel ways to cross the Atlantic Ocean was perpetrated by Jaromir Wagner in the autumn of 1980. Wagner, 41 years old, born in Czechoslovakia but a citizen of West Germany, decided to make the transatlantic crossing on top of the wing of an airplane.

He began his trip from an airfield in Ciessen, West Germany, lashed to the outside of a two-engine, propeller-driven plane. The jaunt took 11 days, with intermediate stops in Scotland, Iceland, Greenland, Newfoundland, Vermont, and New York City, ending in Caldwell, New Jersey. Wagner is the only person known to have crossed the Atlantic Ocean in such a fashion.

The *Double Eagle II* remained remarkably on course during the first half of its voyage through the skies, but on the fourth night ice began to form on the skin of the balloon, as much as 300 pounds of it, the aeronauts estimated. The morning sun, however, melted it and in the process created a small rainstorm that fell on those in the gondola. The following day, the balloon ascended to an altitude of 23,500 feet, but then some strange atmospheric pressures began to play havoc with the craft. Suddenly it began to descend all the way down into the clouds at 4,000 feet, a descent of 19,500 feet in a matter of hours. The three men in the gondola worked furiously, carefully shedding ballast until the craft began to ascend. It finally emerged from the cloud cover to absorb the heat of the afternoon sun, which enabled it to ride its roller coaster all the way back up to a flight zenith of 24,950 feet. It had been their closest call with failure, or perhaps disaster. But they had overcome it and, as night fell, the balloon approached the west coast of Ireland; by morning they were sailing over Great Britain.

At 7:49 P.M., August 17, 1978, *Double Eagle II* set down gently in a barley field near Miserey, France, just outside Paris. Of the more than three tons of ballast they had started out with, only 250 pounds were still aboard when the balloon landed. Even the hang glider had been dumped as ballast. The journey had taken five days, 17 hours, and six minutes. And the Atlantic had finally been conquered by three men riding the winds in a balloon.

Skydiving

Spies and soldiers have been parachuting for decades, but to them it is just a part of the day's work. For skydivers, it is a pastime, a hobby, a way to wrench some of the most exciting thrills from humankind's inventions of adventure. All the elements are there— peril, fear, defiance of nature's laws—and what one can expect of the sport is described in this article by Richard Whittingham, which first appeared in The Thrill Sports, *by the editors of* Consumer Guide.

You thought you never would, but now you've done it. You've decided to leap from an airplane that is cruising 3,000 feet above the ground in order to float lazily to earth under a huge, multicolored canopy. You've put in eight hours of ground training time, and now you're ready to make that first fateful leap into space. It is something you will remember the rest of your life.

In the airplane, you are ready, as ready as you will ever be. Your equipment—all 40-plus pounds of it—has been checked and checked again, and you are feeling all the fears and anxieties inherent in what you are about to do. Soon the plane will reach the drop zone, and despite the butterflies in your stomach, you tell yourself that you will be ready.

Then the jump master signals that your time has come. You move to the open door of the plane, where your static line is checked. You sit in the open door, your legs dangling out 3,000 feet above the ground. You try to guess what you will be thinking about during the next minute of your life.

You hear the jump master shout, "Cut," and the plane's engines are cut back. Then you hear, "Out," and your foot settles on the step outside the plane. Your white-knuckled hands grasp the strut that holds the wing in place, and you feel a sharp blast of the slipstream of air from the plane's propeller. In perhaps the longest second or two that you have ever experienced in your life, you realize that you are completely outside the airplane.

And then you hear the word, "Go," and automatically you push away from the plane. You are falling, and suddenly stark terror grabs your insides as the reality of what you are doing sends involuntary shudders through your body. But then you feel a jerk, and the great colorful canopy blossoms above you. You are not falling anymore; you are floating gently in space. You can see for miles across the checkerboard earth below; you can see life in miniature—tiny trees, buildings, cars, even people—all getting larger ever so gradually. And everything is still and silent.

The descent takes a total of only 2½ minutes, and when it is over you are on your way to becoming a skydiver.

Skydiving is parachuting for sport, and the term is generally applied to free-fall jumps, in which the parachutist has complete control over the opening of the canopy. To become a skydiver is not nearly as difficult as you might think. You simply contact the skydiving club in your area and pay a fee, which generally covers practically everything— your complete ground training by an experienced instructor, the use of a parachute and all other mandatory equipment (with the exception of boots), and the airplane ride up.

Naturally, there are restrictions as to who can become a skydiver. You must meet minimum age and physical fitness requirements, and you must comply with Federal Aviation Administration regulations and any state and/or local ordinances; but if you qualify, you are ready to take part in what is surely one of the most breathtaking sports yet devised. And you will join a select group of adventurers that includes people from all walks of life: housewives, doctors, teachers, laborers, high school students, as well as such famous personalities as Johnny Carson of the *Tonight* show.

Parachuting, which achieved recognition as a sport in the mid-1930s, actually goes back centuries before the airplane was even invented. No one knows who first developed the parachute, but Leonardo da Vinci designed one back in 1495. The first recorded successful parachute jump, however, did not occur for another 300 years. In 1783, Louis-Sebastian Lenormand dove from a tower in Montpellier, France, and drifted to the ground tightly clutching a large, umbrellalike parachute.

It was not until 1912 that someone actually parachuted from an airplane. Captain Albert Berry of the U.S. Army bailed out over St. Louis, Missouri, in that landmark jump. During the 1920s and 1930s, parachuting was pretty much restricted to the barnstormers, wing walkers, and other aerial daredevils of the day who dazzled audiences at air shows and flying circuses.

Then World War II came along. Combat jumping proved to be a training ground for thousands of young parachutists, who afterward took their experience back into civilian life. Quickly, parachuting became a popular pastime and a new form of competition.

As parachuting turned into the sport of skydiving, a spectacular and hair-raising new dimension came into existence—the free-fall. Skydivers would plunge thousands of feet before pulling the rip cord to release their canopies. Master skydivers jumped together and maneuvered to make contact with each other as they fell through space, practicing a technique known as "relative work." They passed batons back and forth as they plummeted toward earth at more than 100 miles an hour, or they guided themselves to a midair rendezvous, where they linked hands to form human chains, stars, or flower petals. A movie stunt man named Rod Pack even leaped from a plane without a parachute, was handed one by another skydiver free-falling alongside, put it on, opened it up, and floated safely to the ground.

U.S. Air Force Captain Joseph Kittinger, another fearless and very professional skydiver equipped with special equipment, made the longest free-fall ever. In 1960, Kittinger exited from a balloon 102,800 feet above ground and plunged 84,700 feet (more than 16 miles) before opening his parachute, a free-fall lasting four minutes, 38 seconds.

Flying for Thrills: The Life of an Aerobatic Pilot

Debbie Gary is a full-time aerobatics instructor in Atlanta, Georgia. Although she is only in her early 30s and the mother of a small child, she has accumulated an uncommon amount of experience in stunt and air-show flying. She has performed her death-defying maneuvers in the skies throughout the United States and Canada and is one of the most highly respected aerobatists in the world today. Here, in her own words, is what the sport is really like.

R.W.: How long have you been into aerobatics?

GARY: For about ten years now.

R.W.: How long were you flying plain old planes, the straight-line shots, before that?

GARY: Four years. So altogether I've got about fourteen years in flying.

R.W.: Fourteen years ago you weren't much more than just a little kid.

GARY: Sort of. I was nineteen then. Now I'm much more conservative. I'm so much more aware of what can go wrong than I was at nineteen or twenty-three. But if I hadn't taken a lot of the chances, the gambles, I'd have never gotten anywhere.

R.W.: Why did you decide to learn how to fly?

GARY: Well, I just sort of stumbled on it, literally. One night, when a boyfriend and I were looking for a bar where they served underage kids, we came upon this airport and there were some airplanes doing touch-and-goes. I was fascinated by it and I saw a sign that said for one hundred and ninety-nine dollars I could learn to fly. I thought, my God, I never even thought of that. What a great idea. A little later I went out and took an introductory lesson and I just fell in love with it.

R.W.: Aerobatics, though, adds a whole different dimension to flying—like danger. What prompted you to go into aerobatics?

GARY: Well, I went from straight flying to glider flying by chance. Right away I got into sport aviation, then I taught glider flying for several years and did some charter flying. I was getting somewhat bored and felt I had to learn something else. I guess I needed to be challenged. Then one day I was demonstrating with a glider—takeoffs and landings—at an air show down in the Virgin Islands. I got talking with the man who was flying aerobatics in the air show. It was called Citaborea—"Aerobatic" spelled backward. I was fascinated. Actually, I had never seen an air show before. I thought, that's exciting, the aerobatic flying, that is. Later, back in California, I thought, that's what I've been looking for. All my friends said, "Don't do it!" Everyone was really afraid for me, but I wasn't. Not because it wasn't scary, it was, but just because I really believed that that is what I was supposed to do. So I started aerobatic lessons with Jim Holland, and I think it was exactly two weeks later I did my first air show.

R.W.: What stunts did you do in your first air show?

GARY: I did everything that was on the basic aerobatic course, which included loops, slow rolls, hammerheads.

R.W.: Describe a hammerhead.

GARY: A hammerhead is one of the most exciting of the basic maneuvers. You pull the airplane straight up and it climbs and climbs and climbs until it almost totally runs out of momentum. At that time you kick the rudder, which pushes the nose in the direction of the left wing. Then the nose drops straight toward the ground, and you make the roll, stop there, and then you allow the airplane to dive toward the ground until you're about down to where you started. Then you pull out—at the last minute.

R.W.: Airplanes are not meant to fly straight up in the air and straight back down again at all.

GARY: No, they aren't, and some airplanes really would let you know they hated that maneuver. With some airplanes you couldn't do this maneuver without the airplane sort of falling over and feeling like it was out of control. Of course, with any good aerobatic airplane you'll feel you're under control the whole time.

R.W.: Your machine has to be absolutely perfect, I know. Do the planes that you are flying now have special carburetion so that they won't stall when you're climbing?

GARY: Yes. In fact, they have fuel injection. In a carbureted engine the engine would quit if inverted, possibly going straight up or straight down. Aerobatic airplanes—not just those that are sort of aerobatic, but the good ones—have special fuel systems for inverted pickup.

R.W.: As aerobatic airplanes become more and more sophisticated, isn't there also a greater danger of machine failure?

GARY: Could be, I guess.

R.W.: Is aerobatic flying a physical strain?

GARY: Sure. The average person would gray out or black out at a certain G force [gravity], but as an aerobatic pilot you're like a ballet dancer. You're out exercising and practicing and building up tolerance, not only just physical stamina, which you need to withstand the hard routine, but you build up a resistance to G forces so that you don't black out under certain Gs. You get so that you physically do what other people can't do.

R.W.: Don't you continually want to push yourself just a little bit further, then a little bit further?

GARY: Sometimes people push themselves beyond their limit and then they make mistakes, have accidents, and they crash. Usually what happens—the reason people crash—is because they begin thinking they are supermen or superwomen and they become complacent. They forget that the reason they're good is because they have always been careful, or a little bit afraid of what could go wrong. I try to remind myself that I'm human every time I get into an airplane. I try to calm myself down because air shows in themselves are very exciting. And I always ask myself: What could go wrong? And I try to be extra-sensitive and look for it. I do push myself. I think anybody who does air shows does that.

R.W.: Do you ever do aerobatics in non-aerobatic planes?

GARY: I have. The Bellanca, for instance.

R.W.: What was that?

GARY: Bellanca Aircraft makes the Super Decathlon and the Citaboria, which are aerobatic airplanes, and it also makes a four-seater called the Super Viking, which is a four-place airplane that happens to be hand-built with a wooden wing and tubular fuselage, which is sort of special and makes it more expensive than other airplanes. So they got the idea of having someone do aerobatic maneuvers in front of the crowd to advertise the airplane, and I agreed to do that. There was an element of risk there. Here I had been flying stock aerobatic airplanes, and now I was flying just a standard fly-around-the-country plane, doing aerobatics.

R.W.: Without fuel injection and the other safety factors?

GARY: It had fuel injection but it didn't have an inverted oil system. I could lose oil pressure inverted. In fact, I did have a couple of emergencies in the airplane because it was a non-aerobatic airplane.

R.W.: Have any of your fellow pilots been killed doing aerobatics?

GARY: I've had eighteen friends killed in airplanes and a lot of them have been air-show pilots. And because it is dangerous, and because I want to live until I'm really old and keep doing this, I keep asking myself, what could it have been that tied all these accidents together? Maybe nothing. But you try to reassure yourself. When you lose someone really close to you, you quit saying it would never happen to me. But I also keep saying, they weren't careful enough. They began to believe in themselves too much. They began to believe they weren't vulnerable. They flew airplanes that were not strong enough. They took them beyond their limits.

R.W.: They didn't do that preflight checkup as carefully as they should because they've done it five thousand times before, is that it?

GARY: There are a lot of factors. There are little problems, in yourself or your equipment, so you have to constantly step back as though you are not you and as though your airplane is not your airplane. You say to yourself: I am looking for what I don't see. Is there a crack somewhere? Is there something rubbing that is going to get stuck and jam my controls? Are the wings as straight as they are supposed to be? And you cannot lose your fear. Another thing, if you start letting other people take care of your airplane for you too much you could get yourself in trouble. They could forget something. You generally have more trust in yourself than in anybody else.

R.W.: Parachutists like to pack their own chutes for the very same reason.

GARY: Exactly.

R.W.: Can you describe some of the more exciting air shows that you've been in?

GARY: Well, for sheer excitement, or challenge, when I flew that Viking from Bellanca, which was not a fully aerobatic aircraft—that was exciting. It was another category, and I had to learn to fly it in a different way from a real aerobatic airplane. The controls were not as sensitive; it wasn't as responsive; and I didn't have as much visibility going through a maneuver. It would take me longer before I would see the ground again, coming around, and it didn't have a way to pick up fuel when I was inverted, and it didn't have a way for the engines to retain oil pressure if I held it level upside-down and sometimes going straight up. I knew that when I started flying it. But one thing I didn't realize, was that if I didn't keep one of the tanks—the left tank—totally propped up full before I began a maneuver, I would get a big gulp of air in the engine that would cause the propeller mechanism to turn too fast and sort of run away. This had happened on a couple of occasions when the plane would take a surge. But on one particular occasion I only had half the fuel in the right tank—and I was sparing off that tank—and I pulled up into a hammerhead, low-level. As I was going straight up I got a big bubble of air that caused a momentary fuel starvation and I lost oil pressure as I was coming straight down. The propeller and the engine started going really fast—over-revving. I thought it would drop back and so I contin-

ued to fly and started to go into my next aerobatic maneuver, which was a four-point roll.

R.W.: Would you describe that maneuver?

GARY: You do a roll, a fast roll, but you stop it at the ninety-degree, or knife-edge, point, and then at the inverted point, and the other knife-edge point, and then back. I did this and held it briefly inverted and once again I got air in the engine. This time the engine just quit. The engine had been going extra fast, really making a lot of noise, and it needed a lot more gas than usual and it got this air bubble instead. There I was, between ten feet and fifty feet off the ground when my engine stopped. Fortunately, I had extra speed that allowed me to pull the airplane up into a climb, but by then I was past the end of the runway, going away from the runway, and so I winged it up into a climbing turn and brought the airplane back around.

This was a retractable-geared airplane which makes it more efficient and cleaner, but I wasn't sure whether I was going to get it aimed straight back down the runway. My mind was going very fast. I thought I would probably have to go across the runway, and then I had this vision of the airplane hitting something, the dust flying, and who knows what, maybe a fire. I brought it around and was lined up with the runway, a couple of feet off, but I still didn't have my gear down. I waited until the very last second to lower my gear. In fact, I was trying to hold the airplane, hold it off. The gear came down and I landed safely. It was very exciting. Oil had streamed all over the side of the airplane and I just sort of coasted up to where I had started. Only one other time an engine quit on me at an air show but I was much higher at that time.

R.W.: What would have happened in that particular case if you were flying inverted as the engine quit?

GARY: It would have taken me longer. Like I said, you fly with extra speed. Even though I could do, say, a loop at one hundred and forty miles per hour in an air show, I would do it at one sixty. Twenty extra miles an hour, something like that, would give you the momentum. But in this case, inverted, I couldn't possibly have gotten right-side up and made it all the way around to the runway exactly at the same point, because I really did pull it around as best as I could and it was the last second before I could get the gear down. There could have been a fire. That is one of the dangers.

R.W.: Why do you think people ski jump, or jump out of airplanes, or race cars, or fly aerobatics? What do you think it is that makes them want to?

GARY: I'm sure that it is the adrenaline that you get when you are afraid. Even people who don't do these things read scary books, and being afraid gives them the shot of adrenaline that lifts them. It intoxicates them. The fear changes what you see. All of a sudden it clarifies your vision, or it makes you excited. It makes you happy, or it makes you feel truly alive.

R.W.: What do you think was the most exciting time that you ever had flying?

GARY: The most exciting time was a period of about a year and a half when I was on a team in Canada. We had five planes. One, the spare plane, was flown by our narrator. The other four we flew in a tight formation like the Blue Angels or the Thunderbirds or one of the military teams. It was run like a military team, and all of the pilots except me were ex-military pilots. It was the most demanding flying I have ever done. It was very hard physically. We flew our airplanes in such a way that we were always pulling and pulling and had to be very strong.

R.W.: You are talking about the physical strength that it takes to pull a plane's nose up, to control the rudders?

GARY: Mostly the pull on the elevator. Particularly in this situation, but anytime you are doing aerobatics, you're pulling and pulling, or pushing, and are really using your strength. And you're twisting because you're moving the stick from side to side to get the fastest roll you can or the hardest pull-up to a certain point. That's one thing. There's also resisting G forces. If you didn't resist the G forces, your body would sort of crumple as you pull G. I've flown with photographers and newspaper people who didn't expect the G forces to be high and suddenly their heads would drop down or they'd drop their cameras. For instance, on this flying team—one of the things about military-type formation design is that in order to be real steady and to look real good you trim the nose of the airplane so if you let go of the nose it would pitch down. This may not make sense to some people, but this way you are always pulling on the control in order to do something. It was either pull or release a pull. We flew a very heavy trip. Right now I am not in the physical condition to go out and do that three hours a day like we used to do.

R.W.: Was that three consecutive hours?

GARY: No. We didn't fly a steady three hours in a row. We'd go out in one-hour sessions. When we did one for a brewery-sponsored air show one season we did seventy-four air show displays. Sometimes that would be at four different locations over a weekend. We really traveled, and it was very exciting and it was very glamorous and it was very difficult. We kept challenging ourselves as a team. As soon as we got really good at all at our routines, we would start experimenting on new maneuvers. For instance, we would all line up in a straight line going the same di-

rection and the two middle airplanes would roll over the top of the two outside airplanes. I scared myself on one occasion with another maneuver that we did. I flew the rear position, the slot position, or the number four position. In this one maneuver I would bring the airplane up while we were in a diamond formation, and it was all four airplanes diving at about a forty-five degree angle and we were all upside-down. I would be above the three airplanes, whereas before I was below. I would roll my airplane up on its side at knife-edge, drop down, and roll back, and I would be right-side up as they were right-side down. Then they would do an outside loop. In this maneuver I just had a couple of seconds to roll into my edge, drop below them, and turn right-side up. As I rolled into a knife-edge I needed to go to full power. Imagine being behind another car and stepping on the throttle—full blast—when you are a couple feet away from it. I had to go to full power because my airplane, with all the drag it was getting, would drop back. I had to allow the airplane to drop down, and going to full power would keep me in position without dropping back. On one particular occasion early in the season when the first leader was learning his timing, there I was, and we're all four upside down, and maybe I delayed or he started to move too soon, and I added full power. And at the same time, instead of him holding the airplane in his dive for a couple of seconds, he sort of pushed the airplane up. You have to remember something, my airplane is above his airplane. If we all started to do an outside loop at that point my airplane ... oh, well.

R.W.: Go on.

GARY: Well, if one airplane is below another and they're both doing a loop together, the one at the top makes a smaller, slower circle than the one at the bottom. So if you're following somebody around the loop, logically you would be alongside them or below them. When you're below them, you sort of add power and move your position so that you're up forward a little bit. That's what I normally did in the slot position in a loop. But here I was upside down, getting ready to do this maneuver that required full power, and the leader starts to push up in this outside loop. Here I am above him in full power, making me go faster instead of throttling back to make me go slower, and so it was like he was pushing up and I was moving forward into his airplane. I just reacted as fast as I could and pushed my airplane up and rolled away from him, but I lost sight of him immediately, and suddenly it was just as if time lasted forever and I was waiting for the airplanes to crash into each other. But we, of course, did not crash. If you ever did hit in a formation situation like that, you wouldn't be around to talk about it later.

R.W.: How close are you in a formation like that?

GARY: Three to five feet depending on the maneuver and your position.

R.W.: That's wing tip to wing tip?

GARY: Or nose to tail. In the slot position, as we got better and learned to fly closer, I would lose a lot of his airplane behind my wing. When I looked up and over my top wing, I would see just the top of his wing above my wing and his tail wing below my top wing. Of course, by then I was very confident in my ability to fly formation, but in the beginning I would just fly a lot farther back or farther away.

R.W.: When you are flying in formation like that you really have to trust the people you are flying with a great deal.

GARY: You bet! I wouldn't fly in a formation team with very many people. There's a possibility that another team may be formed. It depends on sponsorship and that means it may never come to be, but I've been asked to be on that team. They know my experience, and I would fly with them because I know their experience and I trust them. But most people I wouldn't do it with. There is a certain kind of personality that is required, and a great deal of skill. You need somebody who is very steady, very consistent, and very reliable—ones who don't do sudden, cocky-type things.

R.W.: When you go inverted, upside down, I don't see how you ever get over the idea that there are only two little straps holding you inside this plane that is hundreds of feet in the air.

GARY: The reason you can continue to do it is because you believe in those straps. You tighten them so your body does not move when you roll inverted. If you move a half an inch, it feels like a foot. You have to believe in your equipment as well as yourself in order to be able to fly air shows. You have to believe those belts are going to hold you in.

R.W.: And it feels good, the thrill of it all?

GARY: Always.

The Bungee Jumpers

Rush-hour traffic moved at a creeping but steady pace across the great span of the Golden Gate Bridge in San Francisco that Monday in October 1979. It was Columbus Day, but the date would also prove to be memorable because the occupants of one of the cars on the bridge had chosen it to introduce Americans to the art and adventure of Bungee jumping.

The car carrying these intrepid souls came to a halt about midway across the bridge at a point that has been traditionally popular with persons planning suicide. The doors of the sedan swung open and five gentlemanly Britishers, dressed in morning suits and top hats, stepped out along with a young lady, clad appropriately enough in a jumpsuit. The six walked over to the railing of the bridge, toting their Bungee lines (long, thick, elasticized cords— "magnificent rubber bands," as one of the jumpers later described them).

About 220 feet below, in the cold, typically choppy waters of San Francisco Bay, a small boat circled idly. The jumpers carefully attached one end of their Bungee lines to the bridge and the other to the harness that each was wearing. So tethered, they then leaped over the railing and hurtled toward the waves below. The water, looking like a sheet of rippled steel, seemed to rush dizzyingly up at them. But before they could splatter against it, the Bungee lines reached their limit and brought the jumpers to a strained halt, then catapulted them back up toward the bridge. One of the jumpers rebounded so high that he actually touched the underside of the bridge.

Up and down, again and again, they bounced crazily for a matter of minutes before the wide-eyed gazes of the motorists above. Below, and less entertained, officers of the U.S. Coast Guard scurried to get a boat dispatched to the site, while above, members of the California Highway Patrol tried to get through the traffic congestion on the bridge.

When the jumpers finally finished bouncing, they lowered themselves by ropes to the boat that had been waiting for them below. Shortly after, they were arrested, and law enforcement officials, somewhat at a loss for proper charges, could only come up with trespassing, which they later dropped.

Asked why he did it, one of the jumpers replied with a line borrowed from T. S. Eliot's *The Waste Land*. He said there was a real reward for such adventure: "The ecstasy of a moment's surrender, which a lifetime of prudence can never undo."

The Daredevil Professors

"The boldest feat ever attempted" is the way one newspaper writer of 1905 described the little slice of aviation history that took place that year in the sky above Santa Clara, California. And it came about as a result of the unlikely alliance between a quiet college physics professor named John J. Montgomery, and a daredevil circus performer who billed himself as Professor Lascelles.

Montgomery and Professor Lascelles, whose real name was Daniel J. Maloney, had met near Santa Cruz, California, in March 1905. Montgomery, who taught at nearby Santa Clara College, had made his first glider flight back in 1883 and had been experimenting with winged aircraft ever since. Maloney was temporarily employed at a seaside resort to make parachute jumps from a hot-air balloon. A mutual friend of Montgomery and the owner of the resort that employed Maloney thought it might be nice if the two got together

since each was so interested in things airborne, so he arranged for them to meet at a ranch where Montgomery had been testing gliders for two years.

The glider that Montgomery had perfected featured two 24-foot-long wings. They were not stacked one over the other as in most early flying machines, but instead were on the same plane, one behind the other. The wooden support frame was made of ash and the wings were covered with oiled muslin. The sophisticated controls were quite effective. Montgomery would eventually be granted a patent on his Aeroplane, as he called it, but prior to March 1905 it had never flown more than a few feet above the ground or for more than a few dozen yards.

As soon as Dan Maloney saw Montgomery's Aeroplane and heard the professor describe its function, he suggested they attach it to the hot-air balloon he used in his act, take it up a few hundred feet, cut it loose, and see how it would fly. Montgomery, conservative scientist that he was, protested, but Maloney's enthusiasm was irresistible. After only the briefest ground instruction Maloney, astride the riding bar, launched the Aeroplane. Maloney later described the event to a news reporter this way:

> I have become an enthusiast over Professor Montgomery's invention, and while I have had considerable connection and experience with other airships, I believe that he has the key to aerial navigation. At the time of the ascension the atmospheric conditions were far from favorable and at the height of eleven hundred feet, when I struck a strong current of north wind, I cut away from the balloon. I circled about for perhaps three minutes, backward and forward, and then descended lightly in a cleared field nearby.
>
> I tell you I never felt anything like it before in my life, you simply soar through the air as if you were on the back of a bird. The sails [wings] are great things, twenty-four feet long, and the tail sticks out about as far behind. The whole thing only weighs thirty-eight pounds, and you have to do a good deal of the guiding by twisting and balancing the body.

After the flight's success, Montgomery wanted to take the balloon to Santa Clara and demonstrate the Aeroplane to his colleagues and the

An Adventurous Wedding

When Arno Rudolphi and Ann Hayward decided to get married in 1940, they chose to do it above the grounds of the World's Fair in New York City. The couple leaped from an airplane along with a minister from the Church of God, a best man, a maid of honor, and four musicians. The ceremony was performed as they floated to earth under billowy white parachutes, becoming the first persons ever to be united in matrimony in midair.

press. The resort owner saw no profit in an exhibition that far from his resort, so Montgomery hired Maloney on his own. The public demonstration was scheduled for Saturday, April 29, 1905, and invitations were sent to the editors of 25 newspapers. Montgomery's conservatism had vanished, swept away by the sight of his soaring Aeroplane and Dan Maloney's youthful enthusiasm.

On the day of the public exhibition, as the crowd gathered, hot air from a fire burning in a deep pit slowly filled the 30-foot balloon until it strained at the tether lines held by 30 volunteers. The delicate-looking glider rested 15 feet to the side of the balloon, attached to it only by a slender rope. The Aeroplane's wing and tail tips had been painted bright red, and stenciled on the front wing was the name—the *Santa Clara*.

Maloney took his position astride

the lower longeron, while Montgomery directed the winch rope, which ran to the top of the balloon from a tall pole. (The rope was used to ease the inflated balloon over the Aeroplane.) Then Montgomery called to the volunteers to loosen their grips on the restraining ropes and the balloon slowly drifted up and over the Aeroplane. Suddenly, a great gust of wind caught the balloon, breaking the winch rope and jerking the Aeroplane skyward.

Fortunately the *Santa Clara* wasn't damaged and Maloney escaped injury, but there was a slight mishap. A tie-down rope and iron peg were jerked up with the craft. Eventually Maloney cut this loose but it then fell through the roof of a house.

But Maloney was airborne, and his historic flight was described by Thomas Nunan of the San Francisco *Examiner*.

Man has learned to fly. Down at Santa Clara College yesterday, I beheld him use his wings. The individual who has to a very notable degree mastered the art of the birds is a plain good-natured, hardworking scientist, Professor John J. Montgomery.

An Aeroplane, not a flying machine, was towed up through the air until man and machine looked about as large as an eagle, and then the winged aeronaut cut the balloon rope. This is what happened:

The Aeroplane instantly settled on its filmy, silken wings while the huge balloon went tumbling and rolling away on the wind, dwindling in size and falling toward the ground. With the aeronaut poised on the framework at a level lower than that of the wings, slowly and steadily the machine circled to one direction and then the other, repeating these maneuvers several times. Then it headed straight before the wind and took a sudden dive.

"He's steering downward," said inventor Montgomery, in response to my exclamation at the sudden tumble. Then, on the moment, the wings turned gracefully back to the horizontal plane. The Aeroplane glided down in a circle, and after heading back into the wind it mounted perceptibly. Twice the feat of sailing upward on the air was accomplished.

The performer, sailing on wings high above Santa Clara and San Jose, was known to the world as "Professor Lascelles" until Professor Montgomery required him to use his own true name of Daniel Maloney while flying in Santa Clara. He had complete command of the machine. He accomplished just what a bird accomplishes in flight without flapping its wings. He sailed on the air and rose and fell, and tacked one way or the other, just as the hawks and buzzards do.

The flight occupied about 15 minutes. When Maloney had landed in the field near the mill, he folded up the wings and returned to the college with them.

The flight of Montgomery's Aeroplane had started at an altitude of over 2,000 feet, and Maloney had landed at the exact spot preselected before the launch. Not only was it a "bold feat," it was an amazing demonstration of precision flying.

Before that date, no manned, winged aircraft had remained aloft so long or flown anywhere near as high. The quiet college professor and the daring circus performer owned the world altitude and endurance records for aeroplanes.

Both Maloney and Montgomery were killed in later aeroplane crashes. But on that one incredible day in April 1905, they had, as an English newspaper report put it, "gone a long way to solve the problem of centuries."

Hang Gliding the Alps

Forty-year-old Marco Broggi, a weekend mountain climber, ascended the Swiss Alps in April 1980, equipped with little more than his 70-pound, motorized hang glider. He did not want to be encumbered, wishing only, he said, "to be as much like a bird as possible" in his attempt to become the first person to hang glide across the Alps.

Mr. Broggi wanted to make his mark in the record books of the sport, which, according to *The Guinness Book of World Records*, allegedly started in the 11th century, when a monk named Elmer glided away from the 60-foot tower of Malmesbury Abbey in Wiltshire, England, and lived to tell about it.

And so Broggi hiked to an altitude of a little more than 6,900 feet above sea level just outside the town of Altdorf in central Switzerland. His plan was to soar south above the Gotthard Pass to the town of Ambripiotta, a distance of 40 miles, but an 80-mile winding journey under the wing of a hang glider.

There are always a number of risks in such an undertaking—hang gliding by its very nature is a dangerous sport—but most were anticipated by Broggi. Bad weather was a major problem: It was bitterly cold in the mountains the day Broggi set out, with a temperature of 12 degrees Fahrenheit aggravated by erratic, unpredictable, circulating alpine winds; and there were sudden storms to contend with as well.

Undaunted, Broggi, dressed in several layers of clothes to help stave off the brutal effects of the wind and the cold, launched himself from the wind-whipped mountainside and soared above the rugged snow-covered terrain, the put-put of his motor invading the awesome stillness of the mountains. The view was majestic, he said, the experience fantastic.

About halfway to his destination, however, at an altitude of 1¼ miles, the hang glider's motor suddenly began to sputter and then stopped altogether. The glider, now at the mercy of the winds, began to descend at an alarming rate. Broggi guided it as best as he could, working furiously to get the motor started again. Then, as the ground loomed closer, he heard the motor kick over, catch, and hold. Later, he shrugged off the incident, commenting, "There was about 13 feet of snow on the mountain below, so if I hit the ground, I probably wouldn't have been injured, at least seriously."

After a little over two hours of flight time, Broggi saw his targeted destination in the distance. He was guiding the glider in a leisurely descent back toward the earth, his journey just about over, when suddenly gusts of wind up to 35 miles an hour buffeted and battered the craft, hurtling it toward the earth. But as suddenly as the wind blasts had come

up, they subsided, and Broggi was able to land his glider softly on a snow-blanketed slope just outside Ambripiotta.

As he awaited the acclaim of his original and historic feat, and the proud inscription of it in the record books, he was, according to the Chicago Sun-Times's description of the event, "brought back to earth with an expensive thump." Four days after the flight, the Swiss Federal Civil Aviation Bureau fined him $11,500 for illegal flying, along with the admonishment, "If we don't take adequate preventive measures, the air will be full of pilots like Mr. Broggi."

Marco Broggi shrugged that off too. "I somehow suspected that I would be fined," he said. "It was just another risk I was taking."

The *Gossamer Albatross*

Caesar sailed across the English Channel with his Roman legions back in the first century B.C. William the Conqueror crossed it more than 1,100 years later to leave his mark in the course of history. And the largest armada ever assembled by mankind ferried 132,500 troops across the Channel on D day 1944. In 1785, two aeronauts, John Jeffries and Jean Pierre Blanchard, were the first to float across it in a hot-air balloon. Captain Matthew Webb became the first human to swim it in 1875. And the British were the first to traverse it by Hovercraft in 1959. Then, in 1979, came the *Gossamer Albatross*, and for

the first time the Channel was conquered by muscle-powered flight.

For a long time, human beings have attempted to fly under their own power, creating unique if ineffectual devices to help them in the quest. Long before the perfecting of the hang glider, men took to jumping off the sides of mountains or the tops of buildings with a variety of winged contraptions. Some managed to get killed, others merely to injure themselves, but none were ever able to sustain flight under their own muscle power.

Muscle-powered flight was such an intriguing enterprise and fraught with such traditional lack of success that in 1959 British industrialist Henry Kremer offered a monetary award, £5,000 to anyone who could create a muscle-powered aircraft and sustain it in flight over a figure-eight-shaped course that covered approximately three miles. It did not, however, prove to be an easy way to pick up some extra cash. Hundreds of would-be self-powered aviators tried unsuccessfully for 18 years. And as the failures continued to mount up, Kremer continued to enrich his prize. By the mid-1970s, it stood at £50,000.

Then in 1977, that flight barrier was finally broken by two Californians. Paul MacCready, an aeronautical engineer and former international soaring champion from Pasadena, joined forces with Bryan Allen of Bakersfield, a biochemist whose hobbies included bicycle racing and soaring. MacCready designed a strange-looking craft, that at first glance appeared to be the result of a collision between a glider and a bicycle, which he named the *Gossamer Condor*. Allen would be, in MacCready's words, "its pilot and engine." The aircraft had a wingspan of 96 feet (wider than some commercial airliners) and, extended 15 feet out in front, at the end of an aluminum pole, was another wing that served as a stabilizer. The fuselage, if it could be called that, was hardly more than a seat, a pair of pedals, and a large bicycle chain that drove the 13-foot propeller behind it. The entire contraption weighed only 77 pounds and was constructed of such unique materials as lightweight aluminum tubing, cardboard, cellophane tape, and piano wire.

It was described as operating by "pedal power" in the newspapers, but in reality it would be Bryan Allen's leg muscles that would provide the power. A well-trained cyclist in his mid-20s, Allen had the leg strength and the stamina to drive the vehicle, and as an experienced glider pilot he was well equipped for the aviational aspect of the adventure. After some 400 test flights, MacCready and Allen brought their aircraft to a field outside Bakersfield, California. Before a skeptical audience, Allen pedaled it down the runway and into the air. The *Gossamer Condor* never got higher than 12 feet above the ground but it flew for 7½ minutes and completed the prescribed figure-eight course. And MacCready and Allen walked away with Henry Kremer's generous prize. The event was noteworthy enough to earn a place for the unique aircraft *Gossamer Condor* in the Smithsonian Institution in Washington, D.C. And it was exciting enough to stimulate Kremer to a new offer—£100,000 for the first person to complete a muscle-powered flight across the English Channel.

MacCready and Allen decided to accept the new challenge. A new aircraft would be needed, however. The *Condor* had been designed and built for a short flight, and Allen, as strong as he was, could never keep it aloft for the 23-mile flight across the Channel. So, in conjunction with the DuPont Company, the aviationists fabricated a new vehicle and called this one the *Gossamer Albatross*. Using synthetic materials like Mylar and Kevlar, and various other innovations, the *Albatross*, at 57 pounds, was 20 pounds lighter than the *Condor*.

Besides constituting a flight much longer than that of the *Condor*, the Channel crossing would present other profound difficulties—all involving weather and wind conditions. Bucking a headwind would pose an impossible obstacle for Allen and his pedal power. Nor could the fragile aircraft combat gusts of wind above six miles per hour. Even the air turbulences caused by large ships as far away as a mile or small boats much nearer would be enough to wrest control of the *Albatross* from the hands of its pilot.

The flight path chosen was from Folkestone, England, to Cap Gris-Nez, France, 23 miles away, about the narrowest crossing point of the Channel. The *Gossamer Albatross* was shipped from the United States, then MacCready and Allen began the vigil for just the right weather conditions to launch their adventurous enterprise. They waited nearly a month, and finally on June 12, 1979, a rare windless day dawned over the fabled Channel cliffs.

The *Gossamer Albatross* was maneuvered to the end of a special wooden runway that led to the Channel. Allen climbed aboard the seat, set his feet securely in the pedals, and was sealed in the plastic cocoon that was his cabin. The first takeoff attempt was aborted when one of the landing wheels broke. It was replaced and, at 5:51 A.M., the *Gossamer Albatross* again began to move

down the runway with Allen steadily and strongly pedaling, and two helpers running alongside to steady the tips of the 96-foot wing. Moments later, the *Albatross* lifted gently off the runway and slowly rose above the ground. Allen leveled it off at about 15 feet above the surface of the Channel and headed southeast. He kept his speed in the vicinity of 11 to 13 miles an hour by keeping the propeller churning behind him at a rate of 100 revolutions per minute.

Below, but a safe distance away, rescue boats as well as another filled with members of the news media kept pace as Allen pedaled. His was not an uneventful flight, however. At one point a large tanker, its captain unaware of the flimsy aircraft above and the havoc the ship could wreak in the air around it, was closing in. Allen, informed by radio by MacCready, desperately turned his delicate aircraft away from the treacherous turbulence that was approaching. At another point, a headwind arose, causing the *Albatross* to slow, and as it did so to lose altitude. It dipped as close as six inches above the Channel waters before Allen was able to bring it back up.

The heat inside the cabin was also intense, and there was no relief from it. Allen had brought along two liters of water but consumed it before the *Albatross* was halfway across the Channel. Fatigue and leg cramps were ever-increasing problems, and so was dehydration because of the copious amount of perspiring Allen was doing in the steamy cabin.

But, as the flight neared the 2½-

hour mark, Allen could see in the distance the shoreline of France. As he grew weaker, it drew closer. A welcoming party had gathered, watching as the strange, low-flying craft moved slowly toward them. Finally, beneath Allen the water of the Channel turned to the sandy beach of France and, exhausted but elated, he brought the *Gossamer Albatross* to a smooth landing. The first man-powered flight across the English Channel had been completed in two hours and 49 minutes, another epic in the many and varied ways man has crossed that historic waterway.

Climbing Skyscrapers

At 6:30 on the morning of May 26, 1977, George Willig, "the Human Fly," began to ascend the white aluminum facade of the second-tallest building in the world, the South Tower of New York City's 1,350-foot, 110-story World Trade Center. Within seconds of the start of his climb, startled building security guards spotted him inching up the base of the tower. They shouted to Willig in no uncertain terms that he ought to reconsider his actions. From his position on the wall of the South Tower, at that moment about 15 or 20 feet above street level, the Human Fly yelled back: "There is only one way to go. Up!"

Willig had been preparing and training for the stunt for more than a year. During four secret practice sessions conducted at various times near the bottom of the massive structure, Willig had perfected his homemade climbing gear. He developed a variation of a mountain-climbing device called an *ascendeur*, which climbers insert in cracks in the face of a mountain. Willig's refashioned *ascendeurs* were designed to slide and lock into the narrow vertical channels built into the tower's aluminum walls. By sliding the *ascendeurs* upward, and inserting his foot into a rope stirrup attached to each, Willig was able to creep up the face of the building.

By the time Willig had reached the 30th floor, about an hour after starting, huge crowds had gathered on the sidewalks around the building to watch the spectacle. Television broadcaster Tom Brokaw ordered a *Today Show* camera crew to the site, then, along with the program's millions of viewers throughout the country, publicly pondered the identity of the mysterious climber, now visible as a tiny dot on the side of the South Tower.

When a stuntman executes a daredevil feat that electrifies those who witness it, his ambitions often run counter not only to the laws of common sense but also to at least one, and frequently numerous, legal statutes. Some say the legal hurdles are part of the challenge. Consequently, Willig's ground-level assistants, including his brother Steve, were arrested by Port Authority police while the Human Fly, oblivious to it all, kept climbing, sliding his *ascendeurs* up the vertical tracks at a rate of about one floor every two minutes.

The only crisis of the climb developed near the 60th floor, where Willig was met by two policemen on a scaffold that had been lowered from the tower's roof. Prepared even for this eventuality, Willig quickly attached a long coil of nylon rope to an *ascendeur* and used it to swing himself away from the scaffold in a pendulumlike motion. As onlookers at street level gasped, he deftly caught another channel in the aluminum wall to the side of the scaffold, and continued his ascent, exchanging friendly banter with the policemen as he passed next to them on their scaffold.

At approximately 10:00 A.M., 3½ hours after the ascent began, the exhausted but happy Human Fly reached the roof, 1,350 feet above the streets of New York. He was greeted by a throng of policemen who offered congratulations and asked for his autograph before handcuffing him and reading him his rights. Then the Human Fly was served with a summons for disorderly conduct, criminal trespass, and a total disregard for Section 435-10.0(a) of the New York City Administrative Code, which states: "It shall be unlawful to give any exhibition of climbing or scaling on the front or exterior of any house or building." To make matters worse, an official from New York City's Corporation Counsel announced that Willig would be sued for $250,000 to offset the costs of protecting him.

The following day, the New York *Post* heralded Willig's rescue from the dizzying heights of legal liability with the headline: MAYOR CALLS IN HUMAN FLY. Meeting with New York City Mayor Abraham Beame, the conqueror of the World Trade Center agreed to settle for a total fine of $1.10 and a firm promise not to discuss the details of his climb with anyone who, with a strange glint in his eye, might look up to the top of a tall building.

Like so many other landmark adventures, however, the Human Fly's feat was surpassed. Four years after he set foot atop the World Trade Center, another building climber—this one clad in a custom-made blue and orange "Spider-Man" costume—scaled the world's tallest building, the 1,454-foot Sears Tower in Chicago. This "skyscrapereer" was named Dan Goodwin but he billed himself as Spider-Man. (At least he did until he and the license holder of that comic strip character's name agreed that he would cease and desist from using it to avoid a massive lawsuit. Dan Goodwin then became "Spider Dan.")

Spider Dan was 25 years old when he conquered the Sears Tower. Born in Maine, Goodwin was an experienced mountain climber, and had been working as a stuntman in Las Vegas, Nevada, before coming to Chicago to make a name for himself in the world of bizarre adventure.

For months, Dan had been planning his assault on the 110-story sky-scraper. Dressed in his Spider-Dan outfit (which cost him, he claimed, a hefty $450), he arrived at the base of the Sears Tower at about 3:00 A.M. on May 25, 1981, and shortly after took to the wall of the building. Like the Human Fly, he used specially adapted *ascendeurs* that fit into the vertical tracks designed for window-washing scaffolds. For the first three hours, Spider Dan climbed undisturbed. But shortly after 6:00 A.M., workers inside the building discovered that someone was climbing up the outside, and was presently at the 26th-floor level. They reported their findings and soon Chicago police and a contingent of fire fighters arrived at the scene.

At the 30th floor, fire officials tried to coax, then to coerce Goodwin into abandoning his project. As they attempted to stop him, Spider Dan took a pair of strong suction cups that hung from his belt and, like a true "Spider-Man," moved laterally away from them and then continued his ascent.

At the 43rd floor the fire fighters, now aboard a window-washing scaffold, and accompanied by a window-washer familiar with the contraption, bore down on him, but again he simply suction-cupped his way around them.

By 9:30 in the morning, Spider Dan had reached the 55th floor. Still hounded by the fire fighters, he was now playing to a large audience that had gathered in the streets below. The fire fighters told him they would agree to let him continue the climb without further interference (as they admitted later, they could not have

stopped him anyway, and perhaps would only have endangered him further if they continued to try) if he would agree to attach a lifeline around his waist. They would secure it and follow him up on their scaffold, remaining a floor or two below him. Spider Dan reluctantly agreed. From that point on, Spider Dan and the fire fighters on the scaffold had a running conversation while he continued to make his way steadily up the face of the building. As reported in the Chicago Tribune the following day: "Goodwin told the firemen about growing up in Maine and how much he liked Chicago. He sipped a protein drink (which he had brought along), complained that the helicopters hovering overhead were ruining his concentration, and told the firemen about a new adventure he's planning: jumping from high trees with natives in Africa."

At 10:25 A.M., Spider Dan reached the top of the Sears Tower and clambered onto the roof, the first man to conquer the Mount Everest of skyscrapers. Like the Human Fly before him, however, Spider Dan was greeted by officers of the police department and promptly arrested. He was charged with disorderly conduct, for lack of any more specific charges, and later released on a $35 bond.

One of the firemen who talked with Spider Dan from the scaffold said afterward: "He told us it was a thrill to experience things like this. He was an intelligent guy. He wasn't crazy or anything. He just had his own way of getting his kicks. I was surprised how it turned out. It was cold up there and he was freezing. He told us he was tired—but not enough to quit. I really didn't think he'd make it all the way to the top. I didn't think he had the strength." To that, Spider Dan added: "It wasn't child's play. I don't want people to think it's something anyone can do. What I did was sophisticated climbing, with tested equipment and physical training. I don't recommend it to other climbers."

Great Moments in Manned Exploration of Space

Date	Crew	Spacecraft	Importance
Apr. 12, 1961	Yuri Gagarin (USSR)	Vostok 1	First manned earth-orbital flight
May 5, 1961	Alan Shepard (USA)	Mercury-Redstone 3	First American to enter space
Aug. 6–7, 1961	Gherman Titov (USSR)	Vostok 2	First spaceflight to exceed 24 hours (25 hours, 18 minutes)
Feb. 20, 1962	John Glenn (USA)	Mercury-Atlas 6	First American to orbit the earth
Aug. 11–15, 1962	Andrian Nikolayev, Pavel Popovich (USSR)	Vostok 3 and 4	First dual spaceflight and earth orbit
Oct. 3, 1962	Walter Schirra (USA)	Mercury-Atlas 8	Spacecraft brought to splashdown within 4-1/2 miles of target
May 15–16, 1963	Gordon Cooper (USA)	Mercury-Atlas 9	Important findings as to effects of space travel on astronauts
June 16–19, 1963	Valentina Tereshkova (USSR)	Vostok 6	First woman in space (also Vostok 6 was the second dual spaceflight, with Vostok 5, captained by Valery Bykovsky)
Oct. 12, 1964	Vladimir Komarov, Konstantin Feoktistov, Boris Yegorov (USSR)	Voskhod 1	First three-man orbital spaceflight; first without space suits
Mar. 18, 1965	Pavel Belyayev, Aleksei Leonov (USSR)	Voskhod 2	First space walk (Leonov, 10 minutes outside spacecraft)

Date	Crew	Spacecraft	Importance
Mar. 23, 1965	Virgil Grissom, John Young (USA)	Gemini-Titan 3	First manned spacecraft to alter its orbital path
June 3, 1965	James McDivitt, Edward White (USA)	Gemini-Titan 4	First American space walk (White, 20 minutes outside spacecraft)
Dec. 4–18, 1965	Frank Borman, James Lovell (USA) &	Gemini-Titan 7 &	Longest duration Gemini flight (13 days, 18 hours, 35 minutes, 31 seconds); most earth orbits (206); first space rendezvous
Dec. 15–16, 1965	Walter Schirra, Thomas P. Stafford (USA)	Gemini-Titan 6-A	
Mar. 16–17, 1966	Neil Armstrong, David Scott (USA)	Gemini-Titan 8	First docking of two spacecraft
Sept. 12–15, 1966	Charles Conrad, Richard Gordon (USA)	Gemini-Titan 11	First to dock and complete two orbits while tethered
Nov. 11–15, 1966	James Lovell, Edwin Aldrin (USA)	Gemini-Titan 12	First to chalk up 5-1/2 hours of extra-spacecraft activity during a nearly four-day orbital period
Oct. 11–22, 1968	Walter Schirra, Donn Eisele, R. Walter Cunningham (USA)	Apollo-Saturn 7	First manned Apollo flight (10 days, 20 hours, 9 minutes, 3 seconds; 163 orbits of the earth)
Jan. 14–17, 1969	Vladimir Shatalov (USSR) &	Soyuz 4 & Soyuz 5	First docking in which two cosmonauts were transferred from one spacecraft to another (Yeliseyev and Khrunov to Soyuz 4)
Jan. 15, 1969	Boris Volyanov, Aleksei Yeliseyev, Yevgeny Khrunov (USSR)		
Mar. 3–13, 1969	James McDivitt, David Scott, Russell Schweikart (USA)	Apollo-Saturn 9	First manned flight of lunar module (LEM)
May 18–26, 1969	Thomas Stafford, Eugene Cernan, John Young (USA)	Apollo-Saturn 10	First orbit of the moon (in lunar module)
July 16–24, 1969	Neil Armstrong, Edwin Aldrin, Michael Collins (USA)	Apollo-Saturn 11	First lunar landing (Armstrong and Aldrin on lunar surface 21 hours, 36 minutes, 21 seconds)

Date	Crew	Spacecraft	Importance
Oct. 11–16, 1969	Georgi Shonin, Valery Kubasov (USSR) &	Soyuz 6 & Soyuz 7 & Soyuz 8	First time three manned spacecraft orbit at the same time; experiments and tests for lab construction in space carried out
Oct. 12–17, 1969	Anatoly Filipchenko, Vladislav Volkov, Viktor Gorbatko (USSR) &		
Oct. 13, 1969	Vladimir Shatalov, Aleksei Yeliseyev (USSR)		
Nov. 14–24, 1969	Charles Conrad, Richard Gordon, Alan Bean (USA)	Apollo-Saturn 12	Second lunar landing (Conrad and Bean on lunar surface 31 hours, 31 minutes)
Jan. 31–Feb. 9, 1971	Alan Shepard, Stuart Roosa, Edgar Mitchell (USA)	Apollo-Saturn 14	Third lunar landing (Shepard and Mitchell on lunar surface 33 hours, 31 minutes)
Apr. 22–24, 1971	Vladimir Shatalov, Aleksei Yeliseyev, Nikolai Rukavishnikov (USSR)	Soyuz 10	First spacecraft to dock with orbiting space station (Salyut)
June 6–30, 1971	Georgi Dobrovolsky, Vladislav Volkov, Viktor Patsayev (USSR)	Soyuz 11	First crew to be transferred from spacecraft to orbiting space station (Salyut); remained in space station 23 days (crew killed during reentry because of loss of cabin pressure due to mechanical failure)
July 26–28, 1971	David Scott, Alfred Worden, James Irwin (USA)	Apollo-Saturn 15	Fourth lunar landing (Scott and Irwin on lunar surface 66 hours, 55 minutes); first use of lunar land rover; first deep space walk
Apr. 16–27, 1972	Charles Duke, Thomas Mattingly, John Young (USA)	Apollo-Saturn 16	Fifth lunar landing (Duke and Young on lunar surface 71 hours, 2 minutes)

Date	Crew	Spacecraft	Importance
Dec. 7–19, 1972	Eugene Cernan, Ronald Evans, Harrison Schmitt (USA)	Apollo-Saturn 17	Sixth lunar landing (Cernan and Schmitt on lunar surface 75 hours)
May 25–June 22, 1973	Charles Conrad, Joseph Kerwin, Paul Weitz (USA)	Skylab 2	First US manned orbiting space station; remained in earth orbit 28 days, 49 minutes, 49 seconds
July 28–29, 1973	Alan Bean, Jack Lousma, Owen Garriott (USA)	Skylab 3	Extensive tests and experiments in space; remained in earth orbit 59 days, 11 hours, 9 minutes, 4 seconds
Nov. 16, 1973–Feb. 8, 1974	Gerald Carr, Edward Gibson, William Pogue (USA)	Skylab 4	Final Skylab mission; remained in orbit 84 days, 1 hour, 16 minutes, 30 seconds; longest space walk (Carr, 7 hours, 1 minute)
July 15–21, 1975	Aleksei Leonov, Valery Kubasov (USSR) &	Soyuz 19 & Apollo 18	First joint USA-USSR spaceflight and space rendezvous
July 15–24, 1975	Vance Brand, Thomas Stafford, Donald Slayton (USA)		
Dec. 10, 1977–Mar. 16, 1978	Georgi Grechko, Yuri Romanenko (USSR)	Soyuz 26	Docked with Salyut 6 space station
Feb. 26–28, 1979	Vladimir Lyakhov, Valery Ryumin (USSR)	Soyuz 32, 34	Set a new space endurance record of 175 days
June 5, 1980	Yuri Mayyshev, Vladimir Aksenov (USSR)	Soyuz T-2	New model spacecraft successfully tested
Apr. 12–14, 1981	Robert Crippen, John Young (USA)	Columbia	First demonstration of reusable winged spaceship
June 27–July 4, 1982	Thomas Mattingly, Henry Hartsfield (USA)	Columbia	Fourth test flight of winged spacecraft

Extraordinary Occupations

Brahma Bull Rider

Don Gay, of Mesquite, Texas, is the world's foremost rider of Brahma bulls. He has won the world championship six times. Someday the name of Don "Donnie" Gay will go down in the annals of rodeo riding with those of other legendary cowboys. Here he tells about a different and dangerous way to earn a living.

R. W.: Rodeo covers a wide range of events and, I presume, different skills. Do you have a specialty?

GAY: I specialize in riding Brahma bulls—that's my long suit. I've been the world champion six times.

R. W.: But you have done other things in the rodeo?

GAY: Besides bull riding, let's see—bareback riding, steer wrestling, and calf roping. I guess I've done it all. But I did most of those things in my early days of rodeo because then I was a little bit more enthusiastic about it. The bruises didn't seem to be near as severe as they do now.

R. W.: When did you start to ride professionally?

GAY: I've been a professional since I was fifteen—that was about twelve years ago—but I never really got to go any place where I could compete on a full-time basis until I graduated from high school.

R. W.: Where did you first get started?

GAY: Right here in Mesquite, Texas, my hometown. I come from a rodeo family. We have a term here in Mesquite—a "family affair rodeo." My dad was a rodeo contestant in the late forties and early fifties. In nineteen fifty-eight, he was in business with the legendary great in the rodeo business, Jim Shoulders, who's about fifty-two years old now. Shoulders accomplished things that no one else will ever do. He won sixteen world championships, spread over two events, and the all-around title. He won seven bull-riding championships, five bareback championships, and five all-around championships. That's never been equaled. I don't see how anyone could do it in this day and time. Right now, my goal is to win eight bull-riding championships.

R. W.: When you were fifteen and just getting into rodeo, did you start riding bulls right off, or did you have to work up to that?

GAY: I worked up to that. Actually, I was only about five years old when I first got involved with rodeo. Jim Shoulders and my dad were good friends, and they formed a partnership and got into the rodeo stock contracting business. In other words, they were rodeo producers. They bought an old bucking bull, a bronc, and things like that. They built a rodeo here in Mesquite in nineteen fifty-eight. I was just five years old at the time, and we lived rodeo day in and day out back then. I didn't really perform as such till I was fifteen, but our rodeo today began when I was five, right here in Mesquite. Now it's one of only two in the world that are professionally sanctioned rodeos—that means the money you win counts toward championship titles and the contests are run on a weekly basis instead of an annual basis. Our rodeo here runs April through September, six months of the year, every Friday and Saturday night. The only other one runs just on Saturday night about three months out of the year. It's up in Woodstown, New Jersey. Some call it Cow Town, New Jersey. That one used to be televised in the late fifties and early sixties. Most other rodeos are once-a-year affairs.

R. W.: How often do you ride during the year? Is there a kind of rodeo circuit?

GAY: In an average year, I ride around one hundred and sixty times. The term "rodeo circuit" is really not valid. There are six hundred forty professional rodeos throughout the United States and Canada each year, but I'm not under any kind of contract other than being a member of the Professional Rodeo Cowboys Association.

R. W.: You must have to travel quite a bit.

GAY: Sure do. That's the worst part about being a professional cowboy—the traveling. But I own my own airplane, and that's what I use to get to most of the rodeos. I fly it around five or six hundred hours a year.

R. W.: What kind of airplane is it?

GAY: I've got a Bonanza. It's a single-engine, four-place, one-hundred-ninety-mile-per-hour airplane. It's the best airplane that you can buy. It's kinda like the difference between a Cadillac and a Ford.

R. W.: You've won many world championships. Does any one of these stand out in your mind?

GAY: Well, I guess it's the time I recorded the highest score—ninety-five—in the national finals. The perfect score is one hundred. I suppose I should explain how you get to the national finals. The top fifteen money winners in each event qualify. Then in the national finals, you ride ten bulls in eight days. In nineteen seventy-six, it came down to the last bull, the tenth bull. I had to place first in this last go-around to win the world title and the award money. I had to get eighty-two points or more to win, and I set the new record of ninety-five points riding a bull that had only been qualified on two times in seven years. It was a pretty big moment—probably the highest I've ever had in rodeo.

R. W.: How is the scoring done?

GAY: There are two judges—one on

each side of the arena where they can see all the action. The perfect score would be one hundred points. Each judge has fifty of these points, and twenty-five points are allotted on how difficult the animal is to ride and twenty-five on how well the man rides. You can do various things to earn points, but half of it's for the animal—so if you don't have a tough animal, no matter how well you ride, you're still not going to win.

R. W.: You have also been noted in *The Guinness Book of World Records.*

GAY: Right. I scored ninety-seven points in San Francisco at the Cow Palace one year. That was the highest score ever recorded anywhere until nineteen seventy-eight, when Flynn scored ninety-eight points in a rodeo in Palatine, Illinois. So that now is the record.

R. W.: Any other records or highlights?

GAY: I did win the Copenhagen Super Star Championships, a head to head tournament competition in Fort Worth, produced by U. S. Tobacco. That is a new concept in rodeo—sponsored special events. I won twenty thousand dollars at that rodeo. But it's a special event, like I say, and the money you win doesn't count toward championship points. World titles are figured on money won. Whoever wins the most money in a single year in sanctioned rodeos wins the world title.

R. W.: What is the record for that?

GAY: I have broken the money record every year since nineteen seventy-four—this year it's sixty-one thousand six hundred dollars. That's what I earned to win the world championship. I've also received about twenty-five thousand dollars in bonus money from different companies that are starting to get into the rodeo business—sponsors that back the rodeo and use it to promote their products. That's why the rodeo is getting more publicity—the dollars are getting bigger. Of course, it's not on the same scale as what Jack Nicklaus can win or what the pro football players can make. We don't have the TV coverage as yet to make that come about, but it's coming. If you've got a good product, it's just a matter of time before it more or less reaches the top—and we do have a good product. But there are just so many variables in the rodeo business. It's hard for someone who does not have a rodeo background to promote it.

R. W.: I would think that with the great popularity of country music and urban cowboys a lot more interest will be generated for rodeo. People aren't just riding the mechanical bulls at Gilley's in Houston, they're doing it in New York City, Chicago, and Los Angeles.

GAY: Well, the individualism—the man against the beast syndrome—kinda catches people. Also, rodeo is a family entertainment. There's something in the rodeo that goes on during a two-hour performance that everyone in the family can enjoy.

R. W.: How many bulls do you think you have ridden since you first began?

GAY: My gosh, I don't think there's any way I could make an accurate guess—thousands, I'm sure. I think I probably average somewhere around two hundred fifty bulls every year—at least for the past seven or eight years. Before that, I probably quadrupled that figure. I used to ride bulls every day. I can remember riding thirty to forty bulls in a single afternoon when I was practicing. Of course, these weren't all near as tough as the ones that you try to ride in professional rodeo, but some of them were.

R. W.: How do you train for what you do?

GAY: Much like you do for any other sport. There's a lot of time and concentration spent on fundamentals. I run two miles every day. I haven't in the last two weeks because I got hurt—separated my rib—in the national finals. So it's a little hard to run right now.

R. W.: How do you prepare mentally?

GAY: I do a lot of positive mental attitude research. I read. I have a library of everything on the PMA subject—Norman Vincent Peale, Dale Carnegie—the list goes on forever. Positive thinking doesn't apply only to sports or religion—

it will work in any situation. I'm one of those guys who thinks that if I wanted to write a book better than the one you are doing, I could do it. I'm also one of those guys who doesn't think that you have to pay the price for success. You hear that all your life—to do well you have to pay the price. That's just not true. You enjoy it when you succeed, but you pay the price for failure.

R. W.: What would you say are the chief dangers in riding a bull?

GAY: The number one danger is being stepped on. If you get a bull weighing fifteen hundred to twenty-four hundred pounds come crashing down on you, something is going to give, and it's not going to be the bull. That's how serious injuries and deaths have occurred. Very seldom do you see a real serious injury result from being hit by a horn, because the horns are blunted, like the ends of a baseball bat. There have been some puncture wounds—I have been gored where the horn has actually broken the skin. It required sixty-three stitches to close one particular wound up underneath my arm. It looked bad, but it wasn't serious—it didn't damage any nerves or muscles.

R. W.: What other kinds of injuries have you sustained over the years?

GAY: Most of the things have been what I call minor—pinched nerves, broken ribs, separated ribs. I have a big problem with groin muscle injuries. Straddling the bull, the way you sit on the bull, and squeezing with your legs and knees to keep your upper body in position create a dreadful amount of pressure on the groin muscles, and I've torn those on a number of occasions. And there is nothing you can do for it. It's like ribs—the only thing that will help you there is just time.

R. W.: How many bones do you think you've broken?

GAY: Not very many. I think I've broken a total of fifteen ribs in the course of about fifteen years. I've broken my finger and some bones in my hand. And I've broken a toe a time or two—but no serious limb injury, like a broken arm or leg or neck or something like that. Those are what you'd call serious injuries—you are basically bedridden.

R. W.: Have you ever witnessed any bad accidents?

GAY: Yes. I've seen some friends of mine get killed by bulls. It is really a dangerous sport. You have to say it's much like car racing. Richard Petty knows that he can be killed instantly at any time in an automobile race, but he is in tune with his job and knows what he's doing. He's a professional, and he has confidence in his abilities and in his machinery, so he forces out that element of fear. You don't get rid of it, but you learn how to control it and even use it to your advantage.

R. W.: So you do experience fear.

GAY: Yes. Anyone who would tell you he isn't scared to ride a bull or a buckin' horse or he doesn't have a twinge of fear is either crazy or lying. You might think that after you've been doing it for so long it becomes automatic, but you still have that fear. You have to be able to cope with it, understand it, and then use it to your advantage. You can't let it become a dominant factor in your thinking, or you won't do well.

R. W.: A lot of people have never seen a Brahma bull ridden. Could you describe what a ride is like—from the very beginning, when you're in the chute, until it's over?

GAY: To begin with, you hold on to a flat, braided piece of rope. There's a little handle braided into the rope. The rope is looped around the bull's middle and pulled up snug, and the loose end is laid across your hand. You wrap it around and get a good grip on it. You wear spurs. Some people think that spurs hurt the bull, but they just do the holding. They're dulled to the point where they will grab the skin and hold it. If they were sharp, they would cut and that would be to no advantage. The spurs don't do anything to the bulls—their hide is tremendously tough. You can sit there and spur a bull with all your might and not even get him to raise his head. But that's the way you hold on. You sit up close and hold one hand, your free hand, high in the air. It's used as a bal-

(continued on page 340)

Above: Charles Blondin, Monarch of the Cable (left), crosses Niagara Falls in 1859. *Library of Congress* A fly speck against the 110-story World Trade Center, George Willig (right) scales the South Tower in 1977. *United Press International* **Below:** Phillipe Petit balances on a tightrope between the World Trade Center's twin towers during his 1974 feat. *United Press International*

HARRIET QUIMBY- FIRST AMERICAN WOMAN MARTYR TO
AVIATION. LOST HER HEROIC LIFE AT THE BOSTON
AVIATION MEET OF 1912. WAS THE FIRST WOMAN TO
FLY THE ENGLISH CHANNEL. (INSET) ALL THAT WAS
LEFT OF HER BLERIOT MONOPLANE AFTER THE FATAL
PLUNGE.

Harriet Quimby, above, was the first woman to cross the English Channel by
plane; inset, remnants of her aircraft after the crash that took her life in 1912.
Smithsonian Institution Wing walker "Jersey" Ringel, below, starred in early air
shows. *Library of Congress*

"Jersey" Ringel standing on top wing
of aeroplane.

Above: John Montgomery (second from right) and Daniel Maloney (center), the Daredevil Professors, with the Aeroplane, the glider which set a record for manned aircraft in 1905. *University of Santa Clara Archives* **Below:** Skydivers head earthward during a meet. *United Press International*

Aerobatic pilot Debbie Gary (left) is a top air-show performer. *Debbie Gary Callier* Her stubby plane (below) is built to withstand unusual stresses. *Debbie Gary Callier*

Right: Three men in an 11-story-high gas envelope called the *Double Eagle II* make the first transatlantic crossing by balloon, in 1978. *Dick Kent* **Below:** The pilots (left to right), Maxie Anderson, Ben Abruzzo, and Larry Newman, received a tumultuous welcome in France after their five-day, 17-hour journey. *Dick Kent*

Left: Nazi hunter Simon Wiesenthal, a survivor of the death camps, has spent nearly 40 years tracking down war criminals. *United Press International* **Below:** SWAT team members of the Los Angeles Police Department during the 1974 assault on the headquarters of the Symbionese Liberation Army, which kidnapped newspaper heiress Patty Hearst. *United Press International*

Japanese ama divers, above, prepare to harvest the sea bottom. *Japan National Tourist Organization* Garbed as if for outer space, EPA workers, below, check barrels for toxic wastes. *Chicago Tribune Photo, Copyrighted, 1980. Used with permission*

Opposite page: The Great Wallendas (top) before their fall in 1962, in which two died and one was paralyzed. *Circus World Museum* Early movies created death-defying work for Hollywood stuntmen, like this leap from a plane to a moving car (bottom). *Library of Congress* **Above:** Clyde Beatty became world famous in the 1930s as lion trainer for the Hagenbeck-Wallace and Ringling Brothers circuses. *Circus World Museum*

Above: Six thousand perished in the 1900 Galveston, Texas, hurricane and flood, the nation's worst natural disaster. *Library of Congress* **Left:** Las Vegas MGM Grand Hotel guests are rescued from the 15th floor of the burning building by firemen. *United Press International* **Opposite page:** Locked exits (top) contributed to a death toll of 602 in the 1903 Iroquois Theater fire. *Library of Congress* Survivors in two lifeboats (bottom) flee the sinking *Andrea Doria*. *United Press International*

MESSRS. KLAW AND ERLANGER PRESENT
"MR. BLUEBEARD," LATE OF THE
IROQUOIS THEATRE.

ance point—much like you hold your hands out if you're walking a tightwire.

R.W.: Okay, now you're on the bull in the chute. He doesn't buck in the chute, does he?

GAY: Some of them do, but not all of them. They learn after a while that they're going to open the gates. Most of them will stand a little while without causing too much of a ruckus.

R.W.: What goes through your mind at that point?

GAY: At that point, I really don't hear anything else. The bull and I are basically one. I'm trying to tune in on him. I am just thinking about reacting—when that bull makes a move, I'm going to react and make a countermove.

R.W.: Pure concentration—just like in any other professional sport.

GAY: Pure concentration—you have to have that. You can't worry about anything. You have to know the basics, and you have to control all the outside elements so you're not afraid. Most of the bulls will form a general pattern of how they buck in the arena. But just like people, some days some things just happen differently, and a bull might not feel like buckin' the way he normally would and will do something different. You have to be ready for that.

R.W.: What happens when the chute is opened? How would you describe that?

GAY: It's a terribly explosive moment. The bull will jump out, and it's just a brutal thing. It's hard to explain adequately. It's terribly physical, but you don't really realize it till after it's all over. Like I say, you're mentally concentrating on doing well. You're not worried about what really is happening to your body physically at that point in time. You just do as well as you can. I used to give an analogy—it's like standing beside the railroad track and the old five-fifteen roars by at sixty-five miles per hour and you reach out and grab hold of it with a hay hook. It's a tremendous jolt.

R.W.: Have you had anything unusual happen to you while you've been riding?

GAY: I remember one incident that was kind of weird. I was riding a bull out in California, and the bull was really good, but I knew that I was going to make a really good ride and that I was going to win. Then all of a sudden the next thing that I remember is the lights going out. I had hit the ground, and it was all so sudden, I couldn't imagine what had happened to me. The handle in my rope had broken—the power had just jerked the handle apart. One minute I'm riding along and things are going just like I wanted them to, and then the next thing I know, I'd landed right on the back of my head. I picked up my rope and realized what had happened. If the handle hadn't been broken, I'd have been baffled.

The Reluctant Matador

He had been trained in the great tradition of the bullfighter, the same one that had given to the Spanish spectacle such revered names as Juan Belmonte, Manolete, Joselito, Ordóñez, Dominguín, and El Cordobés. Dressed in skintight and richly embroidered silks and satins, the traditional garb of the matador, he stood behind the wooden barrier that separated him from the bullring. The *paseo*, the grand entry procession, was over, and the *corrida* was about to begin. Pepe Currillo, a matador for two years now, gazed out at the jam-packed arena in Bilbao, Spain, that August afternoon in 1980, awaiting the moment of truth.

Across the bullring, the gate to the bull pen was suddenly thrown open and into the arena loped the *toro*, a fine specimen from the Victorino Martin ranch, their thoroughbred bulls known for great size and enormous horns. The huge bull moved about the ring. The crowd was tense, awaiting the matador's formal entrance. Moments passed, but nothing happened. The matador was still standing behind the wooden barrier. More moments passed, but Currillo didn't move. The crowd became restless. Some began to shout.

The bull approached the wooden barrier and Currillo, still behind it, did something that rarely if ever had been done before in a major bullring in Spain. He reached over the barrier and plunged his sword into the massive bull. The crowd was suddenly silent and then jeered madly.

An observer later said, "Pepe Currillo was so panic-stricken by the half-ton bull he just would not go out into the ring and kill it."

Spain has strict bullfight rules, however, and the authorities have the power to punish any *torero* who fails to comport himself properly in the ring. Currillo was fined 5,000 pesetas (about $70), and his career as a matador was considered in serious jeopardy.

R. W.: What is your first impulse when you hit the ground?

GAY: I instinctively start moving, scrambling to get away.

R. W.: Does the bull come after you?

GAY: It depends on the bull. Some bulls are terribly mean. Some of them are gentle—they wouldn't hurt a flea. But I move out of the way of every one of them because the bull's buckin', whether he's trying to get you or not. If you're up off the ground and moving, chances are you won't get stepped on. And some bulls will turn back—they really want to get you. If you can get a step or two on them, the bullfighters and the clowns in the arena will have time to distract the bull.

R. W.: Is that the purpose of the clowns?

GAY: That's their job—to protect the bull riders. They offer their bodies instead of yours. That's what they do. They really are a different breed of cat, I'll tell you.

R. W.: That is something. If you don't get thrown, how do you get off the bull?

GAY: You just kick a leg over and jump. I don't try to land on my feet, unless it's easily done. Most of the time, I'll just kind of roll off to one side and hit on my shoulder and roll and start crawling, moving. If you try to land on your feet and you hit and fall backward or hit wrong and fall down—that might be all it takes to get you underneath the bull.

R. W.: What is the attraction of rodeo riding for you?

GAY: In the first place, of course, it's what I've grown up with, and I just always wanted to be the world champion bull rider. Bull riding is the most exciting event in rodeo and the most dangerous. Everybody has a little bit of thrill seeker in him. The money is good, and it's getting better. It's an event that lets you be your own man. The individualism has a great amount of lure. And it's exciting. I don't think that there's anything that gives you a greater sense of self-satisfaction than riding a bull that maybe has been tried two or three hundred times by your peers, and no one can

qualify on him—and then you do it. There are just not that many opportunities for doing something like that today.

R. W.: How would you advise someone who wanted to get into bull riding? How would you suggest he start?

GAY: First, he should go to an accredited rodeo riding school.

R. W.: How many of those are there?

GAY: I would think that each year, there are probably about one hundred schools that offer sessions. They are listed in the *Rodeo News*, which is a paper put out by our association. There are also listings in national magazines, like the *Western Horseman*. You should take the instruction first, simply because you *can* get hurt. The school will fit you and your ability to the bull, and then you work your way up. Rodeo riding schools are just like miniature training camps. I have my own. My school has about six sessions a year, and they last for three days. What I teach—in a somewhat controlled environment—are the basic fundamentals. I enjoy teaching the sport.

R. W.: More than riding?

GAY: No.

R. W.: Have you any plans to retire?

GAY: I still have a couple more world championships to win.

Working with the Big Cats

As the lights of the arena dim and the brilliant halo of the spotlight focuses on the entryway at one end, a hush of anticipation comes over the audience. Then the band strikes up and suddenly, explosively, the gates fly open and the shaft of light is filled with Gunther Gebel-Williams as he makes his entrance to "The Greatest Show on Earth," the Ringling Brothers and Barnum & Bailey Circus.

And it is a grand entrance. The man whose platinum blond hair looks like a shimmering helmet is standing on the back of a galloping horse, his arms thrust out to the crowd. In one hand he carries a blazing torch, and the myriad sequins on his tight-fitting costume glitter electrically. At the entrance to the caged center ring he leaps from the back of the horse, and the crowd cheers wildly. But it is not his appearance or his entrance that fills the spectators with awe, it is the act he is about to perform, the one that he is justly famous for, the age-old but ever-bedazzling drama of putting the most ferocious animals on earth through their paces.

Gebel-Williams is the latest in a long line of "animal masters," a profession as obviously hazardous as any ever conceived by man. (He performs with a unique menagerie of tigers, leopards, pumas, elephants, and horses.) Such practitioners were once known as "lion tamers," but that is a misnomer. One of the most famous masters of the big cats, Clyde Beatty, pointed out: "No one *tames* a lion or a tiger or a leopard. We train them, get them to do what we want them to, to perform, but we can never make them *tame*. They will always be wild animals."

Because of the ever-present danger in the ring as a master walks among his lions, tigers, leopards, or bears, and commands them to do tricks as one would a pet dog, the wild animal act has always been one of the circus's greatest show-stoppers. Granted, the tightrope walkers, trapeze artists, and the man shot from a cannon cause heart-stopping moments for a circus audience, but none create the sustained thrill of an animal master in all his vulnerability as he conducts his intricate choreography.

The art of training wild animals goes back to ancient times. History records that lions were used to entertain at religious and state occasions in ancient Egypt, perhaps 200 years before the birth of Christ. Most often, they would be walked in parades or taught to perform some basic tricks, like standing to beg on their back paws. Cleopatra had lions imported from central Africa. Her son, Ptolemy VI, was an avowed enthusiast of animal acts that included lions, elephants, water buffalo, giraffes, and even hyenas. The Romans also entertained themselves with wild beasts—on a lesser scale in acts at, say, the Circus Maximus, than in the more grisly scenes with Christians down the Roman road at the Colosseum. Exactly who did the training in those early days or what the methods were, however, has so far eluded historians.

In Europe, trained animals (especially bears) had been a part of the festivities at fairs, and were a sidelight of jousting tournaments as well as religious gatherings since the early Middle Ages. Menageries, somewhat like zoos but with the animals often trained to perform, were common in the 18th and 19th centuries. And as they passed from the scene, the traveling circus came into being and animal acts were quickly incorporated.

From that time forward, lions, tigers, and other big cats have been leaping up onto pedestals, rolling over, playing dead, begging on their hind paws, hurtling through flaming hoops, and doing all those things that one would never expect a giant of the jungle to do at the command of a mere human being.

In the United States, the first of the great animal trainers was Isaac Van Amburgh (1801–1865). His act, featuring a coterie of lions was introduced at the Zoological Institute in New York City. Van Amburgh is also reputed to be the first animal master to put his head into a lion's mouth during a show. It was considered the most daring stunt ever performed in a circus, at least that is the way it was touted by the circus barker then and in all the years after that when other trainers hazarded their heads between the powerful jaws of a lion or tiger. But it really wasn't as perilous as it appeared. As Clyde Beatty ex-

plained in his book *Facing the Big Cats* (with Edward Anthony, Doubleday & Co., 1964):

I've known some pretty reckless trainers, but I have never known or heard of one crazy enough to stick his *head* inside the mouth of a lion. What the trainer does who is supposed to perform this feat is to put an inch or two of his *face* between the open jaws of the animal in a manner and at an angle suggesting that his whole head is about to pop in. First, however, certain precautions are taken. The trainer's right hand rests securely on the lion's upper jaw and his left hand holds the lower jaw firmly. The second the trainer feels the slightest pressure on either hand indicative of a possible clamping together of the jaws, he withdraws his face. . . . I do not know of a single instance of a trainer being seriously injured during the performance of this trick. And I don't recall a single complaint from a spectator to the effect that the trainer had not literally done what the publicity said he would.

Until the emergence of Gunther Gebel-Williams, the most famous of all animal masters had been Clyde Beatty, who manipulated an incredible number of big cats during his 45 years under the big top. (He trained more than 900 tigers alone.) Born in 1904, Beatty joined the circus (Howe's Great London Circus, to be exact) at the age of 15. He was given the job of cageboy, his principal duties to clean up the leavings of the bears and to see that they were fed. By the age of 16, however, he was working the act himself. He made his debut in a cage filled with gargantuan polar bears, and was dressed in the costume of the trainer he was replacing, which was at least three sizes too large for him. Despite his lack of experience, he survived, and became determined to make a career of animal training. It was a matter of only a few years before he became a nationally known figure. His image and notoriety were aided by several Hollywood movies that were made in the 1930s, about the circus in general and Beatty's animal training in particular. The name Clyde Beatty was deeply etched into the American entertainment scene by the early 1930s, and dressed in boots, jodhpurs, and an open-neck safari shirt, a pistol holstered to his side, he was immediately identifiable to millions.

Beatty, when he faced the big cats, carried a chair in one hand and a sharp-cracking whip in the other. The whip was not used to hit the animals, only to get their attention. The crack of the whip also served as an auditory cue in some instances for the animals to perform a certain trick. The blank-cartridge pistol Beatty carried was also used as an attention-grabber, and, Beatty said, "occasionally for reasons of showmanship. The drama of certain situations that develop in the arena is heightened by the bark of a gun." The chair was important in Beatty's defense, his metaphoric sword in the duel with his ferocious adversaries, which the animals *always were* despite how well-trained they were.

In the early 1930s, Beatty was performing for the most famous circus in the world, Ringling Brothers and Barnum & Bailey, and for the Hagenbeck-Wallace Circus, which was under the same management as Ringling Brothers. When he played Madison Square Garden in New York, his dressing room was the focal point for celebrity visitors. Parading through were such luminaries of the day as Jack Dempsey, Gene Tunney, Lowell Thomas, Babe Ruth, Ed Wynn, and Ernest Hemingway. Hemingway went into detail to describe how he saw Beatty's chair as equivalent to the matador's cape in a bullring, and the moves of the animal master as he teased and eluded the big cats as similar in grace and split-second timing to those of the bullfighter.

But the life was hardly all glitter. Training lions, tigers, leopards, panthers, and pumas is an assiduous task, not to mention a dangerous one. Not only must an individual animal be mastered by the trainer, it must also be taught to peacefully coexist with other members of its own species as well as with animals that might be natural enemies (lions and tigers are by nature enemies), and with animals who might be natural prey (such as horses). Animal training is always tense, a stress-filled occupation that demands intense concentration and hair-trigger decisions. As Beatty once explained, "A man can't live through 35 years in the cage with lions and tigers just by cracking a whip—he's got to know exactly what those big cats are thinking, and he's got to be one thought ahead all the way." Gunther Gebel-Williams describes it in his own way: "With a leopard, you have to be very tough. You must let him know who is boss right from the start. . . . But the elephants are the toughest of all. They're the smartest of the animals, and you have to stay ahead of them all the time. If you make one wrong step, they will never forget it."

The element of danger is there every moment. Besides the sharks of the ocean, there are no animals more fearsome to human beings than the big cats (a Siberian tiger may weigh as much as 600 pounds, a lion or a royal Bengal tiger perhaps 500 pounds); their great power, speed, and ferocity are legend. No one knew this better than Beatty himself. His body bore the scars of numerous unpleasant encounters with his co-stars. A near-fatal accident occurred in 1932 at the winter headquarters of the Hagenbeck-Wallace Circus in Peru, Indiana, and the culprit was an enormous male lion named Nero. As Beatty later described it in his book *The Big Cage* (with Edward Anthony, The Century Co., 1933):

> I was putting my lions and tigers through their paces and about two dozen people were looking on. Nero was going over the hurdle. Instead of making a clean jump, the big creature suddenly swerved in his course and came right at me. . . . It was one of those determined charges that an experienced trainer recognizes instantly. The first thing I knew, I was flat on my back on the floor of the arena, with the lion standing over me. Just when I lost my chair I don't recall. . . . As the big lion bent over me and bared the teeth with which he planned to mess up my features, I reached up with my right hand and planted it against his upper lip and nose. Then, with superhuman strength born of desperation, I shoved him away from me. . . . He gave his head a snap to release himself from my palm-hold and as he did I found my hand in his mouth up to the wrist. I yanked it out in a hurry, scraping off patches of skin against his teeth. I don't understand to this day why he failed to bite the whole hand off. . . . He did not make for my face again, contenting himself with seizing what was nearest him. That happened to be the upper part of my leg. He grabbed it midway between the hip and the knee. Having dug his teeth in deeply enough to satisfy himself [it developed later that they had sunk right into the bone], he began to drag me. After he had dragged me about two yards he suddenly let go and made for a nearby lioness. The attack was over as fast as it had begun.

Initially they thought they would have to amputate Beatty's leg, but an operation saved it. He would not walk on the leg again for almost three months. Beatty also bore multiple scars from the claws and teeth of several tigers and one leopard when he died in 1965.

There are other occupational hazards in the animal training business, besides those inflicted by the animals themselves. Beatty went to some length to describe an incident that occurred while he was working closely with a lion named Brutus. The beast turned on him and had Beatty backed to the bars of the caged arena. Beatty used the handle of his whip to give the lion a rap on the snout but in a freak turn of events it recoiled and he smashed himself in the face with the leaded whipstock, breaking the bones above and below one eye. Not only was that eye blinded but the shock of the blow caused him to lose sight in the other eye as well. With Brutus pacing, preparing to attack, Beatty's assistant, outside the caged ring, guided him inch by inch to the safety cage. It was a strange sight—almost a clown comedy routine—and the audience mistook it as an uproarious part of the act. For three weeks after, Beatty remained with bandages covering both eyes.

On another occasion, Beatty was performing with an injured leg (the result of Nero's bite) when another lion got frisky and began taking less than friendly swipes at Beatty with his huge paw. As the trainer dueled with it, the errant lion managed to connect with a savage blow to Beatty's chair, jamming it back against the gun in the holster on his hip. The chair hit in such a way as to trip the trigger, and the gun blasted a blank cartridge down Beatty's leg, the hot wadding scalding his already wounded leg and the flash from it setting his pants on fire. The astonished lion backed off, and Beatty's assistant, outside the cage, grabbed a

bucket of water and threw it on the trainer's leg to put out the fire. A true showman, Beatty finished the act.

The days of the blank-cartridge gun and the chair are gone from the animal training ring—at least in the ring occupied by Gunther Gebel-Williams. He still has the traditional whip (for its sound effects and its symbolism) and a stick that substitutes for the chair that Clyde Beatty wielded. All the rest is much the same: "If you think they don't have teeth or claws, you should look at the scars on my arms," Gebel-Williams pointed out.

Like Beatty, Gunther Gebel joined the circus at an early age. At 12, he became part of the Circus Williams in Cologne, Germany, riding horses as part of an acrobatic act. Shortly afterward, the Williams family, owners of the circus, adopted him and he tacked their name onto his own. By his teens, Gebel-Williams had adopted animal training, and soon rose to become the Circus Williams's superstar. In the late 1960s, Ringling Brothers and Barnum & Bailey wanted to add Gunther Gebel-Williams's name to their marquee. They had to buy the entire Circus Williams to do it, at a purchase price of $2 million. Since then he has become the center of attraction of The Greatest Show on Earth.

Gebel-Williams has added many innovations to the profession of animal training. No one has ever gotten a combination of leopards and pumas to perform together in such intricately woven acts as he has. Gebel-Williams has also combined tigers and elephants in the same ring, something that was hitherto unheard of. He himself is a masterful performer with a stage presence no animal trainer before him could equal. Today, the gemstone of his act is a white tigress named Maharanee. That strange, rare creature was one Clyde Beatty tried desperately to get for his act, but never could. Now, that magnificent beast rides on the back of a black horse around the ring of The Greatest Show on Earth, the dazzling finale to Gunther Gebel-Williams's spectacular act.

Policewoman Decoy

Carol Scannell is an experienced police officer with the Chicago Police Department, but her assignments are far from routine. She works undercover—a decoy who poses as a potential victim for a crime, especially robbery. She does not entice individuals to commit crimes, but she does go to places where such crimes are likely to occur, and, of course, she appears vulnerable. Decoy work is dangerous, exciting, often dramatic, and to Carol a rewarding way to earn a living.

R. W.: As a decoy, you work the transit system mostly—on the Els, in the subway stations—isn't that correct?

SCANNELL: That's right. We concentrate on the Loop, the downtown area, but we do go as far as the Els run in all directions. We go out as far as Ninety-fifth and the Dan Ryan Expressway. Today, we're going all the way out on the Lake Street El, as far west as it goes.

R. W.: Do you work alone or with a team?

SCANNELL: I always work with two male partners—the same ones. We're a kind of team. We have been for a year.

R. W.: How do you communicate with the members of your team when you're on a stakeout?

SCANNELL: We usually refer to our assignments as decoy missions. As for communicating—if you work with somebody for as long as I have with these two officers, you begin to realize what each one is thinking without verbally communicating. For instance, if Frank wanted to change El cars, all he would do is walk to the door and glance, then glance in my direction, and I would know that he saw something better in another car. So that way, when the train came to a stop, I would leave my seat and move to the other car.

R. W.: How many arrests would you

say you've been involved in since you became a decoy?

SCANNELL: About four hundred.

R. W.: In how long a period of time?

SCANNELL: About a year and a half—that's how long I've been a decoy. We usually average at least one a day.

R. W.: What type of arrests were they?

SCANNELL: Theft of person usually—that is, a felony theft. It involves taking property from a person—a purse or something from a purse or a pocket. We use either a lay-down or a pickpocket decoy. As a pickpocket decoy, I would have a wallet in my purse and I would stand at a bus stop or on the El train and wait for somebody to take the wallet from my purse. The second way to get an arrest would be to have one of my partners pose as a down-drunk. He'd lie on the El platform and have in his possession a wallet. My other partner and I would station ourselves in the two utility closets that faced him. Then we'd wait for somebody to come by and grab his wallet. Primarily, it's the same charge—it's just two different ways of achieving it.

R. W.: Have you ever been wounded or attacked during a stakeout?

SCANNELL: Not seriously, no. At least I've never had to take any time off or be hospitalized.

R. W.: Have you ever worried about being in a life-threatening situation?

SCANNELL: There have been times when we were definitely outnum-bered by people who didn't particularly care for us arresting somebody they knew, but we haven't actually had a situation where we've had to use our weapons outright.

R. W.: What goes through your mind, what do you think about, when you're standing on an El platform on a decoy mission?

SCANNELL: Primarily, I just try and make myself aware of what's going on around me. I like to know where the possible offender is in relation to me, and what he has on, in case a foot chase should ensue. I want to at least be able to tell my partners the guy had a red shirt on—that kind of thing.

R. W.: How close is your backup team?

SCANNELL: It varies. If we're on a street level, my partners try to keep a little closer to me, so that if something happens, they are close enough that the offender doesn't outdistance them.

R. W.: And they can always see you?

SCANNELL: Oh, sure.

R. W.: Wouldn't a street-wise criminal become suspicious of three people standing around late at night or when a location is relatively deserted?

SCANNELL: Yes, they would. If we go out tonight to work the Dan Ryan El, that's in a black area, the minute the three of us would step off the El train, some of these people would take off running. The pickpockets who are playing that stop would take one look at us, guess who we are, and would probably take off—jump over barriers and run right across the expressway to get away from us. So that's why we use different outfits—disguises—from time to time—so we can blend in with people.

R. W.: What do you do about people who bolt and run at the sight of you?

SCANNELL: At that point they haven't committed any crime. It's just the fact that they know we are police officers. They haven't done anything, so we don't do anything.

R. W.: Do you ever travel in squad cars?

SCANNELL: No, we don't.

R. W.: So you're really pretty much all on your own?

SCANNELL: That's right, and we've gotten into several foot chases, off the platforms and into areas where you wouldn't want to drive through in a car. For example, we were at the El station at Forty-seventh and Prairie the other day, and some kids were throwing rocks up at us and calling us all sorts of names. So we chased them. And there we were—all three of us going in separate directions in a dangerous, gang-ridden area, walking down the streets, running through the alleys and gangways—and we had no way of summoning help for ourselves if we needed it.

R. W.: What would you do if you were in a dangerous situation or if you were outnumbered and really needed help and there wasn't any immediately available to you? Do

you have any kind of recourse?

SCANNELL: The only recourse we have is the use of our weapons.

R. W.: Do all of you carry service revolvers on your person at all times?

SCANNELL: Yes, we do.

R. W.: You're wearing a white nurse's uniform today. Any particular reason for that outfit?

SCANNELL: Normally, I like to work in blue jeans. But as I mentioned, we like to blend in. Today we're working Lake Street. It's not far from the Cook County medical center. A nurse wouldn't at all be out of place.

R. W.: Do you really enjoy this kind of work?

SCANNELL: Yes, I do. I enjoy it very much.

R. W.: During roll call, you and your partners received honorable mention certificates. Can you tell me what that was about?

SCANNELL: It was for an incident that happened when we were walking down State Street a while back. I was attempting to cross the street, and three males came up behind me. As I stepped off the curb and started to walk across the street, two of them knocked me to the ground, and the third grabbed the purse off my shoulder. He took the wallet from the purse. He threw the purse to the ground, and then all three of them took off running. One of my partners was able to grab the offender with the wallet, and both of them went tumbling to the ground. My other partner and I went after the other two and managed to apprehend all three. That's what that was about—a strong-arm robbery.

R. W.: I understand from speaking with one of the officers prior to our interview that all three of you are very much involved with a special case right now—something to do with gold thefts?

SCANNELL: He was referring to the gold snatchings on the Lake Street line. There had been an incident today at noon—a woman sitting on the train was approached by two men, and when the train came to a stop, they grabbed the gold chain off her neck and ran off the train. This kind of thing has been occurring quite a bit lately on the Lake Street run. That's why my partner gave me this phony gold to wear to work today.

R. W.: You are a very slight person. I assume the idea is to send somebody who appears to be relatively defenseless—an easy target?

SCANNELL: I think that's one of the reasons I've had so much luck with what I'm doing. I don't pose a threat to people. They look at me, and they don't think that I'd be the type that would be able to take care of myself. You must remember the victims of pickpockets are usually women. They generally appear to be the most vulnerable.

R. W.: How do men pose as decoys?

SCANNELL: Men pose as decoys as down-drunks, making themselves appear very vulnerable for a crime to occur. I wouldn't say that if Frank was just to walk on an El platform with a wallet in his possession that somebody might not try to take the wallet from him, but if he's lying on the platform and looking like he's been drinking so much that he's passed out, he's as likely a pickpocket's target as I would be.

R. W.: I suppose that posing as a down-drunk can be a difficult experience.

SCANNELL: It's a frightening experience. While he's lying there he has to keep his eyes closed for the total amount of time it takes. He doesn't know what's going on—he doesn't know who's standing there or what their intentions are or whether they're armed. He simply doesn't know what they're going to do to him. Will they just take the wallet or take the wallet and hurt him? We never know till they act. We just have to watch and be ready to react.

R. W.: It must be nerve-racking.

SCANNELL: It sure is.

R. W.: Can you pick out beforehand the person who's going to go after you?

SCANNELL: After a while, you can almost tell who's going to do what to you. When I step on a crowded train, I just look around, and for some reason I notice a particular individual, and somehow I know that he's going to be the one who's going to take the wallet. So all I do is just stand close enough to him so that he can see the wallet, and within seconds it's gone.

R. W.: Do you ever worry about whether he has a gun?

SCANNELL: I don't think about that. I just assume that he's going to do it the way that I want him to do it. He's just going to reach in and grab the wallet and run.

R. W.: But there must be a possibility.

SCANNELL: Oh, sure, it's a possibility, but I just don't think about that.

R. W.: Have there been decoys killed in Chicago?

SCANNELL: I don't know of anybody who's been killed, but I do know that some officers have been seriously beaten up and hospitalized.

R. W.: What has been your most frightening experience?

SCANNELL: We've had a lot of frightening moments. One that stands out in particular is an incident that occurred when we were working midnights. It was about two in the morning, and we were at Thirty-fifth and State. That is a totally tough area. We were standing on the platform. I was about to board the train when a juvenile approached me and grabbed my purse and grabbed me too. He was with some friends, and we had quite a time getting them on a train to take them to a district where we could process them. A lot of people were beginning to congregate around us on the platform—they were trying to help free the juvenile. It was very touchy.

R. W.: What was your most rewarding experience?

SCANNELL: It's all very rewarding in the fact that we know that what we're doing is a way of protecting other people. Every day, women are the victims of people who are out for one purpose—to pick pockets or rob somebody. And the reward is when we get an offender who has a rap sheet, an arrest record, longer than your arm. We go to court, and we find that even though maybe all those other times he's just been slapped on the hand, now he's going to get what he deserves. We set a trap—and some people say maybe that isn't right—but we're trying to catch people who commit crimes. We don't stand in front of a high school and wait for some kid who's going to make a big mistake. We're after the people who have already committed crimes and are planning others. We just afford them the opportunity to do it one more time to the wrong person.

R. W.: So when you've been a victim or a witness to a crime, you make an arrest. What then do you have to do as a follow-up to that?

SCANNELL: After we make an arrest, we have five days to go to court, because a felony is supposed to be brought before a judge within five days. We usually try to set our court schedule so that we're not going to court every day of the week, but as it turns out we spend a good deal of time in court. Almost every working day we're faced with a subpoena to go to court. Usually by the time we've finished our paperwork and the arrest has been turned over to the lockup, we've already been assigned a court date. But we make an appearance before that court date—I, as the victim, and my partner, as the witness. If the defendant denies the charges and we go to court, we'll be called upon to testify. If the defendant decides, after talking to a public defender or his own private attorney, that he wants to plead guilty and he's an adult, he's usually placed on two years' probation. If he violates the law during the next two years, he'll be sentenced for from two to five years in the penitentiary. If he would rather go to trial and plead not guilty, he can. But we haven't lost a case yet. How can you lose? You have a police officer as a victim and two police officers as witnesses.

R. W.: How many cases have actually gone to court?

SCANNELL: All four hundred of them.

R. W.: So your record is one hundred percent?

SCANNELL: That's right. They can choose to deny it, which they're free to do. They can say, "Oh, they're crazy—this never happened." A lot of them say they found the wallet—that it fell out of my purse. We had one the other day—the guy claimed that he had taken the wallet out of Frank's pocket because he was going to help him. He was going to help him, but he had put the wallet in his pocket and walked thirty yards to board a southbound train when we apprehended him. He was going to help him. We just let them have their say, and then we state the facts.

R. W.: I imagine you don't encounter too many first-time offenders.

SCANNELL: Rarely.

R. W.: Mostly habitual offenders?

SCANNELL: We've had people who haven't been out of Cook County jail for twenty-four hours. We had one juvenile who had been released from the Audy Home—that's a detention home for kids. He'd been there because he killed a woman, but he got out and wasn't out of that home for twenty-four hours before he picked the wallet out of my purse. I've had people pick me twice, and the minute I turn around, they look at me and say, "Oh, no." This one kid picked me on Monday, pleaded guilty in court during the week, and on the following Tuesday he took the wallet out of my purse as I boarded an El at Seventy-ninth and Dan Ryan. I turned around, and he looked at me and said, "Oh, Carol, Carol, why do you do me this way?" And I said, "Well, what did I do to you?" He said, "Well, you told me not to work the Loop!" And I said, "Well, I didn't tell you to come up to Seventy-ninth and Dan Ryan to work." And now we're on a first-name basis.

R. W.: That brings to mind a question. When you make an arrest and have to go to court, don't you worry about blowing your cover and becoming too recognizable?

SCANNELL: I have often thought about that. We don't really protect our identities. When we go to court, it's a crowded court room. We go up there, and we state that we are police officers, where we work, where the particular arrest was made, and the events leading up to the arrest. We state that in front of an open court. The best we can do is try to change our appearance. It is becoming very difficult for us to work the Loop area because we've made so many arrests there. But despite all that, we still manage to come up with about one arrest a day. Now Chicagofest is coming up and that will bring thousands of people downtown and, of course, all those who want to prey upon them. Frank and I worked Chicagofest last year. It was a ten-day deal, and Frank and I alone made twenty-nine arrests. And if we didn't have to spend so much time doing paperwork, we would have grabbed a lot more.

R. W.: Are offenders easy to spot at a big fair like Chicagofest, where thousands of people are milling around?

SCANNELL: Some individuals stand there with towels or newspapers over their arms. The crowd is watching the show or listening to the music, but they're hanging in the back, gazing at purses as the women walk by. This is a much more organized operation than people realize. These offenders actually meet to decide which areas they're going to work and what they're going to do. When they get a woman's wallet, they know exactly where to take it and who will honor the bank credit cards.

R. W.: Did you volunteer for this type of work?

SCANNELL: Yes. I made a request to join this unit. I used to work a beat car. I just wanted to do something different, and this is what I came up with!

Nazi Hunter

Simon Wiesenthal stood on the pavilion, just beyond the gate of the Mauthausen concentration camp in northern Austria on a sunny May morning in 1945, and gazed absently at the U.S. Army tanks lumbering up the road and the soldiers marching beside them. Inside the striped uniform was a 36-year-old man, reduced now to less than 100 pounds, dismally weak, and only in faint touch with reality. He was having great difficulty accepting the fact that the five years of terror, torture, and imprisonment he had endured were at an end and that the war was over—in his words, "the machinery of death had come to a stop."

A few weeks later, Wiesenthal, fattened up to 115 pounds and in basic control of his mind but haunted by the horrors he had witnessed in the Nazi concentration camps, launched his career as a hunter of Nazi criminals. He asked for and was given a job with the U.S. Army War Crimes office based in Linz, Austria.

Simon Wiesenthal had many valid reasons to choose that vocation. He had personally seen thousands die at the hands of the Nazis. He had experienced their criminal neglect, their brutality, their hatred, and their injustice—all the many horrors. And he realized that while millions had perished, he had survived through what could only be described as a chain of miracles.

Wiesenthal was born in 1908, the son of a Jewish sugar merchant in Buczacz (a town in modern-day Poland). He received his first taste of racial and religious hatred when he was only six years old; by that time the Soviets had brought their pogroms to his hometown. He saw townspeople killed by the Soviet soldiers, and others taken away, never to return. But he survived that. When World War II began in 1939, he was married and making a successful living as an architect in Lvov (then a city in eastern Poland). The Soviet Union, having signed a nonagression pact with Germany, sent its army to occupy the city. Soon Wiesenthal saw many of his fellow Jews being put aboard trains bound for forced labor camps in Siberia. He was fortunate enough only to lose his job.

Then the Germans declared war on the Soviet Union, and in late June 1941 they moved into his town. Within two weeks, Wiesenthal lost his home and his freedom. He was arrested along with about 40 other prominent Jews still living in Lvov. Half of them were executed in cold blood that evening, and the others were thrown into a prison cell to await the same fate in the morning. Wiesenthal, however, was luckier than most, experiencing his first miraculous rescue when a former employee of his helped him and a friend to escape.

The freedom was short-lived, however. Not long afterward he and his wife were relocated into a Jewish ghetto and a few months later were sent to the Janowska concentration camp. In late 1941, both of them were assigned to a forced labor camp at a nearby railroad repair works. During the following year, Wiesenthal was consistently reminded of his own relative good fortune as he watched thousands of Jews being herded into boxcars and taken off to grim destinations he had heard about. One of those persons was his mother, whom he would never see again. She would be killed at the Belzec concentration camp.

Simon Wiesenthal suspected that the same horrible fate awaited him and his wife. Through a little ingenuity and some well-placed bribes, he managed to get his wife smuggled out of the forced labor camp and eventually ensconced in an apartment in Warsaw. She assumed a new identity, her forged papers showing her to be a non-Jew (she too would survive the war). But Simon

Wiesenthal could not free himself.

On April 20, 1943, he had his second date with death. That day, he was taken off his job by an SS officer and brought back into the confines of the concentration camp. There he and 43 other Jewish prisoners were marched to a long trench, about six feet deep and perhaps 1,500 feet in length. The group was forced to undress and stand in a line at the edge of the pit. Looking down in it, Wiesenthal could see naked corpses. An SS officer then walked behind the lineup and started to shoot the prisoners one by one in the back of the head. More than half had been shot when Wiesenthal, fully expecting to join the twitching cadavers in the pit, was touched again by the angel of fate. The execution was suddenly interrupted, and his name was called out. He turned away from the trench and identified himself. An SS officer told Wiesenthal to pick up his clothes and follow him. He was then transported back to his job, saved by one of the rarest of creatures, a benevolent SS officer who happened to be his boss. The Nazi had decided to intervene and save him because he wanted him back on the job and also, Wiesenthal believes, because the man did not approve of what was going on and was trying to do what he could to alter it.

About six months later, the same SS officer enabled Wiesenthal to escape. He was able to hide out for a while in Lvov but eventually was discovered and arrested. With him was the diary he had kept that told the horrors he had witnessed. Wiesenthal was quickly marked for death, but before the sentence could be carried out, he managed to slash his wrists. The SS, with a grim if not bizarre form of logic, put Wiesenthal in the prison hospital to recuperate until he was well enough to be executed. There Wiesenthal tried to hang himself.

When he had recovered, he was brought out into the prison courtyard with a large group of other prisoners. They were separated into two groups—one to be executed, the other one to be transported to the Janowska concentration camp. Wiesenthal was put in the group to be killed, but he managed to sneak himself into the group destined for the concentration camp.

At that time, the Soviets were encroaching ever closer from the east. Wiesenthal and the other prisoners now began a continual procession to the west, passing through the concentration camps at Plaszow, Grossrosen, and Buchenwald, eventually arriving at Mauthausen.

As Simon Wiesenthal later observed, of the 149,000 Jews who lived in Lvov at the outbreak of the war, only 34 remained when it was finally over. It was, he thought, a miracle that he was one of the survivors.

Simon Wiesenthal's first job as a Nazi hunter began almost immediately after the war. His role was to escort American army officers around the vicinity of Mauthausen and Linz to flush out the SS officers and other cadre who were responsible for the crimes committed at the concentration camp and who were now hiding from the victors. He even would be given the privilege of arresting some of them himself. At the same time, Wiesenthal began to create his own list of the perpetrators of crimes against his people, the names coming not only from his own experience but from the testimony of other survivors as well.

It was 1947 when Wiesenthal formally established the Jewish Documentation Center in Linz to collect firsthand evidence of Nazi atrocities, to track down those responsible, and to disseminate the information to authorities capable of prosecuting the crimes. He ran the organization for the next seven years but then closed it down until 1961. After Adolf Eichmann was captured, tried, and executed, he reopened the center—this time in Vienna.

Over the years, Wiesenthal has found Nazi hunting both a tedious and dangerous operation. The chore of gathering information and details is an assiduous one; the investigations are long, complex, and often frustrating; and the tracking and the confrontation are perilous. But the Jewish people needed to tell their terrible tales of the extermination camps and the vast number of individual SS men and Gestapo agents who were responsible, and so Wiesenthal's files grew.

Simon Wiesenthal has continually tracked the biggest of them—Martin Bormann, Adolf Eichmann, Heinrich Müller, Franz Stangl, and Dr. Joseph Mengele, but he has also gone after the thousands who were less well-known but no less guilty of genocide.

Wiesenthal has flushed out and helped to bring to trial many war criminals, but he conducts an unending search for those who are still on his list. There is, to his mind, no statute of limitations for the kind of crimes that were committed against the Jewish people in World War II. So the search will go on, Wiesenthal says, until there is no one left to be hunted.

Opening Barrels . . . Carefully

It is at first glance an innocent-looking container, maybe a 50-gallon drum. It is full, weighing maybe 500 pounds. And it is laying out in the open or in a recently opened pit. How it got there no one knows. But that's not the most pressing question. The fact is, it is there. And the urgent question should be: What is in it? Water? Oil? A chemical? Something radioactive? Something that might explode? Something poisonous?

In the 20th century, industries and governments have been dumping a vast amount of varied materials into the earth, the oceans, the lakes, and the rivers. Some is garbage, some harmless wastes, but some of it has the potential of being extraordinarily dangerous. And some of it manages to make it back to the surface.

Who would like to take the chance of opening one of these drums to see if it contains something lethal? Not a lot of people. But someone has to. In the United States, a special branch of the Environmental Protection Agency—the National Investigation Center headquartered in Denver, Colorado—takes on this job. Three five-man teams investigate those sites where hazardous substances may be found.

The investigators are outfitted in specially designed protective suits, which are airtight, have their own self-contained breathing apparatus, and include battery-powered vests that circulate ice water over the chest and back because temperatures can rise to 140 degrees Fahrenheit inside them. These investigators take on the perilous job of discovering just what is inside the barrels. Usually the job is done by taking samples with remote-control equipment. Highly flammable and explosive liquids could be in that particular drum, which could send a fireball hundreds of feet in the air or blast with the intensity of a bomb or a load of dynamite. Or the contents could be the chemical dioxin, a pesticide that has been disposed of underground; it is so lethal that a quart of it in a metropolitan water supply could kill the population of a large city.

The investigator and his team go about the process carefully and only after a thorough planning session has been held. If it is explosive, it can be detonated; if it is toxic, it can be neutralized or destroyed. If it is neither, the investigators are very happy. It is a dangerous job and a full-time one—there are approximately 50,000 known sites of hazardous waste dumps in the continental United States alone.

What type of person applies for this job? "The same kind of guy," an EPA spokesman said, "who gets a kick out of defusing bombs."

Stuntpeople, A Special Breed

Since the motion picture became a part of the entertainment world, there has been a need for a special breed of actor to create the breathtaking, the heart-stopping, the gasp-producing scenes that make movies exciting. Those actors may jump from cliffs; topple off roofs; leap atop speeding trains; have chairs broken over their heads; be dragged by rampaging horses; be knocked through saloon windows; lie amid stampedes of buffalo or elephants; pilot automobiles in high-speed chases or into fiery crashes.

Employing a unique combination of daring and deft illusion stuntpeople make their living from performing such feats, as well as an imaginative variety of others.

These people belong to a small, specialized trade; perhaps no more than 100 of them provide the great majority of stunts for both movies and television, and they include men, women, even children. Their training varies, as do their backgrounds: from rodeo riders to gymnasts to race-car drivers to martial arts experts.

The most celebrated stuntperson in the history of the occupation is Yakima Canutt, who began his career as an actor in the 1920s; turned to stunts in 1927, when Al Jolson in *The Jazz Singer* introduced "talkies"; and later became an "action director," the person who devises a stunt and then is responsible for directing the scene.

Canutt was born in 1895 in the Snake River hill country of the state of Washington. He grew up as a cowboy, then became a rodeo contestant—bronc riding and bulldogging—before coming to Hollywood in 1919. Because of his background, abilities, and penchant for acting, he was a natural to become the counterpart of such actors as Tom Mix and Douglas Fairbanks in the silent adventure films of that age. But his gravelly voice prevented him from making the transition to sound movies. There was still a place for him in the Hollywood film community because the stars have always needed stand-ins, or doubles as they are called in cinematic jargon, for dangerous scenes. (Even purveyor of thrills Evel Knievel, in the film *Viva Knievel,* used a double—stuntman Gary Davis—when he and his motorcycle apparently went soaring over a 120-foot open pen of lions and tigers.)

Over the years, Yakima Canutt has carried out daring deeds on film for John Wayne, Clark Gable, Errol Flynn, Kirk Douglas, and Gregory Peck, among virtually hundreds of others. In the classic western *Stagecoach* it was Canutt, not John Wayne, who leaped from the driver's seat of the stagecoach onto the backs of the team of horses as they raced across the prairie. In another scene from the same movie, Canutt was the Indian shot off his galloping horse by John Wayne. In the famous burning of Atlanta scene in *Gone With the Wind,* the Rhett Butler driving a one-horse hack through the flaming streets was not Clark Gable but Yakima Canutt. According to his filmography, Canutt has appeared or directed stunts in 139 feature films, but that figure would increase two or three times if the listing were to include all the "quickies" and serials that were turned out assembly-line fashion in the 1920s and early 1930s, and which have since been lost to oblivion.

After the silents, Canutt was a regular in many of the "Grade B" westerns that were produced in such abundance in the 1930s by Monogram Productions and subsequently Republic Pictures. He fought with or filled in for all the big names of that genre: John Wayne, Gabby Hayes, Bob Steele, Gene Autrey, and Andy Devine. But his biggest contribution to the art of stuntmanship was a joint effort with John Wayne. Tired of the unrealistic fight scenes that they took part in—in the early days they

Living with Killer Snakes—
A Stunt of a Different Stripe

To the surprise of probably no one, the popularity of snakes has not increased in recent years. The animal, which according to tradition enticed Eve, killed Cleopatra, and menaced humanity in general for centuries, is still considered by most to be totally loathsome. For example, in early 1980, a New York woman sued a dairy company for $3 million after she discovered a six-inch snake in the box with her breakfast eggs. Somewhat later, her husband also sued, just for the torment he said he went through having to listen to his wife's complaints and hysterics.

But snakes do not affect everyone the same way. Take Peter Snyman, for example. Hoping to win a line or two in *The Guinness Book of World Records* by breaking the 36-day record for reptile cohabitation, the 25-year-old carpenter agreed to be imprisoned with two dozen of the world's most deadly snakes. He walked into a small, eight-by-ten foot cage in Hartbeespoort, South Africa, in April 1979.

The serpentine collection included six Egyptian cobras, six black mambas, six puff adders, and six South African boomslangs. A bite from any one of these extraordinarily dangerous snakes could kill a healthy man in a matter of minutes. Snyman roomed with these cagemates for a harrowing 50 days, passing the long, nerve-racking hours trying to eat, sleep, and tend to his other needs recklessly close to his dangerous companions while comfortably cohabiting with them.

No stranger to serpents, Snyman had been a snake collector for more than half his life, a pursuit which on six occasions had resulted in serious bites by members of his prized collection. This herpetological experience helped Snyman decide to establish a round-the-clock antivenin unit and a team of snake watchers to stay close by his side while he roomed with his friends.

Through the 50-day ordeal, no one stayed closer to the South African stuntman than the snakes themselves. Allowed to leave his cage for only 30 minutes out of each 24-hour day, Snyman spent hours in frozen silence as his inquisitive cagemates crawled over his entire body, often particularly interested in inspecting his nostrils, ears, and eyeglasses. At night, when he would only sometimes manage to get in a few hours of restless sleep, a number of the snakes would curl up next to him to keep warm.

Slow, quiet movement was an absolute necessity. The most dangerous moment of the stunt happened when a commotion outside the cage frightened one of the black mambas into striking at Snyman's pillow, leaving a stain of venom where his head had been a few moments earlier.

He survived the ordeal and has found that there has not been a great rush of adventurers out to take his record away.

would simply punch each other on the arms and shoulders—Canutt and Wayne worked out a routine in 1935 in which they could stage what looked like a very real fight. By throwing carefully rehearsed near-miss punches, using deluding camera angles, and with the appropriate SPLAT or THUD dropped in by a sound technician, the modern-day motion picture fight scene was born.

Stunts are only part illusion, however, and most have an exceptionally high degree of danger associated with them. Perhaps no better example exists than the chariot-race scene in the 1958 epic *Ben Hur*, which was highlighted by three incredible collision scenes. The entire race was designed and directed by Canutt; he described it in detail in his autobiography, *Stuntman* (with Oliver Drake, Walker and Company, New York, 1980):

The first wreck was to take place at the end of the spina, the spot where charioteers could skid their chariots dangerously close to the curb to gain a slight advantage. . . .

The driver who was doing the first wreck pulled his team in close to the curb, striking the ramp with the inside wheel, the chariot bounced into the air, flipped upside down and threw the driver end over end, right into the path of an oncoming team. The second driver swerved his chariot as planned, narrowly missing the downed man. Guards from the spina platform ran in, picked the driver up and carried him to safety. As we cut the scene, the driver's brothers and a few close friends ran to him, and for a minute or two it looked like the patch-up of a family feud— they kissed and hugged him and shook his hand.

Our second wreck was staged at the wall beneath the spectators' seats. Messala's chariot had steel blades projecting from the hubs of the heavy wheels. These blades not only looked vicious, they worked. We only used them in close shots, actually cutting the spokes from a chariot's wheels and causing a wreck. However, in all other scenes we used substitutes made of heavy rubber.

In this scene, Messala, doubled by Joe Yrigoyen, slammed his powerful black horses against Ben Hur's white Arabian team, throwing them off stride. He then urged his team ahead so that the vicious wheel blades could try to cut the whites down. This forced Ben Hur's double to swing his team to the right to save them [the double for Charlton Heston as Ben Hur was Canutt's son Joe]. But, in making this move, he crowded another chariot against the wall where we had hidden a one-wheel ramp. As the wheel struck the ramp and bounced the chariot into the air, a trick spring attached to the axle threw the wheel spinning against the wall ten or 12 feet above the ground. The team then dragged the tumbling chariot to the end of the track. The driver was tossed head over heels onto the track just to the rear of Ben Hur's chariot, which sped on in the race.

Our third pileup was a two-chariot wreck caused by teams jamming against each other while fighting for positions. Two ended up in a wheel lock, with one of the teams pinned against the spina wall. The driver on the outside swung his team hard to the right, trying to break out of the lock, but instead of freeing the wheel, the pressure broke the shaft loose from his own chariot, turning it end over end. The driver, who was being dragged by the running horses, freed himself from the runaway team, and rolled out of the way of a team following close behind him, only to end up squarely in front of another oncoming charioteer's team. Here I cut the cameras and substituted for the thrown driver a mechanical dummy. The team and chariot ran over the dummy, which created the thrilling effect of the real driver being killed. The loose team then swung back to the left, collided with the inside team, and wrecked the chariot. Some of the horses fell, but regained their footing and raced away, with harness pieces flying in all directions.

The great chariot-race scene in *Ben Hur* was an incredible feat of staging and performance. But then so were the chase scenes in *The French Connection* and *The Blues Brothers,* and so were the extraordinary effects in the James Bond movies. Without the stuntpeople who take such risks, motion pictures would be tame indeed.

Making a Living with SWAT

One of the most dramatic, exciting, and novel assignments in police work today is the precarious work on a SWAT team. The acronym stands for "Special Weapons and Tactics." Its members are those highly trained individuals called in to handle the most dangerous of confrontations with killers, kidnappers, hostage-holders, the mentally unbalanced, the criminally insane, those under the influence of drugs—in fact anyone who poses an immediate threat to society.

Sergeant Ron McCarthy, a member of the SWAT team of the Los Angeles Police Department, has been in the unit since its inception more than ten years ago. He has participated in hundreds of SWAT actions in the Los Angeles area and was on hand for perhaps the most famous altercation involving SWAT in American criminal annals—the raid that was carried out on the Symbionese Liberation Army's temporary home in Los Angeles (the terrorist group that had abducted Patty Hearst and held her captive).

Here, Sergeant McCarthy tells of some of the SWAT exploits he has participated in and describes what it is like to be a member of that organization.

R. W.: As a member of SWAT, you are involved in a variety of dangerous confrontations. Would you describe a typical one?

McCARTHY: Well, none of them are really typical. Each is pretty unique. But to pick out one, maybe the hostage situation at the Airport Marina Hotel about three or four years ago would give you an idea. That involved a drug dealer who was suffering a lot of depression and paranoia because there were other drug dealers out to kill him. He continually shot up with cocaine himself—with a hypodermic needle, which is kind of unusual, but I guess you get a bigger thrill if you shoot it directly into your bloodstream. But in any event, he took a hostage—his girl friend—and then he barricaded himself in a hotel room for twenty-eight hours.

R. W.: How did you find out about the situation? I mean, how did SWAT get called in?

McCARTHY: There was just a phone call to the hotel's front desk and a kind of frightened female voice saying, "I am being held hostage." The hotel then called the police, and the patrol officers were sent over. They opened the door with a passkey they got from the hotel manager when no one answered inside. When they opened the door, they were met with gunfire—two or three rounds. They took cover, and he

backed into the bathroom area, barricading himself and the hostage in the bathroom. When that situation was assessed, SWAT was called in. We arrived, and it took twenty-eight hours to resolve the situation.

R. W.: Where were you during that time? Were you in the room? How close to him were you?

McCARTHY: At any particular time? Sometimes within eight or ten feet of him, but the bathroom door was between us, of course.

R. W.: Were you alone in the hotel room?

McCARTHY: Oh no. There were a lot of other officers.

R. W.: How many officers were in there?

McCARTHY: Different numbers at different times but usually about five officers.

R. W.: What did you do once you were inside the room?

McCARTHY: The officers involved tried to talk him into coming out. The negotiations were right there at the bathroom door. They went on for twenty-eight hours, and eventually he came out, using her as a shield in an effort to leave the hotel. That's when we had to shoot him.

R. W.: How was he shot without endangering the life of the hostage? What was done?

McCARTHY: The officers were set up

for him, and the circumstances were rehearsed, sort of. This is what we generally try to do. We measure what his options are. He could kill himself and the hostage—that's one option. He could surrender—and that's another option, which involves a different set of tactics. If he says he wants to surrender, for example, we could just say, "Come on out." But how will he come out? With a gun in his hand? And with the hostage? We would plan for any eventuality. But we'd tell him to release the hostage first, and we'd have it set up to take her into custody and get her to a place of safety. Then he would be told to come out without the gun, and we'd arrest him. That would be the easy way. One of his other options, though, is to rush out and start firing. In anticipation of that, we would have set up structural barricades, so that if he did come running out, we'd be protected. Then the other alternative he has, of course, is to use her as a shield and try to march out with a gun to her head. That was considered, and we decided if that was his choice—which it was—and realizing that we were dealing with a deranged doper who was capable of killing anybody at any time, we would have to use deadly force and hope that when we did, the hostage wouldn't be injured.

R. W.: What actually happened?

McCARTHY: Well, we were in position. We placed officers who we had confidence in, in certain positions, so that no matter how he came out with the hostage, one of those officers would have a clear and unobstructed view of him—which means the opportunity to shoot him, to stop him.

R. W.: Do you shoot to kill in a situation like that?

McCARTHY: Well, you have to look at it this way. We are not trying to kill him—our purpose is to stop him. But if we shoot him in the head, he'll be killed—you can predict that. The best information we have is that if you shoot somebody there, in the head—the brain, that is—you have a much smaller chance of his having some kind of reflexive response that would cause his gun to discharge and perhaps shoot the hostage. So we shoot him there. Someone might say we shoot him there for the purpose of killing him, but that is not true. We shoot him there so we can stop him, and he will have absolutely no reflexive response. But it's going to kill him if we shoot him in the brain.

R. W.: And that's what you did in this case?

McCARTHY: Yes. An officer shot him in the head when he came out with the hostage, and he was killed. The hostage wasn't hurt.

R. W.: What part of that situation was the most dangerous to you or to other SWAT officers?

McCARTHY: Probably prior to his coming out of the bathroom. The door was at times the only thing between the officers and him, and because he was under the influence of drugs, he was totally unpredictable. And he did fire five or six rounds through the door.

R. W.: This is more dangerous than a street situation, isn't it?

McCARTHY: No. It's actually far more difficult for an officer on the street, because the suspect usually has more freedom and the officer has fewer tools to solve the problems. He has one other problem—a large audience. And sometimes a large audience is a very critical audience. We have an officer, uniformed, who I've given some instruction to because he works in the projects in south Los Angeles. And one day he confronts a PCP freak armed with a shotgun, and he is holding the weapon down at his side. This officer and his partner approach the man with the shotgun. He is not aiming it at them, but he is screaming and yelling. He was acting in such a way that they weren't sure whether he was going to shoot himself, shoot them, or just give up the shotgun. Because of the tremendous amount of pressure that was generated about police brutality and undue force, this officer decided that he would try to approach the guy and disarm him. Legally and morally, he would have been perfectly right to shoot him. And while all this was going on, the relatives of the armed man were standing there several feet away, screaming, shouting, and harassing the two police officers. Then some

others from the neighborhood joined in. The officer approached the suspect to take him into custody—a suspect who was under the influence of drugs, self-induced insanity, a dope-bag hysterical, if you don't mind me using that kind of terminology—and this officer approaches him and tries to solve the problem without using force. The officer's hand was blown off by the shotgun blast the suspect fired. He has a hook now. I'm sure if he had to do it over again, he would shoot the man who had the shotgun.

R. W.: How did you get into SWAT in the first place?

McCARTHY: Well, first I was just on the force. We all started as regular police officers, and everybody goes to patrol first. SWAT started about ten years into my police career. SWAT is approximately ten years old—a little older than that. When it began, those of us who took an interest in it were more interested in the concept, and the concept was in response to the change in society. Before, there weren't the militants or the organized bands of criminals who had special weapons or the terrorists. Bank robbers used to be individuals with handguns. Now there are militant bank robbers—maybe a team of five or six with radio communications and machine guns. It requires a different kind of police response. In addition, things like barricaded suspects used to be very rare. Now in my city we handle fifty or sixty of these cases a year.

R. W.: What is the concept of SWAT? Why was it founded?

McCARTHY: The concept of SWAT is that it is a lifesaving organization—that the organization itself has the aggressive capability to take the offensive and handle major and unusual police-criminal situations. We are usually called in, in situations involving heavily armed suspects who are often highly skilled and extremely dangerous.

R. W.: Yours is a very combative force then.

McCARTHY: Not necessarily. Although we have that capability, ninety-nine times out of one hundred, our response in solving the problem is without ever firing a shot. Although this year we've handled fifty to sixty situations where suspects have been armed and barricaded, we haven't fired a shot. Suspects have, but we haven't.

R. W.: Are you saying that just the presence of SWAT alone is enough to. . . .

McCARTHY: Cause the suspect to surrender? No. Certainly not the majority of the time. I don't really know the reason why a suspect surrenders—whether it's the circumstances or that he feels intimidated in some way. Of course, there are cases where they don't surrender, and it's necessary to take them in some other way.

R. W.: Such as?

McCARTHY: Tear gas. We can use that to force a person to come out. Many times, we use tear gas and take somebody into custody without firing a shot. Shooting someone is the last resort.

R. W.: Do you think the presence of SWAT at a given scene could be intimidating to the criminal or the person or the persons being confronted?

McCARTHY: The only time that SWAT could be intimidating in my opinion is if the person faced is a rationally thinking person. If he's a psychopath or sociopath—you know, the personality of a typical hardened, violent criminal—no. A person who is a sometime bank robber or a militant might be intimidated. An individual who is mentally deranged—either crazy or under the influence of drugs, like PCP—doesn't have the ability to think and make a good, conscious, solid decision. So then you can expect unusual activity or an "I don't give a damn" attitude. He'll be surrounded by many officers, and the guy will just say go ahead and shoot me. In all of the circumstances involving barricaded suspects that we've been involved in—over four hundred—we've only fired shots in, I believe, a total of fourteen situations. And that's over a period of ten years. There is usually less chance of there being a shooting if SWAT is at the scene.

R. W.: Do you consider SWAT a kind of elite corps?

McCARTHY: We have training and equipment that give us an opportunity to handle the situation differently. A good, solid police officer who has the same training and the same opportunity could probably handle the problem exactly the same way. But not every police officer has that opportunity.

R. W.: Has SWAT in Los Angeles changed much in the ten years it has been in existence?

McCARTHY: We used to spend a lot of time training in strictly military tactics—there were no SWAT tactics to begin with. We knew that the ordinary or regular police tactics were not appropriate. Arriving on the scene in a black-and-white radio-car with a .38 revolver would not solve the problem. So we knew that there had to be a more tactical response than that and better equipment than a .38 revolver, a woefully inefficient weapon. So we first went to the military and tried to use its tactics in a domestic law-enforcement situation. But that wouldn't work. For example, if you had an enemy barricaded in a house in World War II, you'd just blow up the house and that would solve the problem. That would have been the military tactic. Knowing we couldn't do that but we had to protect the citizenry in the area, we had to do something else. So we tried to adapt some military tactics to civilian law-enforcement situations, and gradually over the years we did that.

R. W.: You mentioned special equipment?

McCARTHY: The effectiveness of the equipment and the weapon in accomplishing the job is very important. You have to have the ability to do the job. So that's why we're very selective of the weapons we choose.

R. W.: And some of those weapons are?

McCARTHY: The basic weapon is a .45 automatic pistol, which in our opinion is the safest weapon for the public and the officer for several reasons.

R. W.: Why is that?

McCARTHY: First, the .45 automatic is a low-velocity weapon with a heavy round. The round weighs a lot compared to a .22 or a .25, so that when the round is fired at somebody or something, the round will stop in that somebody or something, and not travel through and come out the other side and perhaps endanger somebody else. A .38 is not as good as a .45 for that reason. If you shoot someone with a .38, hypothetically speaking again, the bullet will travel through him in all probability. But it won't stop him unless you hit him some place where it would disconnect his central nervous system, like the brain, or would sever the spinal cord. But if you shot a person in the heart with a .38, you very probably wouldn't see a reaction until twenty or thirty seconds later. Sometimes you'll read in the newspaper that police officers emptied their guns into someone. The reason they would do that is to stop someone from killing them. See, their first bullet did not stop the person. It takes only approximately two and a half seconds to empty a six-shot revolver. Now, if you fired one shot and it hit the person and he fell down, you would not fire again.

R. W.: And a .45 is that kind of weapon?

McCARTHY: Getting shot with a .45 automatic—a very effective weapon that the military has used since nineteen eleven—is like being hit with a Coke can as opposed to being hit with a pencil. If you are hit with a pencil and the pencil is traveling very fast, it will go right through you and make a hole. You'll be severely injured internally, and eventually you may even die. If you are hit with a Coke can at the same speed, you will be knocked flat on the floor. A .45 bullet will enter you, and if it hits you in the body mass, the torso, where most shots hit, nine out of ten people will be knocked flat with the first round.

R. W.: How dangerous is working in SWAT?

McCARTHY: SWAT is probably a safer place to work than on the street as a patrol officer. We have good equipment—the average patrol officer doesn't have as good equipment as we do. The risk of being shot is there, but I think that good equipment and good training reduce the risk.

R. W.: And you have more extensive training.

McCARTHY: We have the better opportunity to train—that makes our job safer. Our job is not safer from the standpoint of injury. We have a high rate of injury because of the physical demands required of the officer to be a member of SWAT.

R. W.: What are those?

McCARTHY: We have to pass a physical fitness test every three months.

R. W.: And just how strenuous is it?

McCARTHY: We have to do a three-mile run over hilly terrain. And there are sit-ups, push-ups, and chin-ups. There is no variance in scoring for age. In other words, I'm forty-four, and I have to pass at the same score as a man who's, say, twenty-four.

R. W.: That's tough.

McCARTHY: But it's reasonable. The suspect won't ask how old you are before he reacts to you.

R. W.: How many points do you need to pass?

McCARTHY: In order to pass you need two hundred thirty points—so that means you are going to have to average about twenty-five minutes or less in the three-mile run. In other words, you're going to have to average a little over eight-minute miles, five or six chin-ups, sixty sit-ups, and forty push-ups. In addition, we have an obstacle course that requires approximately fifty minutes to an hour to go through. They are all obstacles that you would meet out in the field if you were on a SWAT call. For example, you jump from one roof to another. If you miss, you go to the concrete. We don't put anything underneath it. We jump from one roof to the other with all our equipment on and our weapon. We know that if an officer can meet the requirements of an obstacle course, he will be able to function in a real situation in the street. If we weren't tested this way, we wouldn't have good solid knowledge about how we'd function in a real situation.

R. W.: In addition to physical conditioning, are there other kinds of training you have to go through regularly?

McCARTHY: Yes. We have regular training in weaponry throughout the year. We have to be proficient with the weapons that we use, and that kind of proficiency is obtained with training. But the training goes far beyond that. It goes into the mental aspects of a situation—how to handle various suspects or situations. Our crisis negotiators or hostage negotiators are SWAT officers—that is different from most anywhere else in the United States. Most hostage negotiators are from policy departments. They are not SWAT officers. In our department, the officer who carries the radical-looking equipment and the sophisticated-looking weapons is the same officer who has the ability, the training, and the sensitivity to talk people out of suicide or out of murdering someone or to

talk them into releasing someone they are holding hostage.

R. W.: Who is picked in SWAT as a negotiator?

McCARTHY: First, the officer has to apply for that position. Then he is tested psychologically to see if he has the ability to handle crisis situations and to provide the kind of empathy or identification with a suspect to talk him out of what he is doing or planning to do.

R. W.: What is your specific duty in SWAT?

McCARTHY: My position is the squad leader. My boss is a lieutenant and heads the entire sixty-man unit. The unit is divided into six sections, ten men each, with a sergeant in charge of each squad. I'm one of those six sergeants.

R. W.: What would be your duties during a crisis situation or a confrontation?

McCARTHY: In the average call-out— the average barricade or hostage situation—I would run the squad and make the tactical plan and then implement that plan. My lieutenant is the boss of the entire tactical operation, and I would be directly responsible to him. He would ultimately approve or disapprove of anything that I should decide to do. Actually, there are two individuals who are in charge of five-man teams, and those two officers report directly to me.

R. W.: Do different men within a squad have different capabilities?

McCARTHY: That's right. All of them are cross-trained but some men are team leaders or element leaders. One may be a long-rifle man—he is a sharpshooter, but he will be able to do other things in the squad too. There is also the observer. The observer is the backup to the long-rifle man and is his observation post. Then there's the scout—he is usually a quick, well-experienced, very athletic officer. He's the first man through the door. Then there is the rear guard—the shotgun man. The shotgun man is just that. He carries a shotgun and primarily he covers the movement of the other officers.

R. W.: They all sound relatively perilous.

McCARTHY: The people who are probably in the most danger would be those on an entry team. That's probably the most dangerous thing that an officer does from the standpoint of a life-threatening situation. But if you are doing things tactically correct, then the chances of your being injured are minimized considerably. I think that's where the idea of hazard is best understood. As I said earlier, the job of the regular patrol officers in a tough or high-crime area is probably the most dangerous of all. Those officers have no idea who they are

stopping. When they get a radio call, they have no idea whether it is a legitimate call or how serious the situation is.

R. W.: And when you go out on a call, you know something bad is going to happen—you know that you are dealing with a dangerous situation or otherwise the unit wouldn't be called in.

McCARTHY: True. That's the advantage—before I ever get there, I know that I'll meet a hazardous situation. So, for example, I know to park my car in a position where the suspect won't be able to shoot at me when I get out of it. I know beforehand to get myself in a position where he can't shoot at me. An ordinary patrol officer doesn't have that luxury. And as I said, we have training, and we have knowledge of the situation we're going to meet. I'm not trying to minimize the fact that the job is risky. I'm not trying to be modest. I'm just trying to set the record straight.

R. W.: Working in SWAT is a dangerous occupation.

McCARTHY: It is.

R. W.: Exciting?

McCARTHY: In its own way, yes. Sometimes more so than you'd like.

The Ama Divers of Japan

As they prepare to plunge into the cold ocean waters, the ama divers of Japan present an eerie sight in the early morning sunlight. They look more like participants in some ancient oriental rite or performers in an obscure Kabuki drama than the simple food-gatherers they are in reality. All are women; their faces are painted with a white cream, not for any theatrical effect but merely to protect them against the ravages of saltwater and the sun. These ama are bare-breasted, traditionally garbed only in a pair of tight white trunks and a white bandana to keep the long hair from their eyes.

The ama are part of Japan's fishing industry, a most unique and certainly a hardy, fearless segment of it. These women, who range in age from teenagers to septuagenarians, harvest shellfish and edible seaweeds in the Pacific Ocean and the Sea of Japan during the spring and summer months. Large, open-deck fishing boats bring them out in the morning and again in the afternoon. The women dive to the bottom, anywhere from 50 to 80 feet below the surface of the sea. There, they forage the ocean floor for such morsels as abalone, clams, and a variety of other, more esoteric shellfish, as well as kelp and other undersea vegetation.

What is most astonishing, however, is that they do it without any scuba equipment or other artificial breathing apparatus. The divers simply hold their breath and swim down to pressure-crushing depths, where they remain submerged for about 60 seconds, reaping whatever they can from the rocks and seaweed gardens. An ama may make as many as 100 dives a day, typically diving from 10:00 A.M. until noon, and again from 2:00 P.M. until 4:00 P.M.

The ama divers today use goggles or a one-pane diving mask, wear a pebble-filled belt to help overcome their natural buoyancy, and are attached to the fishing boat by a lifeline. The other end of the lifeline is manned in the boat by a partner, often the diver's husband. (Women do the diving because the greater percentage of subcutaneous fat in their physiques enables them to withstand the cold water for longer periods of time than men.) The principal function of the lifeline is to haul the diver back to the boat when her minute or so of food collecting is finished.

The ama divers are not record-setters for deep-diving. (An Italian woman, Giuliana Treleani, reached a depth of 147½ feet in 1967, the deepest ever plumbed by a woman without breathing aids, and a fellow Italian, Enzo Maiorca, holds the record for a male, 285 feet in 1974.) The ama have little concern with the impressive depths they reach, which they consider merely part of their day-to-day jobs. The records they post, however, in regard to endurance—the number of dives in a given session and the daily nature of the routine—have never been approached by any diver or group of divers.

It is not all work and no play, however. As with fishing folk everywhere, there is that staple called the "shore lunch." Luis Marden described the Japanese ama version in an article in *National Geographic* magazine:

> At noon we ran our boat ashore and jumped out on a rock to have lunch. The ama quickly gathered driftwood and dead pine branches and made a blazing fire. They laid abalone, sazae, and a dozen sea urchins in the embers, where they began to steam and bubble.
>
> In a quarter of an hour we scraped the charred spines from the urchins, broke open the spherical shells, and picked out with chopsticks the orange gonads, sexual organs that looked like highly colored caviar. This and the steamed awabi [abalone], sazae, and rice, with superb Japanese beer, made a seaside meal to be remembered.

The diving of the ama women is a profession that has existed in Japan for more than 2,000 years. Today there are still several thousand ama divers harvesting the fruits of the sea floors off the Japanese coasts, but many have given up the topless tradition and have opted for more protective body coverings such as the neoprene wet suits that western divers commonly employ.

A Modern-Day Bounty Hunter

The profession of bounty hunter seemingly should have gone out of vogue sometime shortly after Wyatt Earp shot up the OK Corral. What with sophisticated police procedures, a computerized FBI, and intricate networks of insurance investigators, it seems there would be little need for the services of a bounty hunter. But apparently there is. Chicago Sun-Times *columnist Roger Simon uncovered just such a person and wrote about him.*

It was all wrong. He should have kicked down the door with one slam of his boot. He should have thrown a hammerlock on me.

He should have slowly tightened his grip until the veins bulged in my forehead. He should have whispered, "Honeymoon's over, sweetheart. We're gonna take a little ride."

Then he should have laughed—evilly.

Instead he wiped a few ashes off his flowered sport shirt, stuck out his hand, and said, "Hi. Is this where I'm supposed to be?"

He is a bounty hunter—a real one. He goes after men and women who have jumped bail. He carries a gun and handcuffs, and in most states he gets to use them.

He tracks people down by tracing them through their cigar suppliers or by dressing up as a dockworker or as a skid row bum. He says he has caught thousands of people in the last 30 years.

His name is Ralph "Papa" Thorson. A movie has been made about his life. It is called *The Hunter*, and he is played by no less than Steve McQueen.

The official Paramount press release describes Thorson as a "huge, full-bearded man; six feet, two inches; three hundred pounds, [who] deals in danger and violence and maintains an arsenal of weapons large enough to arm a SWAT team."

Actually, the guy comes across as a mix between Santa Claus and Rodney Dangerfield. He may be a bounty hunter, but he is a very *nice* bounty hunter—a very *laid-back* bounty hunter.

I asked him about the first time he ever got shot.

"Jeez," he said, "it was the very first time I was in Mexico, and some _____ in a bar shot me."

"And you were after him, right? He was trying to escape, and you pulled out a .357 magnum and. . . ."

"Naw," Thorson said, "I didn't even *know* the guy. He just didn't like gringos, I guess."

"Umm, how about the first time you were ever stabbed?"

"Mexico again," he said. "I was in a bar, and I said to a guy 'excuse me' in what I thought was Spanish. But I don't know Spanish too good, and it turns out that I called him an 'outdoor toilet.' So he stuck a knife in me."

You gotta admit the guy hangs out in some tough bars.

"How did you get into this life?" I asked him.

"I was in college, studying criminology at Berkeley," he said, "and during the summer I was a bartender in a resort. I mixed Campari cocktails for this guy. Have you ever *tasted* a Campari cocktail? My God. They taste like kerosine, vinegar, and battery acid. At least the way I made them they did.

"Anyway, this guy was a bail bondsman, and he offers me a job. He has this client, just an old drunk, not really a bond jumper, but the guy could never stay sober enough to go to court.

"So I just went to his home, got him sober, and brought him in. I got paid twenty dollars, and it was the easiest money I had ever made. I thought this was going to be really sweet.

"In the next case, I damn near got killed. I went after this woman—ninety pounds, five-foot-nothing."

"And she was *tough*?"

"Naw. But she had an eleven-hundred-pound, nine-foot gorilla for an old man. He grabbed me and turned me every which way but loose. I finally took her, but this guy really pounded me. I learned my lesson after that."

"What lesson?"

"I learned that in cases like this, you call four very big cops to go with you—or four very big hoodlums—or take a shotgun."

Thorson works with cops a lot.

Insuring Daredevils

A heartening note for would-be adventurers as well as for the pros is that insurance is available for practically every adventurous escapade or occupation. Ordinary insurance companies cover such diverse and dangerous jobs as oil rig firefighter and stock car driver. Stuntpeople, private investigators, mountain climbers, skydivers—just about all can find a policy if they can pay the premiums.

The most famous insurers of unusual activities or of people involved in out-of-the-ordinary pursuits are the underwriters of Lloyds of London. Among their recent underwritings:

- The stunts of daredevils Evel Knievel and Eddie Kidd. Professional stuntpeople are considered good risks, since they take every possible precaution while performing.
- The high-speed skiing of Jean-Claude Killy for movies and television. During the filming of one television commercial, Killy was to ski down a mountain pursued by a carefully controlled avalanche—but the avalanche detonated too soon and he had to race for his life.
- The British team that flew the Pitts Special aircraft in the 1978 world aerobatic championships.
- The sailing expedition from Ireland to Newfoundland in a 36-foot leather boat undertaken in 1976 by Timothy Severin to recreate the alleged voyage of St. Brendan 1,400 years earlier.
- The 1979 flight of the pedal-powered *Gossamer Albatross* (*see also* Chapter 6), the first muscle-powered flight over the English Channel.
- The voyage in a seagoing bathtub from Dover, England, to Cap Gris Nez, France. A condition of the policy was that the tub's plug remain in place at all times.
- Even Superman—Lloyd's underwriters wrote a $20 million policy to cover the exploits of Christopher Reeve in the making of the motion picture *Superman*.

Since the people he looks for have jumped bail, an arrest warrant has usually been issued for them. And the police are only too happy to cooperate.

He is a licensed private detective, and under an 1872 Supreme Court decision involving bounty hunters, Thorson is allowed to make arrests on his own. "You can use reasonable force to effect an arrest, but you have to use your head," he said. "You just can't go out and start shooting at people."

"So it's you against them," I said. "Good against evil—justice against the criminal—virtue against. . . ."

"Aww, wait a second," he said. "I usually end up drinking with a lot of these guys after it's all over. I know a lot of them. I'm just bringing them back for trial, see?

"Most of them go back and beat the rap anyway. It's just a game. It's cops and robbers. Most of these guys are better off going back to trial.

"In a lot of states, after six months the bail is forfeited. That means I don't get paid. So after six months, I drop the case.

"With a lot of guys, after six months and one day, they'll call me up and 'hoorah' me on the phone. Then they invite me over for a drink or two.

"I got to tell you the truth. Almost everybody I catch winds up as a friend."

Steve McQueen, you might remember, used to play a bounty hunter on the TV series *Wanted Dead or Alive*. And he used to go around with this huge "mare's leg" .44-.40

carbine and blast people to smithereens.

"Well," Thorson said, "I actually try to avoid the whole macho thing. Because no matter how mean and rotten you are, you always find someone meaner and rottener.

"And you know? The older I get, the tougher everybody else seems to get."

He is being modest, of course. In the movie (in which Thorson has a one-line cameo appearance), McQueen jumps on top of a Chicago El train to chase a guy. I asked Thorson if that really happened.

"Naw," he said, "it was only a freight train I jumped on top of."

"What's the single toughest thing you ever did?" I asked.

"This," he said with a little shiver. "I'd rather face a bank robber than these interviews."

Flying Pickup Trucks

If Evel Knievel is the king of motorcycle jumping, then Chuck Strange, from southern California, is the prince of pickup-truck flying. Such a profession is not without its risks. Chuck Strange proved that at the Houston, Texas, Astrodome in early 1978.

The unfortunate incident took place on January 3, when a crowd more accustomed to watching Houston Oiler footballs fly through the air than Chuck Strange's *Star Truck* was stunned into silence. The high-fly-

ing, four-wheel pickup truck roared off the takeoff ramp, sailed over 15 Chevrolets, but crashed into the 16th, which was parked just in front of the landing ramp. Both of Strange's arms were shattered, a rib was broken, his kidney was bruised, and a rescue team had to struggle for 30 minutes to extricate him from the debris. Strange said afterward, however, that he suffered no other serious injuries and planned a strong comeback.

Just a few months before the

Houston mishap, the daredevil stuntman had piloted *Star Truck* to a claimed world record with a 107-foot flight over 18 Datsuns lined up between the takeoff and landing ramps. Actually, the landing ramp wasn't entirely necessary for this event, since Strange missed it completely and landed with a bone-crunching thump well to the right of the intended touchdown point. Not surprisingly, few of Chuck's jumps go precisely by the book. In fact, he points out that many of his fans think he has crashed after executing a relatively clean jump.

Born Charles Othon in Los Angeles, California, Chuck grew up in Phoenix, Arizona, and established a reputation as the champion demolition derby driver in the West while still in his teens. Soon after, he had graduated to daredevil stunts. One of his favorites involved driving a car with a passenger strapped across the hood through a wall of flaming plywood. For Chuck, it was a short jump from car crashing to car flying.

In 1975, Strange flew a car 40 feet into the air, covering a distance of 116 feet, also without the benefit of a landing ramp. He believes that this is still a record for ramp-to-ground car flying.

During his long rest after the crash in the Astrodome, Chuck Strange outlined his plans—and practiced a bit by driving his flashy pickup on its two right wheels around an oval track. One of the stunts he is planning involves a tilted, 12-mile drive around a track to establish a new world record. For a touch of showmanship, of course, an exotically clad young lady will stand in the cargo bed throughout the record-breaking drive.

Another goal is a 200-foot pickup-truck jump across 40 cars, possibly staged back in the Astrodome. But Chuck Strange is also awed by a third possibility—launching and piloting in ramp-to-ramp flight a massive 18-wheel truck.

Misadventures

Stranded in the Alaskan Wilderness

Elmo Wortman had lived off the land and the waters of Alaska by his own resourcefulness for a long time. Sharing that life-style with him were his 16-year-old son Randy, and his two daughters, Cindy, 17, and Jena, 13. Wortman was a carpenter, handyman, hunter, and fisherman, taking on those jobs necessary to sustain himself and his three children in the wilderness.

The Wortmans lived in a small house he had built on a raft, which was anchored in a cove at Port Refugio, a small island in southeast Alaska. Their home was mobile because Elmo Wortman did not like to stay in the same place too long. He would move on, Wortman said, "when the people got too many or the fish too few." But for all his rugged individualism, his self-sufficiency, and his understanding of the wilderness, he was not prepared for the life-threatening ordeal that he and his family would encounter and miraculously survive.

It began on February 14, 1979, when Wortman and his children, aboard *Home*, the 33-foot sailboat that he had built, were caught in a storm as they headed home from Prince Rupert, British Columbia, about 250 miles southeast of their homesite. In the early afternoon, as they were sailing the Pacific just off the coastlines of the Alaskan string of islands known as the Alexander archipelago, the sky turned a steel gray and then the winds suddenly became sharp, slashingly cold, un-

leashing a power that turned the sea into a rolling, heaving mass. Wortman, having seen a variety of storms on the Pacific, knew that this was going to be a terrible one, and so he tried to maneuver the sailboat to the land in sight to the east. But the winds were gusting at about 60 knots, he estimated, and the waves were capping 25 feet high. They were helpless against the storm.

Everyone donned flotation jackets because Wortman knew it would be only a matter of minutes before he and his children would either be washed overboard or his boat would break up beneath them. He also knew the icy water they would be tossed into—bitterly cold at that time of year—offered them a life expectancy of not more than ten or 15 minutes at most. They were wearing heavy boots, which they quickly padded and wrapped to provide some kind of insulation.

Elmo Wortman worked desperately to save what he could. He filled plastic bags with food and pitched them overboard in the hope that they would be washed ashore on the closest island, a desolate and uninhabited slab of rock and ice not far away. He threw other supplies into a small, two-person skiff and then launched it, hoping that it would drift to the island. Then a great wave washed over the boat, and suddenly Wortman and his three children were bobbing about in the freezing ocean waters. Behind them were the remains of their sailboat—stray pieces of wood and other flotsam and jetsam. The whirling, slashing water was so forceful that it tore not only the insulation and padding but also the boots from all four of them, leaving their feet covered only by wool socks. The raging water and the fierce winds were blowing them toward shore, but directly into the rocks that formed a jagged seawall. They were bounced against them, sucked back into the sea, only to be thrust back at the rocks. Finally, 15 minutes later, Wortman and his son were able to clamber onto the shoreline, pulling the two girls ashore after them. Dripping wet, chilled, and his feet frozen to numbness, Wortman set out to gather wood for a fire. In his pocket was their lifeline—a packet of plastic-encased matches.

After starting a fire, he began to search for the things he had thrown overboard. He found very little food—a container of cooking oil and a bag that contained six apples, two onions, and a can of powdered orange juice—most of it having been lost in the sea. The skiff, however, was intact. There was also a sizable amount of plywood, some Styrofoam, several mattress pads, a gallon of diesel fuel, and the large sailcloth from the boat.

By nightfall the storm had subsided, but they were stranded. The family huddled together under the sailcloth, sheltered somewhat from the wind by a huge rock, but the bitterness of the wind and the cold was inescapable.

In the morning, Wortman got the fire going again, but when he tried to warm his frozen feet, he quickly moved away, the heat from the fire creating a pain that was unbearable. He bathed his feet in snow to refreeze them, hoping he would be able to walk again. The pain finally subsided, and Wortman scoured the shoreline and found some of the other provisions, including their boots, that had washed up during the night.

After some exploring, Wortman calculated that they were on a slender spit of land called Long Island, perhaps not more than 15 miles from Dall Island, where Pat Tolson, a friend of his, had a cabin. Tolson would not be there, Wortman knew, because he mentioned he was going to take a trip when the Wortman family had stopped and visited with him on the way to Prince Rupert. But by the unwritten code of the wilderness, the cabin would be unlocked and properly stocked, so that anyone who had been stranded in that hostile environment could find safe refuge.

The family loaded the skiff and began the agonizing trek northward. They planned to reach the northwesternmost point of Long Island, where they would cross a channel to Dall Island to the west. The girls rode on the skiff, Wortman and his son pulling it from the shore by a tether line they had fashioned. On occasion, one of the girls would spell one of the men towing the skiff. They ate the carefully rationed shreds of food they had salvaged and whatever they found along the shore of the sea—shellfish, kelp, mussels, and clams. At night, they built a fire from driftwood that they collected along the way. Wortman warmed his upper body by the fire but continued to pack his boots with ice and snow to keep his feet from thawing. Because of the extreme cold and the great difficulty in towing the skiff, it took them ten days to reach the icy channel.

The four of them would not be able to fit in the skiff for the crossing of the strait, so Wortman dismantled it and used the wood, along with some logs that he found and some of the plywood he had saved, to fashion a raft that would accommodate all four of them. Finally, they launched the makeshift craft and, with the help of some homemade oars, started across the channel. It was a foggy, blustery day, exceptionally cold even for Alaska, but they landed on Dall Island in the afternoon of February 25, 11 days after they had first been shipwrecked.

Everyone was exhausted, drained from the great efforts, the lack of food (they had had nothing to eat in the last two days), and the extended exposure to the elements. Because they were weak and could not combat the winds, the raft was washed ashore at Keg Point, three miles south of their destination, Rose Inlet, where the cabin stood on a hill a few hundred feet from the water's edge.

The two girls, lapsing into delirium from fatigue, said they could not go any farther. So Wortman left them there with the sailcloth and a pair of rubber mattresses, telling them that he and Randy would row to the cabin, return with food, and then, their strength restored, they would all move to the safety of the cabin.

Wortman and his son set out in the raft and paddled the three miles

to the inlet, only to find that the inlet had frozen since their last visit. The only way to get to the cabin would be to trek a half-mile across the ice. So they tied the raft to the shore as best they could and then set out on foot. About halfway across, Wortman accidentally stepped on a thin section of the ice and splashed into the freezing water. Randy quickly lay down, inching forward until he was able to clasp his father's hand, and then slowly pulled him out onto the ice. Chilled and fatigued, they continued walking, eventually reaching the hill that led to the cabin. They barely made it to the cabin door, and once inside, they lapsed into unconsciousness.

When Wortman finally regained his senses, he built a fire, revived his son, and the two of them ate and rested in a hallucinatory state. By the time they were sensible enough to return for the girls, night had fallen and it had begun to snow heavily.

The next morning, the snow continued to fall and drifts were building everywhere. They started down the hill, but when they reached the shore of the frozen inlet, they realized it would be impossible to get across the treacherous ice in such a snowstorm. Finally, the skies cleared for a few minutes, enabling Wortman to search for the skiff. It was gone from its mooring, probably swept out to sea or battered into pieces. Now there was no way that they could get back to the girls.

Day after day went by; the snows had stopped, but the weather remained bitterly cold. Wortman felt certain the girls had died but continually teased himself with hope. After

12 days, the weather suddenly warmed, the temperature climbing above the freezing mark. The snows began to melt, and the inlet broke up into a sea of hundreds of islands of ice. By March 9, the snow had melted enough to reveal part of a small fiberglass boat tied to shore. It probably belonged to Pat Tolson, Wortman thought. Wortman and his son quickly pulled it out of the snow, and began to patch the holes in the bottom of the boat.

By late morning, Wortman decided it was sailable. They immediately set out through the maze of ice chunks in the inlet, carrying the supply of food that Wortman had promised to bring back to his girls 13 days earlier. He also brought along a supply of putty, and he and Randy spent most of the three-mile journey alternating rowing and patching holes.

Finally, they reached the cove at Keg Point, where they had left the girls, but they found no trace of them. He and Randy quickly began a search, gradually moving inland. A few minutes later, Wortman saw the sailcloth on the ground in the shadow of a clifflike wall, with something beneath it. He gently lifted it back. The two girls were lying there, peaceful, their eyes shut, but astonishingly they were not dead. Both of them had survived the 13 days of snow and subfreezing temperatures, eating whatever the ocean washed on shore and huddling together under the sailcloth. The 17-year-old, Cindy, was the first to open her eyes. Still delirious, she asked, "What took you so long, Daddy?"

The four Wortmans rowed back to the cabin. Meanwhile, Pat Tolson had returned to his cabin, had found a note Wortman had left there, and now was on his way to notify the Coast Guard. The next morning, a helicopter arrived and took the worn and frozen Wortman family to a hospital in Ketchikan, Alaska, where they were treated for frostbite, exposure, exhaustion, and hunger. Their frostbite proved to be irreversible: Wortman had some toes and parts of his feet amputated and his children lost parts of their toes, but they had survived 23 days in the brutal Alaskan cold.

Karl Wallenda: Death on the High Wire

It was the kind of act Karl Wallenda, the world's greatest tightrope walker, had performed countless times before. Throughout his career he had often stilled audiences and set their hearts to quivering as he stepped out on a slender wire high above the ground, no net to protect him, only his astonishing talent and catlike balance to sustain him. The walk itself was exciting enough, but sometimes he would garnish it with a stunt, like placing his balance bar perpendicular to the wire and doing a headstand, which was positively breathtaking. Now, at 73 years old, he was going on the wire for what would prove to be the very last time. This wire was strung 120 feet above the street, between two resort hotels in San Juan, Puerto Rico.

"The wire is my life," he once said. And that was surely no over-statement. Karl Wallenda was born into a circus family back in 1905 in Magdeburg, Germany. At the age most children were starting first grade, he was performing acrobatic stunts with the family. While still a teenager, he took to the tightrope. At first, he learned the basics—walking the wire. Then, he mastered the walk with a partner balanced on his shoulders. After that, he began to devise what would become his specialty, a team wire-walk. At the age of 22, in 1927, the same year that talking motion pictures made their debut, Wallenda signed with the Ringling Brothers Circus, known then and for-ever after as The Greatest Show on Earth.

"The Great Wallendas" was the billing he chose because by then Karl's troupe had become a family af-fair—including his wife, Helen, his brother Herman, and later an assort-ment of relatives and in-laws. Karl then devised the most spectacular high-wire stunt ever to be performed above a netless circus ring: "The Great Pyramid." It consisted of two two-man teams on the wire. Each team supported a bar on their shoul-ders, on which another performer was balanced forming a second tier. The two balanced on the second lev-el supported another bar on which was perched a single performer. The three-tiered pyramid would then move slowly, steadily, across the tightrope.

For nearly 15 years, the Great Wallendas performed that magnifi-cent feat before the eyes of virtually millions of circusgoers. But the act came to a sudden and tragic end in 1962 in Detroit, Michigan. Perform-ing there for the Shrine Circus, the troupe had nearly completed its pyr-amid walk when one of the members of the first tier faltered. The pyramid collapsed in a chaos of arms and legs before the horrified eyes and gasps of the audience. Three of the Great Wal-lendas fell to the floor below; two were killed and the other, Karl Wal-lenda's son, broke his back and was paralyzed for life. Karl and his broth-er Herman were able to grab hold of the wire, and the girl who had occu-pied the top tier managed somehow to grab onto Karl's leg as she fell. One walker, incredibly, remained on the wire.

The tragedy ended the famed act; at least it ended the pyramid. Those who survived continued their haz-ardous careers on the tightrope. Karl began to specialize in tightrope walks at extraordinary heights. Wires were strung across canyons, between floors of skyscrapers, any-where that would cause the spec-tators to crane their necks to watch a tiny figure with a long pole delicate-ly move across a threadlike wire.

By the age of 73, Karl Wallenda's name was as famous as any in circus annals. He had done just about ev-erything imaginable for a tightrope walker. Now, he had come to his swan-song performance. Ten stories above a cobblestone street, he stepped with the surefooted grace of an *artiste* who was as comfortable on that thin cable as an average person would be on the sidewalk. Pure concentration. The crowd was silent, in awe, as it always was. He moved steadily across the wire, approaching the window ledge at the terminus of his walk. Suddenly, an upsurge of wind caught him and he stopped, teetering, the pole dipping and rising as he struggled to balance himself. Then another gust of wind and Karl Wallenda knew he was in trouble. He buckled his knees as if to squat on the wire, which would give him leverage against the battering winds. But they were too strong, and they blew him from the wire. With one hand he grasped it, hanging in space for a seemingly endless moment, the long pole clutched in his other hand. He would need it when he climbed back on the wire, he knew. But he was never able to use it because another gust tore him away, and Karl Wallenda plummeted to the ground. The wire that had been his life had also proved to be his death. It was, members of his family agreed afterward, the only way he would have wanted to go.

Tragedy on Mount McKinley

In June 1972, five daring young women from Japan came to Alaska to challenge North America's tallest peak, Mount McKinley. Three of them would perish in the endeavor, blown off the mountain in a storm after apparently conquering the 20,320-foot summit.

The rescue of the other two women was accomplished by Don Sheldon, one of Alaska's most intrepid bush pilots (he was the first to perfect mountainside glacier landings). This article is excerpted from a book about Sheldon's many exploits and daring rescues in Alaska, Wager with the Wind *by James Greiner.*

In the clammy, frost-teased air of the tiny two-man parachute tent, Micheko Sekita clenched her small hands in frustration. The campsite at 9,500 feet was still in deep shadow, and the weak late-June sun illuminated only the high mountain walls around the tent, causing the red nylon to glow. Her fever, the result of a chest cold, seemed to have dissipated somewhat during the long night, and the discomfort she had experienced for several days was forgotten. Micheko Sekita was worried. Five days before, early on the bright morning of June 25, her crew of four had reluctantly bade her farewell and departed for the summit of McKinley. Now all that remained to remind her of them was the feeble hiss of the Sony walkie-talkie, its batteries too weak to function.

The five-woman team had come from Japan in high spirits for their planned ascent of the white mountain and had arrived in Talkeetna on June 5, 1972. As they detrained and piled their 800-pound load of expedition gear aboard Sheldon's venerable jeep, their quiet, laughing voices had a birdlike quality, and the entire world was theirs for the asking. The warm sunshine-flooded air was alive with the sounds of a new spring, and the five women immediately established a permanent niche in Sheldon's heart.

"They were like tiny fragile dolls, and they reminded me of wild flowers as they chattered and laughed at the world around them, but make no mistake, they were athletes in the true sense of the word. I guess the one thing that struck me first was how completely happy they seemed to be. They couldn't have weighed more than 90 pounds apiece, and it didn't require a mathematical genius to figure that, even relaying, they would have to carry packs that would weigh almost as much as they did."

The women were all from the vicinity of Tokyo, where 32-year-old Micheko Sekita was a teacher of handicapped children. Her close companion, Matsuko Inoue, nine years her junior, was also from Tokyo as was Mitsuko Toyama. Nobue Yajimi called the Prefecture of Saitama her home, while the final member, Sachiko Watanabe, came from Sapporo.

These Japanese would represent the first all-woman team from their country to attack the 20,320-foot mountain. In Japan, all-woman mountain-climbing teams are commonplace, but before 1972, McKinley's summit had seen only one all-woman team, the Denali Damsels.

Micheko Sekita had selected experienced climbers, and the McKinley ascent would be done under the banner of the Ryosetsu Climbing Club of Japan. That they were proud of their mission was unmistakable to Sheldon, though Micheko, the leader, was the only member who spoke fair English.

"They had good gear and a tremendous amount of rope. Their food supply seemed adequate and consisted of items that I had seen so many times before on Oriental climbs—powdered vinegar; dried bonito, which is a kind of fish; lots of rice and rice products; instant seaweed soup; and of course, chopsticks. Their gear seemed to be well chosen too, and they carried good snowshoes, which they called *wakans*. They also packed skis."

Ostensibly, the purpose of the Sekita Expedition was to scale McKinley's summit via the Southwest Buttress, a route that would offer the opportunity for rock and ice climbing as well as the necessary work on snow, for which the mountain is famous. But this climb to McKinley's summit had another purpose—to give them experience and to test their climbing abilities. In 1974, Micheko Sekita's team hoped to be the first all-woman team to scale the mighty and inaccessible Everest.

As he watched their preparations

and learned of the route that they would attempt, Sheldon began to feel uneasy. He wondered about their ability on a long and sustained climb in the deep snow and with the associated chill factors on McKinley. . . .

"The last 9,000 feet of the mountain on the route they planned to cover is exposed and along a stretch where many expeditions . . . had already come to grief. The chill factor on the mountain seemed to be the one condition that these gals, like so many other climbers I've flown to the mountain, had not really considered as much as they should have. In spite of the fact that these kids were rock artists in the true sense, McKinley is a different cat than they were used to.

"I took Sekita and her crew of four to the Kahiltna on June 7 and left them chattering amid their 800-pound load of gear. About a half hour later, I overflew them and was amazed that they'd already covered about four lateral miles on skis and couldn't believe my eyes when I saw the packs they carried. They must have weighed at least 60 pounds apiece."

By June 9, the women had established a temporary cache at 7,900 feet on the Kahiltna, after relaying their gear on skis. On June 10, three of them climbed up-glacier to scout for a suitable place at which to locate their base camp. They selected a site at the 9,500-foot level, beneath the base of McKinley's Southwest Buttress. More than a week of constant effort was consumed relaying gear to this place from which the assault of the mountain would begin.

Sheldon, as was his habit, had checked on the progress that the women were making. He again marveled at the stamina they showed, but he would have been even more amazed if he had been aware that the expedition leader, Micheko Sekita, had spent the last several days laboring under the effects of a chest cold and an accompanying fever, which climbed as each day slipped by. By the time the base camp was established at 9,500 feet, she was finding the simple act of breathing increasingly difficult. On the night of June 24, in the glow of the Primus stoves, Micheko decided to stay behind while the rest continued to the summit. This must have been the most difficult decision that she would make on the entire climb, for in Japan, the highest honor accrues when all team members are victorious.

Now, it was early morning on June 30, and she had spent the last five days trying to shake the suffocating effects of the chest cold and fever, which at lower altitudes would be merely uncomfortable. Here at 9,500 feet, in the damp cold of the tent, the thin air, with only about a third of its sea-level complement of the life-sustaining oxygen, aggravated her problem. Then, as if to squelch what little cheer that she had been able to cling to while her teammates ascended above her, the radio had apparently gone dead. The last words that she had heard from her companions had been received at eight o'clock in the evening of June 29. The failure of the radio was now confirmed, for she would certainly have heard more news of the summit team during the long night, through which she had tossed fitfully, half awake and listening to the tiny hiss of the radio beneath her parka, where she kept it to warm the failing batteries. In addition to all these concerns, she had been told that Matsuko Inoue had also become ill, and as a result, had stayed in a bivouac at 17,500 feet. The remaining three women had decided on a dash for the summit, a climb they assumed would take about six hours. In a radio transmission at noon on June 29, they had estimated that they would require "about three hours to reach the summit ridge [19,000 feet]," and at 4:00 P.M., they radioed after negotiating a steep and snow-choked gully that "they would like to get the summit and then go back to Camp V [17,500 feet] where Inoue wait." Mitsuko Toyama's voice had been clearly heard at four o'clock, and Micheko felt that she would soon learn of her party's victory on the summit. Then, at exactly eight o'clock, she had heard the Sony click with an incoming carrier signal and the words "calling you at eight o'clock"—and then complete silence. Had the radio died in Toyama's hand, or had her own set failed? Micheko could not be certain but quickly found that she could no longer contact her companions, for she triggered the transmit button immediately with no success. All she could do was wait.

Micheko Sekita, her thinking clouded by the nagging worry about the fate of her crew and the fever, which though beginning to subside still weakened her, had possibly created further problems with her radio by mistakenly leaving it on during the night. Now, on the morning of June 30, she could wait no longer. She sensed that she was needed above and climbed to a "white peak" at 12,900 feet, where she "waited all day" but saw and heard nothing. She then returned to the camp at 9,500 feet for another miserable night alone.

On July 2, she left the 9,500-foot camp carrying food for her companions and climbed to 14,500 feet. At the day's end, she erected the parachute tent she carried and spent the night.

Above Micheko's position, Matsuko Inoue was also beginning to worry about the summit team. Trying desperately to remain optimistic, she calculated that, due to some unknown emergency, her companions had been forced to descend the mountain via another route. However, this was a theory that she did not really trust, for due to her higher position on the mountain, she had seen and felt the storm that had shrouded the peak late in the afternoon of the day her companions struck out for the summit. The wind had moaned above her campsite, and the top of this mountain that now seemed to rebel at her mere presence became obscured in a whiteout as the southwest wind pushed a great undulating plume of snow over the summit. She tried to summon the strength to go up and look for her teammates, but could not, for the pain in her abdomen was now so severe that she could scarcely stand upright. To climb up would be to invite collapse, and so she did the only other thing that seemed possible; she began to descend with hopes of rejoining her leader.

On July 4, at about 17,000 feet, she met Sekita, who was in the process of ascending. After a brief and depressing reunion, the two sick climbers spent the night there, protected only by their special shelter-type clothing.

The following morning, July 5, Inoue waited while Micheko began to climb the route followed by her team earlier, and in a herculean effort reached the desolate crest of the summit plateau, where she looked upward at the lonely windblown ridge that leads to the top of the world. She saw no sign of her companions and sank into the snow to spend the night, a huddled form exposed to whatever kind of weather the mountain might devise. Her exhausted mind cared little for such things as mere weather. Micheko was now but a short step away from the total despair that would consume her the following morning, July 6, when she topped the highest point on the summit plateau at 19,500 feet. Tears of frustration rolled down her cheeks as she gazed at the last gentle windswept slope between her position and the South Summit. Moaning in despair, she surrendered to the physical and mental exhaustion that had stopped powerful men far short of Denali Pass.

After what would later seem like interminable hours, Micheko arose from the snow and resolutely began to retrace her steps down to the 17,000-foot level where she had left her companion. All she remembers of the descent was that she found herself talking with Matsuko Inoue just before she could have continued no farther. After another night on the mountain without tents, the two continued downward, slowly "inching" their way where but a few days earlier the climbing had been done at a pace that spoke of a victory in the offing. Somehow, they reached the site of the base camp at 9,500 feet and sank into an almost comatose sleep in the tiny two-man shelter that had housed all five of the Sekita Expedition team members simultaneously during the early days of the climb. It was the evening of July 7.

July 8 dawned with Inoue much worse. She now vomited blood and was in desperate need of help. Micheko Sekita knew that she must act swiftly, and she decided to call Sheldon. Before leaving the base camp, she stamped the word SICK in the snow and then prepared to leave, after carefully wrapping Inoue in sleeping bags. She skied down to Sheldon's 7,000-foot landing site, and using a powerful radio transceiver he keeps there, called Talkeetna. It was with this brief transmission that the world learned of the new tragedy that was well under way on Denali, and Sheldon immediately gassed the Cessna and departed for the Kahiltna Glacier.

"I decided to take a quick look. When I arrived over their base camp at 9,500 feet, the first thing that I spotted was the word SICK stamped out in the snow, but I was helpless. I couldn't land there."

Looking down, Sheldon immediately recognized that a change had occurred in the surface of the glacier. Where once there had been a relatively safe landing place, he now detected the swells and undulations on the snow surface that signaled new crevasse activity, which rendered a landing impossible. Without pause, he banked steeply to study the surface of the glacier one more time to be certain that he could not possibly get down and then reached for the mike on his radio.

As he talked with his base at Talkeetna requesting helicopter aid, he was already setting the Cessna up for a landing to pick up Micheko Sekita, who waited farther down the Kahiltna at 7,000 feet. The pilot offered the grieving climber a spare oxygen unit, which she put on as they climbed upward. The vast Kahiltna disappeared beneath the tail of the plane as Sheldon climbed over the route of the ascent, and he quartered the slope until they reached the 16,000-foot level.

"I couldn't get more than 16,000 because of a cloud deck, but we really gave the mountain a going over for about 2½ hours. Even with two sets of eyes looking at everything that might mean something, we drew a blank—no tracks, no nothing. Then the weather began to go sour."

As they circled, Sheldon once more marveled at the strength this tiny climber possessed. She had already been through an exhausting ordeal and now, after 2½ tiring hours flying on oxygen, she was reluctant to abandon the search. Sheldon knew that there was no other choice, for both fuel and oxygen were getting low. He placed the Cessna in a long, gradual glide to a final landing at 7,000 feet. Sekita got out, to climb back on skis to the 9,500-foot camp and her ailing companion.

Sheldon returned to Talkeetna, and as he did, the weather closed in behind him. He watched as the lower levels of the big mountain faded from sight beneath a rapidly moving storm front, and his frustration became almost tangible. It would be four days before McKinley allowed the rescue operation to continue. On July 12, an Air Force helicopter removed both women from the 9,500-foot camp and transported them to Providence Hospital in Anchorage, where Inoue was judged to be critically ill with a badly perforated ulcer. Sekita returned to Talkeetna the following day by train to take up residence with the Sheldons during the search for the missing climbers that would soon begin.

The following two-week period was one of massive confusion. The military directed Ray Genet, who was on the mountain when the search was mounted, to take his group of Special Forces survival trainees to the area where the three women were last heard from. After an extensive search of the area beneath the summit, they returned to their base camp and reported that they had found nothing. The weather was stormy, and high winds pummeled the slopes of the mountain, making sustained search impossible. Genet then left the mountain.

Back in Talkeetna, the news of the apparent disaster on the mountain had Sheldon's office phone ringing constantly.

"A huge press was on. Micheko was on the phone more than she was off it. There were calls from everywhere, reporters from half-a-dozen papers, relatives and loved ones of the climbers, and the Japanese consulate. I couldn't help but notice the trend of the conversations, and both my heart and my wife's went out to the poor girl."

The responsibility that Micheko had assumed as leader of the expedition to McKinley now became a stifling burden. The Japanese consulate demanded that she be personally responsible for all expenses incurred in both the expedition and the rescue or recovery of the climbers from the mountain. Micheko Sekita found that she was bound not only financially but morally, for unless she could comply with the demands of the consulate and the people of her country, she would not be allowed to return home. She would have to somehow return with her whole team or not return at all.

Time began to pass with almost confusing rapidity. Sheldon had taken his second prolonged look on July 12. He was at that time servicing several crews on the mountain, and when he failed to find any trace of the missing team members he overflew four of his expeditions and dropped notes telling the climbers to be on the lookout for them. The weather on the mountain was reasonably mild and offered comparatively good flying conditions. When he could, Sheldon was aloft at these times and flew as long as either the weather or his fuel and oxygen tanks allowed.

"When Micheko and I flew that first day [July 8], I concentrated on the East Approach, because I estimated that if the three gals had been blown off the mountain, the wind, which had been from the west, would have blown them over the East Approach. . . ."

An Air Force C-130 had circled the mountain several times, but no helicopters were pressed into service. Sheldon learned later that the three women had been seen by another team at the 19,000-foot level in Denali Pass, just beneath the mountain's summit. A Dr. Gerstman and his teammates had tried without success to convince the three that they were climbing into a dangerous weather condition. In a statement to Sheldon, Gerstman said that he was appalled that the women did not carry sleeping bags, only small day packs, and were very obviously making a rather desperate dash for the summit. Sheldon's early appraisal of the "flaw" in the Micheko Sekita party's planning was proving to be a chilling reality. Due primarily to his conversation with Dr. Gerstman, he now determined that the missing women had to be somewhere near the summit.

Following his search on July 8 with Micheko on board, Sheldon became obsessed with finding the women, but years of experience looking not only for climbers but for any manner of things on the mountain had taught him patience. He knew that any day he flew could bring success, for the snows of McKinley, or any other mountain, are constantly shifting. With the changing landscape below, each day's search was a completely new one.

Sachiko Watanabe's husband suddenly arrived in Talkeetna from

Sapporo. Each day, he paced aimlessly between Sheldon's hangar and office, watching the sky to the northwest and waiting for news of his lost wife.

On the afternoon of July 22, Sheldon discussed the search with Ray [Pirate] Genet, and though the Pirate was due to join a climb already in progress on the mountain, he agreed to help. His first assistance came in the form of sound advice, and with an almost casual shrug, Genet recalls what happened.

"Watanabe was wandering around there, and it was really sad, so I said, 'Well heck, the best way to look really good is with a helicopter.' I called the Japanese consulate and asked them if they would pay for a helicopter. At that time, nobody really figured that it was a rescue anymore. I figured we were simply looking for bodies. The Air Force wasn't much help, if any, because the limit with their helicopters was about 14,000 feet. The Army had machines that could fly to the summit, but since it was no longer a search for survivors, they wouldn't help us. I figured that a private helicopter would be our only chance."

Genet explained to the consulate in Anchorage why he felt the use of a helicopter would be best at this time and offered to ride the chopper and supply his expert knowledge of the terrain in the search. He was then informed that there was another team of Japanese climbers being staged in Japan and that they would arrive at a later date.

"I said, 'Well, that doesn't make too much sense, because they would all be strangers to the mountain, and too much time would be used up waiting for them. The longer we waited, the better the chances would be that their bodies, wherever they were, would be snowed over and never found.'"

The Japanese consulate reluctantly agreed to Genet's plan but stated that the limit for a helicopter charter would be seven hours of flying time. Genet then contacted Gay Helicopter Service in Anchorage and arranged for use of an Allouette III, a turbo-supercharged machine capable of high-altitude operation.

Chuckling, Genet says, "The pilot, Quakenbush, who finally agreed to fly to McKinley had never been above 10,000 feet. He took the job after the first pilot scheduled 'turned up sick.' We started the search by taking a wide swing around the summit and then flew back and forth over the slopes, gradually losing altitude, until we got to just above 15,000 feet, below the crest of the Southwest Buttress. It was here that I spotted something that at the moment only looked like tiny dots."

Genet asked the pilot to turn around and make another approach, this time at a little lower altitude, which he did.

"As we hovered there, I could see that it was part of the bodies, sticking out of the snow."

Genet carefully marked the spot in his mind and told the chopper pilot to return him to Talkeetna. They had been in the air several hours, and on the way back, he calculated that if they had been required to continue the search for another 30 minutes, they would have reached the charter limit placed upon the flight by the

Japanese consulate. Sheldon met Genet in Talkeetna and quickly learned about the apparent fate of the three climbers.

"From what Ray told me, I could visualize the route that the fall had taken, and it was down at least a 70-percent grade of rock and hard ice. Hell, a guy could parachute down that slope, and it ends almost exactly 1,000 feet above my strip at 14,300 feet. We figured that the gals had made the summit and then got caught in a sudden storm accompanied by tremendous winds. They could probably see the tents of my other people down at the 14,000-foot level and maybe thought that they could take a shortcut down to them. Whatever happened to them, they either fell or were blown over the lip and tumbled at least 4,000 feet."

When asked if he considered the Japanese women experienced enough for the mountain, Genet's laconic reply carried a world of wisdom, "What is experience? On the mountain you learn all the time."

The following day, Sheldon loaded Genet and his vivacious girl friend Marlene Titus, Micheko Sekita, and Sachiko Watanabe's husband into his supercharged Cessna 180 and flew them to 10,000 feet on Kahiltna Pass, within the park boundary. This was done at Genet's request so that his party could become acclimatized to the lower oxygen level in which they would work. Sheldon had asked for and received special permission to land here, since this was a mission to retrieve the bodies of the women as opposed to the routine start of a climb. Prior to leaving Talkeetna, Genet, for very

obvious reasons, had been less than enthusiastic about Watanabe accompanying his group.

After the arrival at 10,000 feet, Genet, Titus, Micheko Sekita, and Watanabe immediately started for the 14,300-foot level and Sheldon's Super Cub landing strip, where they joined one of Genet's expeditions already on the mountain. The climb to this point took the party two full days and consisted of two herculean 18-hour climbing sessions. Once at 14,300 feet, they were in a position to reach the bodies. Genet described the actual recovery with a clinical detachment.

"Titus stayed at 14,300 feet, and we started to climb with a crew of nine, including myself. Micheko Sekita and Watanabe were with us, and we reached the seracs at 15,500 feet, the exact level where the bodies were, in a relatively short time. It took us some time to get the bodies untangled and the drifted snow cleared away, and I then knew that they had fallen a great distance. They were rolled up in the climbing rope that they were tied together with, and several shoes had been lost. We used black plastic sheeting to slide the bodies down to the 14,300-foot level, and it took three guys for each of the bodies. It was so steep we had to belay."

With the bodies recovered and resting at 14,300 feet, Genet explained to Micheko Sekita and Watanabe how and where to tramp down a runway for Sheldon, who would be arriving on July 27. Genet and Titus, along with Genet's expedition, then continued up the mountain. As they climbed, they kept watch over the two Japanese and also watched Sheldon land in the Super Cub. Genet had been in radio contact with the pilot over a small shortwave set that he carries whenever he is on the mountain.

Marlene Titus remembers that Sheldon, for reasons of his own, had chosen to land next to the runway that had been tramped down by the Japanese. Grimacing at the wasted effort, she said, "I'd rather climb the mountain any day than tramp down a runway."

Sheldon explained that he landed "off runway" so that a turn onto the packed area could be made, thus eliminating the danger of bogging down in five feet of soft snow in the turn. If he failed here, it could have easily taken four or five hours to prepare for takeoff.

Whatever Sheldon's reasons for the off-runway landing, his arrival in the Super Cub was as precise as ever, and he immediately relayed the bodies, one at a time, down to the landing site at 10,000 feet, where he would later return with the Cessna and transport them to Talkeetna.

During the next few days, Sheldon returned to the Kahiltna with Micheko Sekita to recover the party's climbing gear at 8,700 feet. Soon all traces of Sheldon's "five little flowers" had been removed from a mountain that remained unchanged by their brief presence.

The bodies of Mitsuko Toyama, Nobue Yajimi, and Sachiko Watanabe were cremated in Anchorage and sent on their long trip home. Micheko Sekita also returned to her homeland to begin the interminable task of forgetting and reimbursing her government for the high cost of a mountain climb that most of her countrymen would consider a failure. Sheldon does not.

"I'm sure that the girls made the summit because of little things that happened, like their watches stopped at nine o'clock by the fall. This would have given them plenty of time to make it, and besides, Genet reported their tracks there at 19,000 feet. I can't say for sure, but I'd never bet against it."

A Family Affair

The *Lucette*, a 43-foot oceangoing sailboat, was cruising smoothly on the open sea due west of the Galápagos Islands on the morning of June 15, 1972. The skipper, Dougal Robertson, a farmer from North Staffordshire, England, who had decided to uproot himself and take his family on a round-the-world voyage, was below deck making navigational calculations. His wife, Lyn, a nurse, his three sons—18-year-old Douglas and 12-year-old twins Neil and Sandy—and Robin Williams, a 22-year-old student who was cruising with the Robertsons as far as New Zealand, were tending to other seafaring duties. It was a pleasant morning with the sun shining warmly on the small swells of the Pacific. But suddenly the schooner was rocked by a tremendous jolt from below, then another and another. The hull groaned and shattered under the impact, and water began to rush into the boat. The *Lucette*, for some inexplicable reason, was being attacked by a school of killer whales.

Robertson knew immediately that the sailboat could not stay afloat and shouted for everyone to abandon ship. A fiberglass dinghy was dropped into the heaving waters and a self-inflatable rubber life raft was uncapped and quickly took shape. Robertson grabbed what he could and then leaped into the raft with the others, just as the *Lucette* slipped below the surface of the sea. The six sat there, stunned, and gazed out across the great silent expanse of the ocean, a few pieces of debris floating on the surface the only things left to remind them of the horror and chaos of the few minutes they had just lived through. The killer whales were gone too, having disappeared back into the deep as quietly and quickly as they had come.

Robertson quickly determined that they had only been able to save enough food and fresh water to last a week if meagerly rationed, or perhaps ten days. Their situation was not at all encouraging, but then it was not hopeless either. Besides the supplies of food and drinkable water, they had been able to salvage a sewing basket, which contained what would prove to be a treasure trove of items that they would later be able to fashion into strategic implements of survival: pins and needles, blades, knitting needles, hat pins, string, even lengths of copper wire. They had also rescued a good-size length of fishing line, a first-aid kit, a container of flares, and one of the *Lucette*'s large sails.

It was precious little for the ordeal Robertson realized lay ahead of them. The Galápagos Islands were only 200 miles to the east, but both the winds and the strong ocean current were against them and it would be impossible to row or even sail (if they could rig one) back in that direction. To the west were the Marquesas Islands, the *Lucette*'s destination, but they were 2,800 miles away. In addition, the shipwrecked crew was miles from any commonly used sealane where normal ship traffic might be encountered.

The only chance they had, Robertson figured, would be if they could somehow sail directly north to the Doldrums, that calm, windless stretch of ocean several hundred miles north of the equator where the ocean current flows back to the east. If they could reach it, they might be able to ride it to land. There, too, were shipping lanes that stretched from Panama out across the Pacific. If the Robertsons could navigate north, then east, they would eventually reach the coast of Central America, but it would be about a 1,000-mile voyage.

One of the first things Robertson decided to do was cut a sail and rig it on the dinghy. The little boat could then serve as a kind of sailing tugboat, towing the larger life raft. The six would ride in the life raft not only because it was roomier but because it had a tentlike canopy that would protect them from the sun and salty air. The flotsam and jetsam they had salvaged from the *Lucette* would be stored in the dinghy.

By nightfall everyone got the message of what the ordeal would be like as Robertson doled out dinner: one biscuit, 1/6 of an orange, one glucose sweet, and one sip of water to each person. A series of watches was also set up—day and night—so that someone would always be scanning the sea for a ship or the sky for an airplane and checking the raft for leaks. The first night also served to remind them that they were not alone. In the darkness they were startled to feel a series of soft bumps from under the rubber floor of the raft. Inquisitive fish, mostly dorado—a game fish that can grow to 30 or 40 pounds—would swim back and forth beneath the raft. The fish also reminded them of the much more threatening creatures that had rammed the *Lucette*, and made them frightfully aware of the dangers that lurked in the sea beneath them. The next day those fears were reinforced when the fin of a large white-tipped shark appeared alongside them.

On the third day Robertson found a welcome surprise when he climbed into the dinghy. On the floor was a flying fish that had ill-chosen the little boat as its point of reentry into the ocean. Its fillets provided a little variation in their diet. Throughout the following weeks of their voyage, the group was graced not only by misguided flying fish but also by better-tasting dorado, which, as predators, would soar from the sea after the smaller flying fish and sometimes land in the dinghy or the life raft.

During the first week a leak sprung in one of the raft's flotation compartments but Robertson was able to repair it. It emphasized the importance of the watches they kept 24 hours a day. Robertson had considered swimming as an exercise routine, the only possible one, but that thought was continually dispelled by the ever-present fins that cut through the water around them. One of the fins belonged to a huge hammerhead shark but most were white-tipped sharks—neither would hesitate, however, to dine on a human being. They had also spied a 50-foot whale, which came to the surface one day like a monstrous submarine, cruised a bit, and then plunged back into the depths.

Seven days adrift, their prayers were suddenly answered, or so they thought. A ship was sighted on the horizon, a cargo ship that Robertson surmised might be on a shipping lane from Panama to Tahiti, and might pass within three miles of them. Robertson clambered into the dinghy with the flares they had saved. When the ship was about as close as it would get to them, he sent a rocket flare soaring into the dull gray sky. Its bright flash scored a great arc, then plummeted into the sea, leaving a telltale wake of smoke in the sky. Robertson then struck a hand flare and waved it high above his head. When it ran its course, he struck another one, all the while keeping his eyes riveted on the ship, waiting to shout to the others at the joyful moment when it would change course and bear down on his signal. But that did not happen. There was only one more rocket flare, and he launched it. But the ship continued unerringly on its course, sliding against the horizon. In desperation he struck another hand flare. But it was to no avail. The source of their sudden hope steamed out of sight. It was a terrible letdown; on the other hand it was evidence that there was help out there, that ships were plying their way from port to port, that rescue was not just a pipe dream. What they did not know was that they would not see another ship during the next month.

As the days passed, their thoughts went from rescue back to basic survival. Their own food and water were now gone and their only hope was to rely on their resourcefulness and the gifts of nature—rainwater and the creatures from the sea. The fish that leaped into their craft provided nutrition in several ways— their flesh could be eaten raw or hung up to dry in the sun and eaten later, and the fluid from their spinal columns could be drunk. As they came closer to the Doldrums another type of creature literally reared its head from the water beckoning to be taken aboard. Large and curious sea turtles were quickly grabbed, heaved into the dinghy, and dispatched. Turtle meat became a new addition to the group's menu. In the absence of rain, there was now turtle blood to drink, which all of them eventually, if reluctantly, imbibed.

On the 15th day, Robertson was startled by a scream from one of his sons—the lashing that connected the dinghy to the life raft had broken and the boy watched with horror as the little boat moved away from them under sail. Robertson reacted instantaneously. He dove into the water and swam frantically after the dinghy, forgetting his weakened condition, driven solely by desperation and adrenaline, and at the same time oblivious to the large shark fin that sliced the water behind and just to the right of him. Those in the raft screamed at him but for some miraculous reason the shark merely kept pace and after a 200-yard swim veered away as Robertson hauled himself into the dinghy.

The importance of saving the dinghy was made abundantly clear two days later when the life raft, soggy and growing limp, passed its threshold of endurance. Robertson realized they would have to abandon it. The tiny dinghy was their only hope. So they salvaged what they could of the raft, cutting up the canopy to be used as capes now that they would be without shelter from the sun and the other elements, and using one flotation chamber to wrap around the bow of the dinghy to give the now-overloaded boat a little extra buoyancy. The interior of the dinghy was not more than eight feet by four feet, but it managed to keep six people and their assortment of supplies, their dried fish and turtle meat, and their hopes afloat.

As they moved farther north, the rains came more frequently, and therefore thirst became less a problem than it had been. But the rain so welcomed by their parched throats and salt-encrusted bodies also brought a new peril. It could come in

Strange Helper

Three men aboard the *Reality,* a 40-foot sloop, were sailing from Maryland to the coastal town of Navarre in the Florida panhandle in January 1980 when the boat began to take on water, swamping so quickly that all the passengers could salvage was a raft, four life preservers, and a poncho.

For five days, 35-year-old Jerry Willis, Doug Dixon, 21, and Chris Napolitano, 19, drifted in the raft off the east coast of Florida with no drinkable water and no food. In the afternoon of the fifth day, as the raft bobbed in the ocean about 95 miles east of Jacksonville, the three weak, listless men were asleep when the raft suddenly bumped something.

Willis was the first to awake. The entire raft now was being jarred; something was ramming it. Willis dragged himself to the rounded rim of the raft. Staring back at him was the snout of a large shark, moving in again for an attack. One bite, Willis knew, and the inflatable raft would fizzle to nothing and they would be in the sea with this huge, probably hungry predator. He quickly grabbed his pocketknife, opened it, and plunged it into the shark just above the dorsal fin as it lunged again toward the raft.

The shark made a swift turn in the water and dived. At that moment, Willis, looking out across the great expanse of water, saw a freighter not too far in the distance. He and his friends began to shout and wave, the hope reviving some strength in all of them.

A mate on the deck of the *Exxon Lexington* saw the movement. A rescue party brought the three men aboard the freighter, and they were then taken to a hospital in Jacksonville to be treated for dehydration, hunger, and exposure. Willis said from his hospital bed, "If that shark hadn't attacked, we would never have seen the tanker. We were so weak from being without food or water that we never would have gotten up to see it, and it would have just glided on by." All three took comfort in the thought that help sometimes comes from unexpected, perhaps paradoxical, sources.

---

such torrential downpours that if they did not bail with almost superhuman efficiency their boat would be swamped. And bailing grew more difficult as they became weaker. The same water that was needed to sustain their lives could ironically be a death-dealing element of nature.

The next two weeks seemed interminable; yet somehow the little boat rode the swells and withstood the occasional battering of whitecaps from a stormy sea. The group grew steadily weaker, although food was still relatively plentiful. Robertson had fashioned fishing lines, baiting them with fish heads or offal, and was able to pull in a few fish himself to supplement those that continued to dive into the dinghy. He had also fashioned some gaffs for spearing fish that skimmed by near the surface. Turtles continued to venture up to the side of the boat and were duly hauled in. And on the 29th day, Robertson, with help from the others, landed the biggest catch of all, a five-foot Mako shark. Its meat proved to be the tastiest fish they had yet caught.

As they entered the fifth week of their ordeal, Robertson turned the corner with his little craft and began to sail east with the Doldrums toward land, although solid ground was still perhaps 400 to 500 miles away. Even with this glimmer of hope, there were growing problems—the patience of the weakened survivors was becoming shorter by the day and tempers were lost, and their grip on reality was loosening noticeably and threateningly.

It was late in the afternoon of the 38th day when everything finally changed. They were sailing along, talking about food—an unending topic of conversation among them— and the heavy cloud cover promised them rain, perhaps in the early eve-

ning. Robertson shook his head suddenly as his eyes caught an alien object out on the vast blue-green plane they were riding. "A ship!" he cried. And it was heading in their direction. As it closed on them, Robertson stood in the center of the dinghy and ripped the cap from a hand flare, its bedazzling red fountain of fire cutting through the gloomy afternoon. When it burned itself down, he threw it as high as he could and watched it arc into the air and then hit the water with a dying hiss. Another flare was passed to him, and he tried to ignite it, but it was a dud.

It didn't matter. The boat had changed its course slightly and was bearing directly down on them. They had been spotted. The ship was the *Toka Maru II*, a Japanese tuna fishing boat, and the crew lined its deck to throw out lines to the emaciated people in the dinghy. Robertson caught one of the lines and they were hauled alongside the ship and brought aboard. They had been adrift for 37 days, eight hours, and 40 minutes. But with incredible ingenuity they had managed to survive.

Surviving the MGM Grand Fire

This bizarre story of survival and death in the tragic 1980 fire at the MGM Grand Hotel in Las Vegas, Nevada, is told by Pulitzer Prize-winning journalist Tom Fitzpatrick, and is reprinted from the Chicago Sun-Times.

She was awake now. She could smell smoke. And she could hear the sounds of shattering glass. There was

pounding at the door of her hotel room. There was shouting, too.

Mary Palacios, 59, wife of the

Laredo, Texas, postmaster, was in a room on the ninth floor of the MGM Grand Hotel.

"Is this the way I'm going to die?" she remembers asking herself. "And I swear, if I knew what was going to happen to me during the next few hours, I would never have let myself wake up."

Palacios, who suffers from rheumatoid arthritis, making it difficult for her to walk or use her hands, had checked into the MGM the night before with a tour group from Laredo.

She speaks Spanish fluently so she knew that the men from another tour group from Guadalajara, Mexico, who were pounding on her door truly needed to get into the room so they could find fresh air to breathe.

Palacios quickly put on a pair of slacks and opened the door. The four men, none of whom could speak English, were terror-stricken.

"I told them not to worry," Palacios said. "I had to keep calm to keep them from panicking."

With the window open, there was enough air to breathe. And after a while, the firemen arrived.

Palacios remembers there were two of them and they looked like knights in shining armor despite the fact that they were covered with soot and wore oxygen masks over their faces.

They told Palacios that a ladder was being run up from the ground and soon would be anchored to the ninth floor. They told Palacios that she would have to climb down the ladder to the street. They assured her she'd make it but she must be careful.

Palacios remembers how efficient the firemen were. She remembers how sure of themselves they seemed. It made her feel better. But she never learned their names.

She remembers them signaling to the men from Guadalajara to come to the window and get on the ladder and begin the descent to the pavement nine stories below.

"I can understand why they were frightened," Palacios said. "They were in a strange country. They didn't understand the language. All they could understand was that some men in uniforms who didn't speak their language wanted them to risk their lives on a ladder."

The men refused to get on the ladder. Palacios tried her best to calm them.

"Look," she said. "It will be all right. These firemen know what they're doing. Even with my arthritis, I can make it. Watch me. It will be easy. Then you can follow."

One of the firemen picked Palacios off the floor and helped her over the ledge to the ladder.

Her hands have been so affected by arthritis that she could hold on to the ladder only by crooking her elbows around the two sides.

She put one foot on the ladder. Then she put her other foot on it. Just as she was putting her left foot down to the next rung she felt the ladder shudder and then it seemed like it was falling.

"I thought I was gone," Palacios said, "but the fireman held on to me. He pulled me back over the window again and into the room.

"My God," she told the fireman,

"I could have been a spot on the sidewalk."

The man who was to get on the ladder next groaned when he saw Palacios being pulled back through the window. He knew she had almost fallen to her death.

He slumped to the floor. Firemen tried to revive him with oxygen.

But he was dead.

"He died of fright," Palacios said. "I felt so sorry for him. It was just that he was so afraid of heights, I guess."

Palacios and the firemen and the other Mexican men put wet towels over their faces and began climbing the stairs toward the roof.

It was painful for her to walk. The firemen helped, sometimes virtually carrying her as the little group slowly made its way to the roof above the 26th floor.

"We walked around over bodies in the hallways," she remembers. "We kept stepping around them in the fire stairs that led to the roof."

And always there was the noise and the thick smoke that made it impossible to see more than two feet ahead. There was the panic, too, as they encountered others who were trying to run down the stairs while Palacios and her group were trying to go up.

Palacios will never forget the roof of the MGM Grand Hotel.

There was a sudden surge of noise and a blast of cold air as they opened the door and climbed onto the roof. And there was the overpowering sound made by the helicopter motors.

Helicopters. To Palacios, they seemed to be everywhere. And there was so much noise and confusion, it was impossible to think.

More importantly, the confusion was so great that Palacios had no power to resist when the firemen pushed her into a chair seat and strapped her in.

One fireman shouted in her ear: "Hold on as hard as you can. Your life depends on it."

Palacios looked directly over her head. She was strapped into the chair seat of an enormous military helicopter and now it was lifting into the air and she was in the air, too.

"I don't know how to describe it," she recalled. "I just knew I was going to swing back and forth and be bashed against the building. I was petrified. I couldn't use my hands to hold on. I just grabbed with the crooks of my elbows onto the lines. I can't describe how horrifying it was to look down and see everything so far below.

"I guess I'll become frightened every time I think of it. I'm afraid I'll dream about it for the rest of my life."

Forced Down in the Himalayas

This is the story of Flight Captain C. J. Rosbert, as told to William Clemens, a saga of survival in the desolate and primitive Himalaya Mountains. Captain Rosbert's incredible tale first appeared in Post True Stories of Daring and Adventure.

During World War II, while the famous Burma Road into southern China was in enemy hands, thousands of American transport pilots regularly flew the "hump" over the Himalayas from India with supplies for the beleaguered Chinese. Lumbering and overloaded, the unarmed transports faced constant danger from Japanese fighter planes.

But the hump pilots faced an even more remorseless foe: Himalayan weather. Once forced down among the forbidding and inaccessible peaks, few returned. Here is a story of two of those gallant men.

. . .

On our last flight from India we took off into a pea-soup fog, and a few minutes out of our base the monsoon rain was flooding down the windshield in torrents. At 12,000 feet the rain turned to snow. We couldn't see our wing tips. That meant we were safe. As well as the enemy liked to take potshots at us, no self-respecting combat pilot would fly in weather like that. With another few thousand feet, we'd be over the hump and the worst would be over.

My copilot, Charles "Ridge" Hammel, was a veteran of Pan American's famed "Africa Corps." A past master at desert flying, he distrusted this land of three-mile-high peaks.

With 17 other Flying Tigers, I had enlisted with Pan American Airways in the China National Aviation Corporation when the U.S. Army took over General Chennault's little squadrons. As our Douglas C-47 kept climbing with her heavy load, Ridge's face broke into a grin and he reached back to pat our Chinese radio operator, Li Wong, on the head.

"We're okay now," he reported. "Another thousand feet and we'll be clear of the hump. Another hour and you'll be home!"

But we couldn't get that last thousand feet. Even while Ridge had his back turned, I could see a thin layer of ice spreading over the windshield, then over the wings. In less time than it takes to tell it, that thin film grew into a layer six inches thick. We started to drop, not in a dive, but slowly. Then we lost the last slit of visibility. All the windows were frozen over solid from the inside. I pressed the palm of my bare hand up against the glass until I could feel the skin stick, then I switched palms. Just before both hands turned numb, I had managed to melt a little two-inch hole. I saw that we were passing through a cloud. Suddenly it opened and dead ahead loomed a jagged peak.

"Look out!" I yelled. "There's a mountain!" Grabbing the controls, with my eye still glued to the tiny opening, I swung the ship violently over into a bank. We missed the face of that cliff by inches. Then my heart stopped. A huge dark object swept by. A terrible scraping noise tore under the cabin; an explosive crash struck right behind me; the engines raced into a violent roar. Something stabbed my ankle, an intense pain shot through my left leg. Then, suddenly, we were not moving. Only the falling snow broke the silence.

I don't know how long I sat there before I heard Ridge's voice. It seemed to come from far away. "Get out of that thing before it catches fire!"

I heard my own voice answer, "Come on back in. You'll freeze to death out there."

My shocked brain told me the ship wouldn't burn. Both engines had been torn off when we hit. The cabin was intact, except for the radio station, which was crumpled like tissue paper. Wong lay sprawled in the aisle behind the cockpit. I struggled out of my seat to reach him. I held his wrist; there was no pulse. I put my arm under him, and a broken neck dropped his head back between his shoulders. . . .

I struggled to stay conscious. Nothing seemed very real. I tried a step, but my left ankle turned under me. The pain almost took my breath away. I looked down. I seemed to be standing on my leg bone, and my foot was lying at a right angle to it. Holding on to the roof supports, I swung myself down beside Ridge. For several minutes we just lay there looking at each other. . . .

We took stock of our situation.

The plane was lying at a 30-degree angle. Outside, a zero wind drove the snow in swirling gusts, but, by huddling close together, we could keep from freezing at night. The first rule of a crash is to stay by the ship. It's much easier for searching parties to spot a plane than it is to sight a person. In our case, we were both in such bad shape that we had no other choice. My leg was continually throbbing and even the slightest movement would send shocks of sickening pain through my whole body.

Ridge was only slightly better off. His left ankle pained him—it proved to be badly sprained—but he managed to move about. Dragging himself over and about a jumbled cargo of machinery, he found our parachutes, which we spread out to lie on. He also found six tins of emergency rations, equivalent to three meals apiece. We figured we could stretch these out for six days, possibly longer. . . .

By daylight, the snow had stopped. The scene almost took my breath away. Glistening, ice-encrusted peaks darted up all round us. Then I looked in the direction in which the plane had been headed, and yelled to Ridge. Together, we stared at the ugly, jagged peak. If we had gone another 50 feet we should have been crushed against it like an eggshell. Our steep bank away from the peak had miraculously paralleled the slope angle of the mountain, so that when we hit, the plane simply slid along the face of the cliff. . . .

We were perched 16,000 feet high, up against one of the peaks of the Himalayas somewhere in the Mishmi Hills, on the frontier of Tibet. We did not know in what direction we should head to get out, what we should look for, how we should plan. The slim chance of our being sighted by searching planes was buried under the two feet of snow which had covered the plane in the night. That meant we'd have to manage our own escape. . . .

In five days, we estimated, our ankles would have improved enough to allow us to move without blacking out every few steps. [They waited only three days.]

We knew we had to make it down to timberline before dark, because we could never live through a night on that unprotected slope. Our injured ankles turned under at every step, and we began to flounder. The slope was so steep that we kept falling, and the struggle to get on our feet again would sap every ounce of strength we could muster. In four hours of almost superhuman effort we had covered scarcely 200 yards. It was hopeless. We just managed to get back to the shelter of the plane with the last streaks of daylight.

Gripped with despair, we lay awake most of that night. We had only one full emergency meal left between us. We had to get down the mountain. But how? Finally, from sheer fatigue, we dozed off. I was awakened by Ridge, who was prying up one of the extra boards used to reinforce the floor. A sled! Now we were riding the crest of hopefulness again. Why hadn't we thought of that before? While it was still dark we pried braces off the side of the cabin and made splints. We tore our

parachutes into strips, bandaged our ankles, then set the splints and wrapped yards of the silk around them until our injured legs were fairly stiff. What was left we wrapped around our hands and feet for protection from the cold, except for two long runners which we used to strap ourselves to the sleds. By daylight we were on our way.

We literally flew for the first 100 yards, but when the slope flattened out, the ends of the boards plowed deep into the soft snow. The struggle to get off, pull them out, set them flat, pile on and get started again was almost as difficult as our walking had been. We threw away everything we could possibly get along without. Even that didn't help enough. Finally, Ridge got his board sliding, only to have it hit a rock and send him sprawling down the slope. He rolled 50 yards before he was able to stop. Inspired, I started rolling after him. I rolled 50 yards too. Then we hit upon a technique. Lying on our backs, holding our injured feet in the air, we slid on the seat of our pants, rolled over on our sides—sometimes on our heads—ten, 20, 50 yards at a time.

The slides grew steeper and steeper until, finally, within sight of timberline, we struck a slope that was almost 500 feet straight down. If getting out of the plane alive was a miracle, we both felt it would take another miracle to get down to the bottom alive. . . .

Soaking wet and so weary that we could scarcely move, we found a cave, so small that the two of us could only half fit onto it. We tried to make a fire by kindling some twigs with what papers we had with us—

our passports, photographs of my wife Marianne, my license cards, address book. In our anxiety to get a tiny bit of warmth, we destroyed every tangible bit of evidence we possessed to prove that we had a home, a family, a country. But the wood was soaked through and we gave up. We took off our wet outer clothes and hung them up, hoping they might dry during the night, and, with our arms around each other, we tried to get some rest.

Looking back on that ordeal now, I cannot see how we could have made it. With our bad ankles, the best we could manage was a painful hobble. We could not follow along the bank because, for the most part, the river flowed through walls of sheer solid rock. We could not use the river itself because it raced through boulder-strewn rapids and over deep falls. Our only chance was to climb over the rough, jungle-covered mountains, keeping the river in sight as best we could.

For three days we crawled up and down those tortuous hills, taking one half bite of our last remaining ration at daylight and dusk, huddling together on the ground at night. Near the end of the eighth day we had to turn back to the river. The peaks were too steep to climb. We struggled over and around the boulders, half in, half out of the water, until, suddenly, the river dropped off into a series of steep falls. It was impossible to go forward. On both sides the walls of the canyon were almost vertical. We were at the end of our strength. We had spread one day's normal emergency minimum over eight days, but had swallowed the last bit of the ration that morning.

Numb, unable to think it out, we sat down beside each other and stared at that solid rock wall. Suddenly, Ridge leaned forward. A long heavy wire or vine was hanging down the side of the cliff. We tried it for strength. It held. Someone had at least been up the river this far. Foot by foot, we pulled and clambered our way up the wall. At the top, we found another sign. Saplings had been notched as if to mark a trail. With lighter spirits than we had had in many days, we hobbled on, and for three days more we drove ourselves through the brush, over boulders, up and down the hills, looking for those all but indistinct marks.

Our first day without even a bite of food left us with an intense empty feeling. After 24 hours, the emptiness turned into a steady dull ache and a feeling of intense weakness which left us wondering, each night, how we could recover enough strength for the next day's march. We searched continually for anything we could get into our mouths. We tried most growing things with stalks or stems.

At the very peak of our hunger, however, another miracle befell us. I fished from the stream a piece of fruit which looked and smelled like a mango. The taste was indescribably vile; it seemed as if someone had struck me a blow in the mouth. I retched horribly and rolled on the ground in agony. But on the verge of starvation you will try anything. Ridge had to try a bite, too, and he went through the same torture. But there is some good in everything. Our stomachs were numb for the next three days. Even starving as we were, we could not bear the thought of food.

On the 13th day we reached the practical end of our endurance. The stream divided and went down two valleys, exactly opposite. Which way should we turn? Because we were facing east, we took that direction. Had we had the strength to think, we would have chosen the westward valley, since in that direction lay Burma and our course from India. To the east, we realized afterward, lay only the wild mountain frontier of Tibet.

That turn to the east was the fourth in our chain of miracles. After an hour, we broke into a clearing. The hut had been burned to the ground, but it was a sign that human beings had lived here. Somehow, we found new strength. Later in the afternoon we found the prints of a child's bare feet in the mud, and then, in the last few minutes of daylight, we dragged ourselves over a hill, and there was a thatched roof. The hut, made entirely of bamboo, stood on stilts about four feet above the ground. The door nearest us was securely latched. So was the center door. When we got no reply to our knock at the last door, Ridge threw himself against it and we sprawled inside. It was so dark and the air was so thick with smoke that we could scarcely see. A big pot was boiling over an open fire in the center of the room. Then we made out the huddled forms of two very old women to whom six nude, wild-looking children were clinging. At the sound of our voices, they appeared to be even more frightened. We tried our few

words of Chinese. Finally, by gestures, we tried to tell them that we were fliers and only wanted food, but the children kept pointing to the old ladies' eyes. One, we learned, was totally blind, the other almost so.

The children later gave us each a gourd. But instead of ladling out the food, one of the old women simply picked up the boiling-hot cooking pot in her bare hands and passed it around while each of us, and then the six children, scooped out a gourdful of the food. Ridge and I were so impressed with this witchery that, starving as we were, we momentarily forgot all about eating—until our gourds got so hot we had to set them on the floor. Almost immediately, with hot food inside and the hot fire outside, we rolled over on the hard bamboo floor and went sound asleep.

Eighteen hours later the hundreds of wood ticks we had attracted in our wanderings chewed us awake. Sunlight was streaming through the open door and some of the smoke had cleared. The faces and bodies of the women—such as showed outside the aged, ragged, blanketlike cloth they wore draped over one shoulder and around their middles—appeared to be encrusted with a lifetime's exposure to dirt and wood smoke. Their hair was long and coarse, and around their heads each wore a wide metal band.

It was on our third day there that the two oldest children disappeared. Late in the afternoon they returned with three men who stepped right out of the Stone Age. They had broad flat foreheads, cheekbones, and noses, and mops of long shaggy hair.

They did not even have sandals on their wide, strong feet, and their legs were bare to the thigh. Each wore a sleeveless leather jerkin that reached to a small loincloth, and carried a long swordlike knife on one hip and a fur-covered pouch on the other. These costumes were typical of all the Mishmi people we saw until we walked out of this strange world nearly a month later. Their long matted hair hung down over their shoulders, from each ear dangled an ornament made from silver coins, and chains of beads, animal teeth, and coins were draped about their necks. They were cheerful, hospitable, interested little men. . . .

After a while they left us, but our act must have made a hit. That same night two others arrived, one a young boy. From their pouch they offered us two eggs, a sweet potato, and a handful of boiled rice, and then invited us to come with them. . . .

Next day, after eight hours of struggling with tortured and bleeding feet over a primitive mountain trail that would have been covered in two hours by our native friends alone, we managed to reach the door of another hut, a bigger one. We fell onto the floor, exhausted.

When we woke, we discovered that friendly hands had carried us inside to a pallet in one corner of the big room. The three men who had brought us were here, and four others, apparently all of the same family. Fifteen women also lived in the house. In the two weeks we were there, Ridge and I never did get all the children counted.

There, in that primitive, smoke-filled hut, deep in the heart of the Himalayas, Ridge and I held court for two incredible weeks, receiving scores of these long-haired, leather-jerkined, bare-legged men of the Stone Age. Their implements were cut from wood or stone and, from what we could learn, they had never heard of Chinese or Indians, let alone Americans. After days on the trail and in their smoke-filled huts, we were as dark-skinned as they. It was not until Ridge felt strong enough to walk and had gone out in the rain that the natives discovered we were white. It produced some awe, at first, and then a curiosity which expressed itself in sly, quizzical looks from all except the children. . . .

They had many peculiar customs, but their one characteristic that never ceased to startle us was their imperviousness to certain kinds of pain. The men would sort through the red-hot coals with their bare hands to find a tinder with which to light their pipes. One of them, trying to get us to unwrap the bandages from our ankles to see what was under them, rubbed his hand over his own ankle in a gesture. For the first time, apparently, he discovered a large round bump, like a cyst, on his ankle bone. He simply drew his knife, sliced off the bump with one deft blow and, with the blood streaming down his foot, returned the knife to the scabbard and kept right on talking to us as though he had simply brushed away a fly.

What work was done was managed by the women. The men, for the most part, sat about the fire, which the women tended, conversing with much raucous laughter, smoking their long bamboo pipes, into which they would stuff dark, stringy, home-cured tobacco. . . .

Late one evening an elderly trader from the Tibetan hills, wearing a great wide bamboo hat and carrying an ancient flintlock musket over his shoulder, appeared. Two bearers lugged huge bags of lumpy red sand, which, we learned, was salt. We told him our story, which by this time had become a mechanical routine. The trader, who told us he had known a white man once and had seen others in his lifetime, wanted us to go with him. We explained that in about five days more our ankles would be strong enough, and then we would follow him. He seemed disappointed, and several times that evening came back to us, motioned for our pencil, which we used for one of our stock demonstrations. We did not want to part with what might be our only means of getting word back to civilization, so we shook our heads. Finally he gave up, signaled to his porters and disappeared into the night.

A few days later his son appeared, a fine-looking youngster wearing earrings and a necklace of large silver coins. With elaborate gestures he presented us with a chicken, a pinch of tea, and a bowl of rice from his bag, and then he, too, evidenced a peculiar interest in the pencil. To keep in his good graces, since his father might be the one to get word to the outside, I tore off a corner of my flying map and wrote: "We are two American pilots. We crashed into the mountain. We will come to your camp in five days."

He snatched the slip of paper from my hand and disappeared. We concluded that he wanted the note for a souvenir, and that in five days he would return to lead us to his father's hut. By noon on the fourth day he was back. Although obviously tired from a long, hurried march, he was beaming. He first sat cross-legged before us, took four eggs out of his pouch and presented them to us, then left the hut and returned with an envelope. It was a standard India state telegraph form sealed with wax. With hearts beating like trip-hammers, Ridge and I clawed the envelope open. It contained a message from Lieutenant W. Hutchings, the commanding officer of a British scouting column then about four days' march away. He was sending rations by the messenger, and a medical officer with aid would follow shortly. . . .

In an hour or so, the porters arrived with the supplies, and we shared cigarettes, matches, salt, and tea with everyone in the hut. The matches and white salt they put in their personal treasure pouches, the tea they brewed, and the cigarettes they smoked with a religious ritual, deeply inhaling each little puff. It was daylight before any of us in the hut slept. It was a night to celebrate.

It took Captain C. E. Lax, the British medical officer, two days longer to make the trip than the native messengers had required—days that seemed hundreds of hours long—but never was anyone made more welcome. He told us that no white man had ever set foot in this country before and, had it not been that the British column, because of the war, had penetrated even as close as four days' march, we might never have been found. It was one chance in a million, and we had hit it. . . .

It took 16 more days of hiking to get out of the mountains, but hiking on a full stomach, resting at night in shelters on grass pallets, swathed in blankets. Over the tough places, our little native helpers, who weighed 50 pounds less than either Ridge or I, carried us, resting in a sling swung from their foreheads. Up the sides of cliffs, along boulder-strewn river beds, on cable-slung bridges that Gurkha engineers built ahead of us over monsoon-fed raging torrents, these little men led or carried us until, finally, we reached the crest of the last mountain range. There, below us, in a lovely green valley on the banks of a great river, lay a little British frontier station, a sight as welcome as the skyline of New York.

The Galveston Hurricane: A First-Person Account

The worst natural disaster ever to strike the United States was the hurricane, tidal waves, and flood that devastated Galveston, Texas, in 1900. About 6,000 people perished in the catastrophe. One who survived to write about it was Isaac Monroe Cline, who gave us this first-person account in his book of memoirs, Storms, Floods and Sunshine. *Cline was also at one time the U.S. Weather Bureau's principal meteorologist.*

History does not record a greater disaster in the United States than that which occurred at Galveston, Texas, on September 8, 1900.

A tropical cyclone appeared early in September and was north of Cuba on September 3, passed through the straits of Florida on September 4 and 5, and traveled in a northwesterly direction through the Gulf of Mexico.

The cyclone was advancing toward the Texas coast at 12 miles per hour, while the winds near its center were of hurricane force and probably exceeded 100 miles per hour.

September 7 was an ideal day as far as weather was concerned, a calm before the storm, but long swells broke on the beach with ominous roaring, and these were building up a tide above the average height. I was up making observations at 5 A.M., September 8, and found the water coming in over the low parts of the city, with the tide 4½ feet above what it should have been.

Early on September 8, I harnessed my horse to a two-wheeled cart, which I used for hunting, and drove along the beach from one end of the town to the other. I warned people residing within three blocks of the beach to move to the higher portions of the city, that their houses would be undermined by the ebb and flow of the increasing storm tide and would be washed away. Summer visitors went home, and residents moved out in accordance with the advice given them. Some 6,000 lives were saved by my advice and warnings.

The swells sent out by the cyclone continued to increase in magnitude and frequency during September 8, and the storm tide rose rapidly. At 3 P.M. on September 8, the storm tide was eight feet on the automatic gauge.

I recognized at 3:30 P. M. that an awful disaster was upon us. I wrote a message to send to the chief of the weather bureau at Washington, D.C., advising him of the terrible situation, and stated that the city was fast going under water, that great loss of life must result, and stressed the need for relief.

I gave this message to my assistant, Joseph L. Cline, who, wading through water nearly to his waist, carried it to the telegraph office but found that all the wires were down. He then went to the telephone exchange and found that they had one wire to Houston that was working intermittently. The telephone company turned this line over to him, and after repeated efforts, he got the message through to the Western Union office in Houston just as this line went out, cutting Galveston off from the outside world and leaving it to the fury of the winds and storm tides.

As I could give no further warning nor advice, my services were terminated by the elements. There remained nothing else I could do to help the people. My wife and three little girls were in our home surrounded by the rapidly rising water, which already covered the island from the Gulf to the bay. In reality, there was no island, just the ocean with houses standing out of the waves that rolled between them.

I waded nearly two miles to my home through the water, often above my waist. Hurricane winds were driving timbers and slates through the air everywhere around me, splitting the paling and weatherboarding of houses into splinters, and roofs of buildings were flying through the air. My house had been built recently, structurally designed to withstand hurricane winds.

After a journey through horrors that were to become worse, I reached my home. Some 50 people had sought safety therein, among whom were the builders of the house and their families. The rapid rise in the storm tide soon forced us to the second story. Here we could see wreckage being tossed by the winds and waves, driven against buildings and breaking them to pieces.

Some of this wreckage hung around our house and formed a dam against which the water banked up to 20 feet above the ground, nearly ten feet higher than the storm tide. We probably would have weathered the storm, but a trestle one-quarter mile long, which the street railway had built out over the Gulf, was torn from its mooring, and the rails held it together as one long piece of wreckage.

The storm swells were pounding the other wreckage against our home. It held firm against these without trembling. But the street railway trestle was carried squarely against the side of the house. The breaking swells drove this wreckage against the house like a huge battering ram. The house creaked and was carried over into the surging waters and torn to pieces. As it went down, my brother, who had come to the house after sending the last message out of the city, stood with my two oldest children near a window, which had one large glass, and as the house commenced giving way, he knocked the glass out of the window and took the children out onto the piece of trestle that was pounding the house to pieces.

I, with my wife and baby, six years old, were in the center of the room. We were thrown by the impact into a triple chimney and were carried down under the wreckage to the bottom of the water. My wife's clothing was entangled in the wreckage, and she never rose from the water. I was pinned under the timbers and thought I would be drowned.

The last thought I remember that passed through my mind was this, "I have done all that could have been done in this disaster. The world will know that I did my duty to the last. It is useless to fight for life. I will let the water enter my lungs and pass on."

However, it was not my time to go. When I regained consciousness, I was floating with my body hanging between heavy timbers, which had pressed the water out of my lungs. A flash of lightning revealed my baby girl floating on wreckage a few feet away. I struggled out of the timbers and reached her. A few minutes later, during another flash, I saw my brother and my other two children clinging to wreckage. I took my baby and joined them on the floating debris. Strange as it may seem, these children displayed no fear, and we, in the shadow of death, did not realize what fear meant. Our only thought was how to win in this disaster.

While being carried forward by the winds and surging waters, through the darkness and terrific downpour of rain, we could hear houses crashing under the impact of the wreckage, hurled forward by the winds and storm tide, but this did not blot out the screams of the injured and dying. Well along in the night, a flash of lightning revealed a child, about four years old, floating on some wreckage with no one else near. We succeeded in rescuing her and placed her with my children. This battle of the storm lasted without interruption from 8:30 P. M. until 11:30 P. M., when the storm tide had receded so that the wreckage we were on touched ground at 28th Street and Avenue P. We spent the remainder of the night in a home near where we landed.

Sunday, September 9, came with a clear sky, a brilliant sunrise, almost a calm and quiet sea with low tide—a most beautiful day. But, oh, the horrible sights that greeted our eyes! The dead, scattered through and hanging out of the wreckage, drowned trying to escape or killed by flying timbers, were to be seen by the thousands—the babe in its mother's arms, riches and poverty side by side with garments torn to shreds, men and women who in health and strength only 24 hours before had looked forward to the future with life's fondest hopes, now dead.

Eddie Foy at the Iroquois Theater

Eddie Foy, a comedian and vaudevillian, had the lead role in a lavish revue entitled Mr. Bluebeard *at the Iroquois Theater in Chicago on December 30, 1903. At the matinee that afternoon, a more-than-capacity crowd in excess of 2,000 people filled the seats and standing room of the theater. Then a fire broke out on stage, and panic raced through the audience.*

Eddie Foy, later dubbed a hero for his efforts to calm the crowd while the stage around him was in flames, here tells the story of the disaster in his own words.

Just before I came on for the second act I heard a commotion on the stage. I got out and saw that up on the fly [the apparatus and walkways above the stage] the border on the big drop had caught fire from a light or wire. The border was muslin, and the fire crept, crept, crept, while the noise on the stage grew louder, and the people began screaming and running. My boy was at the stage door entrance, and as they wouldn't let me go out in front, I grabbed him and gave him to a man, and he rushed him to the outside.

Up in the flies were the German aerial ballet. They were up at the top of the theater, with nothing to bring them down but the elevator. There were about 12 girls up there where the fire was going. On the stage there were 16 girls who were singing *Pearly Moonlight*. They tried to finish the song, but the music stopped and the singers screamed and ran off.

Someone was yelling "Get a stick. Knock it with a pole," referring to the section burning above. But no one did.

Then I ran out on stage. I went out to the footlights half-dressed, with only my tights on, and called to the people to keep quiet. "Don't get excited," I cried. "Don't stampede. It's all right." Then I called to the man to drop the asbestos curtain, and told the leader of the orchestra to play the overture. He stood up, white as a ghost, and beat his baton, but only a few men played. They had lost their heads and were too frightened. The roar from the fire, the stamp of feet rushing to the outside, and the screams of the women drowned out the music. It was like a penny whistle against the north wind.

Then I called to the policeman: "Tell them to go out slowly, to leave the theater slowly." By this time the whole border was on fire. The boy who ran the fly elevator took it up just about into the flames and rescued all the aerialists up there. It was a very brave thing to do.

Then the narrow strips of the wood cracked with a small explosion, and the whole back of the stage was in flames.

The fire curtain had come only halfway down. Maybe the man up in the gallery didn't dare to stay. If the asbestos curtain had come down it would have saved the people in the front of the house, I think.

How did they act in the audience? When I started to talk about 300 people got out in advance, safe, and others were getting out. Then the police came in and tried to stop them. After that, I wasn't there 12 seconds, maybe 15. I'd stayed as long as I could but I was afraid when the scramble came to the back of the stage that my boy Bryan, only six years old, would be hurt.

Eddie Foy survived the Iroquois Theater disaster and so did his son and several hundred others as a result of his actions. But 602 people were killed and hundreds of others were injured.

Cruising on the *Andrea Doria*

On the night of July 25, 1956, the Andrea Doria, an Italian luxury liner carrying 1,709 passengers and crew, was on her way from Genoa, Italy, to New York when she collided with the Swedish-American liner Stockholm in dense fog off the coast of Nantucket. The Stockholm was able to navigate back to New York, but the Andrea Doria, irreparably damaged, had to be evacuated. It finally sank 11 hours after the collision and after everyone had been removed from it. Harrison E. Salisbury, then a writer for the New York Times, reported the misadventures of some of the famous and not-so-famous passengers on that ill-fated ship.

Tales of bravery and sudden tragedy in the night were told yesterday by many of the 760 survivors of the *Andrea Doria* who arrived on the *Ile de France.*

The accent in the stories of the passengers was upon heroism. Apparently there was a minimum of panic and confusion aboard ship.

Because it was the ship's last

night out, many passengers had not retired when the *Stockholm* struck. Many of them cited this as a reason for the comparatively low death toll. Some returned to their cabins to find the walls crushed by the sudden impact of the collision.

One of the most tragic stories was that of Colonel Walter G. Carlin, a prominent Brooklyn Democratic political figure, and his wife.

The Carlins occupied Cabin 46 on the upper deck. It was here that the main brunt of the *Stockholm's* blow was felt.

Shipboard friends of the Carlins, Mr. and Mrs. Alfred Green of New Rochelle, had invited [the Carlins] to join them in the lounge for a drink. But the Carlins were tired and declined. Mrs. Carlin had retired and was reading in her bed. Mr. Carlin was brushing his teeth toward the. end of a fairly long corridor leading from the cabin.

At that moment the collision occurred. Mr. Carlin was knocked from his feet. When he picked himself up, dazed, and made his way toward the cabin, the Greens reported, he saw nothing but a gaping hole. The side of the ship had been sheared off and Mrs. Carlin had vanished, apparently a victim of the tragedy.

Narrow escapes were common. Istvan Rabovsky and his wife, Nora Kovach, ballet dancers who fled from their native Hungary in a spectacular crossing of the Iron Curtain, again came close to tragedy. They occupied a cabin not far from that of the Carlins and had retired before the shock came.

Both rushed to the promenade deck in their underclothes. They reported—as did many passengers—that there was considerable smoke in the area where the ship was hit.

Ruth Roman, the motion picture actress, was returning from Italy with her 3½-year-old son, Dickie. She was dancing in the Belvedere Room when "we heard a big explosion like a firecracker." She said she saw smoke coming from the general area of her cabins, 82 and 84, but when she reached there her son was fast asleep.

Miss Roman and a companion, Mrs. Grace Ellis, awoke the boy and told him: "We are going on a picnic."

There was a considerable wait for lifeboats. Finally, Miss Roman handed the boy over to seamen who lowered him to a boat. She started to climb down a rope ladder to join the boy, but when she was halfway down the lifeboat pulled away. She shouted but it continued away from the *Andrea Doria*.

She was put on the next lifeboat and had received no further word of her youngster as he apparently was put aboard another rescue boat.

Miss Roman was convinced her son was safe. She said she thought he probably would get a thrill out of the excitement without realizing the danger in which he had been.

There were several Roman Catholic sisters aboard the *Andrea Doria*. Among them were Sister Marie Raymond, Grand Rapids, Michigan, and Sister Mary Callistus, London, Ontario, returning after a year of music studies in Florence.

The sisters, traveling together in cabin class, said that a moment after the impact "we heard screaming."

"We had no idea what had happened," one said. "We put on our clothes and our life preservers and got on the deck. We had had boat drill and we went to our muster stations. The people were marvelous. There was a steward there and he made everyone feel very secure. They took off the women and children first. The children were taken by the seamen who tied them together for safety."

Among the passengers also was a group of executives of the Standard Oil Company (New Jersey). They included Dr. Stewart Coleman of Cedarhurst, Long Island, and his family, [and] Marion W. Boyer of Greenwich, Connecticut, and his wife, both directors of the concern; and H. G. Burks, Jr., of Elizabeth, New Jersey, and his wife.

"We were playing bridge on the boat deck when the crash occurred," Mr. Burks said. "It was a substantial jar and it knocked down tables and drinks. We headed for our cabins, which were away from the collision area."

Mr. Burks said his party picked up coats and life preservers and went to the deck. The vessel was listing sharply to starboard.

"We took a place where we thought we would be clear if the ship sank," Mr. Burks said. "After a time the rescue boats arrived and began to take the ladies and children off."

Mr. Burks said the *Andrea Doria* crew behaved well. However, he criticized the failure of the ship's management to make any announcement in English of what had happened.

"It was bad to be left in the dark so far as any official word of what was going on was concerned," he said. "However, both crew and passengers were very orderly."

The bridge party in which the Burks were participating at the moment of the accident included Dr. Coleman and Dr. and Mrs. R. B. Boggs, Manhasset, New York.

Morris Novik, president of radio station WOV, New York, and his wife were in the Belvedere Room at the time of the accident.

The orchestra, Mr. Novik recalled, was playing "Arrivederci Roma."

"They had been playing that tune all night," Mr. Novik said. "They had just started again when the crash came. At first it didn't seem too bad. Of course the tables went over and drinks were spilled."

The fog was very heavy at the time of the crash, Mr. Novik said. By the time the *Ile de France* arrived the fog had lifted a bit and the moon had come out.

Mr. Novik said that the *Andrea Doria* had listed so badly that it was extremely difficult to get people down to the boats.

"We formed chains of hands on the deck," he said, "and passed the women down the chain until a member of the crew picked them up and helped them over the side and down the ladder."

Mayor Richardson Dilworth of Philadelphia and his wife occupied Cabin 80 on the upper deck. The *Stockholm* plowed into the *Andrea Doria* about 60 to 70 feet ahead of the Dilworths' cabin.

"We were in our cabin asleep,"

the mayor said. "The crash not only awoke us—it threw us face to face. Thank God the lights stayed on. We threw on some clothes. There was a lot of smoke in the hall. We had to crawl down the passageway and up the gangways because the boat had tilted so badly. It must have taken us 20 minutes to climb up to the boat deck."

Mayor Dilworth said it was extremely difficult to get the lifeboats off because of the extreme list.

"The decks were like skating rinks," he said. "Half the passengers were over 45. It was quite wonderful to see how they reacted without panic and without pushing around. Quite a few people got broken arms on the slippery decks. Mrs. Dilworth was badly bruised."

Mrs. Ellen Dean of Baltimore said she was in the ballroom, dancing.

"I happened to look out the window," Mrs. Dean said, "and there was another ship. It was right on top of us. A moment later it struck us. I could see its lights and everything. The rails almost touched ours. It was the *Stockholm.*"

Betsy Drake, actress wife of Cary Grant, emerged from the disaster in her stocking feet.

"I was getting ready for bed," she said, "when there was a big bang. Everything flew across the room. My cabin was on the boat deck. I got dressed and found the decks very difficult and slippery. Finally one of the sailors told me to get into a boat and I slid down the deck to the ladder."

A Boat Person's Story

This is the first-person account of Tran Hue Hue, a Vietnamese teenager who fled her homeland in 1978 as one of the "boat people." Her journey began aboard a flimsy vessel with 50 others who sought escape from the troubled poverty of Vietnam. The boat ran onto a coral reef in the South Pacific and was wrecked. During the next 144 days all the other Vietnamese perished; only Tran Hue Hue survived to tell of the terrible ordeal. She was rescued from the reef by a group of fishermen from the Philippines in 1979. Her story appears by permission of The Associated Press.

"To start on this journey is to accept death," my mother warned us as we made our secret preparations to leave Vietnam.

Death soon took my elder brother, my aunt, and 47 others, leaving me alone on the rotting hulk of a wrecked boat with only the sea gulls for food and company. I, too, awaited death.

We had begun our journey aware of the dangers of the sea. My whole family was impatient to leave, our resolve strengthened each time we heard over the BBC radio that other groups of Vietnamese had landed their boats in a free country.

My father was a watch seller in Can-tho, but the Communist authorities had confiscated his supplies. We feared the whole family would be sent to a new economic zone, where life was very hard. My elder brother, Trung, had been notified he would soon be drafted into the army.

I was 17 and tired of life under the watchful eyes of the Communist cadre who distrusted us because we were capitalists.

[On] September 12, [1979,] our gold bribes brought results. We were told to meet that evening at the Ninh Kieu bridge and take sampans to a boat anchored at a sandbar down the river. We made a farewell visit to our ancestors' tombs in the cemetery and burned incense on the altars to ask their pardon for leaving our homeland.

We left the rendezvous in small groups, my elder brother and I pretending to be lovers as we walked hand in hand toward the bridge. But my father, mother, and two younger brothers did not make it to the boat in time. Even though I wept loudly in protest, the captain weighed anchor at midnight. I knew I would never see them again.

"Calm yourself, child," my aunt, Cam Binh, who had come aboard earlier, ordered.

The rain pelted us during the night as the boat had no roof. At daylight I saw we were on an immense ocean with no sign of land.

There were 50 people on board, mostly ethnic Chinese. We traveled for six days, bailing water from our leaking craft much of the time and praying that the sputtering engine would keep going. Three large ships sailed by without stopping.

Our boat drifted onto a coral reef on the evening of September 18, and started sinking. Even though no land was visible we did see a large white ship and believed rescue was imminent. But next day we discovered the white ship also had been wrecked on the reef and was abandoned.

Those who could dive for the large oysters around the reef ate well for a few days. Those who couldn't ate scraps because the food was not equally shared. But the oysters were quickly depleted. Four men, leaving their wives and children behind, were put on a crude raft, given a little milk and water, and sent to find help. They were never seen again.

A few days later everyone walked across the submerged reef to the white ship and with difficulty pulled themselves up the steep ladders to the deck. A larger black vessel was visible in the distance, and beyond that ships could sometimes be seen sailing past. But they never did acknowledge our signals of burning clothing.

After ten days on the white ship my aunt Cam Binh died of hunger and exhaustion. She told me, "Remind grandmother to offer food for my soul." She died silently in a night dark with distress. The others watched, motionless. Someone sighed deeply. Through my tears I could see that Aunt Binh looked awfully thin, a dried corpse sticking to the floor of the ship. She was the first to die.

We tied her corpse to a large board and wrapped around her arm a long strip of white cloth on which we had written in Vietnamese and English, "We are 50 persons, stuck on a coral islet. Please help us. SOS." We pushed the cargo into the water, but the board soon broke and Aunt Binh disappeared.

Two days after her death, a two-year-old girl died of diarrhea. The mother soon followed her. The number of deaths quickly increased. There were days when five or six of us died. The survivors were scared of the dead no longer, with the young men throwing the corpses into the sea like robots.

At night I would hear my companions crying out in their nightmares, "A ship's coming to save us."

It was my brother Trung's turn to have diarrhea. He grew weaker every day, and pain and despair cut deep lines in his face. One early morning he asked me to help him on deck to relieve himself, and then he told me, "Hue, I'm too hungry. Ask around for a piece of dried oyster for me."

Just as I turned, he jumped into the sea. I shouted, "My God, why do you leave me, Trung? Don't you love me?" I threw myself on the deck and wept. Every kind of hardship had befallen me.

After Trung went away I didn't eat and just lay in the cabin weeping, but then our number was down to only seven, and we grew to love each other and share.

We tried one day to reach the larger black ship. But when the tide rose higher and the wind blew stronger we had to go back. I could see sharp spikes of coral and rocks through the green water. The last boy and girl to reach the ladder on our ship were swept away by a wave.

There were five left now. Three women, Huong, 35, Lan, 18, and me, and two boys, Cuong, 18, and Quan, 14. We slept in the same corner and treated one another as blood relatives.

We were no longer a crowd on the ship, and the sea gulls came back. Some nights we caught as many as 20 birds and dried some for the days when we caught none.

But soon we began to weaken. Whenever I wanted to stand up, someone would have to help me. We walked with our hands on the walls. Then we could only crawl on our hands and knees. We could no longer perform the civilized act of bathing in sea water.

Most of us began talking nonsense all day long. Huong died, and a few days later Lan insisted that she go to the black ship. No one stopped her. As we sat there watching, a wave carried her away.

One night Cuong died after saying: "Try to wait. After I die I will call a ship to rescue you." I looked at Quan. He looked at me. Our eyes seemed to ask, who's next?

Nine days after Cuong's death, Quan died in his sleep. I didn't know exactly when. When I tried to wake him in the morning he was dead. I was in a panic, thinking I would have to live alone on this phantom ship, and I cried aloud for a long time.

Around me there was nothing but

dreadful silence. I was not scared of ghosts or demons, not even of Quan's body lying beside me. I was scared of loneliness.

Who was going to talk to me? Who was going to catch sea gulls with me? These thoughts made me cry more.

The sun began to shine, and Quan's face grew paler and paler. His hollow cheeks made his teeth show. With all my strength I sat up, pulled the corpse by its two cold feet to the deck and then let him drop into the sea.

Living by myself, I usually sat up late at night catching sea gulls. They were strong birds that fought back, tearing pieces of skin from my hands. But I never let loose.

There were days when I didn't catch a single bird, and lying there with my stomach empty I would dream of food. One night I found myself sitting with Mom, Dad, and my brothers enjoying a meal of fish cooked by my grandmother, and from then on I always had an excellent meal in my dreams.

Every day I watched for a ship. By now I no longer was scared of death. I sometimes prayed: "If I am sinful, let me die at once. But if I am not sinful, then bring a ship here and don't let me live in prolonged torture."

One night, in a dream, I heard the voices of Cuong and Quan shouting, "Wake up, Hue, a ship is coming tomorrow." It was raining, but I thought I heard an engine. I stood upright for the first time in days and ran out of the cabin. I saw a ship and I waved a white shirt as it came closer. Drops of water were coming down my face from the rain and I touched them lightly, thinking this was just another dream.

But then 19 men were on board and I pointed to myself and said, "Vietnam." I saw that their hair was wavy, and they were tall and dark-skinned. To my questioning eyes, they replied, "Filipinos."

They used sign language to tell me to follow them but my legs were sagging. They carried me in their arms. Everybody on the ship looked at me in surprise, but their eyes were tender. They laughed when I chewed gluttonously on the rice and sugar they gave me, but I was so hungry I was not ashamed.

We searched for my companions but none could be found. I stayed on the Filipino ship for 15 days before landing on Palawan Island. I saw a wall calendar dated February 18, 1979, and I thought, "How could I have lived for so long?"

A week later I was taken to the province capital of Puerto Princesa, where a crowd of Filipinos surrounded me at the airport. I could not understand what they were saying, but then a thin, dark man asked me in Vietnamese, "Are you Hue? My name is Bao. I'm also a Vietnamese refugee. Don't worry."

I was so happy. I hadn't been speaking for so long that my tongue grew stiff. I could not find words to express my happiness.

The sun was high in the sky. I was finding my confidence again. I and other Vietnamese had left our country ready to die along the way. We were seeking freedom. I had lost too much, but I could see beautiful days in the future. My life, my future, would begin from now.

A Long Raft Trip

On November 23, 1942, a British merchant ship, the SS *Ben Lomond*, was torpedoed and sunk by a German U-boat 565 miles off the west coast of central Africa. On board, a steward named Poon Lim, from Hainan Island, off the south coast of China, leaped from the burning deck into the Atlantic Ocean and swam away from the fast-sinking ship. Kept afloat by a Mae West for two hours, he finally spotted a life raft amid the ship's flotsam and jetsam. He climbed aboard it and began what was to become the longest recorded survival at sea by a lone shipwrecked person.

On board the eight-foot-square raft, Poon Lim found a small survival kit, which included a container of fresh water, food tins (mostly biscuits), rope, a flashlight, and several flares. With that meager store, he drifted at the whim of the ocean currents and the winds for the next 133 days.

After several weeks of careful rationing, he exhausted all the food and water from the survival pack. So he used his life jacket to collect rainwater to drink; the wires in his flashlight for hooks to catch fish to eat; and the entrails of the fish to lure sea gulls to his raft, capturing them with his hands after they landed and killing them.

On April 5, 1943, he sighted a fishing boat and was able to attract the attention of the men aboard it. He did not understand the strange language of the Brazilian fishermen but ashore soon learned that he had floated all the way across the equatorial expanse of the Atlantic Ocean and had been rescued only a few miles off the coast of Brazil. During the 4½-month ordeal, he had lost only 20 pounds and was able to walk ashore under his own power.

Poon Lim's response to his world record: "I hope no one will ever have to break it."

Epilogue

The Limit of Human Daring: An Adventurer's View

Octavie LaTour, a circus performer during the first decade of the 20th century, was also a self-proclaimed adventurer of the first rank.

Monsieur LaTour lived during a period when the most intrepid and inquisitive people of civilized lands were deeply committed to the exploration of remote and forbidding regions—the darkest parts of Africa, the wastelands of the Arctic and the Antarctic, the primitive islands of the South Pacific, the jungles and rain forests of South and Central America. But to Monsieur LaTour, adventure was not restricted to the distant, the mysterious, and the foreign. He found adventure in practically every aspect of his own world, the "modern" one, as he described it. The possibilities for bold and perilous undertakings were everywhere—he even found an unusual adventure in New York City, which he denoted as "subwaying."

"Human daring has but one limit: human imagination," he wrote in the New York *World* in April 1905.

> There is the class of the professionally brave, so-called, to which I belong. Our function is to satisfy the public taste for a certain form of excitement that comes from witnessing dangerous feats; the sensation of beholding some human being grappling with death in a hair-raising spectacle relieves the humdrum of modern life.
>
> Courage, not merely moral courage that copes with ethical problems and wins the battles of the soul, but physical courage, is a primitive instinct with us humans. Persons who are not called upon to be brave themselves satisfy their natural inclinations with the admiration of another's thrilling feat.
>
> So we professional heroes and heroines fill a necessary bill in life's vaudeville. We foster the spirit of bravery and daring, and we risk our lives every day and think no more of it, probably less, than a lawyer does of his case at the bar.
>
> And there is nothing too daring to attempt. Demand what feat you will that requires physical skill and physical courage, and we in the circus will attempt it. Nay, we will perform it successfully.
>
> At present I am courting death each day in *La Tourbillon De La Mort*, the supposed limit of human daring. But this act of plunging down the steep incline in an automobile that turns a back somersault in midair and lands on a runway is not really the limit

of human daring. It is only the most perilous act that human imagination has so far devised for human daring. But it is the limit for only a moment. . . .

The trouble is not in finding people with courage to perform the feats, but in working out a stunt more terrible than anything ventured before, that will menace life and all but take it. For hairbreadth as escape must seem, the probability of accident must be really small. . . .

So get your minds fermenting: Give your imagination free play; and invent the real limit of human daring. Show us how to fly to the moon; direct the way to Mars; point the signboards down the roads of human daring. And I for one will go.

An Adventure Sourcebook

On the following pages are listed a wide range of associations, societies, clubs, firms, and publications that provide information and services and offer unique opportunities for do-it-yourself adventurers.

Adventure Vacations

Action Vacations
Times-Mirror Magazines
380 Madison Avenue
New York, NY 10017

Outward Bound
384 Field Point Road
Greenwich, CT 06830

Founded: 1962

Operates schools for wilderness survival training in 17 countries throughout the world; there are seven in the United States. Courses last from four to 26 days.

Sierra Club Outing Dept.
Box 7959, Rincon Annex
San Francisco, CA 94120

See also Sierra Club listings under **Backpacking and Camping** and **Mountain Climbing.**

Archaeology

Archaeological Institute of America
53 Park Place, 8th Floor
New York, NY 10007

Founded: 1879
Members: 7,500
Publications:
　American Journal of Archaeology
　　(quarterly)
　Archaeology (bimonthly)
　Field Opportunities Bulletin (annual)

Composed of archaeologists and other people interested in archaeological research and study. Has founded schools of archaeology in Athens, Rome, the Middle East, and Santa Fe, New Mexico, and is allied with research centers in Turkey and Egypt. Distributes career booklet, offers counseling program and lecture series.

Adventure Travel North America

The easiest way to find out where to go to take part in outdoor adventures in North America is to first look in the pages of a unique book called *Adventure Travel North America*, by Patricia Dickerman, published by Adventure Guides Inc., 36 East 57th Street, New York, NY 10022. Its 27 chapters describe the offerings and provide addresses of all the major facilities, schools, outfitters, expeditions, and guides who cater to the public's whims for adventure on land, water, or in the air. The book is updated periodically. Among the adventures covered:

backpacking	jeeping	scuba diving
ballooning	jet boating	ski touring
biking	mountaineering	snorkeling
canoeing and kayaking	nature expeditions	snowmobiling
cattle drives	pack trips by horse	snowshoeing
covered wagon trips	parachuting	soaring
dog sledding	river running	spelunking
hang gliding	rock climbing	wilderness living
horse trekking	rock hounding	windjammer cruising
houseboating	sailing	

Institute of Nautical Archaeology
Drawer AU
College Station, TX 77840

Founded: 1973
Members: 424
Publication: *Newsletter*

For those interested in the past as revealed in the sea and in marine activities.

Society for American Archaeology
c/o J. E. Ayres
1702 East Waverly
Tucson, AZ 85719

Founded: 1935
Members: 5,513
Publications:
  American Antiquity (quarterly)
  Special Publications (irregular)

For professionals, nonprofessionals, and students interested in American archaeology. On request, it guides the research work of amateurs.

Aviation

Aircraft Owners and Pilots Association
7315 Wisconsin Avenue
Bethesda, MD 20014

Founded: 1939
Members: 220,000
Publications:
  AOPA Airports—U.S.A. (annual)
  AOPA Newsletter (monthly)
  AOPA Pilot (monthly)

This organization works to make flying safer, more enjoyable, and less expensive. It conducts safety and flight-training programs and sponsors research aimed at its goals.

American Institute of Aeronautics and
  Astronautics
1290 Avenue of the Americas
New York, NY 10019

Founded: 1963
Members: 27,000
Publications:
  Astronautics & Aeronautics (monthly)
  International Aerospace Abstracts (semimonthly and semiannual)
  Journal (monthly)
  Journal of Aircraft (monthly)
  Journal of Energy (bimonthly)
  Journal of Guidance & Control
    (bimonthly)

Journal of Hydronautics (quarterly)
Journal of Spacecraft and Rockets
  (monthly)
Roster (biennial)
Student Journal (quarterly)
Technical papers, reports

An organization of scientists and engineers in the aeronautic, astronautic, and hydronautic fields who exchange technological information through meetings and publications. Has a technological information service, library service, abstracting service. Holds an annual convention.

Experimental Aircraft Association
P.O. Box 229
Hales Corners, WI 53130

Founded: 1953
Members: 70,000
Publications:
  Amateur Aircraft Builders Manual
  Chapter Bulletin (monthly)
  Designee Newsletter (monthly)
  Sport Aerobatics (monthly)
  Sport Aviation (monthly)
  The Vintage Airplane (monthly)
  Warbirds (monthly)

For individuals interested in building or improving their own aircraft through experimentation and home engineering. Promotes the construction of airplanes in high school industrial arts classes and the use of aircraft for sport and recreation. Maintains an Air Museum and a library of more than 5,000 volumes. Annual fly-in convention, aircraft exhibit, and air show the first week of August in Oshkosh, Wisconsin.

National Aeronautic Association
821 15th Street, NW
Washington, DC 20005

Founded: 1905
Members: 160,000
Publications:
  Directory and Journal of Aerospace
    Education
  Newsletter (monthly)
  World & USA National and Aviation-
    Space Records (revised quarterly)

This organization is the governing and supervisory body for all official sporting aviation competitions in the United States. It keeps the official world records in aeronautics and astronautics, model flying, gliding and soaring, parachuting, hang gliding, and helicopters. Makes annual major aviation awards.

Backpacking and Camping

American Camping Association
Bradford Woods
Martinsville, IN 46151

Founded: 1910
Members: 6,000
Publications:
  Camping (seven per year)
  Parents Guide to Accredited Camps
    (annual)
  Books on ecology, canoeing, camp
    nursing

Offers a certification program in outdoor living skills. Provides information of interest to camp directors, counselors, camp owners, and individuals interested in organized camping. Maintains a 5,000-volume library and holds an annual meeting.

International Backpackers Association
P.O. Box 85
Lincoln Center, ME 04458

Founded: 1973
Members: 20,000
Publications:
  Directory of American Foot Travelers
    Club Associations & Agencies
  The Trail Voice (quarterly)

The organization promotes activities such as backpacking, mountaineering, hiking, bike and ski touring, and snowshoeing. It encourages protection of national resources, organizes volunteer maintenance of trails, and offers schools in backpacking, camping, and hiking. Maintains its own library and holds an annual convention.

National Campers and Hikers Association
7172 Transit Road
Buffalo, NY 14221

Founded: 1954
Members: 52,000 families (200,000
  individuals)
Publications:
  NCHA News in Woodall Travel Trailer
    (monthly)
  Tent and Trail Bulletin (quarterly)

Disseminates information on outdoor activities and conservation, especially for family campers and hikers. Seeks to improve camping and hiking facilities and establish regional information centers. Aids YMCA and colleges in giving short courses on camping and outdoor recreation. Holds annual convention.

North America Family Campers Association
Box 87
Manchester, CT 06040

Founded: 1957
Members: 4,000
Publications:
  Campfire (25 per year)
  Campfire Chatter (monthly)
  NAFCAgram (irregular)

Sponsored by manufacturers and dealers of camping equipment. Offers information on campsites, equipment, and techniques. Encourages development of campgrounds and improvement of camping conditions.

Sierra Club
530 Bush Street
San Francisco, CA 94108

Founded: 1892
Members: 199,000
Publications:
  National News Report (weekly)
  Sierra Club Bulletin (monthly)
  Books, films, posters

An organization for those interested in learning more about nature and preserving national resources and environment. Conducts campaigns to educate the public, to preserve and restore the environment, and to save threatened natural areas. Holds biennial Wilderness Conferences.

Skyline Hikers of the Canadian Rockies
P.O. Box 3514, Station B
Calgary, AB, Canada T2M 4M2

Founded: 1933
Publication: Skyliner (two or three per
  year)

Encourages hiking in the Canadian Rockies. Members are those who have taken a hike sponsored by this nonprofit association. Each summer the Skyline Hikers sponsor five six-day hikes in a national park in the Canadian Rockies. The organization holds an annual convention.

Trail Riders of the Canadian Rockies
P.O. Box 6742
Postal Station D
Calgary, AB, Canada T2P 2E6

Founded: 1923
Publications: Newsletters and brochures

Sponsors horseback rides into remote areas of the Canadian Rockies. Members are those who have participated in one of the trips. The group works to promote construction of new trails in the Canadian Rockies and to maintain and improve those already in use. Holds an annual convention.

Trail Riders of the Wilderness
American Forestry Association
1319 18th Street, NW
Washington, DC 20036

Founded: 1933
Publication: *Trail Riders of the Wilderness* (annual)

The American Forestry Association works to educate the public on wilderness areas of the United States and the need to conserve them, and conducts horseback expeditions into wilderness areas.

Wilderness Society
1901 Pennsylvania Avenue, NW
Washington, DC 20006

Founded: 1935
Members: 50,000
Publications:
  Annual Report
  The Living Wilderness (quarterly)
  The Wilderness Report (35 per year)

This organization is for individuals interested in preserving the wilderness. It encourages scientific studies of wilderness and issues alerts on critical issues involving threats of destruction of wilderness areas.

Ballooning

Balloon Federation of America
821 15th Street, NW, Suite 430
Washington, DC 20005

Founded: 1961
Members: 2,000
Publications:
  Ballooning (bimonthly)
  Membership List (annual)
  Pilot News (monthly)

For hot-air and gas balloonists who either own their own balloons or belong to clubs that do. Sponsors and supervises official ballooning events, promulgates rules, documents record ascents, and maintains ballooning museum and film library.

Bicycling

Cyclists Touring Club
69, Meadrow
Godalming, Surrey GU7 3HS England

Founded: 1878
Members: 41,000
Publications:
  Cycle Touring (bimonthly)
  Handbook (annual)

Provides touring information, maps, routes, recommended accommodations, insurance, and legal aid. Composed of 200 local groups.

International Bicycle Touring Society
2115 Paseo Dorado
La Jolla, CA 92037

Founded: 1964
Members: 1,000
Publications:
  Newsletter (quarterly)
  Tour Listings (annual)

Open only to men and women over 21. Arranges bicycle tours, led by volunteers and lasting one to three weeks, in the United States and abroad. Participants must be able to cycle 50 miles a day.

League of American Wheelmen
P.O. Box 988
Baltimore, MD 21203

Founded: 1880
Members: 16,000 in 393 local groups
Publications:
  American Wheelmen Magazine (monthly)
  Annual Directory

An organization of persons of all ages interested in bicycling. Sponsors cycling programs, events, rides, and tours. Collects maps of cycle routes in all states and provides an information service.

Birdwatching

American Birding Association
P.O. Box 4335
Austin, TX 78765

Founded: 1969
Members: 4,500
Publications:
  Birding (bimonthly)
  Checklist (irregular)
  Directory (irregular)

Promotes the hobby and sport of birding, educates the public in appreciation of birds and their role in nature, and advances the understanding of birds in their natural habitat.

National Audubon Society
950 Third Avenue
New York, NY 10022

Founded: 1905
Members: 412,000 in 448 local groups
Publications:
  American Birds (bimonthly)
  Audubon (bimonthly)
  Audubon Leader (semimonthly)

For all those interested in conserving and restoring natural resources, particularly wildlife and their habitats, soil, water, and forests. Maintains library, and sponsors summer ecology camps for youth leaders and teachers.

Boating—Canoeing, Kayaking, and Rafting

American Canoe Association
P.O. Box 248
Lorton, VA 22079

Founded: 1880
Members: 5,000
Publications:
  American Canoeist (bimonthly)
  Canoe (bimonthly)

The official organization for canoe and kayak enthusiasts. Conducts activities such as cruises and races as well as training classes, provides information on canoeing, and works to preserve open streams and rivers.

American Whitewater Affiliation
P.O. Box 1483
Hagerstown, MD 21740

Founded: 1954
Members: 1,500
Publications:
  American Whitewater (biennial)
  Safety Code

Promotes boating safety, river access, and conservation particularly as it applies to river travel by various types of paddlecraft.

U.S. Canoe Association
606 Ross Street
Middletown, OH 45042

Founded: 1968
Members: 2,000
Publications:
  Canoe News (bimonthly)
  Directory (annual)

Encourages preservation of waterways and development of recreational and competition paddling. Also offers instruction in paddling skills and disseminates safety information.

Boating—Power Boating

American Power Boat Association
17640 East Nine Mile Road
East Detroit, MI 48021

Founded: 1903
Members: 6,000
Publications:
  Propeller (every three weeks)
  Rule Book & Official Directory (annual)

The official body governing U.S. and international motorboating. Conducts and establishes rules for regattas, and tabulates official records. National authority for Union of International Motorboating (Belgium), which determines world records.

Boat Owners Association of the U.S.
880 South Pickett Street
Alexandria, VA 22304

Founded: 1966
Members: 70,000
Publications:
  BOAT/U.S. Reports (monthly)
  Boating Book Buyers Annual
  Marine Insurance Primer

Maintains Consumer Protection Bureau, which keeps files of consumer experiences. Offers correspondence course on seamanship and safety, marine insurance, and other benefits for boaters such as map services. Represents boaters' interests in conservation and legislation.

National Boating Federation
629 Waverly Lane
Bryn Athyn, PA 19009

Founded: 1966
Members: 1,500,000 in 1,676 clubs
Publications:
  Lookout (quarterly)
  Newsletter (monthly)

Purpose is to encourage amateur boating by providing free classroom instruction on seamanship in cooperation with the Coast Guard. Encourages exchange of information among members and promotes boat safety as well as protection and development of waterways.

U.S. Power Squadrons
P.O. Box 30423
Raleigh, NC 27612

Founded: 1914
Members: 60,000
Publication: *The Ensign* (monthly)

Offers free instruction to pleasure-boat owners interested in studying navigation and acquiring boat skills. Courses include seamanship, celestial navigation, advanced piloting, marine electronics, and engine maintenance.

Boating—River Running and Float Trips

Patrick and Susan Canley
Wild and Scenic, Inc.
Box 2123
Marble Canyon, AZ 86036

Grand Canyon Dories: River Trips
Box 3029
Stanford, CA 94305

James Henry River Journeys
1078 Keith
Berkeley, CA 94708

O.A.R.S.
Box 67
Angels Camp, CA 95222

River Adventure
American River Touring Association
1616 Jackson Street
Oakland, CA 94607

Sobek Expeditions, Inc.
Box 7007
Angels Camp, CA 95222

Western River Guides Association
994 Denver Street
Salt Lake City, UT 84111

Boating—Sailing

United States International Sailing
  Association
P.O. Box 209
Newport, RI 02840

Founded: 1958
Members: 1,250

Publication: *Report* (annual)

Provides financial support, from membership dues and donations, to sailors in international competition. Participates in research projects on sail and hull design.

United States Yacht Racing Union
P.O. Box 209
Newport, RI 02840

Founded: 1925
Members: 18,000
Publications:
  Handbook
  Newsletter (ten per year)
  Yearbook (annual)
  Rule book and time allowance tables

Sponsors and directs sailboat racing in the United States and holds an annual convention. Directs U.S. Sailing Championships, U.S. Women's Championships, U.S. Juniors Championships, and Single-Handed Championships.

Cave Exploration. See Spelunking

Cutter and Chariot Racing

World Championship Cutter and Chariot
  Racing Association
824 Southwood Drive
Murray, UT 84107

Founded: 1964
Members: 36
Publication: *Cutter and Chariot World*
  (monthly)

This organization is made up of local associations for chariot and cutter racing. It conducts a variety of competitions throughout the United States in races featuring teams of horses harnessed to two-wheel cutters or chariots ridden by one person, sets rules and regulations, and maintains records.

Exploration

American Geographical Society
Broadway at 156th Street
New York, NY 10032

Founded: 1852
Members: 1,000
Publications:

Focus (bimonthly)
Geographical Review (quarterly)

For those interested in all aspects of geography, especially research and information dissemination. Sponsors projects.

American Polar Society
98-20 62nd Drive, Apt. 7H
Rego Park, NY 11374

Founded: 1934
Members: 2,367
Publication: *The Polar Times* (semiannual)

Special interests in exploration of the Arctic regions and related sciences.

Explorers Club
46 East 70th Street
New York, NY 10021

Founded: 1904
Members: 2,700
Publications:
    Explorers Journal (quarterly)
    The Explorers Newsletter

An organization of professional explorers and scientists, and clearinghouse for information about exploration and its history. Maintains archives, museum, and a 25,000-volume reference library.

National Geographic Society
17th and M Streets, NW
Washington, DC 20036

Founded: 1888
Members: 10,700,000
Publications:
    National Geographic (monthly)
    National Geographic World (youth monthly)
    Maps (included in issues)

Concerned with all areas of geographic exploration, studies, and related areas of interest. Sponsors expeditions, projects, and other geographic endeavors.

Fishing

International Game Fish Association
3000 East Las Olas Boulevard
Fort Lauderdale, FL 33316

Founded: 1939
Members: 15,000
Publications:
    International Marine Angler (bimonthly)

World Record Game Fishes (annual)

Encourages the study of game-fish angling and factors affecting it. Disseminates information related to commercial and game fishing; maintains and compiles records for freshwater and saltwater fly-rod fishing.

Sport Fishing Institute
608 13th Street, NW, Suite 801
Washington, DC 20005

Founded: 1949
Members: 25,000
Publication: *Bulletin* (ten per year)

Supported by fishing-tackle manufacturers as well as individuals. Provides research grants and publishes information on sport-fish conservation activities.

Handicapped Activities

National Handicapped Sports and
    Recreation Association
Box 18664
Capitol Hill Station
Denver, CO 80218

Founded: 1967
Members: 2,207 in 26 groups
Publications:
    Amputee Ski Technique Manual
    Blind Ski Teaching Manual
    Bulletin

Offers opportunities for amputees and other handicapped persons to participate in various sports through 13 local groups. Sponsors ski clinics.

See also Handy-Cap Horizons under **Travel**

Hang Gliding

U.S. Hang Gliding Association
P.O. Box 66306
Los Angeles, CA 90066

Founded: 1971
Members: 8,600
Publications:
    Hang Glider (monthly)
    Source List for Ultralight Gliders

For those interested in ultralight flight, both as an art and a science. Promotes and educates regarding all types of self-launched ultralight flight, and is especially concerned with safety and disseminating hang-gliding information to enthusiasts.

Hunting

American Archery Council
200 Castlewood Road
North Palm Beach, FL 33408

Founded: 1965
Publications:
  ABCs of Archery
  Newsletter (quarterly)

An organization to promote archery and to serve as a center for all national archery interests. Established the Archery Hall of Fame; holds an annual convention.

National Field Archery Association
Route 2
P.O. Box 514
Redlands, CA 92373

Founded: 1939
Members: 23,412

This organization for field-archery enthusiasts and bow hunters compiles records on hunting and seeks to conserve game and its natural environment. It sponsors contests and operates schools of field archery.

National Rifle Association of America
1600 Rhode Island Avenue, NW
Washington, DC 20036

Founded: 1871
Members: 1,800,000
Publications:
  American Marksman (monthly)
  American Rifleman (monthly)
  Conservation Yearbook
  The Hunter (monthly)
  Hunting Annual

For persons interested in firearms. Promotes firearm safety. Interests are in hunting, gun collecting, and rifle, pistol, and shotgun shooting. Maintains records of shooting competitions and presents awards. Operates a museum of gun collecting, including both antique and modern weapons. Provides speakers and information on proper use of firearms.

Intelligence

American Cryptogram Association
39 Roslyn Avenue
Hudson, OH 44236

Founded: 1929
Members: 1,000
Publication: *The Cryptogram* (bimonthly)

For those interested in solving cipher and code messages.

Association of Former Intelligence Officers
6723 Whittier Avenue, Suite 303A
McLean, VA 22101

Founded: 1975
Members: 3,000
Publication: *Periscope* (bimonthly)

For past employees of U.S. intelligence agencies, but also open to civilians interested in intelligence work.

Mountain Climbing

Adirondack Mountain Club
172 Ridge Street
Glens Falls, NY 12801

Founded: 1922
Members: 8,000
Publications:
  Adirondac (bimonthly)
  Maps and guide

For people interested in hiking, camping, and mountain climbing, especially in the Adirondack region. Conducts recreational and educational activities; maintains trails.

American Alpine Club
113 East 90th Street
New York, NY 10028

Founded: 1902
Members: 1,400
Publications:
  *Accidents in North American
    Mountaineering* (annual)
  American Alpine Journal (annual)
  American Alpine News (quarterly)

For those interested in mountaineering. Conducts expeditions, offers research facilities (museum and library), and holds an annual meeting.

Appalachian Mountain Club
5 Joy Street
Boston, MA 02108

Founded: 1876
Members: 25,000
Publications:
  Appalachia Bulletin (monthly)
  Appalachia Journal (semiannual)

For people interested in exploring the mountain areas of New England and nearby areas. Encourages interest from both a scientific and aesthetic appreciation. Maintains 400 miles of trails, conducts workshops, and offers an extensive mountaineering library.

Iowa Mountaineers
P.O. Box 163
Iowa City, IA 52240

Founded: 1940
Members: 625
Publications:
  Iowa Climber (semiannual)
  News Bulletin (bimonthly)

Conducts classes in rock climbing, mountain climbing, and wilderness survival. Sponsors climbing and camping outings, summer mountain camps, and foreign expeditions.

The Mountaineers (Trail)
719 Pike Street
Seattle, WA 98101

Founded: 1906
Members: 12,000
Publications:
  The Mountaineer (monthly)
  Roster (annual)

For persons over 14 years of age interested in exploring and learning about mountains and forests, mainly of the American Northwest. Conducts hikes and skiing and mountain-climbing trips, provides lessons in mountain climbing, operates five ski lodges and huts, and holds an annual meeting.

Sierra Club
530 Bush Street
San Francisco, CA 94108

Founded: 1892
Members: 199,000
Publications:
  National News Report (weekly)
  Sierra Club Bulletin (monthly)
  Books, films, posters

For those who wish to learn more about natural resources and to conserve and protect wilderness areas. Conducts wilderness outings.

Parachuting

Canadian Sport Parachuting Association
333 River Road
Ottawa, ON, Canada K1L 8B9

Founded: 1956
Members: 6,000 in 100 local groups
Publications:
  Basic Safety Regulations and Technical and Training Manual
  Canadian Parachutist (ten per year)

Promotes safe and enjoyable parachuting, national and international competition, and cooperation among sport parachutists. Sponsors research, safety training, and classes for instructors and riggers.

United States Parachute Association (USPA)
806 15th Street, NW, Suite 444
Washington, DC 20005

Founded: 1957
Members: 17,000 in 500 local groups
Publications:
  Directory and Reference Source (biennial)
  Parachutist (monthly)

A division of the National Aeronautic Association. Stages sport competitions, including the annual National Championship and the annual National Collegiate Parachuting Championship. Coordinates tests on parachuting equipment, sponsors an instructor-training program, and promotes parachuting safety.

Rodeo Riding

International Rodeo Association
American Fidelity Building, Suite 412
Pauls Valley, OK 73075

Founded: 1957
Members: 15,000
Publication: *Rodeo News* (monthly)

Covers all aspects of rodeo riding. Disseminates information about the sport and sponsors clinics.

Professional Rodeo Cowboys Association
101 Pro Rodeo Drive
Colorado Springs, CO 80901

Founded: 1936
Members: 6,237
Publication: *Pro Rodeo Sports News* (22 per year)

An organization for rodeo riders and performers, and the governing body for the sport. Maintains the Pro Rodeo Hall of Champions and Museum of the American Cowboy, open year-round to the public.

Skiing

American Ski Association
5830 South Lake Houston Parkway, T33
Houston, TX 77049

Founded: 1976
Members: 12,040
Publication: *Ski Scoop* (semimonthly
  November–May)

For recreational skiers, ski clubs, and those
who wish to learn to ski. Sponsors skiing excursions, and arranges travel for members
on commercial airlines and American Ski
Association aircraft. Furnishes members
with reports on current conditions for various ski resorts, and arranges ski-area accommodations and social functions.

United States Ski Association
1726 Champa Street, Suite 300
Denver, CO 80202

Founded: 1904
Members: 109,000

This organization has committees that approve Alpine courses. It also sets up Alpine
competition, maintains a skiing Hall of
Fame, promotes Nordic and recreational
skiing and competitions, and holds an annual meeting.

Sled Dog Racing

International Sled Dog Racing Association
Box 446
Nordman, ID 83848

Founded: 1966
Members: 1,150
Publications:
  Directory (annual)
  Info (five per year)

Devoted to encouraging the sport of dogsled
racing. Offers a standardization of rules
for competitions and holds an annual
convention.

Snowmobiling

World Snowmobile Racing Federation
139 Cottonwood Avenue
Hartland, WI 53029

Founded: 1979
Members: 3,000
Publications:
  Newsletter (ten per year)
  Bulletins

Offers information regarding all forms of
snowmobile racing: cross-country, drag,
sprint, enduro, etc. Sanctions all professional snowmobile races in the United States
and Canada, provides insurance, publishes
a rule book, and offers a junior program for
12- to 16-year-olds.

Spelunking

National Speleological Society
Cave Avenue
Huntsville, AL 35810

Founded: 1941
Members: 4,500
Publications:
  Bulletin (quarterly)
  Directory (annual)
  Newsletter (quarterly)
  NSS Monthly News
  Speleo-Digest (annual)

An organization devoted to people interested in caves and their exploration. Disseminates information on the subject of spelunk-
ing, promotes proper preservation of caves
and subterranean environments, maintains
a specialized library, awards research grants
in speleology, and holds an annual
convention.

Stuntmen

Stuntmen's Association of Motion Pictures
4810 Whitsett Avenue
North Hollywood, CA 91607

Founded: 1961
Members: 120
Publication: *Stuntmen's Directory* (annual)

The place to go to find out about stuntmen
and their occupation. Open only to those
who perform stunts in movies or on
television.

Surfing

American Surfing Association
Box 1315
Beverly Hills, CA 90213

Founded: 1974
Members: 12,000
Publication: *The All American Surfer*
  (quarterly)

Promotes surfing as an amateur sport and

establishes standardized rules for surfing competition. Maintains records and bestows awards, and works toward making surfing an Olympic sport.

Travel

Globetrotters' Club
BCM/Roving
London WCIV 6XX England

Founded: 1947
Members: 1,500
Publications:
  Directory (biennial)
  Globe (bimonthly)

Designed to assist those interested in economical travel abroad and in meeting people in the countries they visit. A mutual-aid column helps members looking for traveling companions and for advice regarding specific areas.

Handy-Cap Horizons
3250 East Loretta Drive
Indianapolis, IN 46227

Founded: 1947
Members: 3,000
Publications: Descriptive brochures, quarterly magazine

Conducts tours in the United States and abroad for persons of all ages with any type and degree of handicap. Includes not only handicapped persons but their relatives, attendants, and friends. Also offers tours for nonhandicapped elderly persons who wish to travel at an easy pace.

Treasure Hunting

National Treasure Hunters League
7350 East Jenan Drive
Scottsdale, AZ 85254

Founded: 1968
Members: 50,000
Publication: Journal (quarterly)

All phases of treasure hunting and prospecting are the concerns of this organization, the largest of its type in the world.

Prospectors & Treasure Hunters Guild
210 Exanimo Building
Segundo, CO 81070

Founded: 1971
Members: 6,316
Publication: Newsletter (monthly)

Offers many services for treasure hunters, including guidance, news of the industry, and notification of laws affecting treasure hunting. Maintains a reference library of more than 11,000 volumes.

Prospectors Club International
P.O. Box 2081
Indianapolis, IN 46206

Founded: 1964
Members: 3,500
Publication: The Prospector (quarterly)

For all treasure hunters. Offers a forum for exchanging ideas, information, and treasure-hunting experiences. Disseminates information about treasure locations, and maintains a museum and Hall of Fame.

Underwater Activities

Cousteau Society, Inc.
777 Third Avenue
New York, NY 10017

Founded: 1973
Members: 160,000
Publications:
  Calypso Log (quarterly)
  Calypso Log Dispatch (monthly)
  Special Report (irregular)

Supports education and research of ocean environmental matters. Disseminates information about the work of Jacques Cousteau.

Underwater Society of America
732 50th Street
West Palm Beach, FL 33407

Founded: 1959
Members: 12,000 in 590 local groups
Publication: Underwater Reporter (quarterly)

Sponsors national skin-diving and scuba competition. Encourages underwater exploration, especially as it affects the sports of skin diving, spearfishing, and lung diving.

Water Skiing

American Water Ski Association
S.R. 550 & Carl Floyd Road
Winter Haven, FL 33880

Founded: 1939
Members: 17,000 in 350 local groups
Publications:
  Directory

Water Skier (bimonthly)
Booklets

Promotes both competitive and noncompetitive water skiing in the United States. Establishes rules for competition, certifies performance records, compiles statistics, and maintains a museum.

Wildlife Conservation

National Wildlife Federation
1412 16th Street, NW
Washington, DC 20036

Founded: 1936
Members: 4,600,000

Publications:
Conservation Directory (annual)
Conservation Report (weekly)
International Wildlife Magazine
(bimonthly)
National Wildlife Magazine (bimonthly)
Ranger Rick's Nature Magazine
(monthly)
Conservation teaching materials

Organization strives to promote the proper management of the earth's resources in order to sustain life and to encourage people to appreciate our natural resources. Provides financial aid to local conservation projects, grants fellowships for graduate study of conservation, and holds an annual convention.